L. B. Barrett.
July. 1938.

With best wishes
from F. E. Mitchell.

THE MAJOR PLEASURES
OF LIFE

Gainsboro Rd, Crewe.

THE
MAJOR
PLEASURES
OF LIFE

ༀ*ༀ

Selected and Arranged
by
MARTIN ARMSTRONG

LONDON
VICTOR GOLLANCZ LTD
Covent Garden

First published in 1934
First Cheap Edition Autumn 1936
Reprinted September 1936

Printed in Great Britain by
The Camelot Press Ltd., London and Southampton

PREFACE

IN the majority of anthologies, I suppose, the anthologist is guided in the choice of his material almost entirely by his æsthetic or intellectual preferences. But in an anthology of this kind the motives must often be other than these, and this book, I need hardly say, contains many statements and opinions, interesting in themselves for various reasons, with which I do not at all agree, and occasionally even material which I dislike. In the section on Music, for instance, I have quoted the greater part of Browning's *Master Hughes of Saxe-Gotha*, a poem which, in my opinion, is certainly not poetry and which tells us almost nothing of the nature of the fugue : but the two facts that it was written by a considerable poet *about* a fugue, and that, so far as I know, it is the only poem about a fugue, are enough, I think, to make it necessary to include it. Another instance. In the section on Nature I have printed Wordsworth's *Daffodils*, a poem which is not only much in need of a rest from anthologies, but, as a whole, is not Wordsworth at his best. But I thought it sufficiently interesting to place it beside his sister's prose version written two years before.

In the matter of spelling, in the quotations from earlier writers, I must confess to a lamentable but unavoidable inconsistency. In the verse selections I have used the original spelling whenever, in the time at my disposal, I could get at it (except in the case of *Piers Plowman's Crede*, which I thought it better to modernize). In the prose selections I have done likewise, except when the spelling was so unfamiliar that it seemed likely to fog the average reader.

As for translation, in some cases I have made my own

5

versions, in others I have used translations already existing.

I am indebted to friends and books for putting me on the track of material which I should not have discovered by myself.

M. A.

CONTENTS

§ I THE PLEASURES

The lover is drawn by the thing loved, as the sense is by that which it perceives, and it unites with it, and they become one and the same thing. The work is the first thing born of the union ; if the thing that is loved be base, the lover becomes base. When the thing taken into union is in harmony with that which receives it, there follow rejoicing and pleasure and satisfaction. When the lover is united to that which is loved it finds rest there : when the burden is laid down there it finds rest.

LEONARDO DA VINCI
(from *The Notebooks*—Trans. E. MCCURDY)

Pleasure is the feeling of the furtherance of life, pain of its obstruction.

KANT

The greatest of all evils is pleasure, because by it the soul is riveted to the body.

IAMBLICHUS

Of pleasures, those which occur most rarely give the most delight.

. . . .

If a man should exceed moderation, the things which give him the greatest delight would become the things which give him the least.

. . . . . .

Nothing really pleasant or unpleasant subsists by nature, but has become so by habit.

EPICTETUS

II

There is nothing either good or bad, but thinking makes it so.

SHAKESPEARE

For every Pleasure Money Is Useless.

BLAKE

He who binds to himself a joy
Does the winged life destroy ;
But he who kisses the joy as it flies
Lives in eternity's sun rise.

BLAKE

Abstinence sows sand all over
The ruddy limbs and flaming hair,
But Desire Gratified
Plants fruits of life and beauty there.

BLAKE

So long as the whole soul follows the guidance of the wisdom-loving element without any dissension, each part can not only do its own proper work in all respects, or in other words, be just ; but, moreover, it can enjoy its own proper pleasures in the best and truest shape possible.

PLATO

Live happy in the *Elizium* of a virtuously composed Mind, and let Intellectual Contents exceed the Delights wherein mere Pleasurists place their Paradise. Bear not too slack reins upon Pleasure, nor let complexion or contagion betray thee unto the exorbitancy of Delight. Make Pleasure thy Recreation or intermissive Relaxation, not thy *Diana*, Life, and Profession. Voluptuousness is as insatiable as Covetousness. Tranquility is better than jollity, and to appease pain than to invent pleasure.

SIR THOMAS BROWNE (from *Christian Morals*)

There are some things in which mediocrity is intolerable : poetry, music, painting, and public speaking.

LA BRUYÈRE (from *Les Caractères*)

One can bring no greater reproach against a man than to say that he does not set sufficient value upon pleasure, and there is no greater sign of a fool than the thinking that he can tell at once and easily what it is that pleases him. To know this is not easy, and to extend our knowledge of it is the highest and the most neglected of all arts and branches of education. Indeed, if we could solve the difficulty of knowing what gives us pleasure, if we could find its springs, its inception and earliest *modus operandi*, we should have discovered the secret of life and development, for the same difficulty has attended the development of every sense from touch onwards, and no new sense was ever developed without pains.

SAMUEL BUTLER (from *The Notebooks*)

Whilst you are upon Earth, enjoy the good Things that are there (to that end were they given), and be not melancholy, and wish yourself in Heaven. If a King should give you the keeping of a Castle, with all things belonging to it, Orchards, Gardens, &c., and bid you use them ; withal promise you after twenty years to remove you to the Court, and to make you a Privy Councillor ; if you should neglect your Castle, and refuse to eat of those fruits, and sit down, and whine, and wish that I was a Privy Councillor, do you think the King would be pleased with you ?

Pleasures of Meat, Drink, Clothes, &c., are forbidden those that know not how to use them ; just as Nurses cry *pah !* when they see a Knife in a Child's Hand ; they never say any thing to a Man.

SELDEN (from *Table Talk*)

It is but a sour-faced and joyless superstition that forbids us to be mirthful. For why is it better to assuage thirst and hunger than to drive away care ? My argument is this, and thus have I persuaded myself. No deity, nor any man but an envious, rejoices in my weakness and discomfort, nor accounts as virtues unto us lamentings, sobs, fear, and other such signs of a weak disposition. On the contrary, the more we are stirred to pleasure, the greater the perfection to which we attain, that is, the more fully must we partake of the divine nature. It is the part of a wise man to make use of the things about him and delight in them as much as possible, though not unto surfeit, for therein is no delight. It is the part of a wise man, I say, temperately to enjoy the pleasure of food and drink, perfumes, the beauty of green things, apparel, music, sports, theatres and such things as a man may delight in without harm to his kind

SPINOZA (from *The Ethics*)

Certainly the highest good is to live happily, and not through a life of mortification to expect a happy death. Should we attain felicity in life, death will be easy, as it will be natural and in due season. Whereas by the present system of *religious teaching*, men are enjoined to value chiefly happiness at the end of life, which, if they were implicitly to follow, they would, by neglecting the first great duty, that of innocent enjoyment during existence, effectually preclude themselves from attaining.

COLERIDGE (from *Table Talk*)

Pleasure is very seldom found where it is sought. Our bright blazes of gladness are commonly kindled by unexpected sparks. The flowers which scatter their odours from time to time in the paths of life, grow up without culture from seeds scattered by chance.

Nothing is more hopeless than a scheme of merriment. Wits and humorists are brought together from distant quarters by preconcerted invitations ; they come attended by their admirers, prepared to laugh and to applaud ; they gaze a while on each other, ashamed to be silent, and afraid to speak ; every man is discontented with himself, grows angry with those that give him pain, and resolves that he will contribute nothing to the merriment of such worthless company. Wine inflames the general malignity, and changes sullenness to petulance, till at last none can bear any longer the presence of the rest. They retire to vent their indignation in safer places, where they are heard without attention ; their importance is restored, they recover their good humour, and gladden the night with wit and jocularity.

Merriment is always the effect of a sudden impression. The jest which is expected is already destroyed. The most active imagination will be sometimes torpid under the frigid influence of melancholy, and sometimes occasions will be wanting to tempt the mind, however volatile, to sallies and excursions. Nothing was ever said with un-common felicity, but by the co-operation of chance, and, therefore, wit as well as valour must be content to share its honours with fortune.

All other pleasures are equally uncertain ; the general remedy of uneasiness is change of place ; almost every one has some journey of pleasure in his mind, with which he flatters his expectation. He that travels in theory has no inconvenience ; he has shade and sunshine at his disposal, and wherever he alights finds tables of plenty and looks of gayety. These ideas are indulged till the day of departure arrives, the chaise is called, and the progress of happiness begins.

A few miles teach him the fallacies of imagination. The road is dusty, the air is sultry, the horses are sluggish, and the postillion brutal. He longs for the time of dinner, that he may eat and rest. The inn is crowded, his orders are neglected, and nothing remains but that he devour in haste what the cook has spoiled, and drive on in quest of better entertainment. He finds at night a more commo-dious house, but the best is always worse than he expected.

He at last enters his native province, and resolves to feast his mind with the conversation of his old friends and the recollection of juvenile frolics. He stops at the house of his friend, whom he designs to overpower with pleasure by the unexpected interview. He is not known till he tells his name, and revives the memory of himself by a gradual explanation. He is then coldly received and ceremoniously feasted. He hastens away to another, whom his affairs have called to a distant place, and having seen the house empty, goes away disgusted by a disappointment which could not be intended because it could not be foreseen. At the next house he finds every face clouded with misfortune, and is regarded with malevolence as an unseasonable intruder, who comes not to visit but to insult them.

It is seldom that we find either men or places such as we expect them. He that has pictured a prospect upon his fancy, will receive little pleasure from his eyes ; he that has anticipated the conversation of a wit, will wonder to what prejudice he owes his reputation. Yet it is necessary to hope, though hope should always be deluded ; for hope itself is happiness, and its frustrations, however frequent, are yet less dreadful than its extinction.

SAMUEL JOHNSON (from *The Idler*)

A thing of beauty is a joy for ever :
Its loveliness increases ; it will never
Pass into nothingness ; but still will keep
A bower quiet for us, and a sleep
Full of sweet dreams, and health, and quiet breathing.
Therefore, on every morrow, are we wreathing

A flowery band to bind us to the earth,
Spite of despondence, of the inhuman dearth
Of noble natures, of the gloomy days,
Of all the unhealthy and o'er-darkened ways
Made for our searching : yes, in spite of all,
Some shape of beauty moves away the pall
From our dark spirits. Such the sun, the moon,
Trees old, and young, sprouting a shady boon
For simple sheep ; and such are daffodils
With the green world they live in ; and clear rills
That for themselves a cooling covert make
'Gainst the hot season ; the mid forest brake,
Rich with a sprinkling of fair musk-rose blooms :
And such too is the grandeur of the dooms
We have imagined for the mighty dead ;
All lovely tales that we have heard or read :
An endless fountain of immortal drink,
Pouring unto us from the heaven's brink.
　　Nor do we merely feel these essences
For one short hour ; no, even as the trees
That whisper round a temple become soon
Dear as the temple's self, so does the moon,
The passion poesy, glories infinite,
Haunt us till they become a cheering light
Unto our souls, and bound to us so fast,
That, whether there be shine, or gloom o'ercast,
They always must be with us, or we die.

KEATS (from *Endymion*)

18

By the very right of your senses you enjoy the World. Is not the beauty of the Hemisphere present to your eye? Doth not the glory of the Sun pay tribute to your sight? Is not the vision of the World an amiable thing? Do not the stars shed influences to perfect the Air? Is not that a marvellous body to breathe in? To visit the lungs: repair the spirits, revive the senses, cool the blood, fill the empty spaces between Earth and Heavens; and yet give liberty to all objects? Prize these first: and you shall enjoy the residues: Glory, Dominion, Power, Wisdom, Honour, Angels, Souls, Kingdoms, Ages. *Be faithful in a little, and you shall be master over much.* If you be not faithful in esteeming these; who shall put into your hands the true Treasures? If you be negligent in prizing these, you will be negligent in prizing all. For there is a disease in him who despiseth present mercies, which till it be cured, he can never be happy. He esteemeth nothing that he hath, but is ever gaping after more: which when he hath he despiseth in like manner. Insatiableness is good, but not ingratitude.

Were all your riches here in some little place: all other places would be empty. It is necessary therefore for your contentment and true satisfaction, that your riches be dispersed everywhere. Whether is more delightful; to have some few private riches in one, and other places all void; or to have all places everywhere filled with our proper treasures? Certainly to have treasures in all places. For by this means we are entertained everywhere with pleasures, are everywhere at home honoured and delighted, everywhere enlarged in our own possessions. But to have a few riches in some narrow bounds, though we should suppose a kingdom full, would be to have our delights limited, and infinite spaces dark and empty, wherein we might wander without satisfaction. So that God must of necessity to satisfy his Love give us infinite treasures. And we of necessity seek for our riches in all places.

TRAHERNE (from *Centuries of Meditations*)

All their life was spent not in laws, statutes, or rules, but according to their own free will and pleasure. They rose out of their beds when they thought good ; they did eat, drink, labour, sleep, when they had a mind to it, and were disposed for it. None did wake them, none did offer to constrain them to eat, drink nor do any other thing ; for so had Gargantua established it. In all their rule and strictest tie of their order, there was but this one clause to be observed :

DO WHAT THOU WILT

Because men that are free, well-born, well-bred, and conversant in honest companies, have naturally an *instinct* and spur that prompteth them unto virtuous actions, and withdraws them from vice, which is called *honour*. Those same men, when by base subjection and constraint they are brought under and kept down, turn aside from that noble disposition, by which they formerly were inclined to *virtue*, to shake off that bond of servitude, wherein they are so tyrannously inslaved ; for it is agreeable to the nature of man to long after things forbidden, and to desire what is denied us. By this liberty they entered into a very laudable emulation, to do all of them what they saw did please one. If any of the gallants or ladies should say, "*Let us drink*," they would all drink. If any one of them said, "*Let us play*," they all played. If one said, "*Let us go a walking into the fields*," they went all. If it were to go a hawking, or a hunting, the ladies mounted upon dainty well-paced nags, seated in a stately palfrey saddle, carried on their lovely fists *miniardly begloved* every one of them, either a sparhawk, or a laneret, or a marlin, and the young gallants carried the other kinds of hawks. So nobly were they taught, that there was neither he nor she amongst them, but could read, write, sing, play upon several musical instruments, speak five or six several languages, and compose in them very quaintly, both in verse and prose. Never were seen so valiant *knights*, so noble and worthy, so dexterous and skilful both on foot and horse-back, more brisk and lively, more nimble and quick, or better handling all manner of weapons than were there. Never were seen *ladies* so proper and handsome, so miniard and dainty, less froward, or more ready with their hand, and with their needle, in every honest and free action belonging to that sex, than were there. For this reason, when the time came that any *man* of the said *abbey*, either at the request of his parents, or for some other cause had a mind to go out of it, he carried along with him one of the *ladies*, namely, her, whom he had before that chosen for his *mistress*, and they were married together. And if they had formerly in Theleme lived in good devotion and amity, they did continue therein, and increase it to a greater height in their state of matrimony ; and did entertain that mutual love till the very last day of their life, in no less vigour and fervency than at the very day of their wedding.

RABELAIS (Trans. URQUHART)

Your Heart is the best and greatest gift of God to you ; it is the highest, greatest, strongest, and noblest Power of your Nature ; it forms your whole Life, be it what it will ; all Evil and Good comes from it ; your Heart alone has the key of Life and Death ; it does all that it will ; Reason is but its plaything ; and whether in Time or Eternity, can only be a mere Beholder of the wonders of happiness, or forms of misery, which the right or wrong working of the Heart is entered into.

WILLIAM LAW (from *The Spirit of Love*)

I say again, that the body makes the minde, not that it created it a minde, but forms it a good or a bad minde ; and this minde may be confounded with soul without any violence or injustice to Reason or Philosophy : then the soul it seems is enabled by our Body, not this by it. My Body licenseth my soul to see the worlds beauties through mine eyes : to hear pleasant things through mine ears ; and affords it apt Organs for the conveiance of all perceivable delight. But alas ! my soul cannot make any part, that is not of it self disposed to see or hear, though without doubt she be as able and as willing to see behinde as before. Now if my soul would say, that she enables any part to taste these pleasures, but is her selfe only delighted with those rich sweetnesses which her inward eyes and senses apprehend, shee should dissemble ; for I see her often solaced with beauties, which shee sees through mine eyes, and with musicke which through mine eares she heares. This perfection then my body hath, that it can impart to my minde all his .pleasures ; and my minde hath still many, that she can neither teach

22

my indisposed part her faculties, not to the best espoused parts shew it beauty of Angels, of Musicke, of Spheres, whereof she boasts the contemplation. Are Chastity, Temperance, and Fortitude gifts of the minde ? I appeale to Physitians whether the cause of these be not in the body ; health is the gift of the body, and patience in sicknesse the gift of the minde : then who will say that patience is as good a happinesse, as health, when wee must be extremely miserable to purchase this happinesse. And for nourishing of civill societies and mutuall love amongst men, which is our chief end while we are men ; I say, this beauty, presence, and proportion of the body, hath a more masculine force in begetting this love, than the vertues of the minde : for it strikes us suddenly, and possesseth us immoderately ; when to know those vertues requires some Judgment in him which shall discerne, a long time and conversation between them. And even at last how much of our faith and beleefe shall we be driven to bestow, to assure our selves that these vertues are not counterfeited : for it is the same to be, and seem vertuous, because that he that hath no vertue, can dissemble none, but he that hath a little, may gild and enamell, yea and transforme much vice into vertue : For allow a man to be discreet and flexible to complaints, which are great vertuous gifts of the minde, this discretion will be to him the soule and Elixir of all vertues, so that touched with this, even pride shall be made humility ; and Cowardice, honourable and wise valour. But in things seen there is not this danger, for the body which thou lovest and esteemest faire, is faire : certainly if it be not faire in perfection, yet it is faire in the same degree that thy Judgment is good. And in a faire body, I do seldom suspect a disproportioned minde, and as seldome hope for a good, in a deformed. When I see a goodly house, I assure my selfe of a worthy possessour, from a ruinous weather-beaten building I turn away, because it seems either stuffed with varlets as a Prison, or handled by an unworthy and negligent tenant, that so suffers the wast thereof. And truly the gifts of Fortune, which are riches, are only handmaids, yea Pandars of the bodies pleasure ; with their service we nourish health, and preserve dainty, and wee buy delights ; so that vertue which must be loved for it selfe, and respects no further end, is indeed nothing : And riches, whose end is the good of the body, cannot be so perfectly good, as the end whereto it levels.

DONNE (from *Paradoxes and Problemes*)

SOCRATES. I cannot agree with those who maintain that there is no pleasure except in the cessation of pain, although, as I have said, I make use of their evidence to show that there are some seeming pleasures, not so in reality, and some others, not a few nor small ones, which we imagine to be such, but which are inescapably linked with severe pain of mind or body and with intervals of relief.

PROTARCHUS. And what pleasures, Socrates, are rightly to be esteemed true pleasures ?

SOCRATES. Those which come from beautiful colours and forms and outlines, and many of the pleasures of scents and sounds, and all those things whose absence brings us no discomfort and whose presence is pleasant and satisfying and free from any mixture of pain.

PROTARCHUS. But what exactly do you mean by this kind of pleasures, Socrates ?

24

SOCRATES. What I mean is, assuredly, not at once clear, but let me try to make it so. What I now call beauty of form is not what most people imagine, namely the form of living creatures, or pictures, but rather straight lines and curves, forms such are made by instruments which construct circles and globes and by rulers and squares which make rectangles, if you understand. For I mean that these are not relatively beautiful, like other things, but are always beautiful in themselves and produce pleasures peculiar to them and not dependent on previous irritation. And as for colours, I mean colours of a similar kind, producing the same kind of pleasures. Do you understand my argument?

PROTARCHUS. I am trying to do so, Socrates; but please try, on your part, to make it still plainer.

SOCRATES. Well then, I mean to say that sounds that are clear and smooth and give out one clear, melodious note are not merely relatively beautiful, but beautiful in themselves and produce pleasures peculiar to them.

PROTARCHUS. Yes, no doubt this is so.

SOCRATES. As for the pleasures connected with scents, they are less divine than the pleasures of sound; still, since they are not mingled with pain of mind or body, I consider them to be of the same kind as those I have already mentioned. Well, all these, if you follow me, form two classes of what we generally call pleasures.

PROTARCHUS. I follow you.

SOCRATES. Let us now add to these the pleasures that come from knowledge, if, as I assume, these seem to be free from any previous hunger for knowledge and, consequently, from any distress arising from a lack of it.

PROTARCHUS. I agree.

SOCRATES. Well now, if men have been full of knowledge and have then lost some of it through forgetfulness, do you think they are distressed by this?

PROTARCHUS. No, not instinctively so, though perhaps they may be if they reflect on what they have lost, as men are distressed by the lack of something they have lost.

SOCRATES. But at the moment, my friend, we are discussing actual instinctive feelings and not those that come of reflection.

PROTARCHUS. In that case what you say is true: forgetfulness may come without any feeling of distress.

SOCRATES. Then we must say that the pleasure of knowledge is not mingled with pain.

PLATO (from *Philebus*)

We will entangle buds and flowers and beams
Which twinkle on the fountain's brim, and make
Strange combinations out of common things,
Like human babes in their brief innocence;
And we will search, with looks and words of love,
For hidden thoughts, each lovelier than the last,
Our unexhausted spirits; and like lutes,
Touched by the skill of the enamoured wind,
Weave harmonies divine, yet ever new,
From difference sweet where discord cannot be;
And hither come, sped on the charmèd winds,
Which meet from all the points of heaven, as bees
From every flower aëreal Enna feeds,
At their known island-homes in Himera,
The echoes of the human world, which tell

26

Of the low voice of love, almost unheard,
And dove-eyed pity's murmured pain, and music,
Itself the echo of the heart, and all
That tempers or improves man's life, now free ;
And lovely apparitions,—dim at first,
Then radiant, as the mind, arising bright
From the embrace of beauty (whence the forms
Of which these are the phantoms) casts on them
The gathered rays which are reality—
Shall visit us, the progeny immortal
Of Painting, Sculpture, and rapt Poesy,
And arts, though unimagined, yet to be.
The wandering voices and the shadows these
Of all that man becomes, the mediators
Of that best worship love, by him and us
Given and returned ; swift shapes and sounds, which
    grow
More fair and soft as man grows wise and kind,
And, veil by veil, evil and error fall.

SHELLEY (from *Prometheus Unbound*)

But to those that have a reasonable Nature, what better
thing than reason may be proposed ? If this union bee
agreeable, and if a man will travell in such companie
towardes happie life, let Vertue goe before and pleasure
follow after, as the shadow doth the bodie. It is a small
matter for a great minde to give pleasure for a Hand-maid
to attend on Vertue, which is the most honourablest Mis-
tresse that a man may meete withall. Let Vertue march
before and carrie the Ensigne, yet notwithstanding, we
shall have pleasure, although wee bee Masters and
governours of the same. Shee will presse us to grant her

27

something, but shee cannot constraine us thereunto. But they that have given the superioritie to pleasure, have wanted both, For they loose Vertue. Moreover they have not pleasure ; but pleasure is Lord over them, with whose want they are eyther tormented, or else in aboundance strangled. Wretched if they be forsaken by her, and more wretched if they be overpressed. Like those who are entangled in the Syrtes : now are they left on drie Land, presently hurried away with the violence of the streame. But this falleth out thorow too much intemperance, and the blind love we beare unto the same. He that requireth evill for good, casteth himselfe into great danger if hee obtaine the same. Even as wee hunt wild beastes with labour and hazard, and when we have caught them it is a hard matter to keepe them : for oftentimes they teare their Masters in peices ; so fareth it with those who have great pleasures, for they turne to their great miseries ; and surprize them when they imagine they have the mastrie over them. Which the more and greater they be, so the lesse is he, and more subject and slave unto many whom the common sort call happie. To continue and prosecute the similitude which I have proposed : Even as he that searcheth the haunts of wilde beastes and accounts it a great matter to catch such dumbe Creatures in his nets, and environ some great Forrest with a kennell of hounds, to the end to follow their Tract, forsaketh his better affaires, and renounceth many other offices : so hee that followeth pleasure, neglecteth all other things, respecteth not his former libertie, but dependeth on his belly, neyther buyeth hee pleasures for himselfe, but selleth himselfe to pleasures.

SENECA

(from *Of Blessed Life*—Trans. THOMAS LODGE

28

I may not hope from outward forms to win
The passion and the life, whose fountains are within.

O Lady ! we receive but what we give,
And in our life alone does Nature live :
Ours is her wedding-garment, ours her shroud !
    And would we aught behold, of higher worth,
Than that inanimate cold world allowed
To the poor loveless ever-anxious crowd,
    Ah ! from the soul itself must issue forth
A light, a glory, a fair luminous cloud
        Enveloping the Earth—
And from the soul itself must there be sent
    A sweet and potent voice, of its own birth,
Of all sweet sounds the life and element !

O pure of heart ! thou need'st not ask of me
What this strong music in the soul may be !
What, and wherein it doth exist,
This light, this glory, this fair luminous mist,
This beautiful and beauty-making power.
    Joy, virtuous Lady ! Joy that ne'er was given,
Save to the pure, and in their purest hour,
Life, and Life's effluence, cloud at once and shower,
Joy, Lady ! is the spirit and the power,
Which wedding Nature to us gives in dower,
    A new Earth and new Heaven,
Undreamt of by the sensual and the proud—
Joy is the sweet voice, Joy the luminous cloud—
    We in ourselves rejoice !
And thence flows all that charms or ear or sight,
    All melodies the echoes of that voice,
All colours a suffusion from that light.

        COLERIDGE (from *Dejection : An Ode*)

29

Now 'tis Robert's turn.

MY DEAR ROBERT,

One passage in your Letter a little displeas'd me. The rest was nothing but kindness, which Robert's letters are ever brimful of. You say that " this World to you seems drain'd of all its sweets ! " At first I had hoped you only meant to insinuate the high price of Sugar ! but I am afraid you meant more. O Robert, I don't know what you call sweet. Honey and the honeycomb, roses and violets, are yet in the earth. The sun and moon yet reign in Heaven, and the lesser lights keep up their pretty twink-lings. Meats and drinks, sweet sights and sweet smells, a country walk, spring and autumn, follies and repentance, quarrels and reconcilements, have all a sweetness by turns. Good humour and good nature, friends at home that love you, and friends abroad that miss you, you possess all these things, and more innumerable, and these are all sweet things. . . . You may extract honey from every-thing ; do not go a gathering after gall. The Bees are wiser in their generation than the race of sonnet writers and complainers, Bowles's and Charlotte Smiths, and all that tribe, who can see no joys but what are past, and fill people's heads with the unsatisfying nature of Earthly comforts. I assure you I find this world a very pretty place.

LAMB (from *The Letters*)

Many there be that complain of divine Providence for suffering Adam to transgress. Foolish tongues ! when God gave him reason, he gave him freedom to choose, for rea-son is but choosing ; he had been else a mere artificial

Adam, such an Adam as he is in the motions. We ourselves esteem not of that obedience, or love, or gift, which is of force ; God therefore left him free, set before him a provoking object ever almost in his eyes ; herein consisted his merit, herein the right of his reward, the praise of his abstinence. Wherefore did he create passions within us, pleasures round about us, but that these rightly tempered are the very ingredients of virtue ? They are not skilful considerers of human things, who imagine to remove sin, by removing the matter of sin ; for, besides that it is a huge heap increasing under the very act of diminishing, though some part of it may for a time be withdrawn from some persons, it cannot from all, in such a universal thing as books are ; and when this is done, yet the sin remains entire. Though he take from a covetous man all his treasure, he has yet one jewel left, ye cannot bereave him of his covetousness. Banish all objects of lust, shut up all youth into the severest discipline that can be exercised in any hermitage, ye cannot make them chaste, that came not thither so. . . .

. . . .

If we think to regulate printing, thereby to rectify manners, we must regulate all recreations and pastimes, all that is delightful to man. No music must be heard, no song be set or sung, but what is grave and doric. There must be licensing dancers, that no gesture, motion, or deportment be taught our youth, but what by their allowance shall be thought honest ; for such Plato was provided of. It will ask more than the work of twenty licensers to examine all the lutes, the violins, and the guitars in every house ; they must not be suffered to prattle as they do, but must be licensed what they may say. And who shall silence all the airs and madrigals that whisper softness in chambers ? The windows also, and the balconies, must be thought on ; these are shrewd books, with dangerous frontispieces, set to sale ; who shall prohibit them, shall twenty licensers ? The villages also must have their visitors to enquire what lectures the bagpipe and the rebec reads, even to the ballatry and the gamut of every municipal fiddler ; for these are the countryman's Arcadias, and his Monte Mayors.

Next, what more national corruption, for which England hears ill abroad, than household gluttony ? Who shall be the rectors of our daily rioting ? And what shall be done to inhibit the multitudes that frequent those houses where drunkenness is sold and harboured ? Our garments also should be referred to the licensing of some more sober work-masters, to see them cut into a less wanton garb. Who shall regulate all the mixed conversation of our youth, male and female together, as is the fashion of this country ? Who shall still appoint what shall be discoursed, what presumed, and no further ? Lastly, who shall forbid and separate all idle resort, all evil company ? These things will be, and must be ; but how they shall be least hurtful, how least enticing, herein consists the grave and governing wisdom of a state.

To sequester out of the world into Atlantic and Utopian politics, which never can be drawn into use, will not mend our condition ; but to ordain wisely as in this world of evil, in the midst whereof God hath placed us unavoidably.

MILTON (from *Areopagitica*)

Heark how the birds do sing,
    And woods do ring.
All creatures have their joy, and man hath his.
    Yet, if we rightly measure,
        Mans joy and pleasure
Rather hereafter, than in present, is.

To this life things of sense
    Make their pretence :
In th' other Angels have a right by birth :
    Man ties them both alone,
        And makes them one,
With t' one hand touching heav'n, with th' other
        earth.

In soul he mounts and flies,
    In flesh he dies.
He wears a stuff, whose thread is course and
        round,
    But trimm'd with curious lace,
        And should take place
After the trimming, not the stuff and ground.

Not that he may not here
    Taste of the cheer ;
But as birds drink, and straight lift up their heads
    So must he sip, and think
        Of better drink
He may attain to, after he is dead.

But as his joyes are double,
    So is his trouble.

He hath two winters, other things but one :
   Both frosts and thoughts do nip,
     And bite his lip ;
And he of all things fears two deaths alone.

   Yet ev'n the greatest griefs
     May be reliefs,
Could he but take them right, and in their wayes.
   Happy is he, whose heart
     Hath found the art
To turn his double pains to double praise.

GEORGE HERBERT

Let one Man place his satisfaction in sensual Pleasures, another in the delight of knowledge : though each of them cannot but confess there is great Pleasure in what the other pursues ; (for I think there is no Body so senseless as to deny that there is Pleasure in knowledge and also Pleasure in the taste of good Meats and Drinks) : yet neither of them making the other's delight a part of his happiness, their desires are not moved, but each is satisfied without what the other enjoys, and so his will is not determined to the pursuit of it. But yet as soon as the studious Man's hunger and thirst makes him uneasie, he whose will was never determined to any pursuit of good chear, poinant Sauces, or delicious Wine by the pleasant taste he has found in them, is, by the uneasiness of hunger and thirst, presently determined to eating and drinking, though possibly with great indifferency, what wholesome Food comes in his way. And on the other side, the Epicure buckles to study when shame or the desire to recommend himself to his Mistress shall make him

34

uneasie in the want of any sort of knowledge. Thus, how much soever Men are in earnest and constant in pursuit of happiness, yet they may have a clear view of good, great and confessed good, without being concerned for it or moved by it, if they think they can make up their happiness without it.

. . . .

The Mind has a different relish as well as the Palate, and you will as fruitlessly endeavour to delight all Men with Riches and Glory (which yet some Men place their Happiness in) as you would to satisfy all Men's Hunger with Cheese or Lobsters, which, though very agreeable and delicious fare to some, are to others extremely nauseous and offensive : and many People would with Reason preferr the griping of an hungry Belly to those Dishes which are a Feast to others. Hence it was, I think, that the Philosophers of old did in vain enquire whether *Summum Bonum* consisted in Riches, or bodily Delights, or Virtue, or Contemplation ; and they might have as reasonably disputed whether the best Relish were to be found in Apples, Plumbs, or Nuts, and have divided themselves into Sects upon it. For as pleasant Tastes depend not on the things themselves, but their aggreableness to this or that particular Palate, wherein there is great variety, so the greatest Happiness consists in having those things which produce the greatest pleasure, and the absence of those which cause any disturbance, any pain, which to different Men are very different things. If therefore Men in this life only have Hope, if in this life they can only enjoy, 'tis not strange nor unreasonable they should seek their Happiness by avoiding all things that disease them here and by preferring all that delight them ; wherein it will be no wonder to find

variety and difference. For if there be no Prospect
beyond the Grave, the inference is certainly right, *Let us
eat and drink*, let us enjoy what we delight in, *for tomorrow we shall die*. This, I think, may serve to show us
the Reason why, though all Men's desires tend to Happiness, yet they are not moved by the same Object. Men
may chuse different things, and yet all chuse right, supposing them only like a Company of poor Insects, whereof
some are Bees, delighted with Flowers and their sweetness ; others Beetles, delighted with other kind of Viands ;
which having enjoyed for a Season, they should cease to
be and exist no more for ever.

LOCKE

(from *Essay on the Human Understanding*)

After that Madame Pampinea was thus made Queen
. . . she arose fairely saying : Heere we have Gardens,
Orchardes, Medowes, and other places of sufficient
pleasure, where every one may sport and recreate themselves : but so soone as the ninth houre striketh, then all
to meet here againe, to dine in the coole shade.

This jocund company having received licence from
their Queene to disport themselves, the Gentlemen
walked with the Ladies into a goodly Garden, making
Chaplets and Nosegayes of divers flowers, and singing
silently to themselves. When they had spent the time
limitted by the Queene, they returned into the house,
where they found that Parmeno had effectually executed
his office. For when they entred into the hall, they saw
the Tables covered with delicate white Napery, and the
glasses looking like silver, they were so transparently

36

cleere, all the roome beside strewed with Flowers of Juniper. When the Queen and the rest had washed, according as Parmeno gave order, so every one was seated at the Table : the Viands (delicately drest) were served in, and excellent wines plentifully delivered, none attending but the three servants, and little or no lowd Table-talke passing among them.

Dinner being ended, and the Tables withdrawne (all the Ladies, and the Gentlemen likewise, being skilfull both in singing and dancing, and playing on instruments artificially) the Queene commanded, that divers Instruments should be brought, and (as she gave charge) Dioneus tooke a Lute, and Fiammetta a Violl de gamba, and began to play an excellent daunce. Whereupon, the Queene with the rest of the Ladies, and the other two young Gentlemen (having sent their attending servants to dinner) paced foorth a daunce very majestically. And when the dance was ended, they sung sundry excellent Canzonets, out-wearing so the time, untill the Queene commanded them all to rest, because the houre did necessarily require it. The Gentlemen having their chambers farre severed from the Ladies, curiously strewed with flowers, and their beds adorned in excellent manner, as those of the Ladies were not a jotte inferiour to them ; the silence of the night bestowed sweet rest on them al. In the morning, the Queene and all the rest being risen, accounting over much sleepe to be very hurtfull, they walked abroad into a goodly Meadow, where the grasse grew verdantly, and the beames of the Sun heated not over violently, because the shades of faire spreading Trees gave a temperate calmnesse, coole and gentle winds fanning their sweet breath pleasingly among them. All of them being there set downe in a round ring, and the Queen in the middest, as being the appointed place of eminency, she spake in this manner.

You see (faire company) that the Sunne is highly mounted, the heate (elsewhere) too extreme for us, and therefore here is our fittest refuge, the ayre being so coole, delicate, and acceptable, and our folly well worthy reprehension, if we should walke further, and speede worse. Heere are Tables, Cards, and Chesse, as your dispositions may bee addicted. But if mine advice might passe for currant, I would admit none of those exercises, because they are too troublesome both to them that play, and such as looke on. I could rather wish, that some quaint discourse might passe among us, a tale or fable related by some one, to urge the attention of all the rest. And so wearing out the warmth of the day, one prety Novell will draw on another, untill the Sun be lower declined, and the heates extremity more diminished, to solace our selves in some other place, as to our minds shall seeme convenient. If therefore what I have sayde bee acceptable to you (I purposing to follow in the same course of pleasure), let it appeare by your immediate answere ; for, till the Evening, I thinke we can devise no exercise more commodious for us.

The Ladies and Gentlemen allowed of the motion, to spend the time in telling pleasant tales ; whereupon the Queene saide : Seeing you have approved mine advice, I grant free permission for this first day, that every one shall relate what to him or her is best pleasing. And turning her selfe to Pamphilus (who was seated on her right hand) gave him favour, with one of his Novels, to begin the recreation.

BOCCACCIO
(from *The Decameron*—Nameless translation, 1620)

Of late, in one of those most weary hours,
When life seems emptied of all genial powers,
A dreary mood, which he who ne'er has known
May bless his happy lot, I sat alone ;
And, from the numbing spell to win relief,
Call'd on the Past for thought of glee or grief . . .
O Friend ! long wont to notice, yet conceal,
And soothe by silence what words cannot heal,
I but half saw that quiet hand of thine
Place on my desk this exquisite design.
Boccaccio's Garden and its faery,
The love, the joyaunce, and the gallantry !
An Idyll, with Boccaccio's spirit warm,
Framed in the silent poesy of form . . .
Thanks, gentle artist ! now I can descry
Thy fair creation with a mastering eye,
And all awake. And now in fix'd gaze stand,
Now wander through the Eden of thy hand ;
Praise the green arches, on the fountain clear
See fragment shadows of the crossing deer ;
And with that serviceable nymph I stoop
The crystal from its restless pool to scoop.
I see no longer : I myself am there,
Sit on the ground-sward, and the banquet share.
'Tis I that sweep that lute's love-echoing strings
And gaze upon the maid who gazing sings ;
Or pause and listen to the tinkling bells
From the high tower, and think that there she dwells.
With old Boccaccio's soul I stand possest,
And breathe an air like life, that swells my chest.

The brightness of the world, O thou once free,
And always fair, rare land of courtesy !
O Florence ! with the Tuscan fields and hills

And famous Arno, fed with all their rills ;
Thou brightest star of star-bright Italy !
Rich, ornate, populous, all treasures thine,
The golden corn, the olive, and the vine.
Fair cities, gallant mansions, castles old,
And forests, where beside his leafy hold
The sullen boar hath heard the distant horn,
And whets his tusks against the gnarled thorn ;
Palladian palace with its storied halls ;
Fountains, where Love lies listening to their falls ;
Gardens, where flings the bridge its airy span,
And Nature makes her happy home with man ;
Where many a gorgeous flower is duly fed
With its own rill, on its own spangled bed,
And wreathes the marble urn, or leans its head,
A mimic mourner, that with veil withdrawn
Weeps liquid gems, the presents of the dawn ;—
Thine all delights, and every muse is thine ;
And more than all, the embrace and intertwine
Of all with all in gay and twinkling dance.
'Mid gods of Greece and warriors of romance,
See, Boccace sits, unfolding on his knees
The new-found roll of old Mæonides ;
But from his mantle's fold, and near the heart,
Peers Ovid's Holy Book of Love's sweet smart.
O all-enjoying and all-blending sage,
Long be it mine to con thy mazy page,
Where, half conceal'd, the eye of fancy views
Fauns, nymphs, and winged saints, all gracious to
    thy muse !

Still in thy garden let me watch their pranks,
And see in Dian's vest between the ranks

Of the trim vines, some maid that half believes
The vestal fires, of which her lover grieves,
With that sly satyr peeping through the leaves.

COLERIDGE

When I die, I must depart not only from sensual delights, but from the more manly pleasures of my studies, knowledge, and converse with many wise and godly men, and from all my pleasure in reading, hearing, public and private exercises of religion, &c. I must leave my library, and turn over those pleasant books no more : I must no more come among the living, nor see the faces of my faithful friends, nor be seen of man : houses and cities, and fields and countries, gardens and walks, will be nothing, as to me. I shall no more hear of the affairs of the world, of man, or wars, or other news, nor see what becomes of that beloved interest of wisdom, piety, and peace, which I desire may prosper.

RICHARD BAXTER (from *Dying Thoughts*)

§ II BOOKS AND WRITERS

The Irish antiquaries mention *public libraries* that were before the flood ; and Paul Christian Ilsker, with profounder erudition, has given an exact catalogue of Adam's . . . Some too have noticed astronomical libraries in the Ark of Noah . . . Astle gravely observes that " with respect to *Writings* attributed to the *Antediluvians*, it seems not only decent but rational to say that we know nothing concerning them."

ISAAC D'ISRAELI (from *Curiosities of Literature*)

None writes so ill, that he gives not some thing exemplary, to follow, or flie.

DONNE

Books are not absolutely dead things, but do contain a progeny of life in them to be as active as that soul was whose progeny they are ; nay, they do preserve as in a vial the purest efficacy and extraction of that living intellect that bred them, I know they are as lively and as vigorously productive as those fabulous dragon's teeth ; and, being sown up and down, may chance to spring up armed men.

MILTON (from *Areopagitica*)

Dionysius Alexandrinus was, about the year 240, a person of great name in the church for piety and learning, who had wont to avail himself much against heretics by being conversant with their books, until a certain presbyter laid it scrupulously to his conscience how he durst venture himself among those defiling volumes. The worthy man, loath to give offence, fell into a new debate with himself, what was to be thought ; when suddenly a vision sent from God (it is his own epistle that so avers it) confirmed him in these words : " Read any books whatever come to thy hands, for thou are sufficient both to judge aright and to examine each matter."

MILTON (from *Areopagitica*)

He who would not be frustrate of his hope to write well hereafter in laudable things, ought himself to be a true poem ; that is, a composition and pattern of the best and honourablest things.

MILTON (from *Apology for Smectymnuus*)

The virtue of the poet is bound to that of the man, and it is impossible to be a good poet unless you are in the first place a good man.

STRABO

Blessings be with them and eternal praise,
Who gave us nobler lives and nobler cares—
The poets, who on earth have made us heirs
Of truth and pure delight by heavenly lays.

WORDSWORTH

Now when I beginne this booke, I have no purpose to
come into any mans debt; how my stocke will hold out
I know not; perchance waste, perchance increase in use;
if I doe borrow any thing of Antiquitie, besides that I
make account that I pay it to posterity, with as much and
as good : You shall still finde mee to acknowledge it, and
to thanke not him onely that hath digg'd out treasure for
mee, but that hath lighted mee a candle to the place.

DONNE

They who say our thoughts are not our own, because
they resemble the ancients, may as well say our faces are
not our own, because they are like our fathers : and,
indeed, it is very unreasonable that people should expect
us to be scholars, and yet be angry to find us so.

POPE (from Preface to *The Poems*)

I wish our clever young poets would remember my
homely definitions of prose and poetry; that is, prose
words in their best order; poetry the *best* words in the
best order.

. . . .

I think nothing can be added to Milton's definition or
rule of poetry,—that it ought to be simple, sensuous, and
impassioned ; that is to say, single in conception, abound-
ing in sensible images, and informing them all with the
spirit of the mind.

COLERIDGE (from *Table Talk*)

We will allow a poet to express his meaning, when his meaning is not well known to himself, with a certain degree of obscurity, as it is one source of the sublime.

Obscurity is Neither the Source of the Sublime nor of any Thing Else.

SIR JOSHUA REYNOLDS

(with BLAKE'S comment)

There is something in poetry beyond prose reason ; there are mysteries in it not to be explained, but admired. . . .

. . . .

Genius often then deserves most to be praised when it is most sure to be condemned ; that is, when its excellence, from mounting high, to weak eyes is quite out of sight.

. . . .

Learning . . . is fond and proud of what has cost it much pains ; is a great lover of rules, and boaster of famed examples. As beauties less perfect, who owe half their charms to cautious art, learning inveighs against natural unstudied graces and small harmless inaccuracies, and sets rigid bounds to that liberty to which genius often owes its supreme glory, but the no-genius its frequent ruin. For unprescribed beauties, and unexampled excellence, which are characteristics of genius, lie without the pale of learning's authorities and laws ; which pale, genius must leap to come at them : but by that leap, if genius is wanting, we break our necks, we lose that little credit which possibly we might have enjoyed before. For rules, like crutches, are a needful aid to the lame, though an impediment to the strong.

EDWARD YOUNG

(from *Conjectures on Original Composition*)

BOSWELL. " Then, Sir, what is poetry ? " JOHNSON. " Why, Sir, it is much easier to say what it is not. We all *know* what light is ; but it is not easy to *tell* what it is."

BOSWELL (from *The Life of Samuel Johnson*)

I am inclined to think that both the writers of books, and the readers of them, are generally not a little unreasonable in their expectations. The first seem to fancy that the world must approve whatever they produce, and the latter to imagine that authors are obliged to please them at any rate. Methinks, as on the one hand, no single man is born with a right of controlling the opinions of all the rest ; so on the other, the world has no title to demand, that the whole care and time of any particular person should be sacrificed to its entertainment. Therefore I cannot but believe that writers and readers are under equal obligations, for as much fame, or pleasure, as each affords the other.

POPE (from Preface to *The Poems*)

The pattern, the idea, the ecstasy : it is for these that we must read, not for the word, the fact, the material out of which they are wrought.

T. EARLE WELBY (from *The Dinner Knell*)

Next day he led me into another part of his library. " Here," he said to me, " we have the poets, that is to say those writers whose business it is to put shackles on common sense and to bury reason under decoration, as in former times it was the custom to bury women under their finery. You know them : they are no rarity in the East, where the greater power of the sun, it would seem, heats even the imagination.

" Here are the epics."

" Ah ! And what, if you please, are epics ? "

" To be sure," he said, " I don't know. The authorities assure us that there are only two, and that all others offered under this name are not epics ; but of that also I know nothing. They say, moreover, that it is impossible to write new epics, which is still more surprising.

" Here we have the dramatic poets, who, in my opinion, are the supreme poets, the masters of passion. There are two kinds ; the comic, who stir us so gently, and the tragic, who trouble and disturb us with such violence.

" And here are the lyric poets, whom I despise as much as I esteem the others, whose art is merely a harmonious extravagance.

" Next we see the writers of idylls and eclogues, much appreciated by court society because they give them the idea of a certain tranquility which they do not possess and display them in the character of shepherds.

" Of all the writers we have seen, these next are the most dangerous. It is these that sharpen epigrams, which are little arrows that cause a deep wound beyond reach of remedies.

" Here you see the novels, whose authors are a sort of

poets who strain equally the language of intellect and that of the heart. They pass their lives in a pursuit of nature which is always unsuccessful and their heroes are as foreign to nature as the winged dragon and the hippocentaur."

MONTESQUIEU (from *Lettres Persanes*)

THE POET AS SCIENTIST

As the eyes of Lyncæus were said to see through the earth, so the poet turns the world to glass, and shows us all things in their right series and procession. For, through that better perception, he stands one step nearer to things, and sees the flowing or metamorphosis; perceives that thought is multiform; that within the form of every creature is a force impelling it to ascend into a higher form; and, following with his eyes the life, uses the forms which express that life, and so his speech flows with the flowing of nature. All the facts of the animal economy, sex, nutriment, gestation, birth, growth, are symbols of the passage of the world into the soul of man, to suffer there a change, and reappear a new and higher fact. He uses forms according to the life, and not according to the form. This is true science. The poet alone knows astronomy, chemistry, vegetation, and animation, for he does not stop at these facts, but employs them as signs. He knows why the plain or meadow of space was strown with these flowers we call suns, and moons, and stars; why the great deep is adorned with animals, with men, and gods; for in every word he speaks he rides on them as the horses of thought.

By virtue of this science the poet is the Namer, or

Language-maker, naming things sometimes after their appearance, sometimes after their essence, and giving to every one its own name and not another's, thereby rejoicing the intellect, which delights in detachment or boundary. The poets made all the words, and therefore language is the archives of history, and, if we must say it, a sort of tomb of the muses. For, though the origin of most of our words is forgotten, each word was at first a stroke of genius, and obtained currency, because for the moment it symbolised the world to the first speaker and to the hearer. The etymologist finds the deadest word to have been once a brilliant picture. Language is fossil poetry. As the limestone of the continent consists of infinite masses of the shells of animalcules, so language is made up of images, or tropes, which now, in their secondary use, have long ceased to remind us of their poetic origin. But the poet names the thing because he sees it, or comes one step nearer to it than any other. This expressing, or naming, is not art, but a second nature, grown out of the first, as a leaf out of a tree.

EMERSON (from *The Essays*)

THE ENGLISH GENIUS

Consider that which, even with the Authorized Version, Donne, Sir Thomas Browne, Landor and Pater to set against it, must be esteemed the chief glory of our literature and the most intimate expression of the national genius : our lyrical poetry. What distinguishes English poetry from that of other nations is a quality of atmosphere, corresponding to something in our character. It comes, of course, as I have tried to say elsewhere, very largely from the conditions under which nature presents itself to the eyes in such a climate as ours. The lack of definition in things seen under our usual skies, the mutable face of nature with us as cloud and mist and changing lights work on it, encourage a view of the world in which the bare and enduring fact, independent of its surrounding atmosphere, of the aspect it bears at a choice moment, is negligible. Well, how should such a poetry be taught, how should it yield to a direct and intellectual attack made on it by those who have been educated out of their instincts without being qualified to read it with both innocence and the amplest literary experience ?

T. EARLE WELBY (from The Dinner Knell)

THE ENGLISH METRES

The rooted liberty of flowers in breeze
    Is theirs, by national luck impulsive, terse,
Tethered, uncaptured, rules obeyed " at ease,"
    Time-strengthened laws of verse.

Or they are like our seasons that admit
    Inflection, not infraction : Autumn hoar,
Winter more tender than our thoughts of it,
    But a year's steadfast four ;

Redundant syllables of Summer rain,
    And displaced accents of authentic Spring ;
Spondaic clouds above a dusty plain
    With dactyls on the wing.

Not Common Law, but Equity, is theirs—
    Our metres ; play and agile foot askance,
And distant, beckoning, blithely rhyming pairs,
    Unknown to classic France ;

Unknown to Italy. Ay, count, collate,
  Latins ! with eye foreseeing on the time,
And numbered fingers, and approaching fate
  On the appropriate rhyme.

Nay, nobly our grave measures are decreed :
  Heroic, Alexandrine with the stay,
Deliberate ; or else like him whose speed
  Did outrun Peter, urgent in the break of day.

ALICE MEYNELL

OF STUDIES

Studies serve for delight, for ornament, and for ability.
Their chief use for delight is in privateness and retiring ;
for ornament, is in discourse ; and for ability, is in the
judgment and disposition of business. For expert men can
execute, and perhaps judge of particulars, one by one ; but
the general counsels, and the plots, and marshalling of
affairs, come best from those that are learned. To spend
too much time in studies is sloth ; to use them too much
for ornament is affectation ; to make judgment wholly by
their rules is the humour of a scholar. They perfect
nature, and are perfected by experience : for natural
abilities are like natural plants, that need proyning by
study : and studies themselves do give forth directions too
much at large, except they be bounded in by experience.
Crafty men contemn studies ; simple men admire them ;
and wise men use them : for they teach not their own use ;
but that is a wisdom without them, and above them, won
by observation. Read not to contradict and confute ; nor

to believe and take for granted ; nor to find talk and discourse ; but to weigh and consider. Some books are to be tasted, others to be swallowed, and some few to be chewed and digested : that is, some books are to be read only in parts ; others to be read but not curiously ; and some few to be read wholly, and with diligence and attention. Some books also may be read by deputy, and extracts made of them by others : but that would be only in the less important arguments, and the meaner sort of books : else distilled books are like common distilled waters, flashy things. Reading maketh a full man ; conference a ready man ; and writing an exact man. And therefore, if a man write little, he had need have a great memory ; if he confer little, he had need have a present wit ; and if he read little, he had need have much cunning, to seem to know that he doth not. Histories make men wise ; poets witty, the mathematics subtle ; natural philosophy deep ; moral grave ; logic and rhetoric able to contend. *Abeunt studia in mores*. Nay, there is no stond or impediment in the wit but may be wrought out by fit studies.

BACON (from *The Essays*)

POETRY AND MUSIC

Certain is it, that the great heights and excellency both of poetry and music fell with the Roman learning and empire, and have never since recovered the admiration and applauses that before attended them : yet, such as they are among us, they must be confessed to be the softest and sweetest, the most general and most innocent amusements of common time and life. They still find room in the courts of princes and the cottages of shepherds : they serve to revive and animate the dead calm of poor or idle lives, and to allay or divert the violent passions and perturbations of the greatest and the busiest men. And both these effects are of equal use to human life : for the mind of man is like the sea, which is neither agreeable to the beholder nor the voyager in a calm or in a storm, but is so to both when a little agitated by gentle gales ; and so the mind, when moved by soft and easy passions and affections. I know very well that many, who pretend to be wise by the forms of being grave, are apt to despise both poetry and music as toys and trifles too light for the use or entertainment of serious men ; but whoever find themselves wholly insensible to these charms, would, I think, do well to keep their own counsel, for fear of reproaching their own temper, and bringing the goodness of their natures, if not of their understandings, into question : it may be thought an ill sign, if not an ill constitution, since some fathers went so far as to esteem the love of music a sign of predestination, as a thing divine, and reserved for the felicities of Heaven itself. While the world lasts, I doubt not but the pleasure and requests of these two entertainments will do so too : and happy those that content themselves with these, or any other so easy and so innocent, and do not trouble the world, or other men, because they cannot be quiet themselves, though no body hurts them !

When all is done, human life is, at the greatest and the best, but like a froward child, that must be played with and humoured a little to keep it quiet till it falls asleep, and then the care is over.

SIR WILLIAM TEMPLE (from *Miscellanea*)

THE DEFENCE OF POESIE

Now, therein, of all Sciences (I speake still of humane, and according to the humane conceit, is our *Poet* the *Monarch*. For hee doth not onely shew the way, but giveth so sweete a prospect into the way, as will entice anie man to enter into it : Nay he doth as if your journey should lye through a faire vineyard, at the verie first, give you a cluster of grapes, that, full of that taste, you may long to passe further. Hee beginneth not with obscure definitions which must blurre the margent with interpretations, and loade the memoriē with doubtfulnesse : but hee commeth to you with words set in delightfull proportion, either accompanied with, or prepared for the well-enchanting skill of *Musicke* ; and with a tale forsooth he commeth unto you, with a tale, which holdeth children from play, and olde men from the Chimney corner ; and pretending no more, doth intend the winning of the minde from wickedness to vertue ; even as the child is often brought to take most wholesome things by hiding them in such other as have a pleasaunt taste : which if one should begin to tell them the nature of the *Alloes* or *Rhabarbarum* they should receive, wold sooner take their phisick at their eares then at their mouth. So is it in men, most of which are childish in the best things, til they be cradled in their graves. Glad they will be to heare the tales of *Hercules, Achilles, Cyrus, Æneas*, and hearing them, must needes heare the right description of wisdom, value, and justice ; which if they had bene barely (that is to say Philosophically) set out, they would sweare they be brought to schoole againe. That imitation whereof *Poetrie* is, hath the most conveniencie to nature of al other ; insomuch that as *Aristotle* saith, those things which in

57

themselves are horrible, as cruel battailes, unnatural monsters, are made in poeticall imitation, delightfull.

SIR PHILIP SIDNEY
(from The Defence of Poesie)

ON LITERATURE

To men of letters and leisure, it is not only a noble amusement, but a sweet refuge ; it improves their parts, and promotes their peace ; it opens a back-door out of the bustle of this busy and idle world, into a delicious garden of moral and intellectual fruits and flowers, the key of which is denied to the rest of mankind. When stung with idle anxieties, or stung with fruitless impertinence, or yawning over insipid diversions, then we perceive the blessings of a lettered recess. With what a gust do we retire to our disinterested and immortal friends in our closet, and find our minds, when applied to some favourite theme, as naturally and as easily quieted and refreshed as a peevish child (and peevish children are we all till we fall asleep) when laid to the breast ! Our happiness no longer lives on charity ; nor bids fair for a fall, by leaning on that most precarious and thorny pillow, another's pleasure, for our repose. How independent of the world is he, who can daily find new acquaintance that at once entertain and improve him, in the little world, the minute but fruitful creation of his own mind !

These advantages composition affords us, whether we write ourselves, or in more humble amusement peruse the works of others.

EDWARD YOUNG

THE WORLD IN BOOKS

I go into my library, and all history unrolls before me. I breathe the morning air of the world while the scent of Eden's roses yet lingered in it, while it vibrated only to the world's first brood of nightingales, and to the laugh of Eve. I see the pyramids building; I hear the shoutings of the armies of Alexander; I feel the ground shake beneath the march of Cambyses. I sit as in a theatre,—the stage is time, the play is the play of the world. What a spectacle it is! What kingly pomp, what processions file past, what cities burn to heaven, what crowds of captives are dragged at the chariot-wheels of conquerors! I hear or cry "Bravo" when the great actors come on shaking the stage. I am a Roman Emperor when I look at a Roman coin. I lift Homer, and I shout with Achilles in the trenches. The silence of the unpeopled Syrian plains, the out-comings and in-goings of the patriarchs, Abraham and Ishmael, Isaac in the fields at even-tide, Rebekah at the well, Jacob's guile, Esau's face reddened by desert sun-heat, Joseph's splendid funeral procession—all these things I find within the boards of my Old Testament. What a silence in those old books as of a half-peopled world—what bleating of flocks—what green pastoral rest—what indubitable human existence! Across brawling centuries of blood and war, I hear the bleating of Abraham's flocks, the tinkling of the bells of Rebekah's camels. O men and women, so far separated yet so near, so strange yet so well-known, by what miraculous power do I know ye all! Books are the true Elysian fields where the spirits of the dead converse, and into these fields a mortal may venture unappalled. What king's court can boast such company? What school of Philosophy such wisdom?

The wit of the ancient world is glancing and flashing there. There is Pan's pipe, there are the songs of Apollo. Seated in my library at night, and looking on the silent faces of my books, I am occasionally visited by a strange sense of the supernatural. They are not collections of printed pages, they are ghosts. I take one down and it speaks with me in a tongue not now heard on earth, and of man and things of which it alone possesses knowledge. I call myself a solitary, but sometimes I think I misapply the term. No man sees more company than I do. I travel with mightier cohorts around me than ever did Timour or Genghis Khan on their fiery marches. I am a sovereign in my library, but it is the dead, not the living that attend my levees.

ALEXANDER SMITH (from *Dreamthorpe*)

AN OMNIVOROUS READER

To mind the inside of a book is to entertain one's self with the forced product of another man's brain. Now I think a man of quality and breeding may be much amused with the natural sprouts of his own.—Lord Foppington, in " The Relapse."

An ingenious acquaintance of my own was so much struck with this brilliant sally of his Lordship, that he has left off reading altogether, to the great improvement of his originality. At the hazard of losing some credit on this head, I must confess that I dedicate no inconsiderable portion of my time to other people's thoughts. I dream away my life in others' speculations. I love to lose myself in other men's minds. When I am not walking, I am reading ; I cannot sit and think. Books think for me.

60

I have no repugnances. Shaftesbury is not too genteel for me, nor Jonathan Wild too low. I can read anything which I call *a book*. There are things in that shape which I cannot allow for such.

In this catalogue of *books which are no books*—*biblia a-biblia*—I reckon Court Calendars, Directories, Pocket Books, Draught Boards, bound and lettered on the back, Scientific Treatises, Almanacs, Statutes at Large : the works of Hume, Gibbon, Robertson, Beattie, Soame Jenyns, and generally, all those volumes which " no gentleman's library should be without " : the *Histories* of Flavius Josephus (that learned Jew), and Paley's *Moral Philosophy*. With these exceptions I can read almost anything. I bless my stars for a taste so catholic, so unexcluding.

LAMB (from *The Essays of Elia*)

OF POETS AND POETRY

CÆDMON

In the monastery of the Abbess Hilda of Whitby was a certain brother especially marked by Divine grace, since he was wont to make songs suited to religion and piety, so that whatever he had learned from the Divine writings through interpreters, this he in a little while produced in poetical expressions composed with the greatest harmony and accuracy, in his own tongue, that is, in that of the Angles. By his songs the minds of many were excited to contemn the world, and desire the celestial life. And, indeed, others also after him in the nation of the Angles attempted to compose religious poems, but none could equal him. For he himself did not learn the art of poetry from men, or by being instructed by man ; but, being divinely assisted, received gratuitously the gift of singing, on which account he never could compose any frivolous or idle poem, but those only which pertain to religion suited his religious tongue. For having lived in the secular habit unto the time of advanced age, he had never learned anything of singing. Whence, sometimes at an entertainment, when it was determined for the sake of mirth that all should sing in order, he, when he saw the harp approaching him, used to rise in the midst of his supper, and, having gone out, walk back to his home.

Which, when he was doing on a tune, and having left the house of entertainment had gone out to the stable of the beasts of burden, the care of which was entrusted to him on that night, and there, at the proper hour had resigned his limbs to sleep, a certain one stood by him in a dream, who saluting him and calling him by his name, said, " Cædmon, sing me something." Then he answering said, " I know not how to sing ; and for that reason I went out from the entertainment and returned hither, because I could not sing." Again he who was talking with him said, " Yet you have something to sing to me." " What," said he, " must I sing ? " The other said, " Sing the beginning of created things." Having received this reply, he immediately began to sing verses in praise of God the Creator, which he had never heard, whereof this is the purport :—" Now we must praise the Author of the celestial kingdom, the power of the Creator and His counsel, the deeds of the Father of glory. How He, being

Eternal God, was the author of all wonderful things ; who first created heaven for the sons of men, on the roof of their dwellings, and afterwards created the earth, being the omnipotent guardian of mankind." This is the sense, but not the exact order of the words which he sang in his sleep, for songs, however excellently composed, cannot be translated from one tongue into another, word for word, without some loss of their beauty and spirit. Moreover, on his rising up from sleep, he retained in memory all that he had sung in his dream, and presently added to it more words of song worthy of God, after the same fashion.

And coming in the morning to the steward who was set over him, he told him what a gift he had received ; and having been brought to the Abbess, he was ordered, in the presence of many learned men, to declare his dream, and to repeat the song, that it might be tested, by the judgment of all, what or whence it was that he related. And all concluded that a celestial gift had been granted him by the Lord. And they interpreted to him a certain passage of sacred history or doctrine, and ordered him to transpose it, if he could, into hallowed rhythm. And he, having undertaken it, departed, and returning in the morning, brought back what he was ordered to do, composed in most excellent verse. Whereupon presently the Abbess, embracing heartily the grace of God in the man, instructed him to leave the secular habit and to take the monastic vow ; and having, together with all her people, received him into the monastery, associated him with the company of the brethren and ordered him to be instructed in the whole course of sacred history. And he converted into most sweet song whatever he could learn from hearing, by thinking it over by himself, and, as though a clean animal, by *ruminations* ; and by making it resound more sweetly, made his teachers in turn his hearers.

BEDE (Trans. GIDLEY)

CHAUCER

Chaucer is himself the great poetical observer of men, who in every age is born to record and eternize its acts. This he does as a master, as a father, and superior, who looks down on their little follies from the Emperor to the Miller ; sometimes with severity, oftener with joke and sport. . . .

Of Chaucer's characters, as described in his Canterbury Tales, some of the names or titles are altered by time, but the characters themselves for ever remain unaltered, and consequently they are the physiognomies or lineaments of universal human life, beyond which Nature never steps. Names alter, things never alter. I have known multitudes of those who would have been monks in the age of monkery, who in this deistical age are deists. As Newton numbered the stars, and as Linneus numbered the plants, so Chaucer numbered the classes of men.

BLAKE (from *A Descriptive Catalogue*)

Great thanks, laud, and honour ought to be given unto the clerks, poets, and historiographs that have written many noble books of wisdom of the lives, passions, and miracles of holy saints, of histories of noble and famous

64

acts and faites, and of the chronicles since the beginning of the creation of the world unto this present time, by which we be daily informed and have knowledge of many things of whom we should not have known if they had not left to us their monuments written. Among whom and in especial before all others, we ought to give a singular laud unto that noble and great philosopher Geoffrey Chaucer, the which for his ornate writing in our tongue may well have the name of a laureate poet. For to-fore that he by labour embellished, ornated, and made fair our English, in this realm was had rude speech and incongruous, as yet it appeareth by old books, which at this day ought not to have place ne be compared among, ne to, his beauteous volumes and ornate writings, of whom he made many books and treatises of many a noble history, as well in metre as in rhyme and prose ; and them so craftily made that he comprehended his matters in short, quick, and high sentences, eschewing prolixity, casting away the chaff of superfluity, and showing the picked grain of sentence uttered by crafty and sugared eloquence ; of whom among all others of his books I purpose to print, by the grace of God, the book of the tales of Canterbury, in which I find many a noble history of every state and degree ; first rehearsing the conditions and the array of each of them as properly as possible is to be said ; and after their tales which be of nobleness, wisdom, gentleness, mirth, and also of very holiness and virtue, wherein he finisheth this said book, which book I have diligently overseen and duly examined, to the end that it be made according unto his own making.

CAXTON (from Proem to *Canterbury Tales*)

Beside the pleasant Mill of Trompington
I laughed with Chaucer in the hawthorn shade ;
Heard him, while birds were warbling, tell his tales
Of amorous passion. And that gentle Bard,
Chosen by the Muses for their Page of State—
Sweet Spenser, moving through his clouded heaven
With the moon's beauty and the moon's soft pace,
I called him Brother, Englishman, and Friend.

WORDSWORTH (from *The Prelude*)

EDMUND SPENSER TO GABRIEL HARVEY

To the Worshipfull his very Singular Good Friend,
Maister G. H., Fellow of Trinitie Hall in Cambridge.

Good Master G. I perceive by your most curteous and
frendly Letters your good will to be no lesse in deed than
I alwayes esteemed. In recompence whereof, think I
beseech you, that I wil spare neither speech nor wryting,
nor aught else, whensoever, and wheresoever occasion
shall be offred me. . . As for the twoo worthy Gentlemen,
Master Sidney and Master Dyer, they have me, I thanke
them, in some use of familiarity : of whom and to whome,
what speache passeth for youre credite and estimation,
I leave to your selfe to conceive, having alwayes so well
conceived of my unfained affection and zeale towardes
you. And nowe they have proclaimed in their ἀρειωπάγῳ
a generall surceasing and silence of balde Rymers, and
also of the verie beste to : in steade whereof they have,
by authoritie of their whole Senate, prescribed certaine
Lawes and rules of Quantities of Englishe sillables for
English Verse : having had thereof already great practise,
and drawen mee to their faction. . .

Truste me, your Verses I like passingly well, and envye your hidden paines in this kinde, or rather maligne, and grudge at your selfe, that woulde not once imparte so muche to me. But once or twice you make a breache in Maister Drants Rules : *quod tamen condonabimus tanto Poetæ, tuæque ipsius maximæ in his rebus autoritati.* You shall see when we meete in London (whiche, when it shall be, certifye us) howe fast I have followed after you in that course : beware leaste in time I overtake you. *Veruntamen te solum sequar (ut sæpenumero sum professus,) nunquam sane assequar dum vivam.*

And nowe requite I you with the like, not with the verye beste, but with the verye shortest, namely, with a few Iambickes ; I dare warrant they be precisely perfect for the feete (as you can easily judge), and varie not one inch from the Rule. I will imparte yours to Maister Sidney and Maister Dyer at my nexte going to the Courte. I praye you, keepe mine close to your selfe, or your verie entire friendes, Maister Preston, Maister Still, and the reste.

Unhappie Verse ! the witnesse of my unhappie state,
Make thy selfe fluttring wings of thy fast flying Thought,
And fly forth unto my Love wheresoever she be.

Whether lying restlesse in heavy bedde, or else
Sitting so cheerelesse at the cheerefull boorde, or else
Playing alone carelesse on hir heavenlie Virginals.

If in Bed, tell hir that my eyes can take no reste ;
If at Boorde, tell hir that my mouth can eat no meete ;
If at hir Virginals, tell hir I can heare no mirth.

Asked why ? say : Waking Love suffereth no sleepe ;
Say that raging Love doth appall the weake stomacke,
Say that lamenting Love marreth the Musicall.

Tell hir that hir pleasures were wonte to lull me asleepe,
Tell hir that hir beauty was wonte to feede mine eyes,
Tell hir that hir sweete Tongue was wonte to make me
    mirth.

Now doe I nightly waste, wanting my kindely reste,
Now doe I daily starve, wanting my lively food,
Now doe I always dye, wanting my timely mirth.

And if I waste who will bewaile my heavy chance ?
And if I starve, who will record my cursed end ?
And if I dye, who will saye, *This was Immerito* ?

. . . So once againe, and yet once more, Farewell most
hartily, mine owne good Master H. and love me, as I love
you, and thinke upon poore Immerito, as he thinketh
uppon you.

SPENSER

Leycester House, this 5 of October, 1579.

SHAKESPEARE

                Soul of the age !
The applause ! delight ! the wonder of our stage !
My Shakespeare rise ! I will not lodge thee by
Chaucer, or Spenser, or bid Beaumont lie
A little further, to make thee a room :
Thou art a monument without a tomb,
And art alive still while thy book both live
And we have wits to read, and praise to give.
That I not mix thee so my brain excuses,
I mean with great, but disproportioned Muses :
For if I thought my judgement were of years,

68

I should commit thee surely with thy peers,
And tell how far thou didst our Lyly outshine,
Or sporting Kyd, or Marlowe's mighty line.
And though thou hadst small Latin and less Greek,
From thence to honour thee, I would not seek
For names : but call forth thund'ring Æschylus,
Euripides, and Sophocles to us,
Pacuvius, Accius, him of Cordova dead,
To life again, to hear thy buskin tread
And shake a stage : or when thy socks were on,
Leave thee alone for the comparison
Of all that insolent Greece or haughty Rome
Sent forth, or since did from their ashes come.
Triumph, my Britain, thou hast one to show,
To whom all Scenes of Europe homage owe.
He was not of an age, but for all time !
And all the Muses still were in their prime,
When, like Apollo, he came forth to warm
Our ears, or like a Mercury to charm !
Nature herself was proud of his designs,
And joyed to wear the dressing of his lines !
Which were so richly spun, and woven so fit,
As, since, she will vouchsafe no other wit.
The merry Greek, tart Aristophanes,
Neat Terence, witty Plautus, now not please ;
But antiquated and deserted lie,
As they were not of Nature's family.
Yet must I not give Nature all ; thy Art,
My gentle Shakespeare, must enjoy a part.
For though the poet's matter nature be,
His art doth give the fashion : and, that he
Who casts to write a living line, must sweat,
(Such as thine are) and strike the second heat

Upon the Muses' anvil; turn the same,
And himself with it, that he thinks to frame;
Or for the laurel he may gain a scorn;
For a good poet's made, as well as born.
And such wert thou! Look how the father's face
Lives in his issue, even so the race
Of Shakespeare's mind and manners brightly shines
In his well turnèd and true filèd lines:
In each of which he seems to shake a lance,
As brandisht at the eyes of ignorance.
Sweet Swan of Avon! what a sight it were
To see thee in our waters yet appear,
And make those flights upon the banks of Thames,
That so did take Eliza, and our James!
But stay, I see thee in the hemisphere
Advanced, and made a constellation there!
Shine forth, thou Star of Poets, and with rage,
Or influence, chide or cheer the drooping stage,
Which, since thy flight from hence, hath mourned
    like night,
And despairs day but for thy volume's light.

BEN JONSON

What needs my Shakespear for his honour'd Bones,
The labour of an age in piled Stones,
Or that his hallow'd reliques should be hid
Under a star-ypointing Pyramid?
Dear son of memory, great heir of Fame,
What need'st thou such weak witnes of thy name?
Thou in our wonder and astonishment
Hast built thy self a live-long Monument.

For whilst to th'shame of slow-endeavouring art,
Thy easie numbers flow, and that each heart
Hath from the leaves of thy unvalu'd Book,
Those Delphick lines with deep impression took,
Then thou our fancy of it self bereaving,
Dost make us Marble with too much conceaving ;
And so Sepulcher'd in such pomp dost lie,
That Kings for such a Tomb would wish to die.

MILTON

Others abide our question, thou art free.
We ask and ask—Thou smilest and art still,
Out-topping knowledge. For the loftiest hill,
Who to the star uncrowns his majesty,
Planting his steadfast footsteps in the sea,
Making the heaven of heavens his dwelling-place,
Spares but the cloudy border of his base
To the foil'd searching of mortality ;
And thou, who didst the stars and sunbeams know,
Self-school'd, self-scann'd, self-honour'd, self-secure
Didst tread on earth unguess'd at.—Better so !
All pains the immortal spirit must endure,
All weakness which impairs, all griefs which bow,
Find their sole speech in that victorious brow.

MATTHEW ARNOLD

Shakespeare is the king of poetic rhythm and style, as well as the king of the realm of thought; along with his dazzling prose, Shakespeare has succeeded in giving us the most varied, the most harmonious verse which has ever sounded upon the human ear since the verse of the Greeks.

HENRY COCHIN (Trans. MATTHEW ARNOLD)

He was an eminent instance of the truth of that rule, *Poeta non fit, sed nascitur* : " One is not made, but born a poet." Indeed his learning was very little, so that, as Cornish diamonds are not polished by any lapidary, but are pointed and smoothed even as they are taken out of the earth, so nature itself was all the art which was used upon him.

Many were the wit-combats betwixt him and Ben Jonson, which two I behold like a great Spanish gallion, and an English man-of-war : Master Jonson (like the former) was built far higher in learning ; solid, but slow, in his performances. Shakespeare, with the English man-of-war, lesser in bulk, but lighter in sailing, could turn with all tides, tack about, and take advantage of all winds, by the quickness of his wit and invention.

FULLER (from *The Worthies of England*)

He was the man who of all Modern, and perhaps Ancient Poets, had the largest and most comprehensive soul. All the Images of Nature were still present to him, and he drew them not laboriously, but luckily : when he

72

describes any thing, you more than see it, you feel it too. Those who accuse him to have wanted learning, give him the greater commendation : he was naturally learn'd ; he needed not the spectacles of Books to read Nature ; he look'd inwards, and found her there. I cannot say he is every where alike ; were he so, I should do him injury to compare him with the greatest of Mankind. He is many times flat, insipid ; his Comick wit degenerating into clenches, his serious swelling into Bombast. But he is alwayes great, when some great occasion is presented to him : no man can say he ever had a fit subject for his wit, and did not then raise himself as high above the rest of the Poets,

Quantum lenta solent inter viburna cupressi.

The consideration of this made Mr *Hales* of *Eaton* say, That there was no subject of which any Poet ever writ, but he would produce it much better treated of in *Shakespeare*; and however others are now generally prefer'd before him, yet the Age wherein he liv'd, which had contemporaries with him *Fletcher* and *Johnson*, never equall'd them to him in their esteem : And in the last Kings Court, when *Ben's* reputation was at its highest, Sir *John Suckling*, and with him the greater part of the Courtiers, set our *Shakespeare* far above him.

. . . .

Shakespeare was the *Homer*, or Father of our Dramatick Poets ; *Johnson* was the *Virgil*, the pattern of elaborate writing ; I admire him, but I love *Shakespeare*.

DRYDEN (from *Of Dramatick Poesie*)

ON FIRST LOOKING INTO CHAPMAN'S HOMER

Much have I travell'd in the realms of gold,
And many goodly states and kingdoms seen ;
Round many western islands have I been
Which bards in fealty to Apollo hold.
Oft of one wide expanse had I been told
That deep-brow'd Homer ruled as his demesne ;
Yet did I never breathe its pure serene
Till I heard Chapman speak out loud and bold :
Then felt I like some watcher of the skies
When a new planet swims into his ken ;
Or like stout Cortez when with eagle eyes
He stared at the Pacific—and all his men
Look'd at each other with a wild surmise—
Silent, upon a peak in Darien.

KEATS

MILTON

Reading Milton is like dining off gold plate in a company of kings ; very splendid, very ceremonious, not a little appalling. Him I read but seldom, and only on high days and festivals of the spirit. Him I never lay down without feeling my appreciation increased for lesser men. . . . After long-continued organ-music, the jangle of the Jew's harp is felt as an exquisite relief.

ALEXANDER SMITH (from *Dreamthorpe*)

74

Milton almost requires a solemn service of music to be played before you enter upon him. But he brings his own music, to which, who listens, had need bring docile thoughts, and purged ears.

LAMB (from *The Essays of Elia*)

Milton ! thou shouldst be living at this hour :
England hath need of thee ; she is a fen
Of stagnant waters ; altar, sword, and pen,
Fireside, the heroic wealth of hall and bower,
Have forfeited their ancient English dower
Of inward happiness. We are selfish men ;
Oh ! raise us up, return to us again ;
And give us manners, virtue, freedom, power.
Thy soul was like a star, and dwelt apart ;
Thou hadst a voice whose sound was like the sea ;
Pure as the naked heavens, majestic, free,
So didst thou travel on life's common way
In cheerful godliness ; and yet thy heart
The lowliest duties on herself did lay.

WORDSWORTH

I should not choose this manner of writing, wherein knowing myself inferior to myself, led by the genial power of nature to another task, I have the use, as I may account, but of my left hand. And though I shall be foolish in saying more to this purpose, yet, since it will be such a folly as wisest men go about to commit, having only confessed and so committed, I may trust with more

75

reason, because with more folly, to have courteous pardon. For although a poet, soaring in the high reason of his fancies, with his garland and singing robes about him, might, without apology, speak more of himself than I mean to do; yet for me sitting here below in the cool element of prose, a mortal thing among many readers of no empyreal conceit, to venture and divulge unusual things of myself, I shall petition to the gentler sort it may not be envy to me. I must say, therefore, that after I had for my first years, by the ceaseless diligence and care of my father, (whom God recompense!) been exercised to the tongues and some sciences, as my age would suffer, by sundry masters and teachers, both at home and at the schools, it was found that whether aught was imposed me by them that had the overlooking, or betaken to of mine own choice in English or other tongue, prosing or versing, but chiefly by this latter, the style, by certain vital signs it had, was likely to live. But much latelier in the private academies of Italy, whither I was favoured to resort, perceiving that some trifles which I had in memory, composed at under twenty or thereabout, (for the manner is, that every one must give some proof of his wit and reading there,) met with acceptance above what was looked for; and other things, which I had shifted in scarcity of books and conveniences to patch up amongst them, were received with written enconiums, which the Italian is not forward to bestow on men of this side the Alps; I began thus far to assent both to them and divers of my friends here at home, and not less to an inward prompting which now grew daily upon me, that by labour and intense study, (which I take to be my portion in this life,) joined with the strong propensity of nature, I might perhaps leave something so written to aftertimes as they should not willingly let die. These thoughts at once possessed me, and these other ; that if I were certain to write as men buy leases, for three lives and downward, there ought no regard be sooner had than to God's glory, by the honour and instruction of my country. For which cause, and not only for that I knew it would be hard to arrive at the second rank among the Latins, I applied myself to that resolution which Ariosto followed against the persuasions of Bembo, to fix all the industry and art I could unite to the adorning of my native tongue ; not to make verbal curiosities the end, (that were a toilsome vanity,) but to be an interpreter and relater of the best and sagest things among mine own citizens throughout this island in the mother dialect. That what the greatest and choicest wits of Athens, Rome, or modern Italy, and those Hebrews of old did for their country, I, in my proportion, with this over and above, of being a Christian, might do for mine ; not caring to be once named abroad, though perhaps I could attain to that, but content with these British islands as my world ; whose fortune hath hitherto been, that if the Athenians, as some say, made their small deeds great and renowned by their eloquent writers, England hath had her noble achievements made small by the unskilful handling of monks and mechanics. . . .

The thing which I had to say, and those intentions which have lived with me ever since I could conceive myself anything worth to my country, I return to crave excuse that urgent reason hath plucked from me by an abortive and foredated discovery. And the accomplishment of them lies not but in a power above man's to promise ; but that none hath by more studious ways endeavoured, and with more unwearied spirit that none shall, that I dare almost aver of myself, as far as life and free leisure will extend. . . . Neither do I think it shame to covenant with any knowing reader, that for some years yet I may go on trust with him toward the payment of what I am now indebted,[1] as being a work not to be raised from the heat of youth or the vapours of wine, like that which flows at waste from the pen of some vulgar amourist or the trencher fury of a rhyming parasite ; nor to be obtained by the invocation of dame memory and her siren daughters, but by devout prayer to that eternal Spirit which can enrich with all utterance and knowledge, and sends out his seraphim with the hallowed fire of his altar, to touch and purify the lips of whom he pleases. To this must be added industrious and select reading, steady observation, insight into all seemly and generous arts and affairs ; till which in some measure be compassed, at mine own peril and cost, I refuse not to sustain this expectation from as many as are not loth to hazard so much credulity upon the best pledges that I can give them. Although it nothing content me to have disclosed thus much beforehand, but that I trust hereby to make it manifest with what small willingness I endure to interrupt the pursuit of no less hopes than these, and leave a calm and pleasing solitariness, fed with cheerful and confident thoughts, to embark in a troubled sea of noises and hoarse disputes, put from beholding the bright countenance of truth in the quiet and still air of delightful studies, to come into the dim reflection of hollow antiquities sold by the seeming bulk, and there be fain to club quotations with men whose learning and belief lies in marginal stuffings, who, when they have, like good sumpters, laid ye down their horse-loads of citations and

[1] i.e. *Paradise Lost*.

fathers at your door, with a rhapsody of who and who were bishops here or there, ye may take off their packsaddles, their day's work is done, and episcopacy, as they think, stoutly vindicated.

MILTON (from *The Reason of Church Government*)

Oct. 31, 1779.

MY DEAR FRIEND,

I wrote my last letter merely to inform you that I had nothing to say, in answer to which you have said nothing. I admire the propriety of your conduct though I am a loser by it. I will endeavour to say something now, and shall hope for something in return.

I have been well entertained with Johnson's biography, for which I thank you : with one exception, and that a swingeing one, I think he has acquitted himself with his usual good sense and sufficiency. His treatment of Milton is unmerciful to the last degree. He has belaboured that great poet's character with the most industrious cruelty. As a man, he has hardly left him the shadow of one good quality. Churlishness in his private life, and a rancorous hatred of everything royal in his public, are the two colours with which he has smeared all the canvas. If he had any virtues, they are not to be found in the Doctor's picture of him, and it is well for Milton, that some sourness in his temper is the only vice with which his memory has been charged ; it is evident enough that if his biographer could have discovered more, he would not have spared him. As a poet, he has treated him with severity enough, and has plucked one or two of the most beautiful feathers out of his Muse's wing, and trampled them under his great foot. He has passed sentence of

79

condemnation upon *Lycidas*, and has taken occasion, from that charming poem, to expose to ridicule (what is indeed ridiculous enough) the childish prattlement of pastoral compositions, as if *Lycidas* was the prototype and pattern of them all. The liveliness of the description, the sweetness of the numbers, the classical spirit of antiquity that prevails in it, go for nothing. I am convinced by the way, that he has no ear for poetical numbers, or that it was stopped by prejudice against the harmony of Milton's. Was there ever any thing so delightful as the music of the *Paradise Lost* ? It is like that of a fine organ ; has the fullest and deepest tones of majesty, with all the softness and elegance of the Dorian flute. Variety without end and never equalled, unless perhaps by Virgil. Yet the Doctor has little or nothing to say upon this copious theme, but talks something about the unfitness of the English language for blank verse, and how apt it is, in the mouth of some readers, to degenerate into declamation.

I could talk a good while longer, but I have no room ; our love attends you.

Yours affectionately,

W. C.

WILLIAM COWPER

POPE AND DRYDEN

I told him that Voltaire, in a conversation with me, had distinguished Pope and Dryden thus :—" Pope drives a handsome chariot, with a couple of neat trim nags ; Dryden a coach, and six stately horses." JOHNSON. " Why, Sir, the truth is, they both drive coaches and six ; but Dryden's horses are either galloping or stumbling : Pope's go at a steady even trot."

BOSWELL (from *Life of Samuel Johnson*)

Dryden's genius was of that sort which catches fire by its own motion; his chariot-wheels *get* hot by driving fast.

COLERIDGE (from *Table Talk*)

POPE

If I could flatter myself that this essay has any merit, it is in steering betwixt the extremes of doctrines seemingly opposite, in passing over terms utterly unintelligible, and in forming a temperate yet not inconsistent, and a short yet not imperfect, system of ethics.

This I might have done in prose; but I chose verse, and even rhyme, for two reasons. The one will appear obvious; that principles, maxims, or precepts so written, both strike the reader more strongly at first, and are more easily retained by him afterwards. The other may seem odd, but it is true: I found I could express them more shortly this way than in prose itself; and nothing is more certain, than that much of the force as well as grace of arguments or instructions depends on their conciseness. I was unable to treat this part of my subject more in detail, without becoming dry and tedious; or more poetically, without sacrificing perspicuity to ornament, without wandering from the precision, or breaking the chain of reasoning: if any man can unite all these without diminution of any of them, I freely confess he will compass a thing above my capacity.

(from Preface to *An Essay on Man*)

There are indeed some advantages accruing from a genius to poetry, and they are all I can think of : the agreeable power of self-amusement when a man is idle or alone ; the privilege of being admitted into the best company ; and the freedom of saying as many careless things as other people, without being so severely remarked upon.

(from Preface to *The Poems*)

. . . .

For what I have published, I can only hope to be pardoned ; for what I have burned, I deserve to be praised.

(from Preface to *The Poems*)

POPE

The king of the eighteenth century is still the king of the eighteenth century by general consent. Dryden was the greater poet, *meo judicio*, but he did not represent the eighteenth century so well as Pope. All that was elegant and airy in the polished artificiality of that age reaches its apotheosis in the *Rape of the Lock*. It is Pope's masterpiece, a Watteau in verse. The poetry of manners could no further go than in this boudoir epic, unmatched in any literature. It is useless, I may here say, to renew the old dispute whether Pope was a poet. Call his verse poetry or what you will, it is work in verse which could not have been done in prose, and, of its kind, never equalled. Then the sylph machinery in the *Rape of the Lock* is undoubted work of fancy : the fairyland of powder and patches, *A Midsummer Night's Dream* seen through chocolate-fumes. The *Essay on Man* is naught to us nowadays, as a whole. It has brilliant artificial passages. It has homely aphorisms such as only Pope and Shakespeare could produce—the

quintessence of pointed common sense : many of them
have passed into the language, and are put down, by three
out of five who quote them, to Shakespeare. But as a
piece of reasoning in verse, the *Essay on Man* is utterly
inferior to Dryden's *Hind and Panther*. . . . If the poem had
been half as long, it might have been a masterpiece. As it
is, unless we are to reckon masterpieces by avoirdupois
weight, or to assign undue value to mere symmetry of
scheme, I think we must look for Pope's satirical masterpiece elsewhere. Not in the satire on women, where Pope
seems hardly to have his heart in his work ; but in the
imitations from Horace, those generally known as Pope's
Satires. Here he is at his very best and tersest. They are
as brilliant as anything in the *Dunciad*, and they are brilliant right through ; the mordant pen never flags. It
matters not that they are imitated from Horace. They
gain by it : their limits are circumscribed, their lines laid
down, and Pope writes the better for having these limits
set him, this tissue on which to work. Not a whit does
he lose in essential originality : nowhere is he so much
himself. It is very different from Horace, say the critics.
Surely that is exactly the thing for which to thank poetry
and praise Pope. It has not the pleasant urbane good
humour of the Horatian spirit. No, it has the spirit of
Pope—and satire is the gainer. Horace is the more charming companion ; Pope is the greater satirist. In place of an
echo of Horace (and no verse translation was ever anything but feeble which attempted merely to echo the
original), we have a new spirit in satire ; a fine series of
English satirical poems, which in their kind are unap-
proached by the Roman, and in his kind wisely avoid the
attempt to approach him. *Satires after Horace* would have
been a better title than *Imitations* ; for less imitative

poems in essence were never written. These and the *Rape of the Lock* are Pope's finest title to fame.

FRANCIS THOMPSON (from an Essay on POPE)

DR. JOHNSON

July 4th, 1833. Dr. Johnson's fame now rests principally upon Boswell. It is impossible not to be amused with such a book. But his *bow-wow* manner must have had a good deal to do with the effect produced ; for no one I suppose, will set Johnson before Burke, and Burke was a great and universal talker ; yet now we hear nothing of this except by some chance remarks in Boswell. The fact is, Burke, like all men of genius who love to talk at all, was very discursive and continuous ; hence he is not reported ; he seldom said the short sharp things that Johnson almost always did, which produce a more decided effect at the moment, and which are so much more easy to carry off. Besides, as to Burke's testimony to Johnson's powers, you must remember that Burke was a great courtier ; and after all, Burke said and wrote more than once that he thought Johnson greater in talking than writing, and greater in Boswell than in real life.

COLERIDGE (from *Table Talk*)

Pourtant, pour M. Coleridge, il est tout-à-fait un monologue.

MADAME DE STAËL

Johnson had neither eye nor ear ; for nature, therefore, he cared, as he knew, nothing. His knowledge of town life was minute ; but even that was imperfect, as not being contrasted with the better life of the country.

COLERIDGE (from *Table Talk*)

MY DEAR BOSWELL,

I am surprised that, knowing as you do the disposition of your countrymen to tell lies in favour of each other, you can be at all affected by any reports that circulate among them. Macpherson never in his life offered me a sight of any original or of any evidence of any kind ; but thought only of intimidating me by noise and threats, till my last answer,—that I would not be deterred from detecting what I thought a cheat, by the menaces of a ruffian—put an end to our correspondence.

The state of the question is this. He, and Dr. Blair, whom I consider as deceived, say, that he copied the poem from old manuscripts. His copies, if he had them, and I believe him to have none, are nothing. Where are the manuscripts ? They can be shown if they exist, but they were never shown. *De non existentibus et non apparentibus*, says our law, *eadem est ratio*. No man has a claim to credit upon his own word, when better evidence, if he had it, may be easily produced. But so far as we can find, the Erse language was never written till very lately for the purposes of religion. A nation that cannot write, or a language that was never written, has no manuscripts.

But whatever he has he never offered to show. If old manuscripts should now be mentioned, I should, unless there were more evidence than can be easily had, suppose

85

them another proof of Scotch conspiracy in national falsehood.

Do not censure the expression; you know it to be true. . . .

                    I am, Sir,

                         Your most humble servant,

February 7, 1775.   SAM. JOHNSON

            (from BOSWELL'S *Life of Samuel Johnson*)

            (To " Ossian " Macpherson)

MR. JAMES MACPHERSON,

I received your foolish and impudent letter. Any violence offered me I shall do my best to repel ; and what I cannot do for myself the law shall do for me. I hope I shall never be deterred from detecting what I think a cheat by the menaces of a ruffian.

What would you have me retract ? I thought your book an imposture ; I think it an imposture still. For this opinion I have given my reasons to the public, which I here dare you to refute. Your rage I defy. Your abilities since your Homer are not so formidable, and what I hear of your morals inclines me to pay regard not to what you shall say, but to what you shall prove. You may print this if you will.

                                    SAM. JOHNSON

LAMB ON BLAKE AND BYRON

Blake is a real name, I assure you, and a most extraordinary man, if he be still living. He is the Robert [William] Blake, whose wild designs accompany a splendid

86

folio edition of the *Night Thoughts*, which you may have seen, in one of which he pictures the parting of soul and body by a solid mass of human form floating off, God knows how, from a lumpish mass (fac simile to itself) left behind on the dying bed. He paints in water colours marvellous strange pictures, visions of his brain, which he asserts that he has seen. They have great merit. He has *seen* the old Welsh bards on Snowdon—he has seen the Beautifullest, the Strongest, and the Ugliest Man, left alone from the Massacre of the Britons by the Romans, and has painted them from memory (I have seen his paintings), and asserts them to be as good as the figures of Raphael and Angelo, but not better, as they had precisely the same retro-visions and prophetic visions with himself. The painters in oil (which he will have it that neither of them practised) he affirms to have been the ruin of art, and affirms that all the while he was engaged in his Water paintings, Titian was disturbing him, Titian the Ill Genius of Oil Painting. His Pictures—one in particular the Canterbury Pilgrims (far above Stothard's)—have great merit, but hard, dry, yet with grace. He has written a catalogue of them with a most spirited criticism on Chaucer, but mystical and full of Vision. His poems have been sold hitherto only in Manuscript. I never read them ; but a friend at my desire procured the *Sweep Song*. There is one to a Tiger, which I have heard recited, beginning

Tiger, Tiger, burning bright,
Thro' the desarts of the night,

which is glorious, but, alas ! I have not the Book ; for the man is flown, whither I know not—to Hades or a Mad House. But I must look on him as one of the most extraordinary persons of the age. . . .

So we have lost another Poet. I never much relished his Lordship's mind, and shall be sorry if the Greeks have cause to miss him. He was to me offensive, and I never can make out his great *power*, which his admirers talk of. Why, a line of Wordsworth's is a lever to lift the immortal spirit ! Byron can only move the Spleen. He was at best a Satyrist,—in any other way, he was mean enough. I daresay I do him injustice ; but I cannot love him, nor squeeze a tear to his memory. He did not like the world, and he has left it, as Alderman Curtis advised the Radicals, " If they don't like their Country, damn 'em, let 'em leave it," they possessing no rood of ground in England, and he 10,000 acres. Byron was better than many Curtises.

LAMB (from *The Letters*)

WORDSWORTH

Poet of Nature, thou hast wept to know
That things depart which never may return :
Childhood and youth, friendship and love's first glow,
Have fled like sweet dreams, leaving thee to mourn.

. . . .

Thou wert as a lone star, whose light did shine
On some frail bark in winter's midnight roar :
Thou hast like to a rock-built refuge stood
Above the blind and battling multitude :
In honoured poverty thy voice did weave
Songs consecrate to truth and liberty. . . .

SHELLEY

88

He was no merely amiable, no merely simple, or reverential, or imaginative man, but one eminently masculine and strong : a man of strong intellect, of strong feelings, of sturdy, massive individuality. If I do not apply to him the epithet " intense," it is because I conceive it to belong more properly to a weaker type of man in a state of strain ; but I never met with a mind which to me seemed to work constantly with so much vigour, or with feelings so constantly in a state of fervour ; the strong intellect was, to use his own expression, " *steeped in* " the strong feeling, but the man was always master of both : so broad was the basis of his mental constitution, so powerful the original will which guided and controlled his emotions.

R. P. GRAVES
(from *Afternoon Lectures :*
Recollections of Wordsworth and the Lake Country)

The next day Wordsworth arrived from Bristol at Coleridge's cottage. I think I see him now. He answered in some degree to his friend's description of him, but was more gaunt and Don Quixote-like. He was quaintly dressed (according to the *costume* of that unconstrained period) in a brown fustian jacket and striped pantaloons. There was something of a roll, a lounge in his gait, not unlike his own Peter Bell. There was a severe, worn pressure of thought about his temples, a fire in his eye (as if he saw something in objects more than the outward appearance), an intense, high, narrow forehead, a Roman nose, cheeks furrowed by strong purpose and feeling, and a convulsive inclination to laughter about the mouth,

89

a good deal at variance with the solemn, stately expression of the rest of his face. Chantrey's bust wants the marking traits ; but he was teased into making it regular and heavy : Haydon's head of him, introduced into the *Entrance of Christ into Jerusalem*, is the most like his drooping weight of thought and expression. He sat down and talked very naturally and freely, with a mixture of clear, gushing accents in his voice, a deep guttural intonation, and a strong tincture of the northern *burr*, like the crust on wine. He instantly began to make havoc of the half of a Cheshire cheese on the table, and said, triumphantly, that " his marriage with experience had not been so productive as Mr. Southey's in teaching him a knowledge of the good things of this life." He had been to see the *Castle Spectre* by Monk Lewis, while at Bristol, and described it very well. He said " It fitted the taste of the audience like a glove." This *ad captandum* merit was however by no means a recommendation of it, according to the severe principles of the new school, which reject rather than court popular effect. Wordsworth, looking out of the low, latticed window, said, " How beautifully the sun sets on that yellow bank ! " I thought within myself, " With what eyes these poets see nature ! " and ever after, when I saw the sun-set stream upon the objects facing it, conceived I had made a discovery, or thanked Mr. Wordsworth for having made one for me ! We went over to All-Foxden again the day following, and Wordsworth read us the story of *Peter Bell* in the open air ; and the comment upon it by his face and voice was very different from that of some later critics ! Whatever might be thought of the poem, " his face was a book where men might read strange matters," and he announced the fate of his hero in prophetic tones. There is a *chaunt* in the recitation of both Coleridge and Words-worth, which acts as a spell upon the hearer, and disarms judgment. Perhaps they have deceived themselves by making habitual use of this ambiguous accompaniment. Coleridge's manner is more full, animated, and varied ; Wordsworth's more equable, sustained, and internal. The one might be termed more *dramatic*, the other more *lyrical*. Coleridge has told me that he himself liked to compose in walking over uneven ground, or breaking through the straggling branches of a copse-wood ; whereas Wordsworth always wrote (if he could) walking up and down a straight gravel walk, or in some spot where the continuity of his verse met with no collateral interruption.

HAZLITT (from *Winterslow*)

What is a Poet ? To whom does he address himself ? And what language is to be expected from him ?—He is a man speaking to men : a man, it is true, endowed with more lively sensibility, more enthusiasm and tenderness, who has a greater knowledge of human nature, and a more comprehensive soul, than are supposed to be common among mankind ; a man pleased with his own passions and volitions, and who rejoices more than other men in the spirit of life that is in him, delighting to con-template similar volitions and passions as manifested in the goings-on of the Universe, and habitually compelled to create them where he does not find them. To these qualities he has added a disposition to be affected more than other men by absent things as if they were present ; an ability of conjuring up in himself passions, which are indeed far from being the same as those produced by real events, yet (especially in those parts of the general sympathy which are pleasing and delightful) do more nearly resemble the passions produced by real events, than anything which, from the motions of their own minds merely, other men are accustomed to feel in themselves :—whence, and from practice, he has acquired a greater readiness and power in expressing what he thinks and feels, and especially those thoughts and feelings which, by his own choice, or from the structure of his own mind, arise in him without immediate external excitement. . . .

The knowledge both of the Poet and the Man of science is pleasure ; but the knowledge of the one cleaves to us as a necessary part of our existence, our natural and unalienable inheritance ; the other is a personal and individual acquisition, slow to come to us, and by no habitual and direct sympathy connecting us with our fellow-beings. The Man of science seeks truth as a remote and unknown benefactor ; he cherishes it and loves it in his solitude ; the Poet, singing a song in which all human beings join with him, rejoices in the presence of truth as our visible friend and hourly companion. Poetry is the breath and finer spirit of all knowledge ; it is the impassioned expression which is in the countenance of all Science. Emphatically may it be said of the Poet, as Shakespeare hath said of man, " that he looks before and after." He is the rock of defence for human nature ; an upholder and preserver, carrying everywhere with him relationship and love. In spite of the difference of soil and climate, of language and manners, of laws and customs ; in spite of things silently gone out of mind, and things violently destroyed ; the Poet binds together by passion and knowledge the vast empire of human society, as it is spread over the whole earth, and over all time. The objects of the Poet's thoughts are everywhere ; though the eyes and senses of man are, it is true, his favourite guides, yet he will follow wheresoever he can find an atmosphere of sensation in which to move his wings. Poetry is the first and last of all knowledge—it is as immortal as the heart of man. If the labours of Men of science should ever create any material revolution, direct or indirect, in our condition, and in the impressions which we habitually receive, the Poet will sleep then no more than at present ; he will be ready to follow the steps of the Man of science, not only in those general indirect effects, but he will be at his side, carrying sensation into the midst of the objects of the science itself. The remotest discoveries of the Chemist, the Botanist, or Mineralogist, will be as proper subjects of the Poet's art as any upon which it can be employed, if the time should ever come when these things shall be familiar to us, and the relations under which they are contemplated by the followers of these respective sciences shall be manifestly and palpably material to us as enjoying and suffering beings.

WORDSWORTH (from Preface to *Lyrical Ballads*)

Visionary power
Attends the motions of the viewless winds,
Embodied in the mystery of words :
There darkness makes abode, and all the host
Of shadowy things work endless changes, there,
As in a mansion like their proper home,
Even forms and substances are circumfused

93

By that transparent veil with light divine,
And, through the turnings intricate of verse,
Present themselves as objects recognised.
In flashes, and with glory not their own.

WORDSWORTH (from *The Prelude*)

I have said that poetry is the spontaneous overflow of powerful feelings ; it takes its origin from emotion recollected in tranquility ; the emotion is contemplated till, by a species of re-action, the tranquility gradually disappears, and an emotion, kindred to that which was before the subject of contemplation, is gradually produced, and does itself actually exist in the mind. In this mood successful composition generally begins, and in a mood similar to this it is carried on ; but the emotion, of whatever kind, and in whatever degree, from various causes, is qualified by various pleasures, so that in describing any passions whatsoever, which are voluntarily described, the mind will, upon the whole, be in a state of enjoyment. If Nature be thus cautious to preserve in a state of enjoyment a being so employed, the Poet ought to profit by the lesson held forth to him, and ought specially to .take care that, whatever passions he communicates to his Reader, those passions, if the Reader's mind be sound and vigorous, should always be accompanied with an over balance of pleasure. Now the music of harmonious metrical language, the sense of difficulty overcome, and the blind association of pleasure which has been previously received from works of rhyme or metre of the same or similar construction, an indistinct perception perpetually renewed of language closely resembling that of real life, and yet, in the circumstances of metre, differing from it so widely—all these imperceptibly make up a complex feeling of delight, which is of the most important use in tempering the painful feeling always found intermingled with powerful descriptions of the deeper passions. This effect is always produced in pathetic and impassioned poetry; while, in lighter compositions, the ease and gracefulness with which the Poet manages his numbers are themselves confessedly a principal source of the gratification of the Reader.

WORDSWORTH (from Preface to *Lyrical Ballads*)

COLERIDGE

He is a wonderful man, His conversation teems with soul, mind and spirit. Then he is so benevolent, so good tempered and cheerful, and, like William, interests himself so much about every little trifle. At first I thought him very plain, that is, for about three minutes; he is pale and thin, has a wide mouth, thick lips, and not very good teeth, longish, loose-growing, half-curling, rough, black hair. But if you hear him speak for five minutes you think no more of them. His eye is large and full, not dark but grey; such an eye as would receive from a heavy soul the dullest expression; but it speaks every emotion of his animated mind; it has more of the ' poet's eye in a fine frenzy rolling ' than I ever witnessed. He has fine dark eyebrows, and an overhanging forehead.

DOROTHY WORDSWORTH (from a Letter)

95

You will see Coleridge—he who sits obscure
In the exceeding lustre and the pure
Intense irradiation of a mind,
Which, with its own internal lightning blind,
Flags wearily through darkness and despair—
A cloud-encircled meteor of the air,
A hooded eagle among blinking owls.

SHELLEY (from *Letter to Maria Gisborne*)

At school . . . I enjoyed the inestimable advantage of a
very sensible, though at the same time, a very severe
master. . . . I learned from him that poetry, even that of
the loftiest and, seemingly, that of the wildest odes, had
a logic of its own, as severe as that of science ; and more
difficult, because more subtle, more complex, and dependent on more, and more fugitive causes. In the truly
great poets, he would say, there is a reason assignable, not
only for every word, but for the position of every word ;
and I well remember that, availing himself of the syno-
nymes to the Homer of Didymus, he made us attempt to
show, with regard to each, why it would not have answered
the same purpose ; and wherein consisted the peculiar
fitness of the word in the original text.

. . . .

In poetry, in which every line, every phrase, may pass
the ordeal of deliberation and deliberate choice, it is possible, and barely possible, to attain that *ultimatum* which
I have ventured to propose as the infallible test of a blame-
less style ; namely : its *untranslatableness* in words of the
same language without injury to the meaning. Be it observed, however, that I include in the *meaning* of a word

96

not only its correspondent object, but likewise all the associations which it recalls. For language is framed to convey not the object alone, but likewise the character, mood and intentions of the person who is representing it. In poetry it *is* practicable to preserve the diction uncorrupted by the affectations and misappropriations, which promiscuous authorship, and reading not promiscuous only because it is disproportionally most conversant with the compositions of the day, have rendered general. Yet even to the poet, composing in his own province, it is an arduous work : and as the result and pledge of a watchful good sense, of fine and luminous distinction, and of complete self-possession, may justly claim all the honour which belongs to an attainment equally difficult and valuable, and the more valuable for being rare. It is at *all* times the proper food of the understanding ; but in an age of corrupt eloquence it is both food and antidote.

What is poetry ?—is so nearly the same question with, what is a poet ?—that the answer to the one is involved in the solution of the other. For it is a distinction resulting from the poetic genius itself, which sustains and modifies the images, thoughts, and emotions of the poet's own mind.

The poet, described in ideal perfection, brings the whole soul of man into activity, with the subordination of its faculties to each other according to their relative worth and dignity. He diffuses a tone and spirit of unity, that blends, and (as it were) *fuses*, each to each, by that synthetic and magical power, to which I would exclusively appropriate the name of Imagination. This power, first put in action by the will and understanding, and retained under their irremissive, though gentle and unnoticed, control, *laxis effertur habenis*, reveals itself in the balance or reconcilement of opposite or discordant qualities : of sameness, with difference; of the general with the concrete; the idea with the image ; the individual with the representative; the sense of novelty and freshness with the old and familiar objects ; a more than usual state of emotion with more than usual order ; judgment ever awake and steady self-possession with enthusiasm and feeling profound or vehement ; and while it blends and harmonizes the natural and the artificial, still subordinates art to nature ; the manner to the matter ; and our admiration of the poet to our sympathy with the poetry. Doubtless, as Sir John Davies observes of the soul—(and his words may with slight alteration be applied, and even more appropriately, to the poetic Imagination)—

> Doubtless this could not be, but that she turns
> Bodies to *spirit* by sublimation strange,
> As fire converts to fire the things it burns,
> As we our food into our nature change.
>
> From their gross matter she abstracts *their* forms,
> And draws a kind of quintessence from things ;
> Which to her proper nature she transforms
> To bear them light on her celestial wings.
>
> *Thus* does she, when from *individual states*
> She doth abstract the universal kinds ;
> *Which then re-clothed in divers names and fates*
> *Steal access through the senses to our minds.*

Finally, Good Sense is the Body of poetic genius, Fancy its Drapery, Motion its Life, and Imagination the

Soul that is everywhere, and in each ; and forms all into one graceful and intelligent whole. . . .

No man was ever yet a great poet, without being at the same time a profound philosopher. For poetry is the blossom and the fragrancy of all human knowledge, human thoughts, human passions, emotions, language.

COLERIDGE (from *Biographia Literaria*)

. . . .

The following fragment is here published at the request of a poet of great and deserved celebrity, and, as far as the Author's own opinions are concerned, rather as a psychological curiosity, than on the ground of any supposed *poetic* merits.

In the summer of the year 1797, the Author, then in ill health, had retired to a lonely farm-house between Porlock and Linton, on the Exmoor confines of Somerset and Devonshire. In consequence of a slight indisposition, an anodyne had been prescribed, from the effects of which he fell asleep in his chair at the moment that he was reading the following sentence, or words of the same substance, in *Purchas's Pilgrimage* : " Here the Khan Kubla commanded a palace to be built, and a stately garden thereunto. And thus ten miles of fertile ground were enclosed with a wall." The author continued for about three hours in a profound sleep, at least of the external senses, during which time he has the most vivid confidence that he could not have composed less than from two to three hundred lines ; if that indeed can be called composition in which all the images rose up before him as *things*, with a parallel production of the correspondent expressions, without any sensation or consciousness of effort. On awaking he appeared to himself to have a distinct recollection of the whole, and taking his pen, ink, and paper, instantly and eagerly wrote down the lines that are here preserved. At this moment he was unfortunately called out by a person on business from Porlock, and detained by him above an hour, and on his return to his room, found, to his no small surprise and mortification, that though he still retained some vague and dim recollection of the general purport of the vision, yet, with the exception of some eight or ten scattered lines and images, all the rest had passed away like the images on the surface of a stream into which a stone has been cast, but, alas ! without the after-restoration of the latter !

COLERIDGE (from Biographia Literaria)

. . . . . .

" In Xamdu did Cublai Can build a stately Palace, encompassing sixteene miles of plaine ground with a wall, wherein are fertile Meddowes, pleasant Springs, delightfull Streames, and all sorts of beasts of chase and game, and in the middest thereof a sumptuous house of pleasure."

(from Purchas His Pilgrimage)

. . . . . .

This Citie is three dayes journey Northeastward to the Citie Xandu, which the great Chan Cublay now raigning, built ; erecting therein a marvellous and artificiall Palace of Marble and other stones, which abutteth on the wall on one side, and the midst of the Citie on the other. He included sixteene miles within the circuit of the wall on that side where the Palace abutteth on the Citie wall, into which none can enter but by the Palace. In this inclosure or Parke are goodly meadowes, springs, rivers, red and fallow Deere, Fawnes carryed thither for the Hawkes, (of which are there mewed above two hundred Gerfalcons which he goeth once a weeke to see) and he often useth one Leopard or more, sitting on Horses, which hee setteth upon the Stagges and Deere, & having taken the beast, giveth it to the Gerfalcons, and in beholding this spectacle he taketh wonderfull delight. In the middest in a faire Wood hee hath built a royall House on pillars gilded and vernished, on every one of which is a Dragon all gilt, which windeth his tayle about the pillar, with his head bearing up the loft, as also with his wings displayed on both sides : the cover also is of Reeds gilt and vernished, so that the rayne can doe it no injurie, the reeds being three handfuls thicke and ten yards long, split from knot to knot. The house it selfe also may be sundred, and taken downe like a Tent and erected againe. For it is sustained, when it is set up, with two hundred silken cords. Great Chan useth to dwell there three moneths in the yeare, to wit, in June, July, and August.

(from *Hakluytus Posthumus or Purchas His Pilgrimes*)

. . . .

Just under my feet was an enchanting and amazing chrystal fountain, which incessantly threw up, from dark, rocky caverns below, tons of water every minute, forming a bason, capacious enough for large shallops to ride in, and a creek of four or five feet depth of water, and near twenty yards over, which meanders six miles through green meadows, pouring its limpid waters into the great Lake George . . . About twenty yards from the upper edge of the bason . . . is a continual and amazing ebullition, where the waters are thrown up in such abundance and amazing force, as to jet and swell up two or three feet

above the common surface : white sand and small par-
ticles of shells are thrown up with the waters . . . when
they . . . subside with the expanding flood, and gently
sink again.

WILLIAM BARTRAM (from Travels, 1791)

．　　．　　．　　．　　．　　．　　．

There by divers Pipes answering the divers parts of
those Palaces were seene to runne Wine, Milke, Honey,
and cleere Water. In them hee had placed goodly Domo-
sels skilfull in Songs and Instruments of Musicke and
Dancing, and to make Sports and Delights unto men
whatsoever they could imagine.

(from *Hakluytus Posthumus or Purchas His Pilgrimes*)

July 6, 1833. I could write as good verses now as ever
I did, if I were perfectly free from vexations, and were in
the *ad libitum* hearing of fine music, which has a sensible
effect in harmonising my thoughts, and in animating and,
as it were, lubricating my inventive faculty. The reason
of my not finishing " Christabel " is not, that I don't know
how to do it—for I have, as I always had, the whole plan
entire from beginning to end in my mind ; but I fear I
could not carry on with equal success the execution of the
idea, an extremely subtle and difficult one.

．　　．　　．　　．　　．　　．　　．

If I should finish " Christabel," I shall certainly
extend it and give new characters, and a greater number
of incidents. This the " reading public " require, and this
is the reason that Sir Walter Scott's Poems, though so

loosely written, are pleasing, and interest us by their picturesqueness.

If a genial recurrence of the ray divine should occur for a few weeks, I shall certainly attempt it. I had the whole of the two cantos in my mind before I began it ; certainly the first canto is more perfect, has more of the true wild weird spirit than the last. I laughed heartily at the continuation in *Blackwood*, which I have been told is by Maginn : it is in appearance, and appearance only, a good imitation ; I do not doubt that it gave more pleasure, and to a greater number, than a continuation by myself in the spirit of the first two cantos.

COLERIDGE (from *Table Talk*)

COLERIDGE AND LAMB

Nor has the rolling year twice measured
From sign to sign its steadfast course,
Since every mortal power of Coleridge
Was frozen at its marvellous source ;

The rapt One, of the godlike forehead,
The heaven-eyed creature sleeps in earth :
And Lamb, the frolic and the gentle,
Has vanished from his lonely hearth.

Like clouds that rake the mountain-summits,
Or waves that own no curbing hand,
How fast has brother followed brother
From sunshine to the sunless land !

WORDSWORTH
(from *Extempore Effusion upon the Death of James Hogg*)

LAMB

Once, and once only, have I seen thy face,
Elia! once only has thy tripping tongue
Run o'er my breast, yet never has been left
Impression on it stronger or more sweet.
Cordial old man! what youth was in thy years,
What wisdom in thy levity, what truth
In every utterance of that purest soul!
Few are the spirits of the glorified
I'd spring to earlier at the gate of heaven.

LANDOR

. . . Men, finding in the raptures of the higher poetry
a condition of exaltation, to which they have no parallel
in their own experience, besides the spurious resemblance
of it in dreams and fevers, impute a state of dreaminess
and fever to the poet. But the true poet dreams being
awake. He is not possessed by his subject, but has
dominion over it. In the groves of Eden he walks familiar
as in his native paths. He ascends the empyrean heaven,
and is not intoxicated. He treads the burning marl without
dismay; he wins his flight without self-loss through realms
of chaos 'and old night.' Or if, abandoning himself to
that severer chaos of a ' human mind untuned,' he is content awhile to be mad with Lear, or to hate mankind (a sort
of madness) with Timon, neither is that madness, nor his
misanthropy, so unchecked, but that,—never letting the
reins of reason wholly go, while most he seems to do so,—
he has his better genius still whispering at his ear, with
the good servant Kent suggesting saner counsels, or with

the honest steward Flavius recommending kindlier resolutions. Where he seems most to recede from humanity, he will be found the truest to it. From beyond the scope of Nature if he summon possible existences, he subjugates them to the law of her consistency. He is beautifully loyal to that sovereign directress, even when he appears most to betray and desert her. His ideal tribes submit to policy ; his very monsters are tamed to his hand, even as that wild sea-brood, shepherded by Proteus. He tames, and he clothes them with attributes of flesh and blood, till they wonder at themselves, like Indian Islanders forced to submit to European vesture. Caliban, the Witches, are as true to the laws of their own nature (ours with a difference), as Othello, Hamlet, and Macbeth.

LAMB (from *The Essays of Elia*)

A PARTY AT HAYDON'S

In the morning of this delightful day, a gentleman, a perfect stranger, had called on me. He said he knew my friends, had an enthusiasm for Wordsworth, and begged I would procure him the happiness of an introduction. He told me he was a comptroller of stamps, and often had correspondence with the poet. I thought it a liberty ; but still, as he seemed a gentleman, I told him he might come.

When we retired to tea we found the comptroller. In introducing him to Wordsworth I forgot to say who he was. After a little time the comptroller looked down, looked up, and said to Wordsworth, " Don't you think, sir, Milton was a great genius ? " Keats looked at me, Wordsworth looked at the comptroller. Lamb, who was dozing by the fire, turned round and said, " Pray, sir, did you say Milton was a great genius ? " " No, sir, I asked Mr. Wordsworth if he were not." " Oh," said Lamb, " then you are a silly fellow." " Charles ! my dear Charles ! " said Wordsworth ; but Lamb, perfectly innocent of the confusion he had created, was off again by the fire.

After an awful pause the comptroller said, " Don't you think Newton a great genius ? " I could not stand it any longer. Keats put his head into my books. Ritchie squeezed in a laugh. Wordsworth seemed asking himself, " Who is this ? " Lamb got up, and, taking a candle, said, " Sir, will you allow me to look at your phrenological development ? " He then turned his back on the poor man, and at every question of the comptroller he chaunted :

> Diddle diddle dumpling, my son John,
> Went to bed with his breeches on.

The man in office, finding Wordsworth did not know who he was, said in a spasmodic and half-chuckling anticipation of assured victory, " I have had the honour of some correspondence with you, Mr. Wordsworth." " With me, sir ? " said Wordsworth. " Not that I remember." " Don't you, sir ? I am a comptroller of stamps." There was a dead silence ;—the comptroller evidently thinking that was enough. While we were waiting for Wordsworth's reply, Lamb sung out :

> Hey diddle diddle,
> The cat and the fiddle.

" My dear Charles ! " said Wordsworth,—

> Diddle diddle dumpling, my son John,

chaunted Lamb, and then rising, exclaimed, " Do let me

have another look at that gentleman's organs." Keats and I hurried Lamb into the painting-room, shut the door, and gave way to inextinguishable laughter. Monkhouse followed, and tried to get Lamb away. We went back, but the comptroller was irreconcilable. We soothed and smiled, and asked him to supper. He stayed though his dignity was sorely affected. However, being a good-natured man, we parted all in good humour, and no ill-effects followed.

All the while, until Monkhouse succeeded, we could hear Lamb struggling in the painting-room, and calling at intervals, " Who is that fellow ? Allow me to see his organs once more."

HAYDON (from *The Autobiography*)

BYRON

The fame of Lord Byron's exploit in swimming across the Hellespont, from Sestos to Abydos, in imitation of Leander, had already reached us, and, just as we were passing the molehead, we saw a man jump from it into the sea, whom Lord Sligo recognized to be Lord Byron himself, and, haling him, bade him hasten to dress and to come and join us.

.   .   .   .

" I think he was a strange character," said Lady Hester, recalling him many years later, " his generosity was for a motive, his avarice for a motive ; one time he was mopish, and nobody was to speak to him ; another he was for being jocular with everybody. Then he was a sort of Don Quixote, fighting with the police for a woman of the town ; and then he wanted to make himself something great. But when he allowed himself to be bullied by the Albanians it was all over with him ; you must not show any fear with them. At Athens I saw nothing in him but a well-bred man, like many others ; for, as for poetry, it is easy enough to write verses ; and as for the thoughts, who knows where he got them ? . . . He had a great deal of vice in his looks—his eyes set close together and a contracted brow—so " (imitating it). " Oh, Lord ! I am sure he was not a liberal man, whatever else he might be. The only good thing about his looks was this part " (drawing her hand under the cheek down the front of her neck), " and the curl on his forehead."

CHARLES MERYON
(from *Travels of Lady Hester Stanhope*)

Of its own beauty is the mind diseased,
And fevers into false creation :—where,
Where are the forms the sculptor's soul hath
    seized ?
In him alone. Can Nature show so fair ?
Where are the charms and virtues which we dare
Conceive in boyhood and pursue as men,
The unreached Paradise of our despair,
Which o'er-informs the pencil and the pen,
And overpowers the page where it would bloom
    again ?
BYRON (from *Childe Harold's Pilgrimage*)

108

SHELLEY

At the commencement of Michaelmas term, that is, at the end of October in the year 1810, I happened one day to sit next to a freshman at dinner : it was his first appearance in hall. His figure was slight, and his aspect remarkably youthful, even at our table, where all were very young. He seemed thoughtful and absent. He ate little, and had no acquaintance with any one. I know not how it was that we fell into conversation. . . . I invited the stranger to finish the discussion in my rooms. He eagerly assented. . . . As I felt, in truth, but a slight interest in the subject of his conversation, I had leisure to examine, and I may add, to admire, the appearance of my very extraordinary guest. It was a sum of many contradictions. His figure was slight and fragile, and yet his bones and joints were large and strong. He was tall, but he stooped so much, that he seemed of a low stature. His clothes were expensive, and made according to the most approved mode of the day ; but they were tumbled, rumpled, unbrushed. His gestures were abrupt, and sometimes violent, occasionally even awkward, yet more frequently gentle and graceful. His complexion was delicate, and almost feminine, of the purest red and white ; yet he was tanned and freckled by exposure to the sun, having passed the autumn, as he said, in shooting. His features, his whole face, and particularly his head, were, in fact, unusually small ; yet the last *appeared* of a remarkable bulk, for his hair was long and bushy, and in fits of absence, and in the agonies (if I may use the word) of anxious thought, he often rubbed it fiercely with his hands, or passed his fingers quickly through his locks unconsciously, so that it was singularly wild and rough. In times when it was the mode to imitate stage-coachmen as closely as possible in costume, and when the hair was invariably cropped, like that of our soldiers, this eccentricity was very striking. His features were not symmetrical (the mouth, perhaps, excepted), yet was the effect of the whole extremely powerful. They breathed an animation, a fire, an enthusiasm, a vivid and preternatural intelligence, that I never met with in any other countenance. Nor was the moral expression less beautiful than the intellectual ; for there was a softness, a delicacy, a gentleness, and especially (though this will surprise many) that air of profound religious veneration, that characterises the best works . . . of the great masters of Florence and Rome. . . . I admired the enthusiasm of my new acquaintance, his ardour in the cause of science, and his thirst for knowledge. I seemed to have found in him all those intellectual qualities which I had vainly expected to meet with in an University. But there was one physical blemish that threatened to neutralize all his excellence. ' This is a fine, clever fellow ! ' I said to myself, ' but I can never bear his society ; I shall never be able to endure his voice ; it would kill me. What a pity it is ! ' I am very sensible of imperfections, and especially of painful sounds—and the voice of the stranger was excruciating : it was intolerably shrill, harsh, and discordant ; of the most cruel intension—it was perpetual, and without any remission—it excoriated the ears. . . . When one of the innumerable clocks that speak in various notes during the day and the night at Oxford, proclaimed a quarter to seven, he said suddenly that he must go to a lecture on mineralogy. . . . I invited him to return to tea ; he gladly assented, promised that he would not be absent long, snatched his cap, hurried out of the room, and I heard his footsteps, as he ran through the silent quadrangle, and afterwards along High-street.

. . . .

'Never did a more finished gentleman than Shelley step across a drawing-room!' Lord Byron exclaimed; and on reading the remark in Mr. Moore's *Memoirs*, I was struck forcibly by its justice, and wondered for a moment that, since it was so obvious, it had never been made before.

HOGG (from *Life of Shelley*)

On a poet's lips I slept
Dreaming like a love-adept
In the sound his breathing kept;
Nor seeks nor finds he mortal blisses,
But feeds on the aëreal kisses
Of shapes that haunt thought's wildernesses.
He will watch from dawn to gloom
The lake-reflected sun illume
The yellow bees in the ivy-bloom,
Nor heed nor see, what things they be;
But from these create he can
Forms more real than living man,
Nurslings of immortality.

SHELLEY (from *Prometheus Unbound*)

Poetry is the record of the best and happiest moments of the happiest and best minds. We are aware of evanescent visitations of thought and feeling sometimes associated with place or person, sometimes regarding our own mind alone, and always arising unforseen and departing unbidden, but elevating and delightful beyond all expression : so that even in the desire and regret they leave, there cannot but be pleasure, participating as it does in the nature of its object. It is as it were the interpenetration of a diviner nature through our own ; but its footsteps are like those of a wind over the sea, which the coming calm erases, and whose traces remain only, as on the wrinkled sand which paves it. These and corresponding conditions of being are experienced principally by those of the most delicate sensibility and the most enlarged imagination ; and the state of mind produced by them is at war with every base desire. The enthusiasm of virtue, love, patriotism, and friendship, is essentially linked with such emotions ; and whilst they last, self appears as what it is, an atom to a universe. Poets are not only subject to these experiences as spirits of the most refined organisation, but they can colour all that they combine with the evanescent hues of this ethereal world ; a word, a trait in the representation of a scene or a passion, will touch the enchanted cord, and re-animate, in those who have ever experienced these emotions, the sleeping, the cold, the buried image of the past. Poetry thus makes immortal all that is best and most beautiful in the world ; it arrests the vanishing apparitions which haunt the interlunations of life, and veiling them, or in language or in form, sends them forth among mankind, bearing sweet news of kindred joy to those with whom their sisters abide —abide, because there is no portal of expression from the caverns of the spirit which they inhabit into the universe of things. Poetry redeems from decay the visitations of the divinity in man. . . .

Man is an instrument over which a series of external and internal impressions are driven like the alternations of an ever-changing wind over an Æolian lyre, which move it by their motion to ever-changing melody. . . . To be a poet is to apprehend the true and the beautiful, in a word, the good, which exists in the relation subsisting first between existence and perception, and secondly between perception and expression. . . . Sounds as well as thoughts have relation between each other and towards that which they represent, and a perception of the order of their relations has always been found connected with a perception of the order of the relations of thought. . . . Hence poetic harmony.

SHELLEY (from *A Defence of Poetry*)

KEATS

A loose, slack, not well-dressed youth met Mr. —— and myself in a lane near Highgate. —— knew him, and spoke. It was Keats. He was introduced to me, and stayed a minute or so. After he had left us a little way, he came back and said : " Let me carry away the memory, Coleridge, of having pressed your hand." " There is death in that hand," I said to ——, when Keats was gone ; yet this was, I think, before the consumption had showed itself distinctly.

COLERIDGE (from *Table Talk*)

O Poesy ! for thee I hold my pen
That am not yet a glorious denizen
Of thy wide heaven—Should I rather kneel
Upon some mountain-top until I feel
A glowing splendour round about me hung,
And echo back the voice of thine own tongue ?
O Poesy ! for thee I grasp my pen
That am not yet a glorious denizen
Of thy wide heaven ; yet, to my ardent prayer,
Yield from thy sanctuary some clear air,
Smoothed for intoxication by the breath
Of flowering bays, that I may die a death
Of luxury, and my young spirit follow
The morning sun-beams to the great Apollo
Like a fresh sacrifice ; or, if I can bear
The o'erwhelming sweets, 'twill bring me to the fair
Visions of all places : a bowery nook
Will be elysium—an eternal book
Whence I may copy many a lovely saying
About the leaves, and flowers—about the playing
Of nymphs in woods, and fountains ; and the shade
Keeping a silence round a sleeping maid ;
And many a verse from so strange influence
That we must ever wonder how, and whence
It came. Also imaginings will hover
Round my fire-side, and haply there discover
Vistas of solemn beauty, where I'd wander
In happy silence, like the clear Meander
Through its lone vales ; and where I found a spot
Of awfuller shade, or an enchanted grot,
Or a green hill o'erspread with chequered dress
Of flowers, and fearful from its loveliness,
Write on my tablets all that was permitted,

All that was for our human senses fitted.
Then the events of this wide world I'd seize
Like a strong giant, and my spirit tease
Till at its shoulders it should proudly see
Wings to find out an immortality. . . .

> A drainless shower
Of light is poesy ; 'tis the supreme of power ;
'Tis might half slumb'ring on its own right arm.
The very archings of her eye-lids charm
A thousand willing agents to obey,
And still she governs with the mildest sway :
But strength alone though of the Muses born
Is like a fallen angel : trees uptorn,
Darkness, and worms, and shrouds, and sepulchres
Delight it ; for it feeds upon the burrs
And thorns of life ; forgetting the great end
Of poesy, that it should be a friend
To sooth the cares, and lift the thoughts of man. . . .

What though I am not wealthy in the dower
Of spanning wisdom ; though I do not know
The shiftings of the mighty winds that blow
Hither and thither all the changing thoughts
Of man : though no great minist'ring reason sorts
Out the dark mysteries of human souls
To clear conceiving : yet there ever rolls
A vast idea before me, and I glean
Therefrom my liberty ; thence too I've seen
The end and aim of Poesy.

> KEATS (from *Sleep and Poetry*)

In poetry I have a few maxims, and you will see how far I am from their centre.

1st. I think poetry should surprise by a fine excess, and not by singularity; it should strike the reader as a wording of his own highest thoughts, and appear almost a remembrance.

2nd. Its touches of beauty should never be half-way, thereby making the reader breathless, instead of content. The rise, the progress, the setting of imagery, should, like the sun, come natural to him, shine over him, and set soberly, although in magnificence, leaving him in the luxury of twilight. But it is easier to think what poetry should be, than to write it. And this leads me to

Another axiom—That if poetry comes not as naturally as the leaves to a tree, it had better not come at all. However it may be with me, I cannot help looking into new countries with " Oh, for a muse of fire to ascend ! " If *Endymion* serves me as a pioneer, perhaps I ought to be content, for, thank God, I can read, and perhaps understand, Shakespeare to his depths ; and I have, I am sure, many friends, who, if I fail, will attribute any change in my life and temper to humbleness rather than pride—to a cowering under the wings of great poets, rather than to a bitterness that I am not appreciated. I am anxious to get *Endymion* printed that I may forget it, and proceed.

KEATS (from *The Letters*)

As to the poetical character itself (I mean that sort, of which, if I am anything, I am a member ; that sort distinguished from the Wordsworthian, or egotistical sublime ; which is a thing *per se*, and stands alone), it is not itself—it has no self—it is every thing and nothing—it has no character—it enjoys light and shade—it lives in gusts, be it foul or fair, high or low, rich or poor, mean or elevated—it has as much delight in conceiving an Iago as an Imogen. What shocks the virtuous philosopher delights the cameleon poet. It does no harm from its relish of the dark side of things, any more than from its taste for the bright one, because they both end in speculation. A poet is the most unpoetical of anything in existence, because he has no identity; he is continually in for, and filling, some other body. The sun, the moon, the sea, and men and women, who are creatures of impulse, are poetical, and have about them an unchangeable attribute; the poet has none, no identity. He is certainly the most unpoetical of all God's creatures. If, then, he has no self, and if I am a poet, where is the wonder that I should say I would write no more? Might I not at that very instant have been cogitating on the characters of Saturn and Ops? It is a wretched thing to confess, but it is a very fact, that not one word I ever utter can be taken for granted as an opinion growing out of my identical nature. How can it, when I have no nature? When I am in a room with people, if I am free from speculating on creations of my own brain, then, not myself goes home to myself, but the identity of every one in the room begins to press upon me, so that I am in a very little time annihilated—not only among men; it would be the same in a nursery of children. I know not whether I make myself wholly understood: I hope enough to let you see that no dependence is to be placed on what I said that day.

In the second place, I will speak of my views, and of the life I purpose to myself. I am ambitious of doing the world some good: if I should be spared, that may be the

117

work of future years—in the interval I will assay to reach to as high a summit in poetry as the nerve bestowed upon me will suffer. The faint conceptions I have of poems to come bring the blood frequently into my forehead. All I hope is, that I may not lose all interest in human affairs —that the solitary indifference I feel for applause, even from the finest spirits, will not blunt any acuteness of vision I may have. I do not think it will. I feel assured I should write from the mere yearning and fondness I have for the beautiful, even if my night's labours should be burnt every morning, and no eye ever shine upon them. But even now I am perhaps not speaking from myself but from some character in whose soul I now live.

KEATS (from *The Letters*)

Oh, weep for Adonais !—The quick Dreams,
The passion-wingèd Ministers of thought,
Who were his flocks, who near the living streams
Of his young spirit fed, and whom he taught
The love which was its music, wander not,—
Wander no more, from kindling brain to brain,
But droop there, whence they sprung ; and
        mourn their lot
Round the cold heart, where, after their sweet
        pain,
They ne'er will gather strength, or find a home again.

· · · · · · ·

Go thou to Rome,—at once the Paradise,
The grave, the city, and the wilderness ;
And where its wrecks like shattered mountains
        rise,

118

And flowering weeds and fragrant copses dress
The bones of Desolation's nakedness,
Pass, till the spirit of the spot shall lead
Thy footsteps to a slope of green access
Where, like an infant's smile, over the dead
A light of laughing flowers along the grass is spread ;

 . . . . .

And grey walls moulder round, on which dull
  Time
Feeds, like slow fire upon a hoary brand ;
And one keen pyramid with wedge sublime,
Pavilioning the dust of him who planned
This refuge for his memory, doth stand
Like flame transformed to marble ; and beneath,
A field is spread, on which a newer band
Have pitched in Heaven's smile their camp of
  death,
Welcoming him we lose with scarce extinguished
  breath.

 . . . . . .

The One remains, the many change and pass ;
Heaven's light forever shines, Earth's shadows
  fly ;
Life, like a dome of many-coloured glass,
Stains the white radiance of Eternity.
Until Death tramples it to fragments.—Die,
If thou wouldst be with that which thou dost
  seek !
Follow where all is fled !—Rome's azure sky,
Flowers, ruins, statues, music, words, are weak
The glory they transfuse with fitting truth to speak.

       SHELLEY (from *Adonais*)

Stand still, true poet that you are,
    I know you ; let me try and draw you.
Some night you'll fail us. When afar
    You rise, remember one man saw you,
Knew you, and named a star.

My star, God's glow-worm ! Why extend
    That loving hand of His which leads you,
Yet locks you safe from end to end
    Of his dark world, unless He needs you—
Just saves your light to spend ?

His clenched Hand shall unclose at last
    I know, and let out all the beauty.
My poet holds the future fast,
    Accepts the coming ages' duty,
Their present for this past.

That day, the earth's feast-master's brow
    Shall clear, to God the chalice raising ;
" Others give best at first, but Thou
    For ever set'st our table praising,—
Keep'st the good wine till now."

Meantime, I'll draw you as you stand,
    With few or none to watch and wonder.
I'll say—a fisher (on the sand
    By Tyre the Old) his ocean-plunder,
A netful, brought to land.

Who has not heard how Tyrian shells
    Enclosed the blue, that dye of dyes

Whereof one drop worked miracles,
    And coloured like Astarte's eyes
Raw silk the merchant sells ?

And each bystander of them all
    Could criticise, and quote tradition
How depths of blue sublimed some pall,
    To get which, pricked a king's ambition ;
Worth sceptre, crown and ball.

Yet there's the dye,—in that rough mesh,
    The sea has only just o'er-whispered !
Like whelks, the lip's-beard dripping fresh,
    As if they still the water's lisp heard
Through foam the rock-weeds thresh.

Enough to furnish Solomon
    Such hangings for his cedar-house,
That when gold-robed he took the throne
    In that abyss of blue, the Spouse
Might swear his presence shone

Most like the centre-spike of gold
    Which burns deep in the blue-bell's womb,
What time, with ardours manifold,
    The bee goes singing to her groom,
Drunken and overbold.

Mere conchs ! not fit for warp or woof !
    Till art comes,—comes to pound and squeeze
And clarify,—refines to proof
    The liquor filtered by degrees,
While the world stands aloof.

And there's the extract, flasked and fine,
    And priced, and saleable at last !
And Hobbs, Nobbs, Stokes and Nokes combine
    To paint the future from the past,
Put blue into their line.

Hobbs hints blue,—straight he turtle eats.
    Nobbs prints blue,—claret crowns his cup.
Nokes outdares Stokes in azure feats,—
    Both gorge. Who fished the murex up ?
What porridge had John Keats ?

BROWNING

. . . For your bewilderment more especially noted—how
shall I help that ? We don't read poetry the same way, by
the same law ; it is too clear. I cannot begin writing
poetry till my imaginary reader has conceded licences to
me which you demur at altogether. I *know* that I don't
make out my conception by my language ; all poetry
being a putting of the infinite within the finite. You
would have me paint it all plain out, which can't be ; but
by various artifices I try to make shift with touches and
bits of outlines which *succeed* if they bear the conception
from me to you. You ought, I think, to keep pace with the
thought tripping from ledge to ledge of my ' glaciers,' as
you call them ; not stand poking your alpenstock into the
holes, and demonstrating that no foot could have stood
there ;—suppose it sprang over there ? In *prose* you may
criticise so—because that is the absolute representation of
portions of truth, what chronicling is to history—but in
asking for more *ultimates* you must accept less *mediates*,

122

nor expect that a druid stone circle will be traced for you with as few breaks to the eye as the North Crescent and the South Crescent that go together so cleverly in many a suburb. Why, you look at my little song as though it were Hobbs' or Nobbs' lease of his house, a testament of his devising, wherein, I grant you, not a ' then and there,' ' to him and his heirs,' ' to have and to hold,' and so on, would be superfluous ; and so you begin : ' Stand still,—why ? ' For the reason indicated in the verse, to be sure,—*to let me draw him.* . . . The last charge I cannot answer, for you may be right in preferring it, however unwitting I am of the fact. I *may* put Robert Browning into Pippa and other men and maids. If so, *peccavi* ; but I don't see myself in them at all events.

Do you think poetry was ever generally understood—or can be ? Is the business of it to tell people what they know already, as they know it, and so precisely that they shall be able to cry out—' Here you should supply *this—that*, you evidently pass over, and I'll help you from my own stock ' ? It is all teaching, on the contrary, and the people hate to be taught. They say otherwise,—make foolish fables about Orpheus enchanting stocks and stones, poets standing up and being worshipped,—all nonsense and impossible dreaming. A poet's affair is with God,— to whom he is accountable, and of whom is his reward ; look elsewhere, and you find misery enough. Do you believe people understand *Hamlet* ? . . .

(from a Letter from BROWNING to RUSKIN
concerning the foregoing Poem)

ON PROSE AND STYLE

When we find Milton writing : ' And long it was not after, when I was confirmed in this opinion, that he, who would not be frustrate of his hope to write well hereafter in laudable things, ought himself to be a true poem,'— we pronounce that such a prose has its own grandeur, but that it is obsolete and inconvenient. But when we find Dryden telling us : ' What Virgil wrote in the vigour of his age, in plenty and at ease, I have undertaken to translate in my declining years ; struggling with wants, oppressed with sickness, curbed in my genius, liable to be misconstrued in all I write,'—then we exclaim that here at last we have the true English prose, a prose such as we would all gladly use if we only knew how. Yet Dryden was Milton's contemporary.

MATTHEW ARNOLD (from *The Essays*)

When we behold a natural style we are astonished and enthralled ; for where we looked to behold an author, we find a man.

PASCAL (from *Les Pensées*)

SENECA. Let us reason a little upon style. I would set you right, and remove from before you the prejudices of a somewhat rustic education. We may adorn the simplicity of the wisest.

EPICTETUS. Thou canst not adorn simplicity. What is naked or defective is susceptible of decoration : what is decorated is simplicity no longer. Thou mayest give another thing in exchange for it; but if thou wert master of it, thou wouldst preserve it inviolate. It is no wonder that we mortals, little able as we are to see truth, should be less able to express it.

SENECA. You have formed at present no idea of style.

EPICTETUS. I never think about it. First, I consider whether what I am about to say is true; then, whether I can say it with brevity, in such a manner as that others shall see it as clearly as I do in the light of truth; for, if they survey it as an ingenuity, my desire is ungratified, my duty unfulfilled. I go not with those who dance round the image of Truth, less out of honour to her than to display their agility and address.

SENECA. We must attract the attention of readers by novelty, and force, and grandeur of expression.

EPICTETUS. We must. Nothing is so grand as truth, nothing so forcible, nothing so novel.

SENECA. Sonorous sentences are wanted to awaken the lethargy of indolence.

EPICTETUS. Awaken it to what? Here lies the question; and a weighty one it is. If thou awakenest men where they can see nothing and do no work, it is better to let them rest: but will not they, thinkest thou, look up at a rainbow unless they are called to it by a clap of thunder?

LANDOR (from *Imaginary Conversations*)

PETRARCA. Enter into the mind and heart of your own creatures: think of them long, entirely, solely: never of style, never of self, never of critics, cracked or sound. Like the miles of an open country, and of an ignorant population, when they are correctly measured they become smaller. In the loftiest rooms and richest entablatures are suspended the most spider-webs ; and the quarry out of which palaces are erected is the nursery of nettle and bramble.

BOCCACCIO. It is better to keep always in view such writers as Cicero, than to run after those idlers who throw stones that can never reach us.

PETRARCA. If you copied him to perfection, and on no occasion lost sight of him, you would be an indifferent, not to say a bad writer.

LANDOR (from *The Pentameron*)

As 'tis a greater mystery, in the art
Of painting, to foreshorten any part
Than draw it out, so 'tis in books the chief
Of all perfections to be plain and brief.

SAMUEL BUTLER (1612–1680)

I never knew a writer yet who took the smallest pains with his style and was at the same time readable.

.   .   .   .

Mr Walter Pater's style is, to me, like the face of some old woman who has been to Madame Rachel and had herself enamelled. The bloom is nothing but powder and paint and the odour is cherry-blossom. Mr Matthew Arnold's odour is as the faint sickliness of hawthorn.

SAMUEL BUTLER, 1835–1902 (from *The Notebooks*)

Prose is a more artificial thing than poetry, as a pattern-ing of steps would be more artificial in walking than in dancing ; and artistic prose is always apt to excite offence, as by excess of scruple and ceremony, where verse will be permitted its fastidiousness. The plain man has never been at his ease with prose, and with our literature before him the plain man is indeed unlucky. For whereas French prose, for instance, is often the conversational or episto-lary utterance of men of the world, a beautiful but mun-dane and social thing, English prose is almost wholly the utterance of poets, prophets, eccentrics, humorists, the few fine English writers of social prose being men in the second or third rank. And what is democracy to get directly out of Donne's tremendous sermons, out of Sir Thomas Browne's musings over ' the persons of these ossuaries ' ? . . .

Pride in our poetry and our prose must not blind us to the truth that they are not nearly as good instruments of education for our masses as the French masters of the classic period are for Frenchmen in general. ' All that is not clear is not French,' it has been said ; truly enough if we look at all but comparatively recent French litera-ture. Can any one say, all that is not clear is not English ? Our great writers have a profounder innocence and a rarer command of mystery than any of the French, but they will never tell the merely intelligent reader half as much of the national genius. From those who approach them to be directly educated they keep their secret, and ours.

T. EARLE WELBY (from *The Dinner Knell*)

§III ART AND ARTISTS

ART

Painting is the intermediate somewhat between a
thought and a thing.

COLERIDGE (from *Table Talk*)

We carve and paint, or we behold what is carved and
painted, as students of the mystery of Form. The virtue
of art lies in detachment, in sequestering one object from
the embarrassing variety. Until one thing comes out
from the connection of things, there can be enjoyment,
contemplation, but no thought. Our happiness and
unhappiness are unproductive. The infant lies in a pleasing trance, but his individual character and his practical
power depend on his daily progress in the separation of
things, and dealing with one at a time. Love and all the
passions concentrate all existence around a single form.
It is the habit of certain minds to give an all-excluding
fullness to the object, the thought, the word, they alight
upon, and to make that for the time the deputy of the
world. These are the artists, the orators, the leaders of
society. The power to detach, and to magnify by detach-
ing, is the essence of rhetoric in the hands of the orator
and the poet. This rhetoric, or power to fix the momentary
eminency of an object,—so remarkable in Burke, in
Byron, in Carlyle,—the painter and sculptor exhibit in
colour and in stone. The power depends on the depth of
the artist's insight of the object he contemplates. For
every object has its roots in central nature, and may of
course be so exhibited to us as to represent the world.
Therefore each work of genius is the tyrant of the hour,

and concentrates attention on itself. . . . Though we travel the world over to find the beautiful, we must carry it with us, or we find it not. . . . The traveller who visits the Vatican, and passes from chamber to chamber through galleries of statues, vases, sarcophagi, and candelabra, through all forms of beauty, cut in the richest materials, is in danger of forgetting the simplicity of the principles out of which they all sprung, and that they had their origin from thoughts and laws in his own breast.

EMERSON (from *The Essays*)

PAINTING IS THOUGHT

Shall Painting be confined to the sordid drudgery of facsimile representations of merely mortal and perishing substances, and not be as poetry and music are, elevated into its own proper sphere of invention and visionary conception? No, it shall not be so! Painting, as well as poetry and music, exists and exults in immortal thoughts.

BLAKE

ANCIENTS AND MODERNS

One may say, and assuredly without detriment to the ancients, that in general they did not know, as do the moderns, how to multiply the planes in their pictures how to observe the gradations that these successive planes require, how to bind figure to figure and group to group, how to capture the eye by the prestige of a colour which

132

is not that of Nature but produces the effect of such. Yes, they neglected or were almost ignorant of these things, because they regarded them as mere distractions from the beautiful on which their eyes were fastened, because they held that these secondary portions of art would merely seduce the spectator, and themselves, from that which deserved all their attention.

INGRES
(from DELABORDE'S *Ingres : sa vie et ses travaux*)

People may say what they please about the gradual improvement of the Arts. It is not true of the substance. The Arts and the Muses both spring forth in the youth of nations, like Minerva from the front of Jupiter, all armed : manual dexterity may, indeed, be improved by practice.

Painting went on in power till, in Raffael, it attained the zenith, and in him too it showed signs of a tendency downwards by another path. The painter began to think of overcoming difficulties. After this the descent was rapid, till sculptors began to work inveterate likenesses of perriwigs in marble,—as see Algarotti's tomb in the cemetery at Pisa,—and painters did nothing but copy, as well as they could, the external face of nature. Now, in this age, we have a sort of revivescence,—not, I fear, of the power, but of a taste for the power, of the early times.

COLERIDGE (from *Table Talk*)

THE AMATEUR

—And did you step in, to take a look at the grand picture in your way back ?—'Tis a melancholy daub ! my Lord ; not one principle of the pyramid in any one group ! —and what a price !—for there is nothing of the colouring of Titian—the expression of Rubens—the grace of Raphael—the purity of Domenichino—the correggiescity of Correggio—the learning of Poussin—the airs of Guido —the taste of the Carrachis—or the grand contour of Angelo—Grant me patience, just Heaven !—Of all the cants which are canted in this canting world—though the cant of hypocrites may be the worst—the cant of criticism is the most tormenting !

I would go fifty miles on foot, for I have not a horse worth riding on, to kiss the hand of that man whose generous heart will give up the reins of his imagination into his author's hands—be pleased he knows not why, and cares not wherefore.

STERNE (from *Tristram Shandy*)

LOMBARD SCULPTURE

The entrance to the crypt of St. Zeno . . . is covered by very light but most effective bas-reliefs of jesting subjects : two cocks carrying on their shoulders a long staff, to which a fox is tied by the legs, hanging down between them : the strut of the foremost cock, lifting one leg at right angles, to the other, is delicious. Then a stag hunt, with a centaur horseman drawing a bow ; the arrow has gone clear through the stag's throat, and is sticking there. Several capital hunts with dogs, with fruit trees between, and birds in them ; the leaves, considering the early time, singularly well set, with the edges outwards, sharp, and deep cut ; snails and frogs filling up the intervals, as if suspended in the air, with some saucy puppies on their hind-legs, two or three nondescript beasts ; and, finally, on the centre of one of the arches on the south side, an elephant and castle,—a very strange elephant, yet cut as if the carver had seen one.

These scupltures of St. Zeno are, however, quite quiet and tame compared with those of San Michele of Pavia, which are designed also in a somewhat gloomier mood. . . . They are much earlier than St. Zeno ; of the seventh century at latest. There is more of nightmare, and less of wit in them. . . . The state of mind represented by the west front is more that of a feverish dream, than resultant from any determined architectural purpose, or even from any definite love and delight in the grotesque. One capital is covered with a mass of grinning heads, other heads grow out of two bodies, or out of and under feet ; the creatures are all fighting, or devouring, or struggling which shall be uppermost, and yet in an effectual way, as if they would fight for ever, and come to no decision. Neither sphinxes nor centaurs did I notice, nor a single peacock (I believe peacocks to be purely Byzantine), but mermaids with two tails . . . strange, large fish, apes, stags, bulls, dogs, wolves, and horses, griffins, eagles, long-tailed birds, cocks, hawks, and dragons, without end, or with a dozen of ends, as the case may be ; smaller birds, with rabbits, and small nondescripts, filling the friezes. The actual leaf, which is used in the best Byzantine mouldings at Venice, occurs in parts of these Pavian designs. But the Lombard animals are all *alive*, and fiercely alive too, all impatience and spring ; the Byzantine birds peck idly at the fruit, and the animals hardly touch it with their noses. The cinquecento birds in Venice hold it up daintily, like train-bearers; the birds in the earlier Gothic peck at it hungrily and naturally; but the Lombard beasts gripe at it like tigers, and tear it off with writhing lips and glaring eyes.

RUSKIN

(from The Stones of Venice)

NATURE AND ART

The painter will produce pictures of little merit if he takes the works of others as his standard; but if he will apply himself to learn from the objects of nature he will produce good results. This we see was the case with the painters who came after the time of the Romans, for they continually imitated each other, and from age to age their art steadily declined.

After these came Giotto the Florentine, and he,—reared in mountain solitudes, inhabited only by goats and such like beasts—turning straight from nature to his art, began to draw on the rocks the movements of the goats which he was tending, and so began to draw the figures of all the animals which were to be found in the country, in such a way that after much study he not only surpassed the masters of his own time but all those of many preceding centuries. After him art again declined, because all were imitating paintings already done; and so for centuries it continued to decline until such time as Tommaso the Florentine, nicknamed Masaccio, showed by the perfection of his work how those who took as their standard anything other than nature, the supreme guide of all the masters, were wearying themselves in vain.

Similarly I would say as to these mathematical subjects, that those who study only the authorities and not the works of nature are in art the grandsons and not the sons of nature, which is the supreme guide of the good authorities.

Mark the supreme folly of those who censure such as learn from nature, leaving uncensured the authorities who were the disciples of this same nature !

LEONARDO DA VINCI
(from *The Notebooks*—Trans. E. MCCURDY)

When I sit down to make a sketch from nature, the first thing I try to do is, *to forget that I have ever seen a picture.*

CONSTABLE (from LESLIE'S *Life of Constable*)

The Englishmen seem to be pursuing nature, while we are merely occupied in imitating pictures.

DELACROIX
(from TH. SILVESTRE'S *Histoire des Artistes Vivants*)

A man may be working his eight or nine hours a day from a model and yet not be studying from nature. He is painting but not studying. He is like the man in the Bible who looks at himself in a glass and goeth away forgetting what manner of man he was. He will know no more about nature at the end of twenty years than a priest who has been reading his breviary day after day without committing it to memory will know of its contents. Unless he gets what he has seen well into his memory, so as to have it at his fingers' ends as familiarly as the characters with which he writes a letter, he can be no more held to be familiar with, and to have command over nature, than a man who only copies his signature from a copy kept in his pocket, as I have known French Canadians do, can be said to be able to write. It is painting without nature that will give a man this, and not painting directly from her. He must do both the one and the other, and the one as much as the other.

SAMUEL BUTLER (from *The Notebooks*)

The imitation of nature is as difficult as it is admirable if one can really achieve it and carry it through. But he also may deserve praise who has completely withdrawn himself from nature and has succeeded in placing before our eyes forms and movements which have hitherto existed only in our imagination. . . . Painting, like Poetry, selects from the universe what it can best use for its own ends. It unites, it concentrates in one fantastic figure circumstances and characters which nature has distributed among various individuals. Thanks to this wise and ingenious combination the artist merits the title of an inventor and ceases to be a mere subordinate copyist.

GOYA

In nature there is neither colour nor line, only sun and shade.   Give me a piece of charcoal and I will produce a beautiful picture.

GOYA

However great your genius, if you paint, not from Nature as already copied by you, but directly from the model, you will always be a slave and your picture mere servitude. Raphael, on the contrary, had so thoroughly conquered Nature, he had it so thoroughly in his memory, that instead of Nature commanding him one would rather say that it obeyed him, that it came of its own accord into his work.

. . . .

What is called " touch " is an abuse of execution. It is merely the quality of a false talent, of false artists who divorce themselves from the imitation of Nature simply to display their cleverness. Touch, however skilful, should never be apparent; otherwise it hinders illusion and destroys movement. Instead of the object represented, it displays the process; instead of thought, it betrays the hand.

INGRES (from DELABORDE)

It is not when setting about a design that we should force ourselves to use foot-rules, perpendiculars, and so on. This accuracy must be a confirmed habit which, when we are in the presence of nature, instantly comes to our aid in the stern necessity of reproducing her appearance.

DELACROIX (from TH. SILVESTRE)

No one can ever design till he has learned the language of Art by making many finished copies both of Nature, Art, and of whatever comes in his way, from earliest childhood.

BLAKE

We must always copy nature and learn how to see her rightly. This is why we ought to study the antique and the great masters ; not to imitate them, but, I repeat, to learn how to see.

Do you imagine I send you to the Louvre to find what is called ' Ideal beauty,' a thing outside nature ?

INGRES (from DELABORDE)

No man of Sense ever supposes that copying from Nature is the Art of Painting ; if Art is no more than this, it is no better than any other Manual Labour ; anybody may do it & the fool often will do it best as it is a work of no Mind.

BLAKE

Spiritual War : Israel deliver'd from Egypt, is Art deliver'd from Nature & Imitation.

BLAKE

After having spent years striving to be accurate, we must spend as many more in discovering when and how to be inaccurate.

SAMUEL BUTLER (from *The Notebooks*)

I have not tried to reproduce Nature : I have represented it.

CÉZANNE

ART AND MONEY

There are two causes, it seems, of deterioration of art. And what are they?

Wealth and poverty. Do you think that a potter, after he has grown rich, will care to attend to his trade any longer?

Certainly not.

But he will become more idle and careless than he was before?

Yes, much more.

Then does he not become a worse potter?

Yes, a much worse potter too.

On the other hand, if he is prevented by poverty from providing himself with tools or any other requisite of his trade, he will produce inferior articles, and his sons or apprentices will not be taught their trade so well.

Inevitably.

Then both these conditions, riches and poverty, deteriorate the productions of the artisans, and the artisans themselves.

PLATO (from *The Republic*)

Christianity is Art, and not Money. Money is its Curse.

BLAKE

To give advice to those who are contending for royal liberality, has been for some years the duty of my station in the Academy.

Liberality! We want not Liberality. We want a Fair Price & Proportionate Value & a General Demand for Art.
SIR JOSHUA REYNOLDS

(with BLAKE'S comment)

THE AIM OF ART

Upon the whole it seems to me, that the object and intention of all the Arts is to supply the natural imperfection of things, and often to gratify the mind by realising and embodying what never existed but in the imagination.

It is allowed on all hands, that facts, and events, however they may bind the historian, have no dominion over the poet or the painter. With us, history is made to bend and conform to this great idea of art. And why ? Because these arts, in their highest province, are not addressed to the gross senses ; but to the desires of the mind, to that spark of divinity which we have within, impatient of being circumscribed and pent up by the world which is about us. Just so much as our art has of this, just so much of dignity, I had almost said of divinity, it exhibits ; and those of our artists who possessed this mark of distinction in the highest degree, acquired from thence the glorious appellation of Divine.

SIR JOSHUA REYNOLDS
(from *The Discourses*)

All art constantly aspires towards the condition of music. For while in all other kinds of art it is possible to distinguish the matter from the form, and the understanding can always make this distinction, yet it is the constant effort of art to obliterate it. That the mere matter of a poem, for instance, its subject, namely, its given incidents or situation—that the mere matter of a picture, the actual circumstances of an event, the actual topography of a landscape—should·be nothing without the form, the spirit, of the handling, that this form, this mode of handling, should become an end in itself, should penetrate every part of the matter : this is what all art constantly strives after, and achieves in different degrees.

PATER

Art has no other end in view save the emphasising and recording in the most effective way some strongly felt interest or affection. Where there is neither interest nor desire to record with good effect, there is but sham art, or none at all : where both these are fully present, no matter how rudely and inarticulately, there is great art. Art is at best a dress, important, yet still nothing in comparison with the wearer, and, as a general rule, the less it attracts the attention the better.

SAMUEL BUTLER (from *The Notebooks*)

There is no *inherent* reason why painting should not be used to express the logically inexpressible.

HERBERT READ (from *Art Now*)

The ballet-girl is merely a pretext for the design.

DEGAS

COLOUR

When colour has its richness, form has its fullness.

CÉZANNE

I believe that from the beginning of the world there has never been a true or fine school of art in which colour was despised.

RUSKIN

Colour is eminently subservient to beauty, because it is susceptible of forms, i.e. outline, and yet is a sensation. But a rich mass of scarlet clouds, seen without any attention to the *form* of the mass or of the parts, may be a delightful but not a beautiful object or colour.

COLERIDGE (from *Table Talk*)

ODE ON A GRECIAN URN

Thou still unravish'd bride of quietness,
    Thou foster-child of silence and slow time,
Sylvan historian, who canst thus express
    A flowery tale more sweetly than our rhyme :
What leaf-fring'd legend haunts about thy shape
    Of deities or mortals, or of both,
        In Tempe or the dales of Arcady ?
What men and gods are these ? What maidens loth ?
    What mad pursuit ? What struggle to escape ?
        What pipes and timbrels ? What wild ecstasy ?

Heard melodies are sweet, but those unheard
    Are sweeter ; therefore, ye soft pipes, play on ;
Not to the sensual ear, but, more endear'd,
    Pipe to the spirit ditties of no tone :

Fair youth, beneath the trees, thou canst not leave
     Thy song, nor ever can those trees be bare ;
       Bold lover, never, never canst thou kiss,
Though winning near the goal—yet, do not grieve ;
     She cannot fade, though thou hast not thy bliss,
       For ever wilt thou love, and she be fair !

Ah, happy, happy boughs ! that cannot shed
     Your leaves, nor ever bid the Spring adieu ;
And, happy melodist, unwearied,
     For ever piping songs for ever new ;
More happy love ! more happy, happy love !
     For ever warm and still to be enjoy'd,
       For ever panting and for ever young ;
All breathing human passion far above,
     That leaves a heart high-sorrowful and cloy'd,
       A burning forehead, and a parching tongue.

Who are these coming to the sacrifice ?
     To what green altar, O mysterious priest,
Lead'st thou that heifer lowing at the skies,
     And all her silken flanks with garlands drest ?
What little town by river or sea shore,
     Or mountain-built with peaceful citadel,
       Is emptied of this folk, this pious morn ?
And, little town, thy streets for evermore
     Will silent be ; and not a soul to tell
       Why thou art desolate, can e'er return.

O Attic shape ! Fair attitude ! with brede
     Of marble men and maidens overwrought,
With forest branches and the trodden weed ;
     Thou, silent form, dost tease us out of thought

As doth eternity : Cold Pastoral !
    When old age shall this generation waste,
        Thou shalt remain, in midst of other woe
Than ours, a friend to man, to whom thou say'st,
    " Beauty is truth, truth beauty,"—that is all
        Ye know on earth, and all ye need to know.

KEATS

GREEKS AND ITALIANS

When Greek Art ran and reached the goal,
Thus much had the world to boast *in fructu*—
The truth of Man, as by God first spoken,
Which the actual generations garble,
Was re-uttered,—and Soul (which Limbs betoken)
And Limbs (Soul informs) were made new in
    marble. . .

So, testing your weakness by their strength,
Your meagre charms by their rounded beauty,
Measured by Art in your breadth and length,
You learn—to submit is the worsted's duty.
—When I say " you " 'tis the common soul,
The collective, I mean—the race of Man
That receives life in parts to live in a whole,
And grow here according to God's own plan.

Growth came when, looking your last on them all,
You turned your eyes inwardly one fine day
And cried with a start—What if we so small
Are greater, ay, greater the while than they !

Are they perfect of lineament, perfect of stature?
In both, of such lower types are we
Precisely because of your wider nature:
For time theirs, ours for eternity. . . .

On which I conclude that the early painters,
To cries of " Greek Art and what more wish you? "
Replied, " Become now self-acquainters,
And paint man, man,—whatever the issue!
Make the hopes shine through the flesh they fray,
New fears aggrandise the rags and tatters.
So bring the invisible full into play,
Let the visible go to the dogs—what matters? " . . .

But at any rate I have loved the season
Of Art's spring-birth so dim and dewy,
My sculptor is Nicolo the Pisan;
My painter—who but Cimabue?
Nor ever was man of them all indeed,
From these to Ghiberti and Ghirlandajo,
Could say that he missed my critic meed!
So now to my special grievance—heigh ho!

Their ghosts now stand, as I said before,
Watching each fresco flaked and rasped,
Blocked up, knocked out, or whitewashed o'er
—No getting again what the church has grasped! . . .
Why don't they bethink them of who has merited?
Why not reveal, while their pictures dree
Such doom, that a captive's to be out-ferreted?
Why do they never remember me?

Not that I expect the great Bigordi
Nor Sandro to hear me, chivalric, bellicose;
Nor wronged Lippino—and not a word I
Say of a scrap of Fra Angelico's.
But are you too fine, Taddeo Gaddi,
To grant me a taste of your intonaco—
Some Jerome that seeks the heaven with a sad eye?
No churlish saint, Lorenzo Monaco?

Could not the ghost with the close red cap,
My Pollajolo, the twice a craftsman,
Save me a sample, give me the hap
Of a muscular Christ that shows the draughtsman?
No Virgin by him, the somewhat petty,
Of finical touch and tempera crumbly—
Could not Alessio Baldovinetti
Contribute so much, I ask him humbly?

Margheritone of Arezzo,
With the grave-clothes garb and swaddling barret,
(Why purse up mouth and beak in a pet so,
You bald, saturnine, poll-clawed parrot?)
No poor glimmering Crucifixion,
Where in the foreground kneels the donor?
If such remain, as is my conviction,
The hoarding does you but little honour.

BROWNING
(from *Old Pictures in Florence*)

148

... Just what Dante scorns as unworthy alike of heaven and hell, Botticelli accepts, that middle world in which men take no side in great conflicts, and decide no great causes, and make great refusals. He thus sets for himself the limits within which art, undisturbed by any moral ambition, does its most sincere and surest work. His interest is neither in the untempered goodness of Angelico's saints, nor the untempered evil of Orcagna's *Inferno* ; but with men and women, in their mixed and uncertain condition, always attractive, clothed sometimes by passion with a character of loveliness and energy, but saddened perpetually by the shadow upon them of the great things from which they shrink. His morality is all sympathy ; and it is this sympathy, conveying into his work somewhat more than is usual of the true complexion of humanity, which makes him, visionary as he is, so forcible a realist.

It is this which gives to his Madonnas their unique expression and charm. . . . For with Botticelli she too, though she holds in her hands the " Desire of all nations," is one of those who are neither for Jehovah nor for His enemies ; and her choice is on her face. The white light on it is cast up hard and cheerless from below, as when snow lies upon the ground, and the children look up with surprise at the strange whiteness of the ceiling. Her trouble is in the very caress of the mysterious child, whose gaze is always far from her, and who has already that sweet look of devotion which men have never been able altogether to love, and which still makes the born saint an object almost of suspicion to his earthly brethren. Once, indeed, he guides her hand to transcribe in a book the words of her exaltation, the *Ave*, and the *Magnificat*, and the *Gaude Maria*, and the young angels, glad to rouse her for a moment from her dejection, are eager to hold the inkhorn and to support the book. But the pen almost drops from her hand, and the high cold words have no meaning for her, and her true children are those others, among whom, in her rude home, the intolerable honour came to her, with that look of wistful enquiry on their irregular faces which you see in startled animals—gipsy children, such as those who, in Apennine villages, still hold out their long brown arms to beg of you, but on Sundays become *enfants du chœur*, with their thick black hair nicely combed, and fair white linen on their sunburnt throats.

What is strangest is that he carries this sentiment into classical subjects, its most complete expression being a picture in the *Uffizi*, of Venus rising from the sea, in which the grotesque emblems of the middle age, and a landscape full of its peculiar feeling, and even its strange draperies, powdered all over in the Gothic manner with a quaint conceit of daisies, frame a figure that reminds you of the faultless nude studies of Ingres. At first, perhaps, you are attracted only by a quaintness of design, which seems to recall all at once whatever you have read of Florence in the fifteenth century ; afterwards you may think that this quaintness must be incongruous with the subject, and that the colour is cadaverous or at least cold. And yet, the more you come to understand what imaginative colouring really is, that all colour is no mere delightful quality of natural things, but a spirit upon them by which they become expressive to the spirit, the better you will like this peculiar quality of colour ; and you will find that quaint design of Botticelli's a more direct inlet into the Greek temper than the works of the Greeks themselves even of the finest period. Of the Greeks as they really were, of their difference from ourselves, of the aspects of their outward life, we know far more than Botticelli, or his most learned contemporaries ; but for us long familiarity has taken off the edge of the lesson, and we are hardly conscious of what we owe to the Hellenic spirit. But in pictures like this of Botticelli's you have a record of the first impression made by it on minds turned back towards it, in almost painful aspiration, from a world in which it had been ignored so long ; and in the passion, the energy, the industry of realization, with which Botticelli carries out his intention, is the exact measure of the legitimate influence over the human mind of the imaginative system of which this is perhaps the central myth. The light is indeed cold—mere sunless dawn ; but a later painter would have cloyed you with sunshine ; and you can see the better for that quietness in the morning air each long promontory, as it slopes down to the water's edge. Men go forth to their labours until the evening ; but she is awake before them, and you might think that the sorrow in her face was at the thought of the whole long day of love yet to come. An emblematical figure of the wind blows hard across the grey water, moving forward the dainty-lipped shell on which she sails, the sea " showing his teeth," as it moves, in the thin lines of foam, and sucking in, one by one, the falling roses, each severe in outline, plucked off short at the stalk, but embrowned a little, as Botticelli's flowers always are. Botticelli meant all this imagery to be altogether pleasurable ; and it was partly an incompleteness of resources, inseparable from the art of that time, that subdued and chilled it. But this predilection for minor tones counts also ; and what is unmistakable is the sadness with which he has conceived the goddess of pleasure, as the depositary of a great power over the lives of men.

PATER

(from *Studies in the History of the Renaissance*)

SPRING

By Sandro Botticelli

What masque of what old wind-withered New-Year
Honours this Lady ? Flora, wanton-eyed
For birth, and with all flowrets prankt and pied :
Aurora, Zephyrus, with mutual cheer
Of clasp and kiss : the Graces circling near,
'Neath bower-linked arch of white arms glorified :
And with those feathered feet which hovering glide
O'er Spring's brief bloom, Hermes the harbinger.
Birth-bare, not death-bare yet, the young stems stand
This Lady's temple-columns : o'er her head
Love wings his shaft. What mystery here is read
Of homage or of hope ? But how command
Dead Springs to answer ? And how question here
These mummers of that wind-withered New-Year ?

ROSSETTI

THE CASTING OF THE PERSEUS

I now took courage to myself and banished all those thoughts which from time to time occasioned me great inquietude. . . . I still flattered myself that, if I could but finish my statue of Perseus, all my labours would be converted to delight and meet with a glorious and happy reward. Thus having recovered my vigour of mind, I, with the utmost strength of body and of purse, though indeed I had but little money left, began to purchase several loads of pine-wood from the pine-grove of the Serristori, hard by Monte Lupo; and while I was waiting for it, I covered my Perseus with the earth which I had prepared several months beforehand, that it might have its proper seasoning. After I had made its coat of earth, (for the technical term in our business is *coat*), covered it well and bound it properly with irons, I began by means of a slow fire to draw off the wax, which melted away by many vent holes; for the more of these are made, the better the moulds are filled. When I had entirely stripped off the wax, I made a sort of fence round my Perseus, that is, round the mould above-mentioned, of bricks, piling them one upon another, and leaving several vacuities for the fire to exhale at. I next began to put on the wood, and kept a constant fire for two days and two nights, till the wax being quite off, and the mould well baked, I all on a sudden began to dig a hole to bury my mould in, and observed all those fine methods of proceeding that are prescribed by our art. When I had completely dug the hole, I took my mould, and by means of levers and good strong cables, directed it with care and suspended it a cubit above the level of the furnace, so that it hung exactly in the middle of the hole. I then let it gently down to the very bottom of the furnace and placed it with all the care and exactness I possibly could. After I had finished this part of my task, I began to make a covering of the very earth I had taken off, and in proportion as I raised the earth, I made vents for it, which are a sort of tubes of baked earth, generally used for conduits, and other things of a similar nature. As soon as I saw that I had placed it properly, and that this manner of covering it, by putting on those small tubes in their proper places, was likely to answer, as also that my journeymen thoroughly understood my plan, which was very different from that of all other masters, and I was sure that I could depend upon them, I turned my thoughts to my furnace. I had caused it to be filled with several pieces of brass and bronze, and heaped them upon one another in the manner taught us by our art, taking particular care to leave a passage for the flames, that the metal might the sooner assume its colour and dissolve into a fluid. Thus I with great alacrity excited my men to lay on the pine-wood, which, because of the unctuosity of the resinous matter that oozes from the pine-tree, and that my furnace was admirably well made, burned at such a rate that I was continually obliged to run to and fro, which greatly fatigued me. I, however, bore the hardship ; but, to add to my misfortune, the shop took fire, and we were all very much afraid that the roof would fall in and crush us. From another quarter, that is from the garden, the sky poured in so much rain and wind that it cooled my furnace. Thus did I continue to struggle with these cross accidents for several hours, and exerted myself to such a degree that my constitution, though robust, could no longer bear such severe hardship, and I was suddenly attacked by a most violent intermitting fever. In short, I was so ill that I found myself under a necessity of lying down upon the bed. This gave me great concern, but it was unavoidable. I thereupon addressed myself to my assistants, who were about ten in number, consisting of masters who melted bronze, helpers, men from the country, and the journeymen that worked in the shop, among whom was Bernardino Manellini di Mugello, that had lived with me several years. After having recommended it to them all to take proper care of my business, I said to Bernardino—" My friend, be careful to observe the method which I have shown you, and use all possible expedition, for the metal will soon be ready. You cannot mistake. These two worthy men here will quickly make tubes ; with two such directors you can certainly contrive to manage matters, and I have no doubt but my mould will be filled completely. I at present find myself extremely ill, and really believe that in a few hours this severe disorder will put an end to my life."

Thus I left them in great sorrow and went to bed. As soon as I had lain down, I ordered the maids to carry victuals and drink into the shop for all the men, and told them I did not expect to live till the next morning. They encouraged me notwithstanding, assuring me that my disorder would not last, as it was only the effect of my having over-fatigued myself. In this manner did I continue for two hours in a violent fever. I every moment perceived it to increase, and was incessantly crying out—" I am dying ! I am dying ! " My housekeeper, whose name was Mona Fiore da Castel del Rio, was one of the most sensible women in the world and thoroughly devoted to my interest. She rebuked me for having given way to vain fears and at the same time attended me with the greatest kindness and care imaginable. However, seeing me so very ill, and terrified to such a degree, she could not contain herself, but shed a flood of tears which she endeavoured to conceal from me.

Whilst we were both in this deep affliction, I perceived a man enter the room who in his person appeared to be as crooked and distorted as the letter S. This man began to deliver himself in these terms, with a tone of voice as dismal and melancholy as those who exhort and pray with persons who are going to be executed—" Alas ! poor Benvenuto, your work is spoiled, and the misfortune admits of no remedy." No sooner had I heard these words uttered by this messenger of evil, than I cried out so loud that my voice might be heard as far as the empyreum, and got out of bed. I began immediately to dress, and giving either kicks or cuffs to the maid-servants and the boy as they came to help me on with my clothes, I complained bitterly in these terms—" O you envious and treacherous villains, this is a piece of villany schemed and contrived on purpose ; but I swear by the living God that I will sift it to the bottom and, before I die, give such proofs who I am as shall not fail to astonish the whole world."

Having huddled on my clothes, I went, with a mind boding evil, to the shop, where I found all those whom I had left so alert and in such high spirits, standing in the utmost confusion and astonishment. I thereupon addressed them thus—" Listen all of you to what I am going to say ; and since you either would not or could not follow the method I pointed out, obey me now that I am present. My work is before us, and let none of you offer to oppose or contradict me, for such cases as this require activity and not counsel." Hereupon one Alexander Lastricati had the assurance to say to me—" Look you, Benvenuto, you have undertaken a work which our art cannot compass, and which is not to be effected by human power." Hearing these words, I turned about in such a passion and so bent upon mischief that both he and all the rest unanimously cried out to me—" Give your orders and we will second you in whatever you command, we will assist

you as long as we have breath in our bodies." These kind
and affectionate words they uttered, as I firmly believe,
in a persuasion that I was upon the point of expiring. I
went directly to examine the furnace and saw all the metal
in it concreted. I thereupon ordered two of the helpers to
step over the way to Capretta Beccajo for a load of young
oak which had been above a year drying and been offered
to me by Maria Ginevera, wife to the said Capretta. Upon
his bringing me the first bundles of it, I began to fill the
grate. This sort of oak makes a brisker fire than any other
wood whatever; but the wood of elder-trees and pine-
trees is used in casting artillery, because it makes a mild
and gentle fire. As soon as the concreted metal felt the
power of this violent fire, it began to brighten and glitter.
In another quarter I made them hurry the tubes with all
possible expedition, and sent some of them to the roof
of the house to take care of the fire, which through the
great violence of the wind had acquired new force. And
towards the garden I had caused some tables with pieces
of tapestry and old cloths to be placed, in order to shelter
me from the rain. As soon as I had applied the proper
remedy to each evil, I with a loud voice cried out to my
men to bestir themselves and lend a helping hand, so that
when they saw that the concreted metal began to melt
again, the whole body obeyed me with such zeal and
alacrity that every man did work enough for three. Then
I caused half a mass of pewter to be taken, the weight
about sixty pounds, and thrown upon the metal in the
furnace, which, with other helps, such as the brisk wood
fire and stirring it sometimes with iron and sometimes with
long poles, soon became completely dissolved. Finding
that I had effected what seemed as difficult as to raise the
dead, I recovered my vigour to such a degree that I no

longer perceived whether I had any fever, nor had I the least apprehension of death. Suddenly a loud noise was heard, and a glittering of fire flashed before our eyes as if it had been the darting of a thunderbolt. Upon the appearance of this extraordinary phenomenon, terror seized on all present, and on none more than myself. This tremendous noise being over, we began to stare at each other and perceived that the cover of the furnace had burst and flown off, so that the bronze began to run. I immediately caused the mouths of my mould to be opened ; but finding that the metal did not run with its usual velocity and apprehending that the cause of it was that the quantity of the metal was consumed by the violence of the fire, I ordered all my dishes and porringers, which were in number about two hundred, to be placed one by one before my tubes, and part of them to be thrown into the furnace, so that all present perceiving that my bronze was completely dissolved and that my mould was filling, with joy and alacrity assisted and obeyed me. I for my part was sometimes in one place, sometimes in another, giving my directions and assisting my men, before whom I offered up this prayer—" O God, I address myself to thee, who of thy divine power didst rise from the dead and ascend in glory to heaven. I acknowledge in gratitude this mercy that my mould has been filled : I fall prostrate before thee and with my whole heart return thanks to thy Divine Majesty." My prayer being over, I took a plate of meat which stood upon a little bench, and ate with great appetite. I then drank with my whole company of journeymen and assistants and went joyfully and in good health to bed, for there was still two hours of night ; and I rested as well as if I had been troubled with no manner of disorder.

My good housekeeper, without my having given any

orders, had provided a young capon for my dinner. When I arose, which was not till about noon, she accosted me in high spirits and said merrily—" Is this the man that thought himself dying ! It is my firm belief that the cuffs and kicks which you gave us last night when you were quite frantic and bedevilled, frightened away your fever, and that apprehending lest you should fall upon it in the same manner, it chose to betake itself to flight." So my whole poor family having got over such panics and hardships, without delay procured earthen vessels to supply the place of the pewter dishes and porringers, and we all dined together very cheerfully : indeed I do not remember having ever in my life eaten a meal with greater satisfaction or with a better appetite. After dinner all those who had assisted me in my work, came and congratulated me upon what had happened, returned thanks to the Divine Being for having interposed so mercifully in our behalf, and declared that they had in theory and practice learned such things as were judged impossible by other masters. I thereupon thought it allowable to boast a little of my knowledge and skill in this fine art, and, pulling out my purse, satisfied all my workmen for their labour. . . . Having left my work to cool during two days after it was cast, I began gradually to uncover it. I first of all found the Medusa's head, which had come out admirably by the assistance of the vents. . . . I proceeded to uncover the rest and found that the other head, I mean that of Perseus, was likewise come out perfectly well. This occasioned me still greater surprise because, as it is seen in the statue, it is much lower than that of Medusa, the mouth of that figure being placed over the head and shoulders of Perseus. I found that, where the head of Perseus ends, all the bronze was out which I had in my furnace : this surprised me very much, that there should not be anything over and above what is necessary in casting. My astonishment indeed was raised to such a degree that I looked upon it as a miracle immediately wrought by the Almighty. I went on uncovering it with great success, and found every part turn out to admiration till I had reached the foot of the right leg, where I perceived the heel come out. So proceeding to examine it and finding that the whole was filled up, in one respect I was glad, in another sorry, because I had told the duke that it would not have that effect. Continuing, however, to uncover it, I found that not only the toes were wanting, but part of the foot itself, so that there was almost one half deficient. This occasioned me some new trouble, but I was not displeased at it, because I could thereby convince the duke that I understood my business thoroughly. And though there had come out a great deal more of that foot than I thought there would, the reason was that in consequence of the several accidents that had happened, it was heated much more than it could have been in the regular course of business, especially as the pewter plates had been thrown into the furnace, a thing never done before. I was highly pleased that my work had succeeded so well, and went to Pisa to pay my respects to the duke, who received me in the most gracious manner imaginable. The duchess vied with him in kindness to me, and though the steward had written them an account of the affair, it appeared to them much more wonderful and extraordinary when I related it myself. Upon my speaking to him of the foot of Perseus, which had not come out, (a circumstance of which I had apprized his excellency,) I perceived that he was filled with the utmost astonishment and told the affair to the duchess in the same terms that I had before related to him. Finding that these great personages were become so favourable to me, I availed myself of the opportunity to request the duke's permission to go to Rome. He granted it in the most obliging terms and desired me to return speedily in order to finish my statue of Perseus. He at the same time gave me letters of recommendation to his ambassador Averardo Serristori. This happened in the beginning of the pontificate of Pope Julio de' Monti.

BENVENUTO CELLINI
(from *The Autobiography*—Trans. THOMAS NUGENT)

BACON ON DÜRER

There is no excellent beauty that hath not some strangeness in the proportion. A man cannot tell whether Apelles or Albert Dürer were the more trifler ; whereof the one would make a personage by geometrical proportions ; the other, by taking the best parts out of divers faces, to make one excellent. Such personages, I think, would please nobody but the painter that made them. Not but I think a painter may make a better face than ever was ; but he must do it by a kind of felicity, (as a musician that maketh an excellent air in music) and not by rule.

BACON (from *The Essays*)

RAPHAEL AND MICHAEL ANGELO

Raffaele, it is true, had not the advantage of studying in an Academy ; but all Rome, and the works of Michael Angelo in particular, were to him an Academy. On the sight of the

Capella Sistina, he immediately from a dry, Gothick, and even insipid manner, which attends to the minute accidental discriminations of particular and individual objects, assumed that grand style of painting which improves partial representation by the general and invariable ideas of nature.

Minute Discrimination is Not Accidental. All Sublimity is founded on Minute Discrimination.

I do not believe that Rafael taught Mich. Angelo, or that Mich. Angelo taught Rafael, any more than I believe that the Rose teaches the Lilly how to grow, or the Apple tree teaches the Pear tree how to bear Fruit. I do not believe the tales of Anecdote writers when they militate against Individual Character.

SIR JOSHUA REYNOLDS
(with BLAKE'S comment)

BLAKE ON BLAKE

The character and expression in this picture could never have been produced with Rubens's light and shadow, or with Rembrandt's, or anything Venetian or Flemish. The Venetian and Flemish practice is broken lines, broken masses, and broken colours. Mr. B.'s practice is unbroken lines, unbroken masses, and unbroken colours. Their art is to lose form ; his art is to find form, and to keep it. His arts are opposite to theirs in all things.

BLAKE

BLAKE AMONG THE ARTISTS

The eye that can prefer the Colouring of Titian and Rubens to that of Michael Angelo and Rafael ought to be modest and to doubt its own powers. Connoisseurs talk as if Rafael and Michael Angelo had never seen the Colouring of Titian or Correggio : They ought to know that Correggio was born two years before Michael Angelo, and Titian but four years after. Both Rafael and Michael Angelo knew the Venetian, and contemned and rejected all he did with the utmost disdain, as that which is fabricated for the purpose to destroy art.

Mr. B. appeals to the Public, from the judgment of those narrow blinking eyes that have too long governed art in a dark corner. The eyes of stupid cunning never will be pleased with the work any more than with the look of self-devoting genius. The quarrel of the Florentine with the Venetian is not because he does not understand Drawing, but because he does not understand Colouring. How should he, he who does not know how to draw a hand or a foot, know how to colour it ?

Colouring does not depend on where the Colours are put, but on where the lights and darks are put and all depends on Form or Outline, on where that is put ; where that is wrong, the Colouring can never be right ; and it is always wrong in Titian and Correggio, Rubens and Rembrandt. We shall never equal Rafael and Albert Durer, Michael Angelo, and Julio Romano.

BLAKE

LANDOR AMONG THE ARTISTS

First bring me Raffael, who alone hath seen
In all her purity Heaven's virgin queen,
Alone hath felt true beauty ; bring me then
Titian, ennobler of the noblest men ;
And next the sweet Correggio, nor chastise

His little Cupids for those wicked eyes.
I want not Rubens's pink puffy bloom,
Nor Rembrandt's glimmer in a dusty room.
With those, and Poussin's nymph-frequented
    woods,
His templed hights and long-drawn solitudes
I am content, yet fain would look abroad
On one warm sunset of Ausonian Claude.

LANDOR

TO HIS NEPHEW, TO BE PROSPEROUS IN HIS ART OF PAINTING

On, as thou hast begunne, brave youth, and get
The Palme from Urbin, Titian, Tintarret,
Brugel and Coxu, and the workes out-doe
Of Holben, and that mighty Ruben too.
So draw and paint as none may do the like,
No, not the glory of the world, Vandike.

HERRICK

MICHAEL ANGELO

The David

Michael Angelo now received letters from friends in Florence advising him to return, since he might thus obtain that piece of marble which Pier Soderini, then Gonfaloniere of the city, had talked of giving to Leonardo da Vinci, but was now preparing to present to Andrea dal Monte Sansovino, an excellent sculptor who was making many efforts to obtain it. It was difficult to get a statue out of it without the addition of several pieces, and no one, Michael Angelo excepted, had the courage to attempt it : but he, who had long wished for the block, no sooner arrived in Florence than he made every effort to secure the same. This piece of marble was nine braccia high, and unluckily a certain Maestro Simone da Fiesole had commenced a colossal figure thereon ; but the work had been so grievously injured that the Superintendents had suffered it to remain in the House of Works at Santa Maria del Fiore for many years, without thinking of having it finished, and there it seemed likely to continue.

Michael Angelo measured the mass anew to ascertain what sort of figure he could draw from it, and accommodating himself to the attitude demanded by the injuries which Maestro Simone had inflicted on it, he begged it from the Superintendents and Soderini, by whom it was given to him as a useless thing, they thinking that whatever he might make of it must needs be preferable to the state in which it then lay, and wherein it was totally useless to the fabric. Michael Angelo then made a model in wax, representing a young David with the sling in his hand. . . He commenced his labours in the House of Works, where he formed an enclosure of planks and masonry, which surrounded the marble. There he worked perpetually, permitting no one to see him until the figure was brought to perfection. The marble having been much injured by Simone, did not entirely suffice to the wishes of Michael Angelo, who therefore permitted some of the traces of Simone's chisel to remain : these may still be perceived. . .

When the statue was completed, there arose much discussion as to how it should be transported to the Piazza de' Signori, but Giuliano da Sangallo and Antonio his brother made a strong frame-work of wood, and suspending the figure to this by means of ropes, to the end that it might be easily moved, they thus got it gradually forward with beams and windlasses, and finally placed it on the sight destined to receive the same. The knot of the rope which held the statue was made in such sort that it ran easily, but became tighter as the weight increased, a beautiful and ingenious arrangement, which I now have in my book of designs. . .

When the statue was set up, it chanced that Soderini, whom it greatly pleased, came to look at it while Michael Angelo was retouching it at certain points, and told the artist that he thought the nose too short. Michael Angelo perceived that Soderini was in such a position beneath the figure that he could not see it conveniently, yet to satisfy him he mounted the scaffold with his chisel and a little powder gathered from the floor in his hand, when, striking lightly with the chisel but without altering the nose, he suffered a little of the powder to fall, and then said to the Gonfaloniere who stood below : " Look at it now ! " " I like it better now," replied Piero ; " you have given it life." Michael Angelo then descended, not without compassion for those who desire to appear good judges of matters whereof they know nothing.

VASARI (from Lives of the Painters)

* * * * * * * *

On the 14th day of May 1504 the marble Giant was dragged from the House of Works. They brought it out at the twenty fourth hour, breaking through the wall above the door sufficiently to let it pass through. And that night stones were thrown at the giant with intent to injure it, and it was necessary to mount a guard on it during the night. It moved very slowly, being bound upright : it was hung (so that it did not touch the ground with its feet) with very strong timbers and great ingenuity. It took four days' labour to get it to the Piazza, arriving there on the eighteenth day at the twelfth hour. More than forty men were needed to move it, and it had under it fourteen logs which were changed from hand to hand. They laboured until the 8th day of July 1504 to set it on the base where the Judith used to stand, the which had to be taken away and set on the ground in the palace. And the said Giant had been made by Michael Angelo Buonarroti.

GUALANDI

.   .   .   .

I have seen Michael Angelo, although then sixty years old and not in robust health, strike more chips from the hardest marble in a quarter of an hour than would be carried off by three young stone-cutters in three or four times as long ; a thing incredible to him who has not seen it. He would approach the marble with such impetuosity, not to say fury, that I often thought the whole work must be dashed to pieces. At one blow he would strike off morsels of three and four inches, yet with such exactitude was each stroke given, that a mere atom more would sometimes have spoiled the whole work.

VIGENERO

Michael Angelo was an admirable man, but he knew nothing of painting.

EL GRECO (as reported by PACHECO)

I am still in great distress. For a year I have received nothing from the Pope, and I do not ask him, because it does not seem to me that my work is advancing sufficiently to deserve remuneration. The job is too difficult and, besides, that is not my profession. I am wasting my time in vain. God help me.

MICHAEL ANGELO to his father, 1509

Michael Angelo, through being forced, while painting [the Sistine Chapel], to keep his eyes continually raised to the vault, could see little when he looked downwards ; so that if he had to read a letter or other minute matters, he was constrained to hold it raised above his head. Nevertheless little by little thenceforward he ventured to read once more looking down. From which we may judge what attention and assiduity he brought to his labours.

CONDIVI (from *Vita di Michelagnolo*)

This strain has given me a goitre, such as cats get from the water in Lombardy or wherever they happen to be. My belly has stuck perforce under my chin, my beard points to heaven, my head is bent backwards against my hunched shoulders, my chest is curved like a harp, and my paint-brush keeps dripping a thick coating of paint on my face. My loins are forced up into my paunch and, to balance this, my bottom sticks out like a horse's hind-quarters. My feet grope vainly, since my eyes cannot guide them. Through my bending backwards, my skin is stretched in front and pleated behind. I am bent like a

Syrian bow. Therefore are the judgments of my mind distorted, for it's ill shooting with a bent gun. O save my ruined art, Giovanni, and my honour, for ill it fares, and I . . . I am no painter.

MICHAEL ANGELO
(Prose Translation of a Poem)

LEONARDO DA VINCI

I will not refrain from setting among these precepts a new device for consideration which, although it may appear trivial and almost ludicrous, is nevertheless of great utility in arousing the mind to various inventions. And this is that if you look at any walls spotted with various stains or with a mixture of different kinds of stones, if you are about to invent some scene you will be able to see in it a resemblance to various different landscapes adorned with mountains, rivers, rocks, trees, plains, wide valleys, and various groups of hills. You will also be able to see divers combats and figures in quick movement, and strange expressions of faces, and outlandish costumes, and an infinite number of things which you can then reduce into separate and well conceived forms. With such walls and blends of different stones it comes about as it does with the sound of bells, in whose clanging you may discover every name and word that you can imagine.

LEONARDO DA VINCI
(from *The Notebooks*—Trans. E. MCCURDY)

One who was drinking has left the glass where it was and turned his head towards the speaker. Another twists the fingers of his hands together and turns with set brows to his companion. Another with his hands spread open displays their palms and shrugs his shoulders up towards his ears and gapes in astonishment. Another is speaking in his neighbour's ear, and he who listens turns towards him and gives him hearing, holding in one hand a knife, and in the other the bread half cut through by the knife. Another, as he turns round holding a knife in his hand, has upset with his hand a glass which is upon the table.

Another rests his hands upon the table and watches. Another blows out his mouth. Another bends forward to see the speaker and makes a shade for his eyes with his hand. Another leans back behind the one who is bending forward, and sees the speaker between the wall and him who bends forward.

LEONARDO DA VINCI
Notes for " The Last Supper "
(from *The Notebooks*—Trans. E. MCCURDY)

La Gioconda is, in the truest sense, Leonardo's master-piece, the revealing instance of his mode of thought and work. In suggestiveness, only the *Melancholia* of Dürer is comparable to it ; and no crude symbolism disturbs the effect of its subdued and graceful mystery. We all know the face and hands of the figure, set in its marble chair, in that circle of fantastic rocks, as in some faint light under sea. Perhaps of all ancient pictures time has chilled it least. As often happens with works in which invention seems to reach its limit, there is an element in it given to, not invented by, the master. In that inestimable folio of drawings, once in the possession of Vasari, were certain designs of Verrocchio, faces of such impressive beauty that Leonardo in his boyhood copied them many times. It is hard not to connect with these designs of the elder, by-past master, as with its germinal principle, the unfathomable smile, always with a touch of something sinister in it, which plays all over Leonardo's work. Besides, the picture is a portrait. From childhood we see this image defining itself on the fabric of his dreams; and but for express historical testimony, we might fancy that this was but his ideal lady, embodied and beheld at last. What was the relationship of a living Florentine to this creature of his thought? By what strange affinities had the dream and the person grown up thus apart, and yet so closely together? Present from the first incorporeally in Leonardo's brain, dimly traced in the designs of Verrocchio, she is found present at last in *Il Giocondo's* house. That there is much of mere portraiture in the picture is attested by the legend that by artificial means, the presence of mimes and flute-players, that subtle expression was protracted on the face. Again, was it in four years and by renewed labour never really completed, or in four months and as by stroke of magic, that the image was projected?

The presence that rose thus so strangely beside the waters, is expressive of what in the ways of a thousand years men had come to desire. Hers is the head upon which " all the ends of the world are come," and the eyelids are a little weary. It is a beauty wrought out from within upon the flesh, the deposit, little cell by cell, of strange thoughts and fantastic reveries and exquisite passions. Set it for a moment beside one of those white

Greek goddesses or beautiful women of antiquity, and how would they be troubled by this beauty, into which the soul with all its maladies has passed ! All the thoughts and experience of the world have etched and moulded there, in that which they have of power to refine and make expressive the outward form, the animalism of Greece, the lust of Rome, the mysticism of the middle age with its spiritual ambition and imaginative loves, the return of the Pagan world, the sins of the Borgias. She is older than the rocks among which she sits ; like the vampire, she has been dead many times, and learned the secrets of the grave ; and has been a diver in deep seas, and keeps their fallen day about her ; and trafficked for strange webs with Eastern merchants : and, as Leda, was the mother of Helen of Troy, and, as Saint Anne, the mother of Mary ; and all this has been to her but as the sound of lyres and flutes, and lives only in the delicacy with which it has moulded the changing lineaments, and tinged the eyelids and the hands. The fancy of a perpetual life, sweeping together ten thousand experiences, is an old one ; and modern philosophy has conceived the idea of humanity as wrought upon by, and summing up in itself, all modes of thought and life. Certainly Lady Lisa might stand as the embodiment of the old fancy, the symbol of the modern idea.

PATER

(from *Studies in the History of the Renaissance*)

RAPHAEL

A year ago I could not understand, in the slightest degree, Raphael's Cartoons ; now I begin to read them a little. And how did I learn to do so ? By seeing something done in quite an opposite spirit ; I mean a picture of Guido's, in which all the Saints, instead of that heroic simplicity and unaffected grandeur, which they inherit from Raphael, had, each of them, both in countenance and gesture, all the canting, solemn, melodramatic mawkishness of Mackenzie's Father Nicholas.

KEATS (from *The Letters*)

It is universally admitted that Raphael and Titian hold the first rank among painters, and yet Raphael and Titian considered Nature under very different aspects. . . . The first sought the sublime where it is truly to be found, in form ; the second, in colour.

. . . .

From a letter written in Rome. Ah, my dear friend, I shall return to you the same as I left you, with the same adorations and the same exclusions, putting Raphael above all, because to his divine grace he adds exactly that degree of character and force that is needed, never exceeding the measure. Who can we put in the same rank ? No one ! Unless it be he who in music had a soul like Raphael's, my divine Mozart.

INGRES (from DELABORDE)

A VENETIAN PASTORAL

By *Giorgione*

(IN THE LOUVRE)

Water, for anguish of the solstice :—nay,
But dip the vessel slowly,—nay, but lean
And hark how at its verge the wave sighs in
Reluctant. Hush ! beyond all depth away
The heat lies silent at the brink of day :
Now the hand trails upon the viol-string
That sobs, and the brown faces cease to sing,
Sad with the whole of pleasure. Whither stray
Her eyes now, from whose mouth the slim pipes
    creep
And leave it pouting, while the shadowed grass
Is cool against her naked side ? Let be :—
Say nothing now unto her lest she weep,
Nor name this ever. Be it as it was,—
Life touching lips with Immortality.

ROSSETTI

TITIAN'S BACCHUS AND ARIADNE

Precipitous, with his reeking satyr rout about him,
re-peopling and re-illuming suddenly the waste places,
drunk with a new fury beyond the grape, Bacchus, born
in fire, fire-like flings himself at the Cretan. This is the
time present. With this telling of the story, an artist, and
no ordinary one, might remain richly proud. Guido, in
his harmonious version of it, saw no further. But from
the depths of the imaginative spirit Titian has recalled
past time, and laid it contributory with the present to
one simultaneous effect. With the desert all ringing with

174

the mad cymbals of his followers, made lucid with the presence and new offers of a god,—as if unconscious of Bacchus, or but idly casting her eyes as upon some unconcerning pageant—her soul undistracted from Theseus—Ariadne is still pacing the solitary shore in as much heart-silence, and in almost the same local solitude, with which she awoke at daybreak to catch the forlorn last glances of the sail that bore away the Athenian.

Here are two points miraculously co-uniting; fierce society, with the feeling of solitude still absolute; noon-day revelations, with the accidents of the dull grey dawn unquenched and lingering; the *present* Bacchus, with the *past* Ariadne: two stories, with double Time; separate, and harmonising. Had the artist made the woman one shade less indifferent to the God; still more, had she expressed a rapture at his advent, where would have been the story of the mighty desolation of the heart previous? merged in the insipid accident of a flattering offer met with a welcome acceptance. The broken heart for Theseus was not likely to be pieced up by a God.

CHARLES LAMB (from *Essays of Elia*)

Mr. Severn had had the gratification, from the commencement of their acquaintance, of bringing Keats into communion with the great masters of painting. A notable instance of the impression made on that susceptible nature by those achievements is manifest as early as the Hymn in the fourth book of the *Endymion*, which is, in fact, the " Bacchus and Ariadne " of Titian, now in our National Gallery, translated into verse. Take these images as examples :

And as I sat, over the light blue hills
There came a noise of revellers ; the rills
Into the wide stream came of purple hue—
    'Twas Bacchus and his crew !
The earnest trumpet spake, and silver thrills
From kissing cymbals made a merry din—
    'Twas Bacchus and his kin !
Like to a moving vintage down they came,
Crowned with green leaves, and faces all on
    flame. . . .

.   .   .   .

Within his car, aloft, young Bacchus stood,
Trifling his ivy-dart, in dancing mood,
    With sidelong laughing ;
And near him rode Silenus on his ass,
Pelted with flowers as he on did pass
    Tipsily quaffing.

.   .   .   .

Mounted on panthers' furs and lions' manes,
From rear to van they scour about the plains ;
A three-days' journey in a moment done ;
And always, at the rising of the sun,
About the wilds they hunt with spear and horn,
    On spleenful unicorn.

LORD HOUGHTON
(from *Life and Letters of John Keats*)

HOGARTH

I wished myself a painter, that I might have sent you a sketch of one of the card parties. The long pipe of one gentleman rested on the table, its bole half a yard from his mouth, fuming like a censer by the fish-pool—the other gentleman, who was dealing the cards, and of course had both hands employed, held his pipe in his teeth, which hanging down between his knees, smoked beside his ancles. Hogarth himself never drew a more ludicrous distortion both of attitude and physiognomy, than this effort occasioned : nor was there wanting beside it one of those beautiful female faces which the same Hogarth, in whom the satirist never extinguished that love of beauty which belonged to him as a poet, so often and so gladly introduces, as the central figure, in a crowd of humorous deformities, which figure (such is the power of true genius!) neither acts, nor is *meant* to act as a contrast ; but diffuses through all, and over each of the group, a spirit of reconciliation and human kindness ; and, even when the attention is no longer consciously directed to the cause of this feeling, still blends its tenderness with our laughter ; and thus prevents the instructive merriment at the whims of nature or the foibles or humours of our fellow-men from degenerating into the heart-poison of contempt or hatred.

COLERIDGE (from *Biographia Literaria*)

The hand of him here torpid lies,
    That drew th' essential form of grace ;
Here clos'd in death th' attentive eyes,
    That saw the manners in the face.

SAMUEL JOHNSON (*Epitaph for Hogarth*)

CONSTABLE

That admirable man, Constable, is one of the glories of England. I have told you already of the impression he produced on me at the time I was painting the *Massacre de Scio*. He and Turner are real reformers. They have got clear of the rut of the old landscape-painters. Our school, which abounds to-day in men of talent of this kind, has profited greatly by their example. Géricault came home quite astounded at their great landscapes.

DELACROIX

SOME SAYINGS OF CONSTABLE

On hearing somebody say of the celebrated collection of Raphael's drawings that belonged to Sir Thomas Lawrence, " They inspire," he replied, " They do more, they inform."

. . . .

The amiable but eccentric Blake, looking through one of Constable's sketch books, said of a beautiful drawing of an avenue of fir trees on Hampstead Heath, " Why, this is not drawing, but *inspiration* " ; and he replied, " I never knew it before ; I meant it for drawing."

. . . .

To a lady who, looking at an engraving of a house, called it an ugly thing, he said, " No, madam, there is nothing ugly ; *I never saw an ugly thing in my life* : for let the form of an object be what it may,—light, shade, and perspective will always make it beautiful. It is perspective that improves the form of this."

Speaking of the taste for the *prodigeous* and the *astound-ing*, a taste very contrary to his own, he made use of a quotation from the 1st Book of Kings. " A great and strong wind rent the mountains, and brake in pieces the rocks before the Lord ; but the Lord was not in the wind : and after the wind an earthquake ; but the Lord was not in the earthquake : and after the earthquake a fire ; but the Lord was not in the fire : and after the fire *a still small voice.*"

The attempt to revive styles that have existed in former ages may for a time appear to be successful, but experience may now surely teach us its impossibility I might put on a suit of Claude Lorraine's clothes and walk into the street, and the many who knew Claude but slightly would pull off their hats to me, but I should at last meet with some one more intimately acquainted with him, who would expose me to the contempt I merited. . . .

Imitators always render the defects of their model more conspicuous. Sir George Beaumont, on seeing a large picture by a modern artist, intended to be in the style of Claude, said, " I never could have believed that Claude Lorraine had so many faults, if I had not seen them all collected together on this canvas." It is useful, therefore, to a painter to have imitators, as they will teach him to avoid everything they do.

My dear Fisher, Thank you for your letter of yester-day . . . I am planning a large picture, and I regard all you say ; but I do not enter into that notion of varying one's plans to keep the public in good humour. Change of weather and effect will always afford variety. What if Vander Velde had quitted his sea pieces, or Ruysdael his waterfalls, or Hobbema his native woods. The world would have lost so many features in art. I know that you wish for no material alteration; but I have to combat from high quarters, even from Lawrence, the plausible argument that *subject* makes the picture. . . . I imagine myself driving a nail; I have driven it some way, and by persevering I may drive it home; by quitting it to attack others, though I may amuse myself, I do not advance beyond the first, while that particular nail stands still.

CONSTABLE (from LESLIE)

INGRES

RUGGIERO AND ANGELICA

By Ingres

A remote sky, prolonged to the sea's brim :
One rock-point standing buffeted alone,
Vexed at its base with a foul beast unknown,
Hell-birth of geomaunt and teraphim :
A knight, and a winged creature bearing him,
Reared at the rock : a woman fettered there,
Leaning into the hollow with loose hair
And throat let back and heartsick trail of limb.
The sky is harsh, and the sea shrewd and salt :
Under his lord the griffin-horse ramps blind
With rigid wings and tail. The spear's lithe stem
Thrills in the roaring of those jaws : behind,
That evil length of body chafes at fault.
She does not hear nor see—she knows of them.

ROSSETTI

The sixteenth century produced the greatest men in all the arts. All the artists of that period obeyed this constant and infallible rule, that drawing is the one principle capable of giving to works of art their true beauty and their true form.

.   .   .   .

Drawing does not mean merely the reproduction of outline, nor does it consist merely in line. It is also expression, internal form, plan, modelling. What remains? Drawing comprehends three quarters and a half of what constitutes painting. If I had to put up a sign over my door, it would be : " Drawing School " ; and I am sure that I would produce painters.

.   .   .   .

I recognize that the Flemish and Dutch schools have their particular kind of merit which, I flatter myself, I appreciate as much as any one. But pray do not let us lose our heads. Do not let us admire Rembrandt and the rest without rhyme or reason ; do not let us compare them and their art to the divine Raphael and the Italian school. That would be blasphemy.

.   .   .   .

There is something of the butcher in Reubens. In his thought fresh meat comes first, and the butcher's stall in his settings.

.   .   .   .

Yes, undoubtedly Reubens is a great painter ; but it is this great painter who wrecked everything.

INGRES (from DELABORDE)

181

DELACROIX

Delacroix's chief preoccupation is the study of volume, the analysis of thickness. Moreover he constructs his figures by nuclei, by proportional masses, which, when united, constitute the modelling. Gros worked in a similar way, when he was not turned from his natural bent by a slavish respect for the principles of David. For instance, Gros summarily represented the principal planes of the structure of a horse by a few juxtaposed ovals. Géricault obtained his vigorous relief in the same way. It must also be remarked that if the painter rightly establishes his salient features, he will by this very fact avoid transgressing the imaginary limit known as line or contour, which is nothing more than the termination of each object.... The material procedure of Delacroix bears a close relation to some of the methods of the sculptor ; his broad touches recall Géricault's powerful slashes in the *Radeau de la Méduse* and the thumb-strokes printed on the soft clay by the statuary. At the outset Delacroix sets down in the most luminous tone the culminating point of his salient features and surrounds their volume with a darker tone, so that already we have an indication of the hollows and convexities, as it were the topography of the human figure indicated by the light and shadows.

THÉOPHILE SILVESTRE
(from *Historie des Artistes Vivants*)

DELACROIX TO THÉOPHILE SILVESTRE IN
LONDON, 1858

That period of my life when I was in England (1826) and the memory of the friends of that time are very dear to me. Almost all of them have vanished. Of the English painters who did me the honour to receive me, one and all, with the greatest kindness—for I was then almost unknown—not one, I believe, is left. Wilkie, Lawrence, Fielding, great artists, Coplet especially [Copley ?] in landscape and water-colour, and Etty (dead recently, I think), showed me the greatest goodwill. I say nothing of Bonington, dead in his prime, who was my special friend, and with whom, as with Poterlet (the French painter, he too prematurely dead, a great loss to Painting), I passed my time in London among the delights which that country offers to an enthusiastic youth, the assemblage of hundreds of masterpieces and the spectacle of an extraordinary civilization. I have no desire to see London again. I should find none of those memories there now. And I too have changed ; I should no longer be in a state to enjoy what is to be seen there nowadays. Besides, the English school of painting has changed also. Probably I should find myself compelled to break a lance for Reynolds or for the enchanting Gainsborough, whom you have good reason to love. Not that I am opposed to what is now being done in England ; indeed I have been struck by the prodigious conscientiousness which the English bring to bear even on the things of the imagination. It almost seems as if, in turning once more to an excessive attention to details they are more in their element than when they imitate the Italians and the Flemish colourists. But what do externals matter ? they remain English to the core, despite this apparent transformation. Thus, instead of making pure and simple imitations of the Italian primitives, as has become the fashion with us, they manage to combine a feeling which is infinitely personal with their imitation of the manner of these old schools, and so provide that interest which is derived from the painter's passion, which is precisely what is wanting as a rule in our cold imitations of the style and recipes of schools which have served their time and vanished.

. . . .

TURNER

In 1836 Turner exhibited three pictures in which the characteristics of his later manner were developed with his best skill and enthusiasm. . . . His freak in placing Juliet at Venice instead of Verona, and the mysteries of lamplight and rockets with which he had disguised Venice herself, gave occasion to an article in *Blackwood's Magazine* of sufficiently telling ribaldry, expressing with some force, and extreme discourtesy, the feelings of the pupils of Sir George Beaumont at the appearance of those uncredited views of Nature. The review raised me to the height of " black anger " in which I have remained pretty nearly ever since.

RUSKIN (from *Praeterita*)

No. 52, ' The Dogano ' and 73, ' Campo Santo,' have a gorgeous *ensemble*, and produced by wonderful art, but they mean nothing. They are produced as if by throwing handfuls of white, and blue, and red, at the canvas, letting what chanced to stick, stick ; and then shadowing in some forms to make the appearance of a picture. And yet there is a fine harmony in the highest range of colour to please the sense of vision ; we admire, and we lament to see such genius so employed. But ' Farther on you may fare worse.' No. 182 is a Snow-storm of most unintelligible character —the snow-storm of a confused dream, with a steamboat ' making signals,' and (apparently, like the painter who was in it) ' going by the head.' . . . No. 353 caps all before for absurdity, without even any of the redeeming qualities in the rest. It represents Buonaparte—facetiously des- cribed as ' the exile and the rock limpet,' standing on the seashore of St. Helena. . . . The whole thing is so truly ludicrous, that the *risum teneatis* even of the Amici is absolutely impossible.

(*The Literary Gazette*, May 14, 1842)

This gentleman has on former occasions chosen to paint with cream, or chocolate, yolk of egg, or currant jelly,—here he uses his whole array of kitchen stuff. . . . We cannot fancy the state of eye, which will permit any one cognizant of the Art to treat these rhapsodies as Lord Byron treated ' Christabel ' ; neither can we believe in any future revolution, which shall bring the world round to the opinion of the worshipper, if worshipper such frenzies still possess.

(*The Athenæum*, May 14, 1842)

The stormy blood-red of the horizon, the scarlet of the breaking sunlight, the rich crimson browns of the wet and illumined sea-weed, the pure gold and purple of the upper sky, and, shed through it all, the deep passage of solemn blue, where the cold moonlight fell on one pensive spot of the limitless shore,—all were given with harmony as perfect as their colour was intense.

RUSKIN on "The Exile and the Rock Limpet"
(from *Modern Painters*)

RUSKIN ON WHISTLER'S NOCTURNE IN BLACK AND GOLD (1877)

I have heard and seen much of Cockney impudence before now ; but never expected to hear a coxcomb ask two hundred guineas for flinging a pot of paint in the public's face.

(from *Praeterita*)

COROT

If Corot sees two clouds which appear to him at first sight equally dark, he sets himself to discover the difference which he knows must exist between them, and, after that, he bases on one or other of them his series of tones. When the two extremes of the general effect have been fixed, the intermediate values fall into place and are capable of infinite subdivisions. If the artist observes in a landscape or a figure a colour-scheme composed of four principal values, he records the lightest by a 4, the darkest by a 1, and the two intermediates by 2 and 3. This method enables him to note, in passing, the briefest effects with a pencil and a scrap of paper, from a purely practical point of view, for Corot is not a man to put numbers to his feelings. He begins with his sky, then the first masses to stand out in the centre or to the right or left, then proceeds to organize the objects reflected in water, if there is water,—in fact, establishes his first planes ; so that the objects seem to come alive and emerge, one by one, from the depths of the canvas and arrange themselves in order before the eye of the spectator. Sometimes his method is less regular and he attentively pursues at the same time the form, colour, and movement of the objects, and at each touch casts an anxious eye over every point of the picture to make sure that it responds to all the others. A false touch horrifies him. If he hurries, he may become clumsy and leave here and there inequalities of impasto which he afterwards removes with a razor, as if he were shaving his picture.

His memory holds an immense store of forms, colours, and their relations, and of effects observed at all hours of the day. " These memories," he says, " have sometimes served me better than nature itself would have done."

Having been long misunderstood, Corot is not bored by praise. If you give him praise he cries out, like a child that has asked for a drink : " More, more ! I've had too little." In his anxiety, not while painting his pictures, but when they are on the point of completion, he will consult the first comer, but if the first comer turns out to know nothing about painting he may remark : " One of us two is an imbecile, and I think it's him. . . ."

Corot loathes pedantry and advises his pupils to choose

only subjects that respond to their impressions, considering with reason that the soul of every artist is a mirror in which nature is reflected in a particular fashion. To an artist who had copied him with servility he said : "Do another job like that and I'll shut my studio door in your face." He would never accept a farthing for the lessons he gave.

THÉOPHILE SILVESTRE
(from Histoire des Artistes Vivants)

HARDY ON BONINGTON

January, 1887. After looking at the landscape ascribed to Bonington in our drawing-room I feel that Nature is played out as a Beauty, but not as a Mystery. I don't want to see landscapes, i.e., scenic paintings of them, because I don't want to see the original realities—as optical effects, that is. I want to see the deeper reality underlying the scenic, the expression of what are sometimes called abstract imaginings. The ' simply natural ' is interesting no longer. The much decried, mad, late-Turner rendering is now necessary to create my interest. The exact truth as to material fact ceases to be of importance in art—it is a student's style—the style of a period when the mind is serene and unawakened to the tragic mysteries of life ; when it does not bring anything to the object that coalesces with and translates the qualities that are already there,— half hidden, it may be—and the two united are depicted as the All.

THOMAS HARDY
(from FLORENCE HARDY'S Life of Thomas Hardy)

CÉZANNE

He did not conceive his volumes in outline, geometrically, but in contrasted colours; and that is really the individual distinction of Cézanne: a sensibility to form expressed in colour. "To paint," he said, "was to register his colour sensations." Everything else—all values of atmosphere and perspective—is sacrificed to this end, sacrificed to the organisation of his colour sensations. "When colour has its richness, form has its plenitude" is another of his rare revealing aphorisms. This conception of form built up of colour, a colour synthesis, is perhaps a difficult one to realise, especially for people who are weak in colour sensibility: it is, however, the essential quality of Cézanne's art.

HERBERT READ (from *Art Now*)

DEGAS

Degas was a pupil of Ingres, and any mention of this always pleases him, for he looks upon Ingres as the first star in the firmament of French art. And, indeed, Degas is the only one who ever reflected, even dimly, anything of the genius of the great master. The likeness to Ingres which some affect to see in Flandrin's work is entirely superficial, but in the *Semiramis Building the Walls of Babylon* and in the *Spartan Youths* there is a strange fair likeness to the master, mixed with another beauty, still latent, but ready for efflorescence, even as the beauty of the mother floats evanescent upon the face of the daughter hardly pubescent yet. But if Degas took from Ingres that method of drawing which may be defined as drawing from the character in contradistinction to that of drawing by the masses, he applied the method differently and developed it in a different direction. . . . At the root his drawing is as classical as Ingres', but by changing the subject-matter from antiquity to the boards of the opera-house, and taking curiosity for leading characteristic, he has created an art cognate and co-equal with Goncourt's, rising sometimes to the height of a page by Balzac. With marvellous perception he follows every curve and characteristic irregularity, writing the very soul of his model upon his canvas. . . . And as he sought new subject-matter, he sought for new means by which he might reproduce his subject in an original and novel manner. At one time he renounced oil-painting entirely, and would only work in pastel or distemper. Then, again, it was water-colour painting, and some times in the same picture he would abandon one medium for another. There are examples extant of pictures begun in water colour, continued in gouache, and afterwards completed in oils ; and if the picture be examined carefully, it will be found that the finishing hand has been given with pen and ink. Degas has worked upon his lithographs, introducing a number of new figures into the picture by means of pastel. He has done beautiful sculpture, but not content with taking a ballet-girl for subject, has declined to model the skirt, and had one made by the nearest milliner. In all dangerous ways and perilous straits he has sought to shipwreck his genius : but genius knows no shipwreck, and triumphs in spite of obstacles. Not even Wagner has tested more thoroughly than Degas the invincibility of genius.

If led to speak on the marvellous personality of his art, Degas will say, " It is strange, for I assure you no art was ever less spontaneous than mine. What I do is the result of reflection and study of the great masters; of inspiration, spontaneity, temperament—temperament is the word—I know nothing. When people talk about temperament it always seems to me like the strong man in the fair, who straddles his legs and asks some one to step up on the palm of his hand."

. . . .

When he is in company with any one who knew Manet, his *confrère* and compeer in realistic pictorial art, and the friend of his life, he loves to allude to those little childishnesses of disposition which make Manet's memory a well-beloved, even a sacred thing.

"Do you remember," Degas said, as he hurried his friend along the Rue Pigalle, "how he used to turn on me when I wouldn't send my pictures to the Salon? He would say, 'You, Degas, you are above the level of the sea, but for my part, if I get into an omnibus and some one doesn't say M. Manet, how are you, where are you going? I am disappointed, for I know then that I am not famous.'" Manet's vanity, which a strange boyishness of disposition rendered attractive and engaging, is clearly one of Degas' happiest memories, but all the meanness of *la vie de parade*, so persistently sought by Mr. Whistler, is bitterly displeasing to him. Speaking to Mr. Whistler, he said, "My dear friend, you conduct yourself in life just as if you had no talent at all." Again speaking of the same person, and at the time when he was having numerous photographs taken, Degas said, "You cannot talk to him; he throws his cloak around him—and goes off to the photographer."

GEORGE MOORE
(from *Impressions and Opinions*)

Autumn, 1883. If you hear a voice within you saying : " you are no painter," *then paint by all means*, lad, and that voice will be silenced, but only by working ; he who, when he feels thus, goes to friends and tells his troubles, loses part of his manliness, part of the best that is in him ; your friends can only be those who themselves struggle against it, who raise your activity by their own example of action. One must undertake it with confidence, with a certain assurance that one is doing a reasonable thing, as the farmer drives his plough, or like our friend in the sketch below, who harrows, even drags the harrow himself. If one has no horse, one is one's own horse—many people do so here.

There is a saying by Gustave Doré which I have always admired : " j'ai la patience d'un bœuf." I find in it a certain goodness, a certain resolute honesty, in short, it has a deep meaning that saying, it is the word of a real artist. When one thinks of the men from whose heart such a saying sprang, all the arguments one too often hears of art dealers about " natural gifts," seem to become a terrible raven's croaking.

. . . .

Spring, 1885. Study well that question of colours, etc. I also try to do so, and I will gladly and thankfully read also what you may find of that kind. At present I am busy putting in practice, on the drawing of a hand and arm, what Delacroix said about drawing : " Ne pas prendre par la ligne mais par le milieu." That gives opportunity enough to proceed from ellipses. And what I try to acquire is, not to draw a *hand*, but the gesture, not mathematically correctly a head, but the *expression* at large. For instance, when a digger looks up and sniffs the wind or speaks. In short, *life*.

. . . . .

Arles, 21/2/88. Before getting to Tarascon I noticed a magnificent country of huge yellow rocks, piled up in the strangest and stateliest forms. In the little village between these rocks were rows of small round trees with olive-green or grey-green leaves, which might quite likely be lemon trees.

But here at Arles the country seems flat. I have seen some splendid red stretches of soil planted with vines with a background of mountains of the most delicate lilac. And the landscapes in the snow, with the summits white against a sky as luminous as the snow, were just like the winter landscapes that the Japanese have painted.

. . . . .

Spring, 1888. I have been working on a canvas of 20 in the open air in an orchard, lilac ploughland, a reed fence, two rose coloured peach trees, against a sky of glorious blue and white. Probably the best landscape I have done.

. . . . .

Spring, 1888. Yesterday I saw another bull fight, where five men played the bull with darts and cockades. One toreador damaged himself jumping the barricade. He was a fair man with grey eyes, plenty of sang-froid ; people say he'll be ill long enough. He was dressed in sky blue and gold, just like the little horseman in our Monticelli, the three figures in a wood. The arenas are a fine sight when there's sunshine and a crowd. . . .

I shall be all in when the orchards are over, for they are canvases of 25 and 30 and 20. We would not have too many of them, even if I could bring off twice as many. It seems to me that this may really break the ice in Holland. Mauve's death was a terrible blow to me. You will see that the rose coloured peach trees were painted with a sort of passion.

I must also have a starry night with cypresses, or perhaps above all, a field of ripe corn : there are some wonderful nights here. I am in a continual fever of work.

.   .   .   .

Spring, 1888. You were right to tell Tasset that he must put in the geranium lake all the same ; he has sent it, I have just checked it. *All the colours that the Impressionists have brought into fashion are unstable*, so there is all the more reason boldly to use them too crude ; time will tone them down only too well.

So, of all the colours I ordered, the three chromes, (orange, yellow, lemon yellow), the Prussian blue, the emerald, the crimson lakes, the Malachite green, or the orange lead, hardly one of them is to be found on the Dutch palette, in Maris, Mauve, or Israels. It is only to be found in Delacroix, who has a passion for the two colours which are most condemned, and with most reason, lemon yellow and Prussian blue. All the same, I think he did superb things with them—the blues and the lemon yellows.

.   .   .   .

Summer, 1888. The last canvas absolutely kills all the others ; it is only a still-life with coffee-pots and cups and plates in blue and yellow ; it stands quite by itself.

It must be because of the drawing.

Instinctively these days I keep remembering what I have seen of Cézanne, because he has just got—as in the " Harvest " we saw at Portier's—the harsh side of

Provence. It has become very different from what it was in spring, and yet I have certainly no less love for this countryside, burnt up as it begins to be from now on. Everything now here is old gold, bronze copper one might say, and this with the green azure of the sky blanched with heat : a delicious colour, extraordinarily harmonious, with the blended tones of Delacroix.

If Gaugin were willing to join in, I think it would be a step forward for us. It would establish us squarely as the exploiters of the South, and nobody could complain of that. I must manage to get the firmness of colouring that I got into that picture that kills the rest. I'm thinking of what Portier used to say, that seen by themselves the Cézannes had looked nothing, but bring them near other pictures and they washed the colour out of everything else. He used to say too that the Cézannes did well in gold, which means that the gamut of colour was pitched very high. So perhaps, perhaps I am on the track, and I am getting my eye in for this kind of country. We must wait and make sure.

This last picture can bear the surroundings of red brick, with which my studio is paved. When I put it on the ground, with this background of red, *very red* brick, the colour of the picture does not become hollow or bleached. The country near Aix where Cézanne works is just the same as this, it is still the Crau. If coming home with my canvas I say to myself " Look ! I've got the very tones of old Cézanne ! " I only mean that Cézanne like Zola is so absolutely part of the countryside, and knows it so intimately that you must make the same calculations in your head to arrive at the same tones. Of course, if you saw them side by side together, they would go together, but there would be no resemblance.

195

With a handshake, I hope you will be able to write one of these days.

Yours,

VINCENT

(from *The Letters of Vincent van Gogh*)

PAUL GAUGIN TO CHARLES MORICE

April, 1903. You were mistaken that time when you said that I was wrong to call myself a savage. For it is true. I am a savage. And civilized people feel it to be so. All that is surprising and bewildering in my work is that " savagery that comes up in spite of myself." That is what makes my work inimitable. The work of a man is the explanation of a man. And there are two sorts of beauty ; one is the result of instinct, the other of study. A combination of the two, with the resulting modifications, brings with it a very complex richness, which the art critic ought to try to discover. Now you are an art critic. Let me not guide you, but rather advise you to open your own eyes to what I want to explain, though rather mysteriously, in a few lines. The great science of Raphael does not bewilder me, nor does it in the least prevent me from feeling, seeing and understanding his foundation, which is the instinct for beauty.

Raphael was born beautiful. All else in him is simply a modification of that. We have just passed through a long period of error in art, caused by the knowledge of physical and mechanical chemistry and by the study of nature. Artists having lost their savagery, and no longer able to rely upon instinct, one might better say imagination,

have strayed off on many different paths to find the productive elements they have no longer the strength to
create, and now they cannot work except in disorderly
crowds, feeling frightened, almost lost if left to themselves. That is why it is useless to advise solitude for
everyone ; one must be strong enough to endure it and
to work alone. All that I learned from others has only
hampered me. So I can say : no one has taught me anything. It is true I know very little. But I prefer that little
which is my own. And who knows but that even this
little, when exploited by others, may not become something great ? How many centuries it takes to create even
the appearance of movement.

(from *The Letters of Paul Gaugin*—
Trans. RUTH PIELKOVO)

I'm just finishing a sort of carved Kanaka's head lying
against a white cushion, in a palace I invented, and surrounded by women, also of my own imagination. I think
it is a pretty bit of painting. Yet it's not altogether mine,
for I stole the idea from a pine plank. You must not say
anything about it, for one does one's best, and when
marble or wood insist on tracing a head for you, it is very
tempting to steal.

GAUGIN (from *The Letters*)

MATISSE

It is an art which, in its constant reference to our age-
long pictorial tradition, can afford endless reservations
and ellipses. An art which dares to rely on the spectator's

realizing all that is sub-understood and merely hinted at or implied. Hence perhaps only an artist can fully estimate the miracles of tact, of inventive fertility, of suppressed pictorial science which this allusive-elliptical method implies. And it is only because of Matisse's extraordinary gifts that such a method becomes possible. But it is not only the magnitude of his gifts, it is their peculiarity which is essential. Let us try to enumerate them—first of all we must place an astonishing sense of linear rhythm, a rhythm which is at once extremely continuous and extremely elastic, that is to say it is capable of extraordinary variations from the norm without loss of continuity. The phrase can be held on to through all its changes. Imagine the rhythm rendered the least bit tight and mechanical in its regularity and the whole system of allusion and ellipsis would break down and become ridiculous. Secondly, and this is perhaps Matisse's most obvious gift, an impeccable sense of colour harmony. But here, too, we must distinguish clearly. Matisse has in the first place the gift that we note in almost all Mahommedan art, the gift of finding rich new and surprising harmonies of colour notes placed in apposition upon a flat surface. And like the best of Oriental craftsmen Matisse is never content with a perfect accord of all the colours, there is always with this an element of surprise, there are always appositions which make us say to ourselves " How the Devil did it occur to him that that colour would fit into that scheme, and yet how perfectly acceptable it is." It is this element of surprise that gives its extraordinary freshness and vitality to his schemes even viewed as pure decoration, viewed as we might view some rare Persian rug.

But Matisse's colour has a further quality without which his equivocal method could never have its full effect. He has an almost uncanny gift of situating each colour in its place in the scheme viewed as a vision of plastic reality, as a world of volumes in a space. That is to say, the colour of, let us suppose, a painted window shutter seen on a house in the distance out of a window remains at the distance from the eye which the whole design indicates ; and the colour of a pot or a flower on the table is just the due amount nearer to the eye. At each point its colour holds the plane in its due position. What is peculiarly uncanny about this gift is that Matisse can give the most wilful interpretation to natural colour—making a distant bridge bright magenta perhaps—and yet not violate the plastic consistency.

ROGER FRY (from *Henri-Matisse*)

· · · · · · · ·

The only time that Matisse revealed to me his usual practice or method, he told me that when he is in the South he sets out with his tackle immediately after breakfast. He looks for a subject, sets up his easel. At mid-day, either he has finished his sketch, and signs it ; or considering it spoilt, he decides to do another the next day. It is the extravagance of a dandy who throws to the wash first one white tie, then another, if he has crumpled them in knotting, and will go on using up ties until his skill has triumphed. The ' fait du premier coup,' the hit-or-miss method of Matisse is at the other extreme of Cézanne's slowness.

JACQUES ÉMILE BLANCHE
(Trans. HERBERT READ in *Art Now*)

· · · · · · · ·

Expression for me is not to be found in the passion which blazes from face to face or which is made evident by some violent gesture. It is in the whole disposition of my picture—the place occupied by the figures, the empty space around them, the proportions—everything plays its part. Composition is the art of arranging in a decorative manner the various elements which the painter uses to express his sentiments. In a picture every separate part will be visible and will take up that position, principal or secondary, which suits it best. Everything which has no utility in the picture is for that reason harmful. A work of art implies a harmony of everything together (une harmonie d'ensemble) : every superfluous detail will occupy, in the mind of the spectator, the place of some other detail which is essential.

MATISSE
(Trans. HERBERT READ in *Art Now*)

PICASSO

" I see for others ; that is to say, so that I can put on canvas the sudden apparitions which force themselves on me. I don't know in advance what I am going to put on the canvas, any more than I decide in advance what colours to use. Whilst I work, I take no stock of what I am painting on the canvas. Every time I begin a picture, I feel as though I were throwing myself into the void. I never know if I shall fall on my feet again. It is only later that I begin to evaluate more exactly the result of my work."

* * * * * * * *

The moments of creation with Picasso are dominated by anguish. This anguish Picasso analysed for me recently. His only wish has been desperately to be himself; in fact, he acts according to suggestions which come to him from beyond his own limits. He sees descending upon him a superior order of exigences, he has a very clear impression that something compels him imperiously to empty his spirit of all that he has only just discovered, even before he has been able to control it, so that he can admit other suggestions. Hence his torturing doubts. But this anguish is not a misfortune for Picasso. It is just this which enables him to break down all his barriers, leaving the field of the possible free to him, and opening up to him the perspectives of the unknown.

ZERVOS (Trans. HERBERT READ in *Art Now*)

SURRÉALISME

The artist, whether poet or mystic or painter, does not seek a symbol for what is clear to the understanding and capable of discursive exposition; he realises that life, especially the mental life, exists on two planes, one definite and visible in outline and detail, and the other—perhaps the greater part of life—submerged, vague, indeterminate. A human being drifts through time like an iceberg, only partly floating above the level of the consciousness. It is the aim of the Surréaliste, whether as a painter or as a poet, to try and realise some of the dimensions and characteristics of his submerged being, and to do this he resorts to the significant imagery of dreams and dreamlike states of mind.

HERBERT READ (from *Art Now*)

§ IV LOVE

Only that soul is happy which loves.

GOETHE

Intellectual passion drives out sensuality.

LEONARDO DA VINCI

If I love you, what is that to you?

OLD SAYING

It is only the truly virtuous man who can love, or who can hate, others.

CONFUCIUS

"Fishes pine away for love and wax lean," if Gomesius's authority may be taken, and are rampant too, some of them.

ROBERT BURTON

Thou hast ravished my heart, my Sister, my Spouse; thou hast ravished my heart with one of thine eyes, with one chain of thy neck. How fair is thy love, my Sister, my Spouse! how much better is thy love than wine! and the smell of thine ointments than all spices! Thy lips, O my Spouse, drop as the honeycomb; honey and milk are under thy tongue, and the smell of thy garments is like the smell of Lebanon.

A garden inclosed is my Sister, my Spouse, a spring shut up, a fountain sealed. Thy plants are an orchard of pomegranates with pleasant fruits; camphire with spikenard. Spikenard and saffron, calamus and cinnamon, with all trees of frankincense ; myrrh and aloes, with all the chief spices ; a fountain of gardens, a well of living waters and streams from Lebanon.

. . . . . .

I sleep, but my heart waketh. It is the voice of my Beloved that knocketh, saying, Open to me, my Sister, my Love, my Dove, my Undefiled ; for my head is filled with dew, and my locks with the drops of the night. I have put off my coat : how shall I put it on ? I have washed my feet : how shall I defile them ?

My Beloved put in his hand by the hole of the door and my heart was moved for him. I rose up to open to my Beloved, and my hands dropped with myrrh and my fingers with sweet-smelling myrrh upon the handles of the lock.

My Beloved is white and ruddy, the chiefest among ten thousand. His head is as the most fine gold, his locks are bushy and black as a raven. His eyes are as the eyes of doves by the rivers of waters, washed with milk and fitly set. His cheeks are as a bed of spices, as sweet flowers. His lips like lilies dropping sweet-smelling myrrh. His hands are as gold rings set with the beryl ; his belly is as bright ivory overlaid with sapphires. His legs are as pillars of marble set upon sockets of fine gold ; his countenance is as Lebanon, excellent as the cedars. His mouth is most sweet ; yea, he is altogether lovely.

. . . . . .

I am my Beloved's and my Beloved is mine : he feedeth among the lilies. Thou art beautiful, O my Love, as Tirzah, comely as Jerusalem, terrible as an army with banners. Turn away thine eyes from me, for they have overcome me.

Set me as a seal upon thy heart, as a seal upon thine arm. For love is strong as death, jealousy is cruel as the grave : the coals thereof are coals of fire which hath a most vehement flame.

Many waters cannot quench love, neither can the floods drown it. If a man would give all the substance of his house for love, it would utterly be contemned.

THE BIBLE (from *The Song of Solomon*)

DUKE

O spirit of love ! how quick and fresh art thou,
That, notwithstanding thy capacity
Receiveth as the sea, nought enters there,
Of what validity and pitch soe'er,
But falls into abatement and low price,
Even in a minute : so full of shapes is fancy,
That it alone is high fantastical.

CURIO

Will you go hunt, my lord ?

DUKE   What, Curio ?

CURIO   The hart.

DUKE

Why, so I do, the noblest that I have.
O ! when mine eyes did see Olivia first,
Methought she purged the air of pestilence.
That instant was I turn'd into a hart,
And my desires, like fell and cruel hounds,
E'er since pursue me. How now ! What news from her ?

VALENTINE

So please my lord, I might not be admitted;
But from her handmaid do return this answer:
The element itself, till seven years' heat,
Shall not behold her face at ample view;
But, like a cloistress, she will veiled walk,
And water once a day her chamber round
With eye-offending brine: all this to season
A brother's dead love, which she would keep fresh
And lasting in her sad remembrance.

DUKE

O! she that hath a heart of that fine frame
To pay this debt of love but to a brother,
How will she love, when the rich golden shaft
Hath kill'd the flock of all affections else
That live in her: when liver, brain, and heart,
These sovereign thrones, are all supplied, and fill'd
Her sweet perfections with one self king.
Away before me to sweet beds of flowers;
Love-thoughts lie rich when canopied with bowers.

SHAKESPEARE (from *Twelfth Night*)

My Love is of a birth as rare
As 'tis for object strange and high:
It was begotten by despair
Upon Impossibility.

Magnanimous Despair alone
Could show me so divine a thing,
Where feeble Hope could ne'er have flown
But vainly flapt its Tinsel Wing.

And yet I quickly might arrive
Where my extended Soul is fixt,
But Fate does Iron wedges drive,
And alwaies crouds it self betwixt.

For Fate with jealous Eye does see
Two perfect Loves ; nor lets them close :
Their union would her ruine be,
And her Tyrannick pow'r depose.

And therefore her Decrees of Steel
Us as the distant poles have plac'd,
(Though Loves whole World on us doth wheel)
Not by themselves to be embrac'd.

Unless the giddy Heaven fall,
And Earth some new Convulsion tear ;
And, us to joyn, the World should all
Be cramp'd into a *Planisphere*.

As Lines so Loves *oblique* may well
Themselves in every Angle greet :
But ours so truly *Paralel*,
Though infinite can never meet.

Therefore the Love which us doth bind,
But Fate so enviously debarrs,
Is the Conjunction of the Mind,
And Opposition of the Stars.

MARVELL

There is a lady sweet and kind ;
Was never face so pleased my mind ;
I did but see her passing by,
And yet I love her till I die.

Her gesture, motion, and her smiles,
Her wit, her voice, my heart beguiles :
Beguiles my heart, I know not why,
And yet I love her till I die.

Cupid is wingèd and doth range ;
Her country so my love doth change :
But change she earth, or change she sky,
Yet will I love her till I die.

ANONYMOUS

Lord, there were a thousand things I remembered after
you were gone that I should have said, and now I am to
write not one of them will come into my head. Sure as I
live it is not settled yet ! Good God ! the fears and
surprises, the crosses and disorders of that day, 'twas
confused enough to be a dream, and I am apt to think
sometimes it was no more. But no, I saw you ; when shall
I do it again, God only knows ! Can there be a romancer
story than ours would make if the conclusion proved
happy ? Ah ! I dare not hope it ; something that I cannot
describe draws a cloud over all the light my fancy discovers sometimes, and leaves me so in the dark with all
my fears about me that I tremble to think on't. But no
more of this sad talk. . . . Before you go I must have a ring
from you, too, a plain gold one ; if I ever marry it shall be

my wedding ring ; when I die I'll give it you again. What a dismal story this is you sent me ; but who could expect better from a love begun upon such grounds ? I cannot pity neither of them, they were both so guilty. Yes, they are the more to be pitied for that.

Here is a note comes to me just now, will you do this service for a fine lady that is my friend ; have I not taught her well, she writes better than her mistress ? How merry and pleased she is with her marrying because there is a plentiful fortune ; otherwise she would not value the man at all. This is the world ; would you and I were out of it ; for, sure, we were not made to live in it. Do you remember Arme and the little house there ? Shall we go thither ? that's next to being out of the world. There we might live like Baucis and Philemon, grow old together in our little cottage, and for our charity to some ship-wrecked strangers obtain the blessing of dying both at the same time. How idly I talk ; 'tis because the story pleases me—none in Ovid so much. I remember I cried when I read it. Methought they were the perfectest characters of a contented marriage, where piety and love were all their wealth, and in their poverty feasted the gods when rich men shut them out. I am called away,—farewell !

Your faithful.

(from *Letters of Dorothy Osborne*)

Ah ! when will this long weary day have end,
And lende me leave to come unto my love ?
How slowly do the houres theyr numbers spend ?
How slowly does sad Time his feathers move ?

Hast thee, O fayrest Planet, to thy home,
Within the Westerne fome :
Thy tyred steedes long since have need of rest,
Long though it be, at last I see it gloome,
And the bright evening-star with golden creast
Appeare out of the East.
Fayre child of beauty! glorious lampe of love!
That all the host of heaven in rankes doost lead,
And guydest lovers through the nights sad dread,
How chearefully thou lookest from above,
And seemst to laugh atweene thy twinkling light,
As joying in the sight
Of these glad many, which for joy doe sing,
That all the woods them answer, and their eccho
    ring!

Now ceasse, ye damsels, your delights fore-past;
Enough it is that all the day was youres :
Now day is doen, and night is nighing fast,
Now bring the Bryde into the brydall boures.
The night is come, now soon her disarray.
And in her bed her lay;
Lay her in lillies and in violets,
And silken courteins over her display,
And odourd sheets, and Arras coverlets.
Behold how goodly my faire love does ly,
In proud humility!
Like unto Maia, when as Jove her took
In Tempe, lying on the flowry gras,
Twixt sleepe and wake, after she weary was,
With bathing in the Acidalian brooke.
Now it is night, ye damsels may be gon,
And leave my love alone,

And leave likewise your former lay to sing :
The woods no more shall answere, nor your eccho
    ring.

Now welcome, night! thou night so long ex-
    pected,
That long daies labour doest at last defray,
And all my cares, which cruell Love collected,
Hast sumd in one, and cancelled for aye :
Spread thy broad wing over my love and me,
That no man may us see ;
And in thy sable mantle us enwrap,
From feare of perill and foule horror free.
Let no false treason seeke us to entrap,
Nor any dread disquiet once annoy
The safety of our joy ;
But let the night be calme, and quietsome,
Without tempestuous storms or sad afray :
Lyke as when Jove with fayre Alcmena lay,
When he begot the great Tirynthian groome :
Or lyke as when he with thy selfe did lie
And begot Majesty.
And let the mayds and yongmen cease to sing,
Ne let the woods them answer nor theyr eccho
    ring.

But let stil Silence trew night-watches keepe,
That sacred Peace may in assurance rayne,
And tymely Sleep, which is the tyme to sleepe,
May poure his limbs forth on your pleasant playne ;
The whiles an hundred little winged loves,
Like divers-fethered doves.
Shall fly and flutter round about your bed,

213

And in the secret darke, that none reproves,
Their prety stealthes shal worke, and snares shal
    spread
To filch away sweet snatches of delight,
Conceald through covert night.
Ye sonnes of Venus, play your sports at will !
For greedy pleasure, carelesse of your toyes,
Thinks more upon her paradise of joyes,
Than what ye do, albe it good or ill.
All night therefore attend your merry play,
For it will soone be day :
Now none doth hinder you, that say or sing ;
Ne will the woods now answer, nor your Eccho ring.

SPENSER (from *Epithalamion*)

I wonder, by my troth, what thou and I
Did, till we lov'd ? were we not wean'd till then ?
But suck'd on countrey pleasures, childishly ?
Or snorted we in the seaven sleepers den ?
T'was so ; But this, all pleasures fancies bee.
If ever any beauty I did see,
Which I desir'd, and got, t'was but a dreame of thee.

And now good morrow to our waking soules,
Which watch not one another out of feare ;
For love, all love of other sights controules,
And makes one little roome, an every where.
Let sea-discoverers to new worlds have gone,
Let Maps to other, worlds on worlds have showne,
Let us possesse one world, each hath one, and is one.

My face is thine eye, thine in mine appeares,
And true plaine hearts doe in the faces rest,
Where can we finde two better hemispheares
Without sharpe North, without declining West?
What ever dyes, was not mixt equally;
If our two loves be one, or, thou and I
Love so alike, that none doe slacken, none can die.

DONNE

IN THE ORCHARD

Leave go my hands, let me catch breath and see;
Let the dew-fall drench either side of me;
   Clear apple-leaves are soft upon that moon
Seen sidelong like a blossom in the tree;
   Ah God, ah God, that day should be so soon.

The grass is thick and cool, it lets us lie.
Kissed upon either cheek and either eye,
   I turn to thee as some green afternoon
Turns toward sunset, and is loth to die;
   Ah God, ah God, that day should be so soon.

Lie closer, lean your face upon my side,
Feel where the dew fell that has hardly dried,
   Hear how the blood beats that went nigh to swoon;
The pleasure lives there when the sense has died;
   Ah God, ah God, that day should be so soon.

O my fair lord, I charge you leave me this:
Is it not sweeter than a foolish kiss?
   Nay take it then, my flower, my first in June,

My rose, so like a tender mouth it is :
  Ah God, ah God, that day should be so soon.

Love, till dawn sunder night from day with fire,
Dividing my delight and my desire,
  The crescent life and love the plenilune,
Love me though dusk begin and dark retire ;
  Ah God, ah God, that day should be so soon.

Ah, my heart fails, my blood draws back ; I know,
When life runs over, life is near to go ;
  And with the slain of love love's ways are strewn,
And with their blood, if love will have it so ;
  Ah God, ah God, that day should be so soon.

Ah, do thy will now ; slay me if thou wilt ;
There is no building now the walls are built,
  No quarrying now the corner-stone is hewn,
No drinking now the vine's whole blood is split ;
  Ah God, ah God, that day should be so soon.

Nay, slay me now ; nay, for I will be slain ;
Pluck thy red pleasure from the teeth of pain,
  Break down thy vine ere yet grape-gatherers prune,
Slay me ere day can slay desire again ;
  Ah God, ah God, that day should be so soon.

Yea, with thy sweet lips, with thy sweet sword ; yea,
Take life and all, for I will die, I say ;
  Love, I gave love, is life a better boon ?
For sweet night's sake I will not live till day ;
  Ah God, ah God, that day should be so soon.

Nay, I will sleep then only; nay, but go.
Ah sweet, too sweet for me, my sweet, I know
   Love, sleep, and death go to the sweet same tune;
Hold my hair fast, and kiss me through it so.
   Ah God, ah God, that day should be so soon.

SWINBURNE

Vulcan met two lovers, and bid them ask what they would and they should have it; but they made answer, *O Vulcane faber deorum, &c.* " O Vulcan the gods' great smith, we beseech thee to work us anew in thy furnace, and of two make us one; which he presently did, and ever since true lovers are either all one, or else desire to be united." Many such tales you shall find in Leon Hebræus, *dial.* 3. and their moral to them. The reason why Love was still painted young (as Phornutus and others will), " is because young men are most apt to love; soft, fair, and fat, because such folks are soonest taken; naked, because all true affection is simple and open; he smiles, because merry and given to delights; hath a quiver, to show his power, none can escape; is blind, because he sees not where he strikes, whom he hits," &c. His power and sovereignty is expressed by the poets, in that he is held to be a god, and a great commanding god, above Jupiter himself; Magnus Dæmon, as Plato calls him, the strongest and merriest of all the gods according to Alcinous and Athenæus. *Amor virorum rex, amor rex deum,* Euripides, the god of gods and governor of men; for we must all do homage to him, keep a holiday for his deity, adore in his temples, worship his image (*numen enim hoc non est nudum nomen*), and sacrifice to his altar, that conquers all, and rules all :

> Mallem cum icone, cervo et apro Æolico,
> Cum Anteo et Stymphalicis avibus luctari
> Quam cum amore—

" I had rather contend with bulls, lions, bears, and giants, than with Love ; " he is so powerful, enforceth all to pay tribute to him, domineers over all, and can make mad and sober whom he list ; insomuch that Cæcilius in Tully's Tusculans, holds him to be no better than a fool or an idiot, that doth not acknowledge Love to be a great god.

> Cui in manu sit quem esse dementem velit,
> Quem sapere, quem in morbum injici, &c.

That can make sick and cure whom he list. Homer and Stesichorus were both made blind, if you will believe Leon Hebræus, for speaking against his godhead ; and though Aristophanes degrade him, and say that he was scornfully rejected from the council of the gods, had his wings clipped besides, that he might come no more amongst them, and to his farther disgrace banished heaven for ever, and confined to dwell on earth, yet he is of that power, majesty, omnipotency, and dominion, that no creature can withstand him.

> Imperat Cupido etiam diis pro arbitrio,
> Et ipsum arcere ne armipotens potest Jupiter.

He is more than quarter-master with the gods.

Tenet

> Thetide æquor, umbras Æaco, cœlum Jove :

and hath not so much possession as dominion. Jupiter

himself was turned into a satyr, shepherd, a bull, a swan, a golden shower, and what not, for love ; that as Lucian's Juno right well objected to him, *ludus amoris tu es*, thou art Cupid's whirligig : how did he insult over all the other gods, Mars, Neptune, Pan, Mercury, Bacchus, and the rest ? Lucian brings in Jupiter complaining of Cupid that he could not be quiet for him ; and the moon lamenting that she was so impotently besotted on Endymion, even Venus herself confessing as much, how rudely and in what sort her own son Cupid had used her being his mother, "now drawing her to Mount Ida, for the love of that Trojan Anchises, now to Libanus for that Assyrian youth's sake. And although she threatened to break his bow and arrows, to clip his wings, and whipped him besides on the bare buttocks with her phantophle, yet all would not serve, he was too headstrong and unruly." . . . Your bravest soldiers and most generous spirits are enervated with it, *ubi mulieribus blanditiis permittunt se, et inquinantur amplexibus*. Apollo, that took upon him to cure all diseases, could not help himself of this ; and therefore Socrates calls Love a tyrant, and brings him triumphing in a chariot, whom Petrarch imitates in his Triumph of Love, and Fracastorius in an elegant poem expresseth at large, Cupid riding, Mars and Apollo following his chariot, Psyche weeping, &c.

In vegetal creatures what sovereignty Love hath, by many pregnant proofs and familiar examples may be proved, especially of palm-trees, which are both he and she, and express not a sympathy but a love-passion, and by many observations have been confirmed. . . . Constantine *de Agric. lib.* 10 *cap.* 4. gives an instance out of Florentius his Georgics of a palm-tree that loved most fervently, " and would not be comforted until such time her love applied himself unto her; you might see the two trees bend, and of their own accords stretch out their boughs to embrace and kiss each other: they will give manifest signs of mutual love." Ammianus Marcellinus, *lib*. 24, reports that they marry one another, and fall in love if they grow in sight; and when the wind brings the smell to them they are marvellously affected. Philostratus *in Imaginibus*, observes as much, and Galen, *lib*. 6. *de locis affectis, cap*, 5. they will be sick for love; ready to die and pine away, which the husbandmen perceiving, saith Constantine, " stroke many palms that grown together, and so stroking again the palm that is enamoured, they carry kisses from one to the other " : or tying the leaves and branches of the one to the stem of the other, will make them both flourish and prosper a great deal better: " which are enamoured they can perceive by the bending of the boughs, and inclination of their bodies. If any man think this which I say to be a tale, let him read that story of two palm-trees in Italy, the male growing at Brundusium, the female at Otranto (related by Jovianus Pontanus in an excellent poem, sometimes tutor to Alphonsus junior, King of Naples, his secretary of state, and a great philosopher) " which were barren, and so continued a long time," till they came to see one another growing up higher, though many stadiums asunder. . . .

If such fury be in vegetals, what shall we think of sensible creatures, how much more violent and apparent shall it be in them!

ROBERT BURTON
(from *The Anatomy of Melancholy*)

It was upon a holiday,
When shepheardes groomes han leave to playe,
  I cast to goe a shooting.
Long wandring up and downe the land,
With bowe and bolts in either hand,
  For birds in bushes tooting,
At length within an Yvie todde,
(There shrouded was the little God)
  I heard a busie bustling.
I bent my bolt against the bush,
Listening if any thing did rushe,
  But then heard no more rustling :
Tho, peeping close into the thicke,
Might see the moving of some quicke,
  Whose shape appeared not ;
But were it faerie, feend, or snake,
My courage earnd it to awake,
  And manfully thereat shotte.
When that sprong forth a naked swayne
With spotted winges, like Peacocks trayne,
  And laughing lope to a tree ;
His gylden quiver at his backe,
And silver bowe, which was but slacke,
  Which lightly he bent at me :
That seeing, I levelde againe
And shott at him with might and maine,
  As thicke as it had hayled.
So long I shott, that al was spent ;
Tho pumie stones I hastly hent
  And threwe ; but nought availed :
He was so wimble and so wight,

From bough to bough he pelled light,
  And oft the pumies latched.
Therewith afrayd, I ranne away ;
But he, that earst seemd but to playe,
  A shaft in earnest snatched,
And hit me running in the heele :
For then I little smart did feele,
  But soone it sore encreased ;
And now in rancleth more and more,
And inwardly it festreth sore,
  Ne wote I how to cease it.

WILLYE

Thomalin, I pittie thy plight,
Perdie with Love thou diddest fight :
  I know him by a token :
For once I heard my father say,
How he him caught upon a day,
  (Whereof he wil be wroken)
Entangled in a fowling net,
Which he for carrion Crowes had set
  That in our Peere-tree haunted :
Tho sayd, he was a winged lad,
But bowe and shafts as then none had,
  Els had he sore been daunted.
But see, the Welkin thicks apace,
And stouping Phebus steepes his face :
  Yts time to hast us homeward.

                SPENSER (from *The Shepheards Calender*)

The man's desire is for the woman ; but the woman's desire is rarely other than for the desire of the man.

A woman's friendship borders more closely on love than man's. Men affect each other in the reflection of noble or friendly acts ; whilst women ask fewer proofs, and more signs and expressions of attachment.

. . . .

Every one who has been in love, knows that the passion is strongest, and the appetite weakest, in the absence of of the beloved object, and that the reverse is the case in her presence.

. . . . . .

Love, however sudden, as when we fall in love at first sight, (which is, perhaps, always the case of love in its highest sense,) is yet an act of the will, and that too one of its primary, and therefore ineffaceable acts. This is most important ; for if it be not true, either love itself is all a romantic *hum*, a mere connection of desire with a form appropriated to excite and gratify it, or the mere repetition of a day-dream ;—or if it be granted that love has a real, distinct, and excellent being, I know not how we could attach blame and immorality to inconstancy, when confined to the affections and a sense of preference. Either, therefore, we must brutalize our notions with Pope :—

> Lust, thro' some certain strainers well refined,
> Is gentle love and charms all woman-kind :

or we must dissolve and thaw away all bonds of morality by the irresistible shocks of an irresistible sensibility with Sterne.

. . . .

The torch of love may be blown out wholly, but not that of Hymen. Whom the flame and its cheering light and genial warmth no longer bless, him the smoke stifles ; for the spark is inextinguishable, save by death :—

Nigro circumvelatus amictu
Mæret Hymen, fumantque atræ sine lumine tædæ.

. . . .

There is no condition (evil as it may be in the eye of reason), which does not include, or seem to include when it has become familiar, some good, some redeeming or reconciling qualities. I agree, however, that marriage is not one of these. Marriage has, as you say, no *natural* relation to love. Marriage belongs to society ; it is a social contract. It should not merely include the conditions of esteem and friendship, it should be the ratification of their manifestation. Still I do not know how it can be replaced ; *that* belongs to the future, and it is a question which the future only can solve. I however agree that we can now, better than at any former time, say what *will not*, what *cannot* be.

COLERIDGE (from *Table Talk and Omniana*)

All love, at first, like generous wine,
Ferments and frets until 'tis fine ;
But, when 'tis settled on the lee,
And from th'impurer matter free,
Becomes the richer still the older,
And proves the pleasanter the colder.

SAMUEL BUTLER (1612–1680)

In our last book we have been obliged to deal pretty much with the passion of love; and in our succeeding book shall be forced to handle this subject still more largely. It may not therefore in this place be improper to apply ourselves to the examination of that modern doctrine, by which certain philosophers, among many other wonderful discoveries, pretend to have found out, that there is no such passion in the human breast. . . .

To avoid, however, all contention, if possible, with these philosophers, if they will be called so; and to show our own disposition to accommodate matters peaceably between us, we shall here make them some concessions, which may possibly put an end to the dispute.

First, we will grant that many minds, and perhaps those of the philosophers, are entirely free from the least traces of such a passion.

Secondly, that what is commonly called love, namely, the desire of satisfying a voracious appetite with a certain quantity of delicate white human flesh, is by no means that passion for which I here contend. This is indeed more properly hunger; and as no glutton is ashamed to apply the word love to his appetite, and to say he *loves* such and such dishes; so may the lover of this kind, with equal propriety, say, he *hungers* after such and such women.

Thirdly, I will grant, which I believe will be a most acceptable concession, that this love for which I am an advocate, though it satisfies itself in a much more delicate manner, does nevertheless seek its own satisfaction as much as the grossest of all our appetites.

And, lastly, that this love, when it operates towards one of a different sex, is very apt, towards its complete gratification, to call in the aid of that hunger which I have mentioned above; and which it is so far from abating, that it heightens all its delights to a degree scarce imaginable by those who have never been susceptible of any other emotions than what have proceeded from appetite alone.

In return to all these concessions, I desire of the philosophers to grant, that there is in some (I believe in many) human breasts a kind and benevolent disposition, which is gratified by contributing to the happiness of others. That in this gratification alone, as in friendship, in parental and filial affection, as indeed in general philanthropy, there is a great and exquisite delight. That if we will not call such disposition love, we have no name for it. That though the pleasures arising from such pure love may be heightened and sweetened by the assistance of amorous desires, yet the former can subsist alone, nor are they destroyed by the intervention of the latter. Lastly, that esteem and gratitude are the proper motives of love, as youth and beauty are to desire, and, therefore, though such desire may naturally cease, when age or sickness overtakes its object ; yet these can have no effect on love, nor ever shake or remove, from a good mind, that sensation or passion which hath gratitude and esteem for its basis. . . .

Examine your heart, my good reader, and resolve whether you do believe these matters with me. If you do, you may now proceed to their exemplification in the following pages : if you do not, you have, I assure you, already read more than you have understood ; and it would be wiser to pursue your business, or your pleasures (such as they are), than to throw away any more of your time in reading what you can neither taste nor comprehend. To treat of the effects of love to you, must be as absurd as to discourse on colours to a man born blind ; since possibly your idea of love may be as absurd as that which we are told such blind man once entertained of the colour scarlet ; that colour seemed to him to be very much like the sound of a trumpet : and love probably may, in your opinion, very greatly resemble a dish of soup, or a surloin of roast-beef.

FIELDING (from *Tom Jones*)

Hear, ye ladies that despise
What the mighty Love has done ;
Fear examples and be wise :
Fair Callisto was a nun ;
Leda, sailing on the stream
To deceive the hopes of man,
Love accounting but a dream,
Doted on a silver swan ;
Danaë, in a brazen tower,
Where no love was, loved a shower.

Hear, ye ladies that are coy,
What the mighty love can do ;
Fear the fierceness of the boy :
The chaste Moon he makes to woo ;
Vesta, kindling holy fires,
Circled round about with spies,
Never dreaming loose desires,
Doting at the altar dies ;
Ilion, in a short hour, higher
He can build, and once more fire.

FLETCHER

MRS. MILLAMANT. Mirabell, did you take exceptions last night ? O, ay, and went away.—Now I think on't I'm angry—no, now I think on't I'm pleased—for I believe I gave you some pain.

MIRABELL. Does that please you ?

MRS. MILLAMANT. Infinitely : I love to give pain.

MIRABELL. You would affect a cruelty which is not in your nature ; your true vanity is in the power of pleasing.

MRS. MILLAMANT. Oh I ask your pardon for that—one's cruelty is one's power ; and when one parts with one's cruelty, one parts with one's power, and when one has parted with that, I fancy one's old and ugly.

MIRABELL. Ay, ay, suffer your cruelty to ruin the object of your power, to destroy your lover—and then how vain, how lost a thing you'll be ! Nay, 'tis true ; you are no longer handsome when you've lost your lover ; your beauty dies upon the instant ; for beauty is the lover's gift, 'tis he bestows your charms—your glass is all a cheat. The ugly and the old, whom the looking-glass mortifies, yet after commendation can be flattered by it, and discover beauties in it ; for that reflects our praises, rather than your face.

MRS. MILLAMANT. O the vanity of these men !—Fainall, d'ye hear him ? If they did not commend us, we were not handsome ! Now you must know they could not commend one, if one was not handsome. Beauty the lover's gift ! —Lord, what is a lover, that it can give ? Why, one makes lovers as fast as one pleases, and they live as long as one pleases, and they die as soon as one pleases ; and then, if one pleases, one makes more.

WITWOUD. Very pretty. Why, you make no more of making lovers, madam, than of making so many card-matches.

MRS. MILLAMANT. One no more owes one's beauty to a lover, than one's wit to an echo. They can but reflect what we look and say; vain empty things if we are silent or unseen, and want a being.

MIRABELL. Yet to those two vain empty things you owe the two greatest pleasures of your life.

MRS. MILLAMANT. How so?

MIRABELL. To your lover you owe the pleasure of hearing yourselves praised; and to an echo the pleasure of hearing yourselves talk.

WITWOUD. But I know a lady who loves talking so incessantly, she won't give an echo fair play; she has that everlasting rotation of tongue, that an echo must wait till she dies, before it can catch her last words.

MRS. MILLAMANT. O fiction!—Fainall, let us leave these men.

CONGREVE (from *The Way of the World*)

ANGELICA. Nay, Mr. Tattle, if you make love to me, you spoil my design, for I intend to make you my confidant.

TATTLE. But, madam, to throw away your person, such a person, and such a fortune, on a madman?

ANGELICA. I never loved him till he was mad; but don't tell anybody so.

TATTLE. Tell, madam! alas, you don't know me—I have much ado to tell your ladyship how long I have been in love with you; but encouraged by the impossibility of Valentine's making any more addresses to you, I have ventured to declare the very inmost passion of my heart.

Oh, madam, look upon us both ; there you see the ruins of a poor decayed creature,—here a complete and lively figure, with youth and health, and all his five senses in perfection, madam ; and to all this, the most passionate lover——

ANGELICA. O fy, for shame ! hold your tongue ; a passionate lover and five senses in perfection ! when you are as mad as Valentine, I'll believe you love me, and the maddest shall take me.

CONGREVE (from *Love for Love*)

Love was the mother of poetry, and still produces, among the most ignorant and barbarous, a thousand imaginary distresses and poetical complaints. It makes a footman talk like Oroondates, and converts a brutal rustic into a gentle swain. The most ordinary plebeian or mechanic in love bleeds and pines away with a certain elegance and tenderness of sentiments which this passion naturally inspires.

These inward languishings of a mind infected with this softness, have given birth to a phrase which is made use of by all the melting tribe, from the highest to the lowest, I mean that of " dying for love."

Romances, which owe their very being to this passion, are full of these metaphorical deaths. Heroes and heroines, knights, squires, and damsels, are all of them in a dying condition. There is the same kind of mortality in our modern tragedies, where every one gasps, faints, bleeds, and dies. Many of the poets, to describe the execution which is done by this passion, represent the fair sex as basilisks that destroy with their eyes ; but I think

Mr. Cowley has with greater justness of thought compared a beautiful woman to a porcupine, that sends an arrow from every part.

I have often thought, that there is no way so effectual for the cure of this general infirmity, as a man's reflecting upon the motives that produce it. When the passion proceeds from the sense of any virtue or perfection in the persons beloved, I would by no means discourage it ; but if a man considers that all his heavy complaints of wounds and deaths rise from some little affectations of coquetry, which are improved into charms by his own fond imagination, the very laying before himself the cause of his distemper, may be sufficient to effect the cure of it.

It is in this view that I have looked over the several bundles of letters which I have received from dying people, and composed out of them the following bill of mortality, which I shall lay before my reader without any further preface, as hoping that it may be useful to him in discovering those several places where there is most danger, and those fatal arts which are made use of to destroy the heedless and unwary.

Lysander, slain at a puppet-show on the third of September.

Thyrsis, shot from a casement in Piccadilly.

T. S., wounded by Zelinda's scarlet stocking, as she was stepping out of a coach.

Will Simple, smitten at the opera by the glance of an eye that was aimed at one who stood by him.

Thos. Vainlove, lost his life at a ball.

Tim. Tattle, killed by the tap of a fan on his left shoulder by Coquetilla, as he was talking carelessly with her in a bow-window. . . .

Philander, mortally wounded by Cleora, as she was adjusting her tucker. . . .

F. R., caught his death upon the water, April the first.

W. W., killed by an unknown hand, that was playing with the glove off upon the side of the front-box in Drury Lane.

Sir Christopher Crazy, Bart., hurt by the brush of a whalebone petticoat.

Sylvius, shot through the sticks of a fan at St. James's church.

Damon, struck through the heart by a diamond necklace.

Thomas, Trusty, Francis Goosequill, William Meanwell, Edward Callow, Esqrs., standing in a row, fell all four at the same time by an ogle of the Widow Trapland.

Tom Rattle, chancing to tread upon a lady's tail as he came out of the play-house, she turned full upon him, and laid him dead upon the spot.

Dick Tastewell, slain by a blush from the Queen's box in the third act of the *Trip to the Jubilee*. . . .

Ned Courtly, presenting Flavia with her glove (which she had dropped on purpose), she received it and took away his life with a curtsey.

John Gosselin, having received a slight hurt from a pair of blue eyes, as he was making his escape was despatched by a smile.

Strephon, killed by Clarinda as she looked down into the pit.

Charles Careless, shot flying by a girl of fifteen, who unexpectedly popped her head upon him out of a coach.

Josiah Wither, aged three score and three, sent to his long home by Elizabeth Jettwell, spinster. . . .

William Wiseacre, Gent., drowned in a flood of tears by Moll Common.

232

John Pleadwell, Esq. of the Middle Temple, barrister at law, assassinated in his chambers the sixth instant by Kitty Sly, who pretended to come to him for his advice.

(The Spectator, Tuesday, May 13, 1712)

ADDISON

God is Love. I dare say. But what a mischievous devil Love is !

SAMUEL BUTLER

—I am half distracted, captain *Shandy*, said Mrs. *Wadman*, holding up her cambrick handkerchief to her left eye, as she approach'd the door of my uncle *Toby's* sentry-box—a mote—or sand—or something—I know not what, has got into this eye of mine—do look into it—it is not in the white——

In saying which, Mrs. *Wadman* edged herself close in beside my uncle *Toby*, and squeezing herself down upon the corner of his bench, she gave him an opportunity of doing it without rising up—Do look into it—said she.

Honest soul ! thou didst look into it with as much innocency of heart, as ever child look'd into a raree-shew-box ; and 'twere as much a sin to have hurt thee.

—If a man will be peeping of his own accord into things of that nature—I've nothing to say to it——

My uncle *Toby* never did : and I will answer for him, that he would have sat quietly upon a sofa from *June* to *January* (which, you know, takes in both the hot and cold months), with an eye as fine as the *Thracian Rodope's* beside him, without being able to tell, whether it was a black or a blue one.

233

The difficulty was to get my uncle *Toby* to look at one at all.

'Tis surmounted. And

I see him yonder with his pipe pendulous in his hand, and the ashes falling out of it—looking—and looking—and then rubbing his eyes—and then looking again, with twice the good-nature that ever *Galileo* look'd for a spot in the sun.

—In vain ! for by all the powers which animate the organ—Widow *Wadman's* left eye shines this moment as lucid as her right—there is neither mote, or sand, or dust, or chaff, or speck, or particle of opake matter floating in it—There is nothing, my dear paternal uncle ! but one lambent delicious fire, furtively shooting out from every part of it, in all directions, into thine—

—If thou lookest, uncle *Toby*, in search of this mote one moment longer—thou art undone.

An eye is for all the world exactly like a cannon, in this respect ; That it is not so much the eye or the cannon, in themselves, as it is the carriage of the eye—and the carriage of the cannon, by which both the one and the other are enabled to do so much execution. I don't think the comparison a bad one ; However, as 'tis made and placed at the head of the chapter, as much for use as ornament, all I desire in return is, that whenever I speak of Mrs. *Wadman's* eyes (except once in the next period) that you keep it in your fancy.

I protest, Madam, said my uncle *Toby*, I see nothing whatever in your eye.

It is not in the white ; said Mrs. *Wadman* : my uncle *Toby* look'd with might and main into the pupil——

Now of all the eyes which ever were created—from your own, Madam, up to those of *Venus* herself, which certainly

were as venereal a pair of eyes as ever stood in a head—
there never was an eye of them all, so fitted to rob my
uncle *Toby* of his repose, as the very eye, at which he was
looking—it was not, Madam, a rolling eye—a romping
or a wanton one—nor was it an eye sparkling—petulant
or imperious—of high claims and terrifying exactions,
which would have curdled at once that milk of human
nature, of which my uncle *Toby* was made up—but 'twas
an eye full of gentle salutations—and soft responses—
speaking—not like the trumpet stop of some ill-made
organ, in which many an eye I talk to, holds coarse converse—but whispering soft—like the last low accent of
an expiring saint—" How can you live comfortless, captain *Shandy*, and alone, without a bosom to lean your
head on—or trust your cares to ? "

It was an eye——

But I shall be in love with it myself, if I say another
word about it.

—It did my uncle *Toby's* business.

LAURENCE STERNE (from *Tristram Shandy*)

ANGELICA. Therefore I ask your advice Sir Sampson :
I have fortune enough to make any man easy that I
can like ; if there were such a thing as a young agreeable man with a reasonable stock of good-nature and
sense.—For I would neither have an absolute wit nor
a fool.

SIR SAMPSON. Odd, you are hard to please, madam ; to
find a young fellow that is neither a wit in his own eye,
nor a fool in the eye of the world, is a very hard task.
But, faith and troth, you speak very discreetly ; for
I hate both a wit and a fool.

ANGELICA. She that marries a fool, Sir Sampson, forfeits
the reputation of her honesty or understanding : and
she that marries a very witty man is a slave to the
severity and insolent conduct of her husband. I should
like a man of wit for a lover, because I would have such
a one in my power ; but I would no more be his wife
than his enemy. For his malice is not a more terrible
consequence of his aversion than his jealousy is of his
love.

CONGREVE (from *Love for Love*)

The stage is more beholding to love, than the life of
man. For as to the stage, love is ever matter of comedies,
and now and then of tragedies : but in life, it doth much
mischief : sometimes like a siren ; sometimes like a fury.
You may observe, that amongst all the great and worthy
persons, (whereof the memory remaineth, either ancient
or recent) there is not one that hath been transported to
the mad degree of love : which shows, that great spirits,
and great business, do keep out this weak passion. You
must except, nevertheless, Marcus Antonius, the half-
partner of the Empire of Rome ; and Appius Claudius the
decemvir, and lawgiver : whereof the former was indeed
a voluptuous man, and inordinate ; but the latter was an
austere, and wise man : and therefore it seems (though
rarely) that love can find entrance, not only into an open
heart ; but also into a heart well fortified ; if watch be not
well kept. It is a poor saying of Epicurus ; *Satis magnum
alter alteri theatrum sumus* : as if man, made for the contemplation of heaven, and all noble objects, should do
nothing but kneel before a little idol, and make himself

subject, though not of the mouth (as beasts are) yet of the eye; which was given him for higher purposes. It is a strange thing, to note the excess of this passion; and how it braves the nature, and value of things; by this, that the speaking in a perpetual hyperbole is comely in nothing, but in love. Neither is it merely in the phrase; for whereas it hath been well said, that the arch-flatterer, with whom all the petty flatterers have intelligence, is a man's self; certainly, the lover is more. For there was never proud man thought so absurdly well of himself, as the lover doth of the person loved: and therefore, it was well said, that it is impossible to love, and to be wise. Neither doth this weakness appear to others only, and not to the party loved; but to the loved, most of all: except the love be reciproque. For it is a true tale, that love is ever rewarded, either with the reciproque, or with an inward, and secret contempt. By how much more, men ought to beware of this passion, which loseth not only other things, but itself. As for the other losses, the poet's relation doth well figure them; that he that preferred Helena quitted the gifts of Juno, and Pallas. For whosoever esteemeth too much of amorous affection quitteth both riches, and wisdom. This passion hath his floods, in the very times of weakness; which are, great prosperity; and great adversity; though this latter hath been less observed. Both which times kindle love, and make it more fervent, and therefore show it to be the child of folly. They do best, who, if they cannot but admit love, yet make it keep quarter; and sever it wholly from their serious affairs, and actions of life: for if it check once with business, it troubleth men's fortunes, and maketh men that they can no ways be true to their own ends. I know not how, but martial men are given to love: I think it is but as they are given to wine; for perils commonly ask to be paid in pleasures. There is in man's nature a secret inclination, and motion, towards love of others; which, if it be not spent upon some one, or a few, doth naturally spread itself towards many, and maketh men become humane, and charitable; as it is seen sometimes in friars. Nuptial love maketh mankind; friendly love perfecteth it; but wanton love corrupteth, and imbaseth it.

BACON (*Essays*)

Those that have loved longest love best. A sudden blaze of kindness may by a single blast of coldness be extinguished, but that fondness which length of time has connected with many circumstances and occasions, though it may for a while be suppressed by disgust or resentment, with or without a cause, is hourly revived by accidental recollection. To those who have lived long together, every thing heard and every thing seen recalls some pleasure communicated, or some benefit conferred, some petty quarrel, or some slight endearment. Esteem of great powers, or amiable qualities newly discovered, may embroider a day or a week, but a friendship of twenty years is interwoven with the texture of life. A friend may be often found and lost, but an *old friend* never can be found, and nature has provided that he cannot easily be lost.

SAMUEL JOHNSON (*Letters*)

Love comes suddenly and spontaneously, through temperament or through weakness. A sudden beauty

238

fixes us, resolves us. Friendship, on the contrary, is formed little by little, with time, goodness of heart, attachment, services and kindnesses between friends, until after many years it has effected less than is sometimes effected in a moment by a beautiful face or a beautiful hand.

Time, which strengthens friendship, weakens love

While love endures, it subsists of itself, and sometimes by things which, one would think, would quench it,— by whims, spite, absence, or jealousy. Friendship, on the contrary, must be assisted : it will die for lack of care, confidence, and kindness.

It is more common to see an excessive love than a perfect friendship.

Love and friendship exclude one another.

Once only do we love truly, and that is in our first love. The loves that follow are more deliberate.

The love that comes suddenly is the slowest to cure.

Love that grows by slow degrees is too much akin to friendship to be a violent passion.

He who loves enough to wish to love a million times more, is second in love only to him who loves more than he wishes.

Men often desire to love and fail to do so : they court

slavery and fail to achieve it, and so, if I dare say so, they are bound to remain free.

. . . . .

To be with those that one loves is enough : to dream, to speak with them, to refrain from speaking, to think of them, to think of more indifferent matters, but always at their side,—it is all one.

. . . . . .

It would seem that, since there is a strange, unjust, and baseless suspicion which has once and for all been called jealousy, that other jealousy which is a just and natural sentiment, based on reason and experience, deserves another name.

. . . . . .

Women who consider us in nothing and spare us no occasions for jealousy, would deserve no jealousy of us, if only we were guided more by their sentiments and behaviour than by our hearts.

. . . . .

The beginnings and the decline of love are to be perceived by the embarrassment of lovers when they find themselves alone together.

. . . . . .

To love is a weakness : it is often another weakness to cease to love.

. . . . .

If a man love an ill-favoured woman, he loves her to distraction ; for he loves her either by a strange weakness in himself, or because she has charms more secret and invincible than those of beauty.

. . . . . .

He can accept, who tastes as delicate a pleasure in receiving as his friend feels in giving.

There are those who desire a certain thing with such
ardour and determination, that, for fear of missing it,
they omit none of those things that will insure their
missing it.

LA BRUYÈRE (from *Les Caractères*)

He is starke mad, who ever sayes
    That he hath been in love an houre,
Yet not that love so soone decayes,
    But that it can tenne in lesse space devour ;
Who will beleeve mee, if I sweare
That I have had the plague a yeare ?
    Who would not laugh at mee, if I should say,
    I saw a flaske of powder burne a day ?

Ah, what a trifle is a heart,
    If once into loves hands it come !
All other griefes allow a part
    To other griefes, and aske themselves but some ;
They come to us, but us Love draws,
Hee swallows us, and never chawes :
    By him, as by chain'd shot, whole rankes doe
        dye,
    He is the tyran Pike, our hearts the Frye.

If 'twere not so, what did become
    Of my heart, when I first saw thee ?
I brought a heart into the roome,
    But from the roome I carried none with mee :
If it had gone to thee, I know
Mine would have taught thine heart to show
    More pitty unto mee : but Love, alas,
    At one first blow, did shiver it as glasse.

Yet nothing can to nothing fall,
  Nor any place be empty quite,
Therefore I thinke my breast hath all
  Those peeces still, though they be not unite ;
And now as broken glasses show
A hundred lesser faces, so
  My ragges of heart can like, wish, and adore,
  But after one such love, can love no more.

DONNE

The blessed Francis enjoined that to speak with and
to gaze upon women, which things have already made
many to fall, should be altogether cut off, for he said
that thereby the weak spirit is broken and the strong
spirit made weak. And the blessed Francis said that it
is as hard a matter for a man who converses with women,
if he be not of a proved uprightness, not to fall into the
defilement of sin as to walk through the fire and not to
burn his feet. But the blessed Francis had so utterly
turned away his eyes from their regard that hardly ever
did he look any woman in the face, as he once told his
companions. And he said moreover that it is not safe for
a man to dwell at all upon the forms of women when they
rise in the imagination, for, if he do so, it rarely happens
that even the most chaste soul is not thereby stricken
and defiled.

Moreover he said that it was a vain and evil thing to
talk with women, except for confession or for a few words
of instruction such as belongs to honesty and salvation of
body and soul. And what talk and what intercourse, said
the blessed Francis, can the Man of God have with

women, save to bring them to penitence or to give them
counsel of bettering their lives according to religion?
For it is through excess of self-confidence that a man
ceases to guard against the Enemy who, if he gain but a
hair of the Man of God, will soon make it grow into a
beam.

SAINT BONAVENTURA
(from *The Life of St. Francis*)

A certain brother was travelling on a road, and his
aged mother was with him, and they came to a river
which the old woman was not able to cross; and her son
took his shoulder cloth and wound it round his hands so
that they might not touch his mother's body, and in this
manner he carried her across the river. Then his mother
said unto him, " My son, why didst thou first wrap round
thy hands with the cloth, and then take me across? "
and he said, " The body of a woman is fire, and through
thy body there would have come to me the memory of
another woman, and it was for this reason that I acted
as I did."

PALLADIUS
(from *The Paradise of the Fathers*—
Trans. E. A. WALLIS BUDGE)

*How St. Bennet Overcame A Great Temptation of the
Flesh.*

Saint Bennet, upon a certain day being alone, the
Tempter was at hand: for a little black bird, commonly
called a merle or an ousel, began to fly about his face,
and that so near as the holy man, if he would, might have

taken it with his hand : but after he had blessed himself
with the sign of the cross, the bird flew away : and forthwith the holy man was assaulted with such a terrible
temptation of the flesh, as he never felt the like in all his
life. A certain woman there was which some time he had
seen, the memory of which the wicked spirit put into his
mind, and by the representation of her did so mightily
inflame with concupiscence the soul of God's servant,
which did so increase that, almost overcome with pleasure,
he was of a mind to have forsaken the wilderness. But,
suddenly assisted with God's grace, he came to himself ;
and seeing many thick briers and nettle-bushes to grow
hard by, off he cast his apparel, and threw himself into
the midst of them, and there wallowed so long that, when
he rose up, all his flesh was pitifully torn : and so by the
wounds of his body, he cured the wounds of his soul, in
that he turned pleasure into pain, and by the outward
burning of extreme smart, quenched that fire which, being
nourished before with the fuel of carnal cogitations, did
inwardly burn in his soul : and by this means he overcame
the sin, because he made a change of the fire. From which
time forward, as himself did afterward report unto his
disciples, he found all temptation of pleasure so subdued,
that he never felt any such thing.

ST. GREGORY THE GREAT
(from *Dialogus Beati Gregorii*—Trans. P.W., 1608)

The joyes of love, if they should ever last
Without affliction or disquietnesse
That worldly chaunces doe amongst them cast,
Would be on earth too great a blessednesse,
Liker to heaven then mortall wretchednesse :

244

Therefore the winged God, to let men weet
That here on earth is no sure happinesse,
A thousand sowres hath tempred with one sweet,
To make it seeme more deare and dainty, as is
   meet.

SPENSER (from *The Faerie Queene*)

" Sophocles, the poet, was once asked in my presence :
' How do you feel concerning love, Sophocles ? Are you
still capable of it ? ' to which he replied : ' Hush, if you
please ! To my great delight I have escaped from it, and I
feel as if I had escaped from a frantic and savage master.' "

PLATO (from *The Republic*)

Odi et amo. Quare id faciam, fortasse requiris.
Nescio, sed fieri sentio et excrucior.

CATULLUS

From the southern sea-board of Cilicia may be seen
to the south the beautiful island of Cyprus, which was
the realm of the goddess Venus ; and many there have
been, who, impelled by her loveliness, have had their
ships and rigging broken upon the rocks that lie among
the seething waves. Here the beauty of some pleasant
hill invites the wandering mariners to take their ease
among its flowery verdure, where the zephyrs continually
come and go, filling with sweet odours the island and the
encompassing sea. Alas ! How many ships have foundered
there !

LEONARDO DA VINCI
(from *The Notebooks*—Trans. EDWARD MCCURDY)

245

In a Dreame, Love bad me go
To the Gallies there to Rowe ;
In the Vision, I askt why ?
Love as briefly did reply :
'Twas better there to toyle, than prove
The turmoiles they endure that love.
I awoke, and then I knew
What Love said was too too true :
Henceforth therefore I will be
As from Love, from trouble free.
None pities him that's in the snare,
And warn'd before, wo'd not beware.

HERRICK

Beshrew that heart that makes my heart to groan
For that deep wound it gives my friend and me !
Is't not enough to torture me alone,
But slave to slavery my sweet'st friend must be ?
Me from myself thy cruel eye hath taken,
And my next self thou harder hast engrossed :
Of him, myself, and thee, I am forsaken ;
A torment thrice threefold thus to be crossed.
Prison my heart in thy steel bosom's ward,
But then my friend's heart let my poor heart bail ;
Who'er keeps me, let my heart be his guard ;
Thou canst not then use rigour in my gaol :
And yet thou wilt ; for I, being pent in thee,
Perforce am thine, and all that is in me.

So now I have confess'd that he is thine
And I myself am mortgaged to thy will,
Myself I'll forfeit, so that other mine

Thou wilt restore, to be my comfort still :
But thou wilt not, nor he will not be free,
For thou are covetous and he is kind ;
He learn'd but surety-like to write for me,
Under that bond that him as fast doth bind.
The statute of thy beauty thou wilt take,
Thou usurer, that put'st forth all to use,
And sue a friend came debtor for my sake ;
So him I lose through my unkind abuse.
Him have I lost ; thou hast both him and me :
He pays the whole, and yet I am not free.

SHAKESPEARE

When by thy scorne, O murdresse, I am dead,
And that thou thinkst thee free
From all solicitation from mee,
Then shall my ghost come to thy bed,
And thee, fain'd vestall, in worse armes shall see ;
Then thy sicke taper shall begin to winke,
And he, whose thou art then, being tyr'd before,
Will, if thou stirre, or pinch to wake him, thinke
    Thou call'st for more,
And in false sleepe will from thee shrinke.
And then poore Aspen wretch, neglected thou
Bath'd in a cold quicksilver sweat wilt lye
    A veryer ghost than I ;
What I will say, I will not tell thee now,
Lest that preserve thee ; and since my love is spent,
I'had rather thou shouldst painfully repent,
Than by my threatnings rest still innocent.

DONNE

247

The expense of spirit in a waste of shame
Is lust in action ; and, till action, lust
Is perjur'd, murderous, bloody, full of blame,
Savage, extreme, rude, cruel, not to trust ;
Enjoy'd no sooner but dispised straight ;
Past reason hunted ; and, no sooner had,
Past reason hated, as a swallowed bait,
On purpose laid to make the taker mad :
Mad in pursuit, and in possession so ;
Had, having, and in quest to have, extreme ;
A bliss in proof, and, proved, a very woe ;
Before, a joy proposed ; behind, a dream.
All this the world well knows ; yet none knows well
To shun the heaven that leads men to this hell.

SHAKESPEARE

Never give all the heart, for love
Will hardly seem worth thinking of
To passionate women if it seem
Certain, and they never dream
That it fades out from kiss to kiss ;
For everything that's lovely is
But a brief, dreamy, kind delight.
O never give the heart outright,
For they, for all smooth lips can say,
Have given their hearts up to the play.
And who could play it well enough
If deaf and dumb and blind with love ?
He that made this knows all the cost,
For he gave all his heart and lost.

YEATS

Though nurtured like the sailing moon
In beauty's murderous brood,
She walked awhile and blushed awhile,
And on my pathway stood
Until I thought her body bore
A heart of flesh and blood.

But since I laid a hand thereon
And found a heart of stone
I have attempted many things
And not a thing is done,
For every hand is lunatic
That travels on the moon.

She smiled and that transfigured me
And left me but a lout,
Maundering here, and maundering there,
Emptier of thought
Than the heavenly circuit of its stars
When the moon sails out.

YEATS

Thou blind mans marke, thou fooles selfe chosen snare,
Fond fancies scum, and dregs of scattred thought,
Band of all evils, cradle of causelesse care,
Thou web of will, whose end is never wrought.
Desire, desire I have too dearely bought
With prise of mangled mind thy worthlesse ware,
Too long, too long asleepe thou hast me brought,
Who should my mind to higher things prepare.
But yet in vaine thou hast my ruine sought,
In vaine thou madest me to vaine things aspire,
In vaine thou kindlest all thy smokie fire.

For vertue hath this better lesson taught,
Within my selfe to seeke my onelie hire :
Desiring nought but how to kill desire.

     .   .   .   .   .   .

Leave me, O Love, which reachest but to dust,
And thou my mind aspire to higher things :
Grow rich in that which never taketh rust :
What ever fades, but fading pleasure brings.
Draw in thy beames, and humble all thy might
To that sweet yoke where lasting freedomes be ;
Which breakes the clowdes and opens forth the light ;
That doth both shine and give us sight to see.
O take fast hold, let that light be thy guide,
In this small course which birth drawes out to death,
And thinke how evill becommeth him to slide
Who seeketh heav'n and comes of heav'nly breath.
Then farewell world, thy uttermost I see,
Eternall Love maintaine thy life in me.

SIDNEY

    Who breathes to thee the holiest prayer,
      O love ! is ever least thy care.
Alas ! I may not ask thee why 'tis so . . .
      Because a fiery scroll I see
      Hung at the throne of Destiny,
Reason with Love and register with Woe.

    Few question thee, for thou art strong,
      And, laughing loud at right and wrong,
Seizest, and dashest down, the rich, the poor ;
      Thy sceptre's iron studs alike
      The meaner and the prouder strike,
And wise and simple fear thee and adore.

LANDOR

Never seek to tell thy love
Love that never told may be ;
For the gentle wind does move
Silently, invisibly.

I told my love, I told my love,
I told her all my heart,
Trembling, cold, in ghastly fears—
Ah, she doth depart.

Soon as she was gone from me
A traveller came by
Silently, invisibly—
O, was no deny.

BLAKE

Go, piteous heart, rasèd[1] with deadly woe,
Piercèd with pain, bleeding with woundès smart,
Bewail thy fortune, with veinès wan and blo.[2]
O Fortune unfriendly, Fortune unkind thou art
To be so cruel and so overthwart,
To suffer me so carefully to endure
That where I love best I dare not discure[3] !

One there is, and ever one shall be,
For whose sake my heart is sore diseasèd ;
For whose love welcome disease to me !
I am content so all parties be pleasèd :
Yet, an God would, I would my pain were easèd !
But Fortune forceth me so carefully to endure
That where I love best I dare not discure !

SKELTON

[1] torn.   [2] blue.   [3] reveal.

251

The world is governed by its ideals, and seldom or never has there been one which has exercised a more profound and, on the whole, a more salutary influence than the mediæval conception of the Virgin. For the first time woman was elevated to her rightful position, and the sanctity of weakness was recognised as well as the sanctity of sorrow. No longer the slave or toy of man, no longer associated only with ideas of degradation and of sensuality, woman rose, in the person of the Virgin Mother, into a new sphere, and became the object of a reverential homage of which antiquity had had no conception. Love was idealised. The moral charm and beauty of female excellence were fully felt. A new type of character was called into being : a new kind of admiration was fostered. Into a harsh and ignorant and benighted age this ideal type infused a conception of gentleness and of purity unknown to the proudest civilisations of the past. In the pages of living tenderness which many a monkish writer has left in honour of his celestial patron, in millions who in many lands and in many ages, have sought with no barren desire to mould their characters into her image, in those holy maidens who, for the love of Mary, have separated themselves from all the glories and pleasures of the world, to seek in fastings and vigils and humble charity to render themselves worthy of her benediction, in the new sense of honour, in the chivalrous respect, in the softening of manners, in the refinement of tastes displayed in all the walks of society : in these and in many other ways we detect its influence. All that was best in Europe clustered around it, and it is the origin of many of the purest elements of our civilisation.

LECKY (from *History of Rationalism*)

HÉLOISE TO ABÉLARD. A consolatory letter of yours to a friend happened some days since to fall into my hands : my knowledge of the writing and my love of the hand gave me the curiosity to open it. In justification of the liberty I took, I flattered myself I might claim a sovereign privilege over everything which came from you. But how dear did my curiosity cost me ! I met with my name a hundred times ; I saw yours too, equally unhappy. These mournful but dear remembrances put my heart into such violent motion that I thought it was too much to offer comfort to a friend for a few slight disgraces. Alas ! my memory is perpetually filled with bitter remembrances of past evils. Be not then unkind, nor deny me, I beg of you, that little relief which you only can give. Let me have a faithful account of all that concerns you ; I would know everything, be it ever so unfortunate. We may write to each other ; so innocent a pleasure is not denied us. Let us not lose through negligence the only happiness which is left us. That writing may be no trouble to you, write always to me carelessly and without study ; I had rather read the dictates of the heart than of the brain. I cannot live if you will not tell me that you still love me ; but that language ought to be so natural to you, that I believe you cannot speak otherwise to me without violence to yourself. Irresolute as I am I still love you, and yet I must hope for nothing. I have renounced life and stript myself of everything, but I find I neither have nor can renounce my Abélard. Though I have lost my lover I still preserve my love. O vows ! O convent ! I have not lost my humanity under your inexorable discipline. You have not turned me to marble by changing my habit ; my heart is not hardened by my imprisonment ; I am still sensible to what has touched me, though, alas ! I ought not to be. Without offending your commands permit a lover to exhort me to live in obedience to your rigorous rules. Remember I still love you, and yet strive to avoid loving you. What a terrible saying is this ! I shake with horror, and my heart revolts against what I say. I shall blot all my paper with tears. I end my letter wishing you, if you desire it (would to Heaven I could !), for ever adieu !

.   .   .   .

ABÉLARD TO HÉLOISE. When love has once been sincere how difficult it is to determine to love no more ! 'Tis a thousand times more easy to renounce the world than love. I hate this deceitful, faithless world ; I think no more of it ; but my wandering heart still eternally seeks you, and is filled with anguish at having lost you, in spite of all the powers of my reason. There are some whom God saves by suffering. Let my salvation be the fruit of your prayers ; let me owe it to your tears and your exemplary holiness. Though my heart, Lord, be filled with the love of Thy creature, Thy hand can, when it pleases, empty me of all love save for Thee. To love Héloise truly is to leave her to that quiet which retirement and virtue afford. I have resolved it : this letter shall be my last fault. Adieu. If I die here I will give orders that my body be carried to the House of the Paraclete. You shall see me in that condition, not to demand tears from you, for it will be too late ; weep rather for me now and extinguish the fire which burns me. You shall see me in order that your piety may be strengthened by horror of this carcase, and my death be eloquent to tell you what you brave when you love a man. I hope you will be willing, when you have finished this mortal life, to be buried near me. Your cold ashes need then fear nothing, and my tomb shall be the more rich and renowned.

. . . . . .

HÉLOISE TO ABÉLARD. My dear Husband (for the last time I use that title!), shall I never see you again? Shall I never have the pleasure of embracing you before death? What dost thou say, wretched Héloise? Dost thou know what thou desirest? Couldst thou behold those brilliant eyes without recalling the tender glances which have been so fatal to thee? That mouth cannot be looked upon without desire. Ask no more therefore to see Abélard: if the memory of him has caused thee so much trouble, Héloise, what would not his presence do? What desires will it not excite in thy soul? How will it be possible to keep thy reason at the sight of one so lovable?

I will own to you what makes the greatest pleasure in my retirement: after having passed the day in thinking of you, full of the repressed idea, I give myself up at night to sleep. Then it is that Héloise, who dares not think of you by day, resigns herself with pleasure to see and hear you. How my eyes gloat over you! Sometimes you tell me stories of your secret troubles, and create in me a felt sorrow: sometimes the rage of our enemies is forgotten and you press me to you and I yield to you, and our souls, animated with the same passion, are sensible of the same pleasures. But O delightful dreams and tender illusions, how soon do you vanish away! I awake and open my eyes to find no Abélard: I stretch out my arms to embrace him and he is not there: I cry, and he hears me not. But do you, Abélard, never see Héloise in your sleep? How does she appear to you? Do you entertain her with the same tender language as formerly, and are you glad or sorry when you wake? Pardon me, Abélard, pardon a mistaken lover. I must no longer expect from you that vivacity which once marked your every action ; no more must I require from you the correspondence of desires. We have bound ourselves to severe austerities and must follow them at all costs. Let us think of our duties and our rules, and make good use of that necessity which keeps us separate. You, Abélard, will happily finish your course : your desires and ambitions will be no obstacle to your salvation. But Héloise must weep, she must lament for ever without being certain whether all her tears will avail for her salvation. I begin to perceive, Abélard, that I take too much pleasure in writing to you : I ought to burn this letter. It shows that I still feel a deep passion for you, though at the beginning I tried to persuade you to the contrary. I am sensible of waves both of grace and passion, and by turns yield to each. Have pity, Abélard, on the condition to which you have brought me, and make in some measure my last days as peaceful as my first have been uneasy and disturbed.

. . . .

ABÉLARD TO HÉLOISE. Write no more to me, Héloise, write no more to me : 'tis time to end communications which make our penances of nought avail. We retired from the world to purify ourselves, and, by a conduct directly contrary to Christian morality, we became odious to Jesus Christ. Let us no more deceive ourselves with remembrance of our past pleasures : we but make our lives troubled and spoil the sweets of solitude. Let us make good use of our austerities and no longer preserve the memories of our crimes amongst the severities of penance. Ah, Héloise, how far are we from such a happy temper ! Your heart still burns with that fatal fire you cannot extinguish, and mine is full of trouble and unrest.

Think not, Héloise, that I here enjoy perfect peace : I will for the last time open my heart to you : I am not yet disengaged from you, and though I fight against my excessive tenderness for you, in spite of all my endeavours I remain but too sensible of your sorrows and long to share in them. Your letters have indeed moved me : I could not read with indifference characters written by that dear hand. I sigh and weep, and all my reason is scarce sufficient to conceal my weakness from my pupils.

Farewell, Héloise. This is the last advice of your dear Abélard : for the last time let me persuade you to follow the rules of the Gospel. Heaven grant that your heart, once so sensible of my love, may now yield to be directed by my zeal. May the idea of your loving Abélard, always present to your mind, be now changed into the image of Abélard truly penitent ; and may you shed as many tears for your salvation as you have done for our misfortunes.

(from *The Love Letters of Abélard and Héloise*—
Anonymous translation, 1722)

An ancient chronicle of Tours records that when they deposited the body of the Abbess Eloisa in the tomb of her lover Peter Abélard, who had been there interred twenty years, this faithful husband raised his arms, stretched them, and closely embraced his beloved Eloisa. Du Chesne, the father of French history, not only relates this legendary tale of the ancient chroniclers, but gives it as an incident well authenticated.

ISAAC D'ISRAELI (from *Curiosities of Literature*)

Oh, Love ! no habitant of earth thou art—
An unseen Seraph, we believe in thee,—
A faith whose martyrs are the broken heart,—
But never yet hath seen, nor e'er shall see
The naked eye, thy form, as it should be ;
The mind hath made thee, as it peopled Heaven,
Even with its own desiring phantasy,
And to a thought such shape and image given,
As haunts the unquenched soul, parched, weary,
      wrung, and riven.

BYRON (from *Childe Harold*)

We were two lovers standing sadly by
While our two loves lay dead upon the ground ;
Each love had striven not to be first to die,
But each was gashed with many a cruel wound.
Said I : " Your love was false while mine was true."
Aflood with tears he cried : " It was not so,
'Twas your false love my true love falsely slew—
For 'twas your love that was the first to go."
Thus did we stand and said no more for shame
Till I, seeing his cheek so wan and wet,
Sobbed thus : " So be it ; my love shall bear the
      blame ;
Let us inter them honourably." And yet
I swear by all truth human and divine
'Twas his that in its death throes murdered mine.

SAMUEL BUTLER (1835–1902)

Western wind, when wilt thou blow,
The small rain down can rain?
Christ, if my love were in my arms,
And I in my bed again!

ANONYMOUS

25 College Street.
Postmark, 13 October, 1819.

MY DEAREST GIRL,

This moment I have set myself to copy some verses
out fair. I cannot proceed with any degree of content.
I must write you a line or two and see if that will assist in
dismissing you from my Mind for ever so short a time.
Upon my Soul I can think of nothing else. The time is
passed when I had power to advise and warn you against
the unpromising morning of my Life. My love has made
me selfish. I cannot exist without you. I am forgetful of
everything but seeing you again—my Life seems to stop
there—I see no further. You have absorb'd me. I have
a sensation at the present moment as though I was dis-
solving—I should be exquisitely miserable without the
hope of soon seeing you. I should be afraid to separate
myself far from you. My sweet Fanny, will your heart
never change? My love, will it? I have no limit now to my
love. . . . Your note came in just here. I cannot be happier
away from you. 'Tis richer than an Argosy of Pearles. Do
not threat me even in jest. I have been astonished that
Men could die Martyrs for religion—I have shuddered
at it. I shudder no more—I could be martyr'd for my
Religion—Love is my religion—I could die for that.
I could die for you. My Creed is Love and you are its only

tenet. You have ravish'd me away by a Power I cannot resist ; and yet I could resist till I saw you ; and even since I have seen you I have endeavoured often " to reason against the reasons of my Love." I can do that no more—the pain would be too great. My love is selfish. I cannot breathe without you.

Yours for ever
JOHN KEATS

Bright star ! would I were steadfast as thou art—
Not in lone splendour hung aloft the night,
And watching, with eternal lids apart,
Like Nature's patient, sleepless Eremite,
The moving waters at their priestlike task
Of pure ablution round earth's human shores,
Or gazing on the new soft fallen mask
Of snow upon the mountains and the moors—
No ; yet still steadfast, still unchangeable,
Pillow'd upon my fair love's ripening breast,
To feel for ever its soft fall and swell,
Awake for ever in a sweet unrest,
Still, still to hear her tender-taken breath,
And so live ever, or else swoon to death.

KEATS

SWEETEST FANNY,

You fear, sometimes, I do not love you so much as you wish ? My dear Girl, I love you ever and ever and without reserve. The more I have known the more I have lov'd. In every way—even my jealousies have been agonies of Love, in the hottest fit I ever had I would have died for you. I have vex'd you too much. But for Love ! Can I help it ? You are always new. The last of your kisses was ever the sweetest ; the last smile the brightest ; the last movement the gracefullest. When you pass'd my window home yesterday, I was fill'd with as much admiration as if I had then seen you for the first time. You uttered a half complaint once that I only lov'd your beauty. Have I nothing else then to love in you but that ? Do not I see a heart naturally furnish'd with wings imprison itself with me ? No ill prospect has been able to turn your thoughts a moment from me. This perhaps should be as much a subject of sorrow as joy—but I will not talk of that. Even if you did not love me I could not help an entire devotion to you : how much more deeply then must I feel for you knowing you love me. My Mind has been the most discontented and restless one that ever was put into a body too small for it. I never felt my Mind repose upon anything with complete and undistracted enjoyment —upon no person but you. When you are in the room my thoughts never fly out of the window : you always concentrate my whole senses. The anxiety shown about our Loves in your last note is an immense pleasure to me : however you must not suffer such speculations to molest you any more : nor will I any more believe you can have the least pique against me. Brown is gone out— but here is Mrs. Wylie—when she is gone I shall be awake for you.—Remembrances to your Mother.

Your affectionate

J. KEATS

'Tis said that some have died for love :
And here and there a churchyard grave is found
In the cold North's unhallowed ground,—
Because the wretched man himself had slain,
His love was such a grievous pain.
And there is one whom I five years have known ;
He dwells alone
Upon Helvellyn's side :
He loved—the pretty Barbara died,
And thus he makes his moan :
Three years had Barbara in her grave been laid
When thus his moan he made—

" Oh, move, thou cottage, from behind that oak !
Or let the aged tree uprooted lie,
That in some other way yon smoke
May mount into the sky !
The clouds pass on ; they from the heavens depart :
I look—the sky is empty space ;
I know not what I trace ;
But when I cease to look, my hand is on my heart.

" Oh ! what a weight is in these shades ! Ye leaves,
That murmur once so dear, when will it cease ?
Your sound my heart of rest bereaves,
It robs my heart of peace.
Thou thrush, that singest loud—and loud and free,
Into yon row of willows flit,
Upon that alder sit ;
Or sing another song, or choose another tree.

" Roll back, sweel rill ! back to thy mountain bounds,
And there for ever be thy waters chained !
For thou dost haunt the air with sounds

That cannot be sustained ;
If still beneath that pine-tree's ragged bough
Headlong yon waterfall must come,
Oh, let it then be dumb !—
Be anything, sweet rill, but that which thou art now.

" Thou eglantine, so bright with sunny showers,
Proud as a rainbow spanning half the vale,
Thou one fair shrub, oh ! shed thy flowers,
And stir not in the gale.
For thus to see thee nodding in the air,—
To see thy arch thus stretch and bend,
Thus rise and thus descend,—
Disturbs me till the sight is more than I can bear."

The man who makes this feverish complaint
Is one of giant stature, who could dance
Equipped from head to foot in iron mail.
Ah gentle love ! if ever thought was thine
To store up kindred hours for me, thy face
Turn from me, gentle love ! nor let me walk
Within the sound of Emma's voice, nor know
Such happiness as I have known today.

WORDSWORTH

Sweet for a little even to fear, and sweet,
O love, to lay down fear at love's fair feet ;
Shall not some fiery memory of his breath
Lie sweet on lips that touch the lips of death ?
Yet leave me not ; yet, if thou wilt, be free ;
Love me no more, but love my love of thee.
Love where thou wilt, and live thy life ; and I,

One thing I can, and one love cannot—die.
Pass from me ; yet thine arms, thine eyes, thine
    hair,
Feed my desire and deaden my despair.
Yet once more ere time change us, ere my cheek
Whiten, ere hope be dumb or sorrow speak,
Yet once more ere thou hate me, one full kiss ;
Keep other hours for others, save me this.
Yea, and I will not (if it please thee) weep,
Lest thou be sad ; I will but sigh, and sleep.
Sweet, does death hurt ? thou canst not do me
    wrong :
I shall not lack thee, as I loved thee, long.
Hast thou not given me above all that live
Joy, and a little sorrow shalt not give ?
What even though fairer fingers of strange girls
Pass nestling through thy beautiful boy's curls
As mine did, or those curled lithe lips of thine
Meet theirs as these, all theirs come after mine ;
And though I were not, though I be not, best,
I have loved and love thee more than all the rest.
O love, O lover, loose or hold me fast,
I had thee first, whoever have thee last ;
Fairer or not, what need I know, what care ?
To thy fair bud my blossom once seemed fair.
Why am I fair at all before thee, why
At all desired ? seeing thou art fair, not I.
I shall be glad of thee, O fairest head,
Alive, alone, without thee, with thee, dead ;
I shall remember while the light lives yet,
And in the night-time I shall not forget.
Though (as thou wilt) thou leave me ere life leave,
I will not, for thy love I will not, grieve ;

Not as they use who love not more than I,
Who love not as I love thee though I die ;
And though thy lips, once mine, be oftener prest
To many another brow and balmier breast,
And sweeter arms, or sweeter to thy mind,
Lull thee or lure, more fond thou wilt not find.

SWINBURNE

Fain would I change that note
　To which fond love hath charm'd me
Long, long to sing by rote,
　Fancying that that harm'd me :
Yet when this thought doth come,
" Love is the perfect sum
　Of all delight,"
I have no other choice
Either for pen or voice
　To sing or write.

O Love, they wrong thee much
　That say thy sweet is bitter,
When thy ripe fruit is such
　As nothing can be sweeter.
Fair house of joy and bliss
Where truest pleasure is,
　I do adore thee ;
I know thee what thou art,
I serve thee with my heart,
　And fall before thee.

ANONYMOUS

" She will change," I cried,
" Into a withered crone "
The heart in my side,
That so still had lain,
In noble rage replied
And beat upon the bone :

" Uplift those eyes and throw
Those glances unafraid :
She would as bravely show
Did all the fabric fade ;
No withered crone I saw
Before the world was made."

Abashed by that report,
For the heart cannot lie,
I knelt in the dirt.
And all shall bend the knee
To my offended heart
Until it pardon me.

YEATS

There is none, O none but you,
    That from me estrange your sight,
Whom mine eyes affect to view
    Or chained ears hear with delight.

Other beauties others move,
    In you I all graces find ;
Such is the effect of love,
    To make them happy that are kind.

Women in frail beauty trust,
   Only seem you fair to me :
Yet prove truly kind and just,
   For that may not dissembled be.

Sweet, afford me then your sight,
   That, surveying all your looks,
Endless volumes I may write
   And fill the world with envied books :

Which when after-ages view,
   All shall wonder and despair,
Woman to find man so true,
   Or man a woman half so fair.

CAMPION

Sweetest love, I do not goe,
   For wearinesse of thee,
Nor in hope the world can show
   A fitter Love for mee ;
      But since that I
Must dye at last, 'tis best,
To use my selfe in jest
   Thus by fain'd deaths to dye ;

Yesternight the Sunne went hence,
   And yet is here to day,
He hath no desire nor sense,
   Nor halfe so short a way :
      Then feare not mee,
But beleeve that I shall make

Speedier journeyes, since I take
  More wings and spurres than hee.

O how feeble is mans power,
  That if good fortune fall,
Cannot adde another houre,
  Nor a lost houre recall !
    But come bad chance,
And wee joyne to'it our strength,
And wee teach it art and length,
  It selfe o'r us to'advance.

When thou sigh'st, thou sigh'st not winde,
  But sigh'st my soule away,
When thou weep'st, unkindly kinde,
  My lifes blood doth decay.
    It cannot bee
That thou lov'st mee, as thou say'st,
If in thine my life thou waste,
  That art the best of mee.

Let not thy divining heart
  Forethinke me any ill,
Destiny may take thy part,
  And may thy feares fulfill ;
    But thinke that wee
Are but turn'd aside to sleepe ;
They who one another keepe
  Alive, ne'r parted bee.

DONNE

268

We two will rise, and sit, and walk together,
Under the roof of blue Ionian weather,
And wander in the meadows, or ascend
The mossy mountains, where the blue heavens bend
With lightest winds, to touch their paramour ;
Or linger, where the pebble-paven shore,
Under the quick, faint kisses of the sea
Trembles and sparkles as with ecstasy,—
Possessing and possessed by all that is
Within that calm circumference of bliss,
And by each other, till to love and live
Be one :—or, at the noontide hour, arrive
Where some old cavern hoar seems yet to keep
The moonlight of the expired night asleep,
Through which the awakened day can never peep ;
A veil for our seclusion, close as night's,
Where secure sleep may kill thine innocent lights ;
Sleep, the fresh dew of languid love, the rain
Whose drops quench kisses till they burn again.
And we will talk, until thought's melody
Become too sweet for utterance, and it die
In words, to live again in looks, which dart
With thrilling tone into the voiceless heart,
Harmonizing silence without a sound.
Our breath shall intermix, our bosoms bound,
And our veins beat together ; and our lips
With other eloquence than words, eclipse
The soul that burns between them, and the wells
Which boil under our being's inmost cells,
The fountains of our deepest life, shall be
Confused in Passion's golden purity,
As mountain-springs under the morning sun.
We shall become the same, we shall be one

Spirit within two flames, oh ! wherefore two ?
One passion in twin-hearts, that grows and grew,
Till like two meteors of expanding flame,
Those spheres instinct with it become the same,
Touch, mingle, are transfigured ; ever still
Burning, yet ever inconsumable :
In one another's substance finding food,
Like flames too pure and light and unimbued
To nourish their bright lives with baser prey,
Which point to Heaven and cannot pass away :
One hope within two wills, one will beneath
Two overshadowing minds, one life, one death,
One Heaven, one Hell, one immortality,
And one annihilation. Woe is me !
The wingèd words on which my soul would pierce
Into the height of Love's rare Universe,
Are chains of lead around its flight of fire—
I pant, I sink, I tremble, I expire !

SHELLEY (from *Epipsychidion*)

Perchance she droops within the hollow gulf
Which the great wave of coming pleasure draws,
Not guessing the glad cause !
Ye Clouds that on your endless journey go,
Ye Winds that westward flow,
Thou heaving Sea
That heav'st 'twixt her and me,
Tell her I come ;
Then only sigh your pleasure, and be dumb ;
For the sweet secret of our either self
We know.

Tell her I come,
And let her heart be still'd.
One day's controlled hope, and then one more,
And on the third our lives shall be fulfill'd !
Yet all has been before :
Palm placed in palm, twin smiles, and words astray.
What other should we say ?
But shall I not, with ne'er a sign, perceive,
Whilst her sweet hands I hold,
The myriad threads and meshes manifold
Which Love shall round her weave :
The pulse in that vein making alien pause
And varying beats from this ;
Down each long finger felt, a differing strand
Of silvery welcome bland ;
And in her breezy palm
And silken wrist,
Beneath the touch of my like numerous bliss
Complexly kiss'd,
A diverse and distinguishable calm ?
What should we say !
It all has been before ;
And yet our lives shall now be first fulfill'd,
And into their summ'd sweetness fall distill'd
One sweet drop more ;
One sweet drop more, in absolute increase
Of unrelapsing peace.
  O, heaving Sea,
That heav'st as if for bliss of her and me,
And separatest not dear heart from heart,
Though each 'gainst other beats too far apart,
For yet awhile
Let it not seem that I behold her smile.

O, weary Love, O, folded to her breast,
Love in each moment years and years of rest,
Be calm, as being not.
Ye oceans of intolerable delight,
The blazing photosphere of central Night,
Be ye forgot.
Terror, thou swarthy Groom of Bride-bliss coy,
Let me not see thee toy.
O, Death, too tardy with thy hope intense
Of kisses close beyond conceit of sense ;
O, Life, too liberal, while to take her hand
Is more of hope than heart can understand ;
Perturb my golden patience not with joy,
Nor, through a wish, profane
The peace that should pertain
To him who does by her attraction move.
Has all not been before ?
One day's controlled hope, and one again,
And then the third, and ye shall have the rein,
O Life, Death, Terror, Love !
But soon let your unrestful rapture cease,
Ye flaming Ethers thin,
Condensing till the abiding sweetness win
One sweet drop more ;
One sweet drop more in measureless increase
Of honied peace.

COVENTRY PATMORE

Walking thus towards a pleasant Grove,
   What did, it seem'd, in new delight
   The pleasures of the time unite,
To give a triumph to their love,

They stay'd at last, and on the Grass
   Reposed so, as o'r his breast
   She bow'd her gracious head to rest,
Such a weight as no burden was.

When with a sweet, though troubled look,
   She first brake silence, saying, Dear friend,
   O that our love might take no end,
Or never had beginning took!

I speak not this with a false heart,
   (Wherewith his hand she gently strain'd)
   Or that would change a love maintain'd
With so much faith on either part.

Nay, I protest, though Death with his
   Worst Counsel should divide us here,
   His terrors could not make me fear,
To come where your lov'd presence is.

Only if loves fire with the breath
   Of life be kindled, I doubt,
   With our last air 'twill be breath'd out,
And quenched with the cold of death.

Then with a look, it seem'd, deny'd
   All earthly pow'r but hers, yet so,
   As if to her breath he did ow
This borrow'd life, he thus repli'd;

O you, wherein, they say, Souls rest,
    Till they descend pure heavenly fires,
    Shall lustful and corrupt desires
With your immortal seed be blest?

And shall our Love, so far beyond
    That low and dying appetite,
    And which so chast desires unite,
Not hold in an eternal bond?

Is it, because we should decline,
    And wholly from our thoughts exclude
    Objects that may the sense delude,
And study only the Divine?

O no, Belov'd, I am most sure,
    Those vertuous habits we acquire,
    As being with the Soul intire,
Must with it evermore endure.

Else should our Souls in vain elect,
    And vainer yet were Heavens laws,
    When to an everlasting Cause
They gave a perishing Effect.

Nor here on earth then, nor above,
    Our good affection can impair,
    For where God doth admit the fair,
Think you that he excludeth Love?

These eyes again then, eyes shall see,
    And hands again these hands enfold,
    And all chast pleasures can be told
Shall with us everlasting be.

For if no use of sense remain
  When bodies once this life forsake,
  Or they could no delight partake,
Why should they ever rise again?

And if every imperfect mind
  Make love the end of knowledge here,
  How perfect will our love be, where
All imperfection is refin'd?

Let then no doubt, Celinda, touch,
  Much less your fairest mind invade,
  Were not our souls immortal made,
Our equal loves can make them such.

So when one wing can make no way,
  Two joyned can themselves dilate,
  So can two persons propagate,
When singly either would decay.

So when from hence we shall be gone,
  And be no more, nor you, nor I,
  As one anothers mystery,
Each shall be both, yet both but one.

This said, in her up-lifted face,
  Her eyes which did that beauty crown,
  Were like two stars, that having faln down,
Look up again to find their place:

While such a moveless silent peace
  Did seize on their becalmed sense,
  One would have thought some influence
Their ravish'd spirits did possess.

LORD HERBERT OF CHERBURY
(from *An Ode upon a Question Moved . . .*)

The hunchèd camels of the night
Trouble the bright
And silver waters of the moon.
The Maiden of the Morn will soon
Through Heaven stray and sing,
Star gathering.

Now while the dark about our loves is strewn,
Light of my dark, blood of my heart, O come !
And night will catch her breath up, and be dumb.

Leave thy father, leave thy mother,
And thy brother ;
Leave the black tents of thy tribe apart !
Am I not thy father and thy brother,
And thy mother ?
And thou—what needest with thy tribe's black
    tents
Who hast the red pavilion of my heart ?

FRANCIS THOMPSON

TO THE BODY

Creation's and Creator's crowning good ;
Wall of infinitude ;
Foundation of the sky,
In Heaven forecast
And long'd for from eternity,
Though laid the last ;
Reverberating dome,
Of music cunningly built home
Against the void and indolent disgrace

Of unresponsive space ;
Little, sequester'd pleasure-house
For God and for His Spouse ;
Elaborately, yea, past conceiving, fair,
Since, from the graced decorum of the hair,
Ev'n to the tingling, sweet
Soles of the simple, earth-confiding feet,
And from the inmost heart
Outwards unto the thin
Silk curtains of the skin,
Every least part
Astonish'd hears
And sweet replies to some like region of the
    spheres ;
Form'd for a dignity prophets but darkly name,
Lest shameless men cry " Shame ! '
So rich with wealth conceal'd
That Heaven and Hell fight chiefly for this field ;
Clinging to everything that pleases thee
With indefectible fidelity ;
Alas, so true
To all thy friendships that no grace
Thee from thy sin can wholly disembrace ;
Which thus 'bides with thee as the Jebusite,
That, maugre all God's promises could do,
The chosen People never conquer'd quite ;
Who therefore lived with them,
And that by formal truce and as of right,
In metropolitan Jerusalem.
For which false fealty
Thou needs must, for a season, lie
In the grave's arms, foul and unshriven,
Albeit, in Heaven,

Thy crimson-throbbing Glow
Into its old abode aye pants to go,
And does with envy see
Enoch, Elijah, and the Lady, she
Who left the roses in her body's lieu.
O, if the pleasures I have known in thee
But my poor faith's poor first-fruits be,
What quintessential, keen ethereal bliss
Then shall be his
Who has thy birth-time's consecrating dew
For death's sweet chrism retain'd,
Quick, tender, virginal, and unprofaned !

COVENTRY PATMORE

True Love in this differs from gold and clay,
That to divide is not to take away.
Love is like understanding, that grows bright,
Gazing on many truths ; 'tis like thy light,
Imagination ! which from earth and sky,
And from the depths of human fantasy,
As from a thousand prisms and mirrors, fills
The Universe with glorious beams, and kills
Error, the worm, with many a sun-like arrow
Of its reverberated lightning. Narrow
The heart that loves, the brain that contemplates,
The life that wears, the spirit that creates
One object, and one form, and builds thereby
A sepulchre for its eternity. . . .
If you divide suffering and dross, you may
Diminish till it is consumed away ;
If you divide pleasure and love and thought,
Each part exceeds the whole ; and we know not

How much, while any yet remains unshared,
Of pleasure may be gained, of sorrow spared.

SHELLEY (from *Epipsychidion*)

Imagination having been our theme,
So also hath that intellectual Love,
For they are each in each, and cannot stand
Dividually.—Here must thou be, O Man !
Power to thyself ; no Helper hast thou here ;
Here keepest thou in singleness thy state :
No other can divide with thee this work :
No secondary hand can intervene
To fashion this ability ; 'tis thine,
The prime and vital principle is thine
In the recesses of thy nature, far
From any reach of outward fellowship,
Else is not thine at all. But joy to him,
Oh, joy to him who here hath sown, hath laid
Here the foundation of his future years !
For all that friendship, all that love can do,
All that a darling countenance can look
Or dear voice utter, to complete the man,
Perfect him, made imperfect in himself,
All shall be his : and he whose soul hath risen
Up to the height of feeling intellect
Shall want no humbler tenderness ; his heart
Be tender as a nursing mother's heart ;
Of female softness shall his life be full,
Of humble cares and delicate desires,
Mild interests and gentlest sympathies.

WORDSWORTH (from *The Prelude*)

279

There is nothing can please a man without love, and if a man be weary of the wise discourses of the Apostles, and of the innocency of an even and a private fortune, or hates peace or a fruitfull year, he hath reaped thorns and thistles from the choicest flowers of Paradise. *For nothing can sweeten felicity it self, but love ;* but when a man dwels in love, then the brests of his wife are pleasant as the droppings upon the hill of Hermon, her eyes are fair as the light of heaven, she is a fountain sealed, and he can quench his thirst, and ease his cares, and lay his sorrows downe upon her lap, and can retire home as to his sanctuary and refectory, and his gardens of sweetnesse and chast refreshments. No man can tell but he that loves his children, how many delicious accents make a mans heart dance in the pretty conversation of those dear pledges ; their childishnesse, their stammering, their little angers, their innocence, their imperfections, their necessities, are so many little emanations of joy and comfort to him that delights in their persons and society. But he that loves not his wife and children, feeds a Lionesse at home and broods a nest of sorrowes ; and blessing it self cannot make him happy ; so that all the commandments of God injoining a man to *love his wife,* are nothing but so many necessities and capacities of joy. *She that is lov'd is safe, and he that loves is joyfull.* Love is a union of all things excellent ; it contains in it proportion and satisfaction, and rest, and confidence.

JEREMY TAYLOR (from *Sermons*)

Let our love be firm, constant, and inseparable, not coming and returning like the tide, but descending like a never-failing river, ever running into the Ocean of Divine excellency, passing on in the chanels of duty and a constant obedience, and never ceasing to be what it is till it comes to be what it desires to be ; still being a river till it be turned into sea and vastness, even the immensity of a blessed Eternity.

JEREMY TAYLOR (from *Holy Living*)

Ev'n like two little bank-dividing brooks,
   That wash the pebbles with their wanton streams,
And having rang'd and search'd a thousand nooks,
   Meet both at length in silver-breasted Thames,
     Where in a greater current they conjoin :
So I my Best-Beloved's am ; so He is mine.

Ev'n so we met ; and after long pursuit,
   Ev'n so we joined ; we both became entire ;
No need for either to renew a suit,
   For I was flax, and He was flames of fire :
     Our firm-united souls did more than twine ;
So I my Best-Beloved's am ; so He is mine.

If all those glittering Monarchs, that command
   The servile quarters of this earthly ball,
Should tender in exchange their shares of land,
   I would not change my fortunes for them all :
     Their wealth is but a counter to my coin :
The world's but theirs ; but my Beloved's mine.

QUARLES

If I speak with the tongues of men and of angels, but have not love, I am become sounding brass or a clanging cymbal. And if I have the gift of prophecy, and know all mysteries and all knowledge ; and if I have all faith, so as to move mountains, but have not love, I am nothing. And if I bestow all my goods to feed the poor, and if I give my body to be burned, but have not love, it profiteth me nothing. Love suffereth long, and is kind ; love envieth not ; love vaunteth not itself, is not puffed up, doth not behave itself unseemly, seeketh not its own, is not provoked, taketh not account of evil ; rejoiceth not in unrighteousness, but rejoiceth with the truth : beareth all things, believeth all things, hopeth all things, endureth all things. Love never faileth : but whether there be prophecies, they shall be done away ; whether there be tongues, they shall cease ; whether there be knowledge, it shall be done away. For we know in part, and we prophesy in part ; but when that which is perfect is come, that which is in part shall be done away. When I was a child, I spake as a child, I felt as a child, I thought as a child : now that I am become a man, I have put away childish things. For now we see in a mirror, darkly : but then face to face : now I know in part ; but then shall I know even as also I have been known. But now abideth faith, hope, love, these three ; and the greatest of these is love.

ST. PAUL (I *Corinthians* xiii)

Very great is Love, a great good above all good. It maketh easy every load, and suffereth evenly all this is uneven. For it beareth burdens without burden and maketh sweet and savoury all that is bitter. . .

282

Love flieth aloft and will not be held back by lowly matters. Love longeth to be free and to be estranged from all earthly affection, lest its inner longing be hindered, lest it be shackled by any temporal comfort or sink beneath any temporal distress.

Nothing is sweeter than Love, nothing stronger, nothing higher, nothing broader, nothing more pleasant, nothing better nor more full in earth or heaven ; because Love is born of God, nor can it find rest beyond all things created save in God.

Love flieth, runneth, and rejoiceth : it is free and cannot be held.

It giveth all for all things and holdeth all in all things, because it resteth in one supreme thing above all things, from which every good floweth and proceedeth.

It respecteth not gifts, but turneth itself, above all goods, to the giver.

Often Love knoweth no limit, flaming like fire above every limit.

Love feeleth no burden, reckoneth no labours, desireth above its strength, considereth nought impossible, because it holdeth all things to be lawful and possible unto itself.

Therefore it is strong unto all things, and undertaketh and fulfilleth many things, where he that loveth not fainteth and is laid low.

Love keepeth watch and sleeping sleepeth not. In weariness it is not weary, in oppression not oppressed, in terrors it is not perturbed. But as a living flame and a burning torch it leapeth aloft and winneth unto safety.

If any loveth, he knoweth what this voice calleth.

A great cry in the ears of God is this burning affection of the spirit, which saith : My God thou art my Love :

thou art all mine and I am all thine. Enlarge me in love, that I may learn to taste with the inner mouth of the heart how sweet it is to love and to be melted and to swim in love.

Let me be possessed by Love, and lifted out of myself in the fervour of ecstasy.

I will sing the song of Love, I will follow thee, my Beloved, on high : my soul shall grow faint in thy praise, exulting in love.

I will love thee more than myself, loving myself only in thee, and, in thee, all who truly love thee, even as the Law of Love, which shineth forth from thee, commandeth.

Love is swift, sincere, dutiful, jocund and pleasant ; strong, patient, faithful, prudent, long-suffering, and brave. Love seeketh not its own. For where any seeketh his own, there he falleth from Love.

Love is circumspect, humble, and right ; not soft nor light nor following after vain things : sober, chaste, constant and quiet, keeping watch upon all its affections.

Love is submissive and obedient to authority, holdeth itself cheap, is devout and thankful unto God, trusting and hoping always in him, yea, even when God is not a sweet savour unto it ; because no man liveth in love without sorrow.

He who is not ready to suffer all things and to hold himself at the will of the Beloved, is not worthy to be called a Lover. For the Lover must embrace all hard and bitter things for the sake of the Beloved, nor ever be turned away from him by any evil chance.

THOMAS À KEMPIS
(from *The Imitation of Christ*)

284

Love in the fountain and Love in the stream are both the same. And therefore they are both equal in Time and Glory. For love communicateth itself : and therefore love in the fountain is the very love communicated to its object. Love in the fountain is love in the stream, and love in the stream equally glorious with love in the fountain. Though it streameth to its object it abideth in the lover, and is the love of the lover.

   .   .   .   .   .   .

You are as prone to love, as the sun is to shine ; it being the most delightful and natural employment of the Soul of Man : without which you are dark and miserable. Consider then the extent of Love, its vigour and excellency, For certainly he that delights not in Love makes vain the universe, and is of necessity to himself the greatest burden. The whole world ministers to you as the theatre of your Love. It sustains you and all objects that you may continue to love them. Without which it were better for you to have no being. Life without objects is sensible emptiness, and that is a greater misery than Death or Nothing. Objects without Love are a delusion of life. The Objects of Love are its greatest treasures : and without Love it is impossible they should be treasures. For the Objects which we love are the pleasing Objects, and delightful things. And whatsoever is not pleasing and delightful to you can be no treasure : nay it is distasteful, and worse than nothing, since we had rather it should have no being.

That violence wherewith sometimes a man doteth upon one creature, is but a little spark of that love, even towards all, which lurketh in his nature. We are made to love, both to satisfy the necessity of our active nature, and to answer the beauties in every creature. By Love our Souls are married and solder'd to the creatures : and it is our duty like God to be united to them all, We must love them infinitely, but in God, and for God : and God in them : namely all His excellencies manifested in them. When we dote upon the perfections and beauties of some one creature, we do not love that too much, but other things too little. Never was anything in this world loved too much, but many things have been loved in a false way : and all in too short a measure.

Suppose a river, or a drop of water, an apple or a sand, an ear of corn, or an herb : God knoweth infinite excellencies in it more than we : He seeth how it relateth to angels and men ; how it proceedeth from the most perfect Lover to the most perfect Beloved ; how it representeth all His attributes ; how it conduceth in its place, by the best of means to the best of ends : and for this cause it cannot be beloved too much. God the Author and God the End are to be beloved in it ; Angels and men are to be beloved in it ; and it is highly to be esteemed for all their sakes. O what a treasure is every sand when truly understood ! Who can love anything that God made too much ? What a world would this be, were everything beloved as it ought to be !

Suppose a curious and fair woman. Some have seen the beauties of Heaven in such a person. It is a vain thing to say they loved too much. I dare say there are ten thousand beauties in that creature which they have not seen. They loved it not too much, but upon false causes. Nor so much upon false ones, as only upon some little ones. They love a creature for sparkling eyes and curled hair, lily breasts and ruddy cheeks : which they should love moreover for being God's Image, Queen of the Universe, beloved by Angels, redeemed by Jesus Christ, an heiress of Heaven, and temple of the Holy Ghost : a mine and fountain of all virtues, a treasury of graces, and a child of God. But these excellencies are unknown. They love her perhaps, but do not love God more : nor men as much : nor Heaven and Earth at all. And so, being defective to other things, perish by a seeming excess to that. We should be all Life and Mettle and Vigour and Love to every-thing ; and that would poise us. I dare confidently say that every person in the whole world ought to be beloved as much as this : And she if there be any cause of difference more than she is. But God being beloved infinitely more, will be infinitely more our joy, and our heart will be more with Him, so that no man can be in danger by loving others too much, that loveth God as he ought.

TRAHERNE (from *Centuries of Meditations*)

If yet I have not all thy love,
    Deare, I shall never have it all,
I cannot breathe one other sigh, to move,
    Nor can intreat one other teare to fall,
And all my treasure, which should purchase thee,
Sighs, teares, and oathes, and letters I have spent.
    Yet no more can be due to mee,
    Than at the bargaine made was ment,
If then thy gift of love were partiall,
That some to mee, some should to others fall,
    Deare, I shall never have Thee All.

Or if then thou gavest mee all,
    All was but All, which thou hadst then ;

287

But if in thy heart, since, there be or shall
New love created bee, by other men,
Which have thier stocks intire, and can in teares,
In sighs, in oathes, and letters outbid mee,
This new love may beget new feares,
For this love was not vowed by thee.
And yet it was, thy gift being generall,
The ground, thy heart, is mine, what ever shall
   Grow there, deare, I should have it all.

Yet I would not have all yet,
Hee that hath all can have no more,
And since my love doth every day admit
New growth, thou shouldst have new rewards in
   store ;
Thou canst not every day give me thy heart,
If thou canst give it, then thou never gavest it :
Loves riddles are, that though thy heart depart,
It stayes at home, and thou with losing savest it :
But wee will have a way more liberall,
Than changing hearts, to joyne them, so wee shall
   Be one, and one anothers All.

DONNE

. . . When men contract friendships, they inclose the
Commons ; and what Nature intended should be every
mans, we make proper to two or three. Friendship is like
rivers and the strand of the seas, and the ayre, common
to all the world ; but Tyrants, and evil customes, warrs,
and want of love have made them proper and peculiar.

JEREMY TAYLOR (from Friendship)

And they also say that there was a certain self-denying and ascetic brother who wished to go to the city to sell his handiwork, and to buy the things which he needed ; and he called a brother, and said unto him, " Come with me, and let us go and return together." And when they had gone as far as the gate of the city, the man of abstinence said unto his companion, " Sit down here, O my brother, and wait for me while I go in and perform my business ; and I will return speedily." And having gone into the city, and wandered round about in the streets, a certain rich woman tried her blandishments upon him, and he stripped off his monk's garb and took her to wife. Then he sent a message to his companion, saying, " Arise, get thee to thy cell, for I can never see thee again." Now the man who had been sent to him with this message related unto him the whole matter, even as it had happened, and he said to the messenger, " God forbid that such things should be spoken about my holy brethren, and God forbid that I should depart from this place until my brother cometh, according to his word to me." And having tarried there a long time, and ceasing not from weeping and pray- ing either by night or by day, the report of him was heard throughout the city, and the clergy, and the monks, and the governors of the city entreated him to depart to his monastery, but he would not hearken unto their supplica- tion, and he said, " I cannot trangress my brother's com- mand, and I cannot leave this place until we go back together to the monastery." So he stayed there for seven years, being burned by heat in the summer, and dried up by the cold and ice in the winter, and with hunger, and thirst, and weeping, and watching, he made supplication on behalf of his brother. Then at length one day his former companion came unto him, dressed in costly garments, and said unto him, " O So-and-So, I am he who was with thee the monk So-and-so; arise, get thee gone to thy monastery "; and the brother looked at him and said, " Thou art not, for he was a monk, and thou art a man in the world." Then God looked upon the trouble of that brother, and at the end of seven years the woman died, and the brother who had married her repented, and again put on the garb of the monk, and went out to his companion; and when he saw him, he rose up, and embraced and kissed him, and he took him with gladness, and they went forth to the monastery. Then that brother renewed his former ascetic works, and he was worthy of the highest grade of perfection. Thus by the patience of one man the other lived, and the saying, " A brother is helped by his brother, even as a city is helped by its fortress," was fulfilled.

PALLADIUS

(from *The Paradise of the Fathers*—
Trans. E. A. WALLIS BUDGE)

If Love dwelt not in Trouble it could have nothing to love. But its substance which it loves, namely the poor soul, being in trouble and pain, it hath thence cause to love this its own substance and to deliver it from pain, that so itself may be it be again beloved. Neither could any one know what Love is, if there were no Hatred; or what friendship is, if there were no foe to contend with. Or, in one word, if Love had not something which it might love, and manifest the virtue and power of love in working out deliverance to the Beloved from all pain and trouble.

Love is higher than the Highest. Love is greater than the Greatest. Yes, it is *in a certain sense* greater than God ; while yet, in the highest sense of all, God is Love, and Love is God. Love being the highest principle is the virtue of all virtues ; from whence they flow forth. Love, being the greatest Majesty, is the Power of all Powers, from whence they severally operate. And it is the Holy Magical Root, a Ghostly Power from whence all the wonders of God have been wrought by the hands of his elect servants, in all their generations successively. Whoever finds it, finds *Nothing* and *All Things*.

Love is the principal cause of all created beings, both spiritual and corporeal, by virtue whereof the second causes do move and act occasionally, according to certain Eternal Laws, from the beginning implanted in the very constitution of things thus originated. The virtue which is in Love is the very life and energy of all the principles of Nature, superior and inferior. It reaches to all Worlds, and to all manner of beings in them contained, they being the workmanship of Divine Love, and is the *first mover* and *first movable*, both in heaven above, and in the earth beneath, and in the water under the earth.

JACOB BOEHME (Trans. WILLIAM LAW)

By love subsists
All lasting grandeur, by pervading love ;
That gone, we are as dust.—Behold the fields
In balmy spring-time full of rising flowers
And joyous creatures ; see that pair, the lamb

And the lamb's mother, and their tender ways
Shall touch thee to the heart ; thou callest this love,
And not inaptly so, for love it is,
Far as it carries thee. In some green bower
Rest, and be not alone, but have thou there
The One who is thy choice of all the world :
There linger, listening, gazing with delight
Impassioned, but delight how pitiable !
Unless this love by a still higher love
Be hallowed, love that breathes not without awe ;
Love that adores, but on the knees of prayer,
By heaven inspired ; that frees from chains the soul
Lifted, in union with the purest, best,
Of earth-born passions, on the wings of praise
Bearing a tribute to the Almighty's Throne.

WORDSWORTH (from *The Prelude*)

§V MUSIC AND MUSICIANS

SOME SAYINGS ABOUT MUSIC

The excellence of Music is to be measured by pleasure. But the pleasure must not be that of chance persons ; the fairest music is that which delights the best and best educated, and especially that which delights the one man who is pre-eminent in virtue and education.

When a man surrenders himself to music and flute-playing and suffers his soul to be flooded through the funnel of his ears with those sweet and soft and plaintive harmonies . . . and spends his whole life in warbling and delighting himself with song, such a man at the outset tempers like steel whatever portion of the spirited element he possesses, and makes it useful, instead of brittle and useless. If, however, he relaxes not in his devotion, but yields to the enchantment, he then begins to liquefy and waste away, till the spirit is melted out of him and the sinews of his soul are extirpated and he is made " a feeble wielder of the lance."

PLATO (from *The Republic*)

I believe that wine itself, though a man be guilty of habitual intoxication, does not more debauch and befool the natural understanding than music—always music, music in season and out of season—weakens and destroys the spiritual discernment.

COWPER (from *The Letters*)

Some to church repair,
Not for the doctrine, but the music there.

POPE

Some Fathers went so far as to esteem the love of music a sign of predestination, as a thing divine, and reserved for the felicities of Heaven itself.

SIR WILLIAM TEMPLE

An ordinary fiddler makes better music for a shilling than a gentleman will do after spending forty.

PEPYS

To know whether you are enjoying a piece of music or not you must see whether you find yourself looking at the advertisements of Pears' soap at the end of the programme.

SAMUEL BUTLER

Away! Away, Music! Thou speakest to me of things which in all my endless life I have not found, and shall not find.

JEAN PAUL RICHTER

One, being asked to go hear a man who exactly counterfeited the voice of a nightingale, answered, " Sir, I have heard the nightingale itself."

PLUTARCH

The nightingale does not sing well.

JEAN COCTEAU

It is the province of painting to describe. Poetry, too, can esteem itself happy in that respect, in comparison with music : its domain is not so limited as mine. On the other hand, mine spreads further into other regions and it is not so easy to attain my empire.

BEETHOVEN

Music is the most modern of all arts : it began as the simple exponent of joy and sorrow (major and minor). The uneducated can scarcely believe that it has the power of expressing particular passions ; therefore it is difficult for them to understand the more individual masters, such as Beethoven and Schubert. We have learned to express the finer shades of feeling by penetrating more deeply into the mysteries of harmony.

SCHUMANN

Reader, be you professional or amateur, do not look for a profound intention in my pieces. To my mind there is no other rule in music worthy of a man of genius than to please that sense to which music appeals.

DOMENICO SCARLATTI

Some music is above me ; most music is beneath me. I like Beethoven and Mozart—or else some of the aërial compositions of the elder Italians, as Palestrina and Carissimi—And I love Purcell. . .

Good music never tires me, nor sends me to sleep. I feel physically refreshed and strengthened by it, as Milton says he did.

In this country there is no general reverence for the fine arts ; and the sordid spirit of a money-amassing philosophy would meet any proposition for the fostering of art, in a genial and extended sense, with the commercial maxim,—*Laissez faire*. Paganini, indeed, will make a fortune, because he can actually sell the tones of his fiddle at so much a scrape ; but Mozart himself might have languished in a garret for anything that would have been done for him here.

COLERIDGE (from *Table Talk*)

MUSIC IN POETRY

This folk, of which I telle you so,
Upon a carole wenten tho.
A lady caroled hem, that highte
Gladnesse, the blisful, the lighte ;
Wel coude she singe and lustily,
Non half so wel and semely.
And make in song swich refreininge,
It sat hir wonder wel to singe.
Hir vois ful cleer was and ful swete.
She was nought rude ne unmete,
But couthe y-now of swich doing
As longeth unto caroling :
For she was wont in every place
To singen first, folk to solace ;
For singing most she gaf hir to ;
No craft had she so leef to do.
    Tho mightest thou caroles seen,
And folk ther daunce and mery been,

And make many a fair tourning
Upon the grene gras springing.
Ther mightest thou see these floutours,
Minstrales, and eek jogelours,
That wel to singe dide hir peyne.
Somme songe songes of Loreyne ;
For in Loreyne hir notes be
Ful swetter than in this contree.

CHAUCER (from *The Romaunt of the Rose*)

Ther herde I pleyen on an harpe
That souned bothe wel and sharpe,
Orpheus ful craftely,
And on his syde, faste by,
Sat the harper Orion,
And Eacides Chiron,
And other harpers many oon,
And the Bret Glascurion ;
And smale harpers with her glees
Seten under hem in sees,
And gonne on hem upward to gape,
And countrefete hem as an ape,
Or as craft countrefeteth kinde.
    Thou saugh I stonden hem behinde,
A-fer from hem, al by hemselve,
Many thousand tymes twelve,
That maden loude menstralcyes
In cornemuse, and shalmyes,
And many other maner pype,
That craftely begunne pype

Bothe in doucet and in rede,
That ben at festes with the brede ;
And many floute and lilting-horne,
And pypes made of grene corne,
As han thise litel herde-gromes,
That kepen bestes in the bromes.

Ther saugh I than Atiteris,
And of Athenes dan Pseustis,
And Marcia that lost her skin,
Bothe in face, body, and chin,
For that she wolde envyen, lo !
To pypen bet then Apollo.
Ther saugh I famous, olde and yonge,
Pypers of the Duche tonge,
To lerne love-daunces, springes,
Reyes, and these straunge thinges.

Tho saugh I in another place
Stonden in a large space,
Of hem that maken blody soun
In trumpe, beme, and clarioun ;
For in fight and blood-shedinge
Is used gladly clarioninge.

Ther herde I trumpen Messenus,
Of whom that speketh Virgilius.
Ther herde I Joab trumpe also,
Theodomas, and other mo ;
And alle that used clarioñ
In Cataloigne and Aragon,
That in hir tyme famous were
To lerne, saugh I trumpe there.

Ther saugh I sitte in other sees,
Pleyinge upon sondry glees,
Whiche that I cannot nevene,
Mo then sterres been in hevene,

Of whiche I nil as now not ryme,
For ese of yow, and losse of tyme :
For tyme y-lost, this knowen ye,
By no way may recovered be.

CHAUCER (from *The Hous of Fame*)

If music be the food of love, play on ;
Give me excess of it, that, surfeiting,
The appetite may sicken, and so die.
That strain again ! it had a dying fall :
O ! it came o'er my ear like the sweet sound
That breathes upon a bank of violets,
Stealing and giving odour. Enough ! no more :
'Tis not so sweet now as it was before.

SHAKESPEARE (from *Twelfth Night*)

Or sweetest Shakespear fancies childe,
Warble his native wood-notes wilde,
And ever against eating Cares
Lap me in soft Lydian Aires,
Married to immortal verse
Such as the meeting soul may pierce
In notes, with many a winding bout
Of lincked sweetness long drawn out,
With wanton heed, and giddy cunning,
The melting voice through mazes running ;
Untwisting all the chains that ty
The hidden soul of harmony.

MILTON (from *L'Allegro*)

Can any mortal mixture of Earths mould
Breathe such divine inchanting ravishment ?
Sure somthing holy lodges in that brest,
And with these raptures moves the vocal air
To testifie his hidd'n residence ;
How sweetly did they float upon the wings
Of silence, through the empty-vaulted night
At every fall smoothing the Raven doune
Of darknes till it smil'd : I have oft heard
My mother Circe with the Sirens three,
Amid'st the flowry-kirtl'd Naiades
Culling their potent hearbs, and baleful drugs,
Who as they sung, would take the prison'd soul,
And lap it in Elysium.

MILTON (from *Comus*)

There is sweet music here that softer falls
Than petals from blown roses on the grass,
Or night-dews on still waters between walls
Of shadowy granite, in a gleaming pass ;
Music that gentlier on the spirit lies,
Than tir'd eyelids upon tir'd eyes ;
Music that brings sweet sleep down from the bliss-
       ful skies.
Here are cool mosses deep,
And thro' the moss the ivies creep,
And in the stream the long-leaved flowers weep,
And from the craggy ledge the poppy hangs in
       sleep.

TENNYSON (from *The Lotus-Eaters*)

Let but thy voice engender with the string,
And Angels shall be born while thou dost sing.

HERRICK

Music, thou Queen of Heaven, Care-charming spell
That strik'st a stilnesse into hell :
Thou that tam'st Tygers, and fierce storms (that rise)
With thy soule-melting Lullabies :
Fall down, down, down, from those thy chiming
    spheres,
To charm our soules, as thou enchant'st our eares.

HERRICK

Many love music but for music's sake,
Many because her touches can awake
Thoughts that repose within the breast half-dead,
And rise to follow where she loves to lead.
What various feelings come from days gone by !
What tears from far-off sources dim the eye !
Few, when light fingers with sweet voices play
And melodies swell, pause, and melt away,
Mind how at every touch, at every tone,
A spark of life hath glisten'd and hath gone.

LANDOR

What though I lean o'er thee to scan
    The written music cramped and stiff ;—
'Tis dark to me, as hieroglyph
    On those weird bulks Egyptian.

But as from those, dumb now and strange,
A glory wanders on the earth,
Even so thy tones can call a birth
From these, to shake my soul with change.

O swift, as in melodious haste
Float o'er the keys thy fingers small ;
O soft, as is the rise and fall
Which stirs that shade within thy breast.

ROSSETTI

MUSIC IN ATLANTIS

We have also sound-houses, where we practise and
demonstrate all sounds, and their generation. We have
harmonies which you have not, of quarter-sounds, and
lesser slides of sounds. Divers instruments of music likewise to you unknown, some sweeter than any you have ;
together with bells and rings that are dainty and sweet.
We represent small sounds as great and deep ; likewise
great sounds, extenuate and sharp ; we make divers
tremblings and warblings of sounds, which in their
original are entire. . . We have also means to convey
sounds in trunks and pipes, in strange lines, and distances.

BACON (from *The New Atlantis*)

Musicke a sister to Poetry, next craveth your acquaintance (if your *Genius* be so disposed). I know there are many, who are *adeo* ἄμουσοι and of such disproportioned spirits, that they avoid her company. . . Never wise man (I thinke) questioned the lawfull use hereof, since it is an immediate gift of heaven, bestowed on man, whereby to praise and magnifie his Creator ; to solace him in the midst of so many sorrowes and cares, wherewith life is hourely beset. . .

The Physitians will tell you, that the exercise of Musicke is a great lengthener of the life, by stirring and reviving of the Spirits, holding a secret sympathy with them ; Besides, the exercise of singing openeth the breast and pipes ; it is an enemy to melancholly and dejection of the mind, which *S. Chrysostome* truely calleth, *The Divels Bath.* Yea, a curer of some diseases : in *Apuglia*, in *Italy*, and thereabouts, it is most certaine, that those who are stung with the *Tarantula*, are cured onely by Musicke. Beside the aforesaid benefit of singing, it is a most ready helpe for a bad pronunciation, and distinct speaking, which I have heard conformed by many great Divines : yea, I my selfe have knowne many Children to have bin holpen of their stammering in speech, onely by it.

Plato calleth it, *A divine and heavenly practice*, profitable for the seeking out of that which is good and honest.

Homer saith, Musitians are worthy of Honor, and regard of the whole world ; and we know, albeit *Lycurgus* imposed most streight and sharpe Lawes upon the *Lacedemonians*, yet he ever allowed them the exercise of Musicke.

Aristotle averreth Musicke to bee the onely disposer of

the mind to Vertue and Goodnesse; wherefore he reckoneth it among those foure principall exercises, wherein he would have children instructed.

Tully saith, there consisteth in the practice of singing and playing upon Instruments, great knowledge, and the most excellent instruction of the mind : and for the effect it worketh in the mind, he tearmeth it, *Stabilem Thesaurum, qui mores instituit, componitque, ac mollit irarum ardores, &c.* A lasting Treasure, which rectifieth and ordereth our manners, and allayeth the heat and fury of our anger, &c.

I might runne into an infinite Sea of the praise and use of so excellent an Art, but I onely shew it you with the finger, because I desire not that any Noble or Gentleman should (save at his private recreation and leisureable houres) proove a Master in the same, or neglect his more weighty imployments : though I avouch it a skill worthy the knowledge and exercise of the greatest Prince.

King *Henry* the eight could not onely sing his part sure, but of himselfe composed a Service of foure, five, and sixe parts ; as *Erasmus* in a certaine Epistle testifieth of his own knowledge. . .

I desire no more in you than to sing your part sure, and at the first sight, withall, to play the same upon your Violl, or the exercise of the Lute, privately to your selfe.

To deliver you my opinion, whom among other Authors you should imitate and allow for the best, there being so many equally good, is somewhat difficult ; yet as in the rest herein you shall have my opinion.

For Motets and Musicke of piety and devotion, as well for the honour of our Nation, as the merit of the man, I preferre above all other our *Phoenix, M. William Byrd,* whom in that kind, I know not whether any may equall,

I am sure none excell, even by the judgement of *France* and *Italy*, who are very sparing in the commendation of strangers, in regard of that conceipt they hold of themselves. His *Cantiones Sacrae*, as also his *Gradualia*, are meere Angelicall and Divine; and being of himselfe naturally disposed to Gravity and Piety, his veine is not so much for light Madrigals or Canzonets, yet his *Virginellae* and some others in his first Set, cannot be mended by the best *Italian* of them all.

HENRY PEACHAM
(from *The Compleat Gentleman*)

THE LUTE-PLAYER

... His hands sprightly as fire he flings,
And with a quavering coyness tastes the strings.
The sweet-lipp'd sisters, musically frighted,
Singing their fears, are fearfully delighted,
Trembling as when Apollo's golden hairs
Are fann'd and frizzled in the wanton airs
Of his own breath, which married to his lyre
Doth tune the spheres, and make Heaven's self look
      higher.
From this to that, from that to this he flies,
Feels Music's pulse in all her arteries;
Caught in a net which there Apollo spreads,
His fingers struggle with the vocal threads.
Following those little rills, he sinks into
A sea of Helicon; his hand does go
Those paths of sweetness which with nectar drop,
Softer than that which pants in Hebe's cup.

The humorous strings expound his learned touch
By various glosses ; now that seem to grutch
And murmur in a buzzing din, then gingle
In shrill-tongued accents, striving to be single.
Every smooth turn, every delicious stroke
Gives life to some new grace ; thus doth he invoke
Sweetness by all her names ; thus, bravely thus,
(Fraught with a fury so harmonious)
The Lute's light genius now does proudly rise,
Heaved on the surges of swollen rhapsodies,
Whose flourish (meteor-like) doth curl the air
With flash of high-born fancies ; here and there
Dancing in lofty measures, and anon
Creeps on the soft touch of a tender tone ;
Whose trembling murmurs melting in wild airs
Runs to and fro, complaining his sweet cares,
Because those precious mysteries that dwell
In Music's ravish'd soul he dares not tell,
But whisper to the world : thus do they vary
Each string his note, as if they meant to carry
Their Master's blest soul (snatch'd out at his ears
By a strong ecstasy) through all the spheres
Of Music's heaven ; and seat it there on high
In th'empyrean of pure harmony.
At length (after so long, so loud a strife
Of all the strings, still breathing the best life
Of blest variety, attending on
His fingers' fairest revolution,
In many a sweet rise, many as sweet a fall)
A full-mouthed diapason swallows all.

CRASHAW (from *Music's Dual*)

CHURCH-MUSICK

Sweetest of sweets, I thank you ; when displeasure
  Did through my body wound my kind,
You took me thence, and in your house of pleasure
  A dainty lodging me assign'd.

Now I in you without a body move,
  Rising and falling with your wings :
We both together sweetly live and love,
  Yet say sometimes, *God help poor Kings.*

Comfort, I'le die ; for if you post from me,
  Sure I shall do so, and much more :
But if I travel in your companie,
  You know the way to Heavens door.

GEORGE HERBERT

AT A SOLEMN MUSICK

Blest pair of Sirens, pledges of Heav'ns joy,
Sphear-born harmonious Sisters, Voice and Vers,
Wed your divine sounds, and mixt power employ
Dead things with inbreath'd sense able to pierce,
And to our high-rais'd phantasie present
That undisturbed Song of pure content,
Ay sung before the saphire-colour'd throne
To him that sits thereon
With Saintly shout and solemn Jubily,

Where the bright Seraphim in burning row
Their loud up-lifted Angel trumpets blow,
And the Cherubick host in thousand quires
Touch their immortal Harps of golden wires,
With those just Spirits that wear victorious Palms,
Hymns devout and holy Psalms
Singing everlastingly :
That we on Earth with undiscording voice
May rightly answer that melodious noise ;
As once we did, till disproportion'd sin
Jarr'd against natures chime, and with harsh din
Broke the fair musick that all creatures made
To their great Lord, whose love their motion
    sway'd
In perfect Diapason, whilst they stood
In first obedience, and their state of good.
O may we soon again renew that Song,
And keep in tune with Heav'n, till God ere long
To his celestial consort us unite
To live with him, and sing in endles morn of
    light.

MILTON

TO MR. H. LAWES, ON HIS AIRES

Harry, whose tuneful and well measur'd Song
First taught our English Musick how to span
Words with just note and accent, not to scan
With Midas Ears, committing short and long ;
Thy worth and skill exempts thee from the throng,

With praise enough for Envy to look wan;
To after age thou shalt be writ the man
That with smooth aire couldst humor best our
     tongue.
Thou honour'st Verse, and Verse must send her
     wing
To honour thee, the Priest of Phoebus Quire
That tun'st their happiest lines in Hymn, or Story.
Dante shall give Fame leave to set thee higher
Then his Casella, whom he woo'd to sing
Met in the milder shades of Purgatory.

                                              MILTON

A SONG FOR ST. CECILIA'S DAY

From harmony, from heavenly harmony,
     This universal frame began:
     When nature underneath a heap
          Of jarring atoms lay,
     And could not heave her head,
The tuneful voice was heard from high,
     "Arise, ye more than dead!"
Then cold, and hot, and moist, and dry,
     In order to their stations leap,
          And Music's power obey.
From harmony, from heavenly harmony,
     This universal frame began:
          From harmony to harmony
Through all the compass of the notes it ran,
The diapason closing full in Man.

What passion cannot Music raise and quell?
When Jubal struck the chorded shell,
His listening brethren stood around,
And, wondering, on their faces fell
To worship that celestial sound:
Less than a God they thought there could not
dwell
Within the hollow of that shell
That spoke so sweetly and so well.
What passion cannot Music raise and quell? . . .

The soft complaining flute,
In dying notes, discovers
The woes of hopeless lovers,
Whose dirge is whisper'd by the warbling lute.

Sharp violins proclaim
Their jealous pangs and desperation,
Fury, frantic indignation,
Depth of pains, and height of passion,
For the fair, disdainful dame.
But O, what art can teach,
What human voice can reach,
The sacred organ's praise?
Notes inspiring holy love,
Notes that wing their heavenly ways
To mend the choirs above.

Orpheus could lead the savage race;
And trees uprooted left their place,
Sequacious of the lyre;
But bright Cecilia raised the wonder higher:
When to her organ vocal breath was given,
An angel heard, and straight appear'd
Mistaking Earth for Heaven.

312

As from the power of sacred lays
       The spheres began to move,
And sung the great Creator's praise
       To all the Blest above ;
So when the last and dreadful hour
This crumbling pageant shall devour,
The trumpet shall be heard on high,
The dead shall live, the living die,
And Music shall untune the sky !

DRYDEN

MUSIC AND LOVE

How oft, when thou, my music, music play'st,
Upon that blessed wood whose motion sounds
With thy sweet fingers, when thou gently sway'st
The wiry concord that mine ear confounds,
Do I envy those jacks that nimble leap
To kiss the tender inward of thy hand,
Whilst my poor lips, which should that harvest reap,
At the wood's boldness by thee blushing stand !
To be so tickled, they would change their state
And situation with those dancing chips,
O'er whom they fingers walk with gentle gait,
Making dead wood more blest than living lips.
Since saucy jacks so happy are in this,
Give them thy fingers, me thy lips to kiss.

.   .   .   .   .   .

Music to hear, why hear'st thou music sadly ?
Sweets with sweets war not, joy delights in joy.
Why lov'st thou that which thou receiv'st not gladly,
Or else receiv'st with pleasure thine annoy ?

If the true concord of well tuned sounds,
By unions married, do offend thine ear
They do but sweetly chide thee, who confounds
In singleness the parts that thou shouldst bear.
Mark how one string, sweet husband to another,
Strikes each in each by mutual ordering;
Resembling sire and child and happy mother,
Who, all in one, one pleasing note do sing:
Whose speechless song, being many, seeming one,
Sings this to thee; " Thou single wilt prove none."

SHAKESPEARE

ON THE POWER OF SOUND

Thy functions are ethereal,
As if within thee dwelt a glancing mind,
Organs of vision! And a Spirit aerial
Informs the cell of Hearing, dark and blind;
Intricate labyrinth, more dread for thought
To enter than oracular cave;
Strict passage, through which sighs are brought,
And whispers for the heart, their slave;
And shrieks, that revel in abuse
Of shivering flesh; and warbled air,
Whose piercing sweetness can unloose
The chains of frenzy, or entice a smile
Into the ambush of despair;
Hosannas pealing down the long-drawn aisle,
And requiems answered by the pulse that beats
Devoutly, in life's last retreats!

Oblivion may not cover
All treasures hoarded by the miser, Time.
Orphean insight ! Truth's undaunted lover,
To the first leagues of tutored passion climb,
When Music deigned within this grosser sphere
Her subtle essence to unfold,
And voice and shell drew forth a tear
Softer than Nature's self could mould.
Yet strenuous was the infant Age :
Art, daring because souls could feel,
Stirred nowhere but an urgent equipage
Of rapt imagination sped her march
Through the realms of woe and weal :
Hell to the lyre bowed down ; the upper arch
Rejoiced that clamorous spell and magic verse
Her wan disasters could disperse.

.   .   .   .

The Gift to king Amphion
That walled a city with its melody
Was for belief no dream :—thy skill, Arion !
Could humanize the creatures of the sea,
Where men were monsters. A last grace he craves,
Leave for one chant ;—the dulcet sound
Steals from the deck o'er willing waves,
And listening dolphins gather round.
Self-cast, as with a desperate course,
'Mid that strange audience, he bestrides
A proud One docile as a managed horse ;
And singing, while the accordant hand
Sweeps his harp, the Master rides ;
So shall he touch at length a friendly strand,
And he, with his preserver, shine star-bright
In memory, through silent night.

. . . Ye wandering Utterances, has earth no scheme
No scale of moral music—to unite
Powers that survive but in the faintest dream
Of memory ?—O that ye might stoop to bear
Chains, such precious chains of sight
As laboured minstrelsies through ages wear !
O for a balance fit the truth to tell
Of the Unsubstantial, pondered well !

.   .   .   .

By one pervading spirit
Of tones and numbers all things are controlled,
As sages taught, where faith was found to merit
Initiation in that mystery old.
The heavens, whose aspect makes our minds as
      still
As they themselves appear to be,
Innumerable voices fill
With everlasting harmony ;
The towering headlands, crowned with mist,
Their feet among the billows, know
That Ocean is a mighty harmonist ;
Thy pinions, universal Air,
Ever waving to and fro,
Are delegates of harmony, and bear
Strains that support the Seasons in their round ;
Stern Winter loves a dirge-like sound.

.   .   .   .

Break forth into thanksgiving,
Ye banded instruments of wind and chords ;
Unite, to magnify the Ever-living,
Your inarticulate notes with the voice of words !

Nor hushed be service from the lowing mead,
Nor mute the forest hum of noon ;
Thou too be heard, lone eagle ! freed
From snowy peak and cloud, attune
Thy hungry barkings to the hymn
Of joy, that from her utmost walls
The six-days' Work by flaming Seraphim
Transmits to Heaven ! As Deep to Deep
Shouting through one valley calls,
All worlds, all natures, mood and measure keep
For praise and ceaseless gratulation, poured
Into the ear of God, their Lord !

   .   .   .   .   .   .

A Voice to Light gave Being ;
To Time, and Man his earth-born chronicler ;
A Voice shall finish doubt and dim fore-seeing,
And sweep away life's visionary stir ;
The trumpet (we, intoxicate with pride,
Arm at its blast for deadly wars)
To archangelic lips applied,
The grave shall open, quench the stars.
O Silence ! are Man's noisy years
No more than moments of thy life ?
Is Harmony, blest queen of smiles and tears,
With her smooth tones and discords just,
Tempered into rapturous strife,
Thy destined bond-slave ? No ! though earth be
    dust
And vanish, though the heavens dissolve, her stay
Is in the Word, that shall not pass away.

WORDSWORTH

By music, minds an equal temper know,
Nor swell too high, nor sink too low.
If in the breast tumultuous joys arise,
Music her soft, assuasive voice applies ;
Or when the soul is pressed with cares,
Exalts her in enlivening airs.

Music the fiercest grief can charm,
And fate's severest rage disarm :
Music can soften pain to ease,
And make despair and madness please :
Our joys below it can improve,
And antedate the bliss above.

POPE (from *Ode on St. Cecilia's Day*)

MEDICAL MUSIC

In the Philosophical Magazine for May, 1806, we find
that " several of the medical literati on the continent are
are present engaged in making enquiries and experiments
upon the *influence of music in the cure of diseases.*" The
learned Dusaux is said to lead the band of this new tribe
of *amateurs* and *cognoscenti.*

The subject excited my curiosity, though I since have
found that it is no new discovery.

There is a curious article in Dr. Burney's History of
Music, " On the medicinal Powers attributed to Music
by the Ancients," which he derived from the learned
labours of a modern physician, M. Burette, who doubtless
could play a tune to, as well as prescribe one to, his

patient. He conceives that music can relieve the pains of the sciatica ; and that independent of the greater or less skill of the musicians, by flattering the ear, and diverting the attention, and occasioning certain vibrations of the nerves, it can remove those obstructions which occasion this disorder. M. Burette, and many modern physicians and philosophers, have believed that music has the power of affecting the mind, and the whole nervous system, so as to give a temporary relief in certain diseases, and even a radical cure. De Mairan, Bianchini, and other respectable names, have pursued the same career. . . .

Music and the sounds of instruments, says the lively Vigneul de Marville, contribute to the health of the body and the mind ; they quicken the circulation of the blood, they dissipate vapours, and open the vessels, so that the action of perspiration is freer. He tells a story of a person of distinction, who assured him, that once being suddenly seized by violent illness, instead of a consultation of physicians, he immediately called a band of musicians ; and their violins played so well in his inside, that his bowels became perfectly in tune, and in a few hours were harmoniously becalmed.

ISAAC D'ISRAELI
(from *Curiosities of Literature*)

THE FUGUE

First you deliver your phrase
    —Nothing propound, that I see,
Fit in itself for much blame or much praise—
    Answered no less, where no answer needs be :
Off start the Two on their ways !

Straight must a Third interpose,
  Volunteer needlessly help—
In strikes a Fourth, a Fifth thrusts in his nose,
  So the cry's open, the kennel's a-yelp,
Argument's hot to the close !

One dissertates, he is candid—
  Two must discept,—has distinguished !
Three helps the couple, if ever yet man did :
    Four protests, Five makes a dart at the thing
      wished—
Back to One goes the case bandied !

One says his say with a difference—
  More of expounding, explaining !
All now is wrangle, abuse, and vociference—
    Now there's a truce, all's subdued, self-restraining
Five, though, stands out all the stiffer hence.

One is incisive, corrosive—
  Two retorts, nettled, curt, crepitant—
Three makes rejoinder, expansive, explosive—
    Four overbears them all, strident and strepitant—
Five . . . O Danaides, O Sieve !

Now, they ply axes and crowbars—
  Now, they prick pins at an issue
Fine as a skein of the casuist Escobar's
  Worked on the bone of a lie. To what issue ?
    Where is our gain at the Two-bars ?

Est fuga, volvitur rota!
   On we drift. Where looms the dim port?
One, Two, Three, Four, Five, contribute their
      quota—
   Something is gained, if one caught but the
      import—
Show it us, Hughes of Saxe-Gotha!

What with affirming, denying,
      Holding, riposting, subjoining,
All's like . . . it's like . . . for an instance I'm trying . . .
   There! See our roof, its gilt moulding and
      groining
Under those spider-webs lying!

So your fugue broadens and thickens,
   Greatens and deepens and lengthens,
Till one exclaims—" But where's music, the dickens?
   Blot ye the gold, while your spider-web
      strengthens,
Blacked to the stoutest of tickens? " . . .

Hughes! I advise *mea pœna*
   (Counterpoint glares like a Gorgon)
Bid One, Two, Three, Four, Five, clear the arena!
   Say the word, straight I unstop the Full-Organ,
Blare out the *mode Palestrina.*

BROWNING
(from *Master Hughes of Saxe-Gotha*)

Would that the structure brave, the manifold music I
    build,
  Bidding my organ obey, calling its keys to their
    work,
Claiming each slave of the sound, at a touch, as when
    Solomon willed
  Armies of angels that soar, legions of demons that
    lurk,
Man, brute, reptile, fly,—alien of end and of aim,
  Adverse, each from the other heaven-high, hell-deep
    removed,—
Should rush into sight at once as he named the ineffable
    Name,
  And pile him a palace straight, to pleasure the princess
    he loved !

Would it might tarry like his, the beautiful building of
    mine,
  This which my keys in a crowd pressed and importuned
    to raise !
Ah, one and all, how they helped, would dispart now and
    now combine,
  Zealous to hasten the work, heighten their master his
    praise !
And one would bury his brow with a blind plunge down
    to hell,
  Burrow awhile and build, broad on the roots of
    things,
Then up again swim into sight, having based me my
    palace well,
  Founded it, fearless of flame, flat on the nether springs.

And another would mount and march, like the excellent
    minion he was,
  Ay, another and yet another, one crowd but with many
    a crest,
Raising my rampired walls of gold as transparent as glass,
  Eager to do and die, yield each his place to the rest :
For higher still and higher (as a runner tips with fire,
  When a great illumination surprises a festal night—
Outlining round and round Rome's dome from space to
    spire)
  Up, the pinnacled glory reached, and the pride of my
    soul was in sight.

In sight ? Not half ! for it seemed, it was certain, to match
    man's birth,
  Nature in turn conceived, obeying an impulse as I ;
And the emulous heaven yearned down, made effort to
    reach the earth,
  As the earth had done her best, in my passion, to scale
    the sky :
Novel splendours burst forth, grew familiar and dwelt
    with mine,
  Not a point nor peak but found and fixed its wandering
    star ;
Meteor-moons, balls of blaze : and they did not pale nor
    pine,
  For earth had attained to heaven, there was no more
    near nor far.

Nay more ; for there wanted not who walked in the glare
    and glow,
  Presences plain in the place ; or, fresh from the
    Protoplast,

Furnished for ages to come, when a kindlier wind should
blow,
Lured now to begin and live, in a house to their liking
at last ;
Or else the wonderful Dead who have passed through the
body and gone,
But were back once more to breathe in an old world
worth their new :
What never had been, was now ; what was, as it shall be
anon ;
And what is,—shall I say, matched both ? for I was
made perfect too.

All through my keys that gave their sounds to a wish of
my soul,
All through my soul that praised as its wish flowed
visibly forth,
All through music and me ! For think, had I painted the
whole,
Why, there it had stood, to see, nor the process so
wonder-worth :
Had I written the same, made verse—still, effect proceeds
from cause,
Ye know why the forms are fair, ye hear how the tale is
told ;
It is all triumphant art, but art in obedience to laws,
Painter and poet are proud in the artist-list enrolled :—

But here is the finger of God, a flash of the will that
can,
Existent behind all laws, that made them and, lo, they
are !

And I know not if, save in this, such gift be allowed to
　　man,
　That out of three sounds he frame, not a fourth sound,
　　but a star,
Consider it well : each tone of our scale in itself is nought ;
　It is everywhere in the world—loud, soft, and all is said :
Give it to me to use ! I mix it with two in my thought :
　And, there ! Ye have heard and seen : consider and bow
　　the head !

BROWNING (from Abt Vogler)

ON A PIECE OF MUSIC

How all's to one thing wrought !
The members, how they sit !
O what a tune the thought
Must be that fancied it.

Nor angel insight can
Learn how the heart is hence :
Since all the make of man
Is law's indifference.

What makes the man and what
The man within that makes :
Ask whom he serves or not
Serves and what side he takes.

For good grows wild and wide,
Has shades, is nowhere none ;
But right must seek a side,
And choose for chieftain one.

Who built these walls made known
The music of his mind,
Yet here he had but shewn
His ruder-rounded rind.

Not free in this because
His powers seemed free to play :
He swept what scope he was
To sweep and must obey.

Though down his being's bent
Like air he changed in choice,
That was the instrument
Which overvaulted voice.

Therefore this masterhood,
This piece of perfect song,
This fault-not-found-with good,
Is neither right nor wrong.

No more than red and blue,
No more than Re and Mi,
Or sweet the golden glue
That's built for by the bee.

GERARD MANLEY HOPKINS

TO SILENCE

*" Space, the Bound of a Solid " : Silence, then, the
Form of a Melody*

Not, Silence, for thine idleness I raise
My silence-bounded singing in thy praise,
But for thy moulding of my Mozart's tune,
Thy hold upon the bird that sings the moon,
   Thy magisterial ways.

Man's lovely definite melody-shapes are thine,
Outlined, controlled, compressed, complete,
   divine.
Also thy fine intrusions do I trace,
Thy afterthoughts, thy wandering, thy grace,
   Within the poet's line.

Thy secret is the song that is to be.
Music had never stature but for thee,
Sculptor ! strong as the sculptor Space whose
   hand
Urged the Discobolus and bade him stand.

Man, on his way to Silence, stops to hear and see.

ALICE MEYNELL

TITLE AND PREFACE OF BYRD'S FIRST VOLUME OF MADRIGALS

Psalmes, Sonets & songs of Sadnes and pietie, made into Musicke of five parts ; whereof some of them going abroad among divers in untrue coppies are heere truely corrected, and th'other being Songs very rare and newly composed, are heere published, for the recreation of all such as delight in Musicke : by William Byrd, one of the Gent of the Queenes Maiesties honorable Chappell. Printed by Thomas East the assigne of W. Byrd, and are to be sold at the dwelling house of the said T. East, by Paules Wharfe. 1588 cum privilegio Regiae Maiestatis.

Reasons briefly set downe by th'auctor, to perswade every one to learne to sing.

First, it is a knowledge easely taught, and quickly learned, where there is a good Master, and an apt Scoller.

2. The exercise of singing is delightfull to Nature, & good to preserve the health of Man.

3. It doth strengthen all the parts of the brest, & doth open the pipes.

4. It is a singuler good remedie for a stutting & stamering in the speech.

5. It is the best meanes to procure a perfect pronunciation, & to make a good Orator.

6. It is the onely way to know where Nature hath bestowed the benefit of a good voyce : which guift is so rare, as there is not one among a thousand, that hath it : and in many, that excellent guift is lost, because they want Art to expresse Nature.

7. There is not any Musicke of Instruments whatsoever, comparable to that which is made of the voyces of Men, where the voyces are good, and the same well sorted and ordered.

8. The better the voyce is, the meeter it is to honour and serve God there-with : and the voyce of man is chiefly to be imployed to that ende.

Omnis spiritus laudet Dominum

Since singing is so good a thing,
I wish all men would learne to sing.

WILLIAM BYRD

A MUSICAL COMPETITION BETWEEN WILLIAM BYRD AND ALFONSO FERRABOSCO. *Circa* 1597

I would counsell you diligentlie to peruse those waies which my loving Maister (never without reverence to be named of the musicians) M. *Bird*, and M. *Alphonso* in a vertuous contention in love betwixt themselves, made upon the plainsong of *Miserere*, but a contention, as I saide, in love : which caused them strive every one to surmount another, without malice, envie or backbiting : but by great labour, studie, and paines, ech making other censure of that which they had done. Which contention of theirs (specially without envie) caused them both become excellent in that kind, and winne such a name, and gaine such credite, as will never perish so long as Musicke indureth. Therefore, there is no waie readier to cause you become perfect, than to contend with some one or other, not in malice (for so is your contention uppon passion, not for love of vertue) but in love shewing your adversarie your worke, and not skorning to bee corrected of him, and to amende your fault if hee speake with reason : but of this enough. To return to M. *Bird*, and M. *Alphonso*, though either of them made to the number of fortie waies and could have made infinite more at their pleasure, yet hath one manne, my friend and fellow M. *George Waterhouse*, upon the same plain-song of *Miserere*, for varietie surpassed all who ever laboured in that kinde of studie. For, hee hath alreadie made a thousand waies (yea and though I should talke of halfe as manie more, I should not be farre waide of the truth) every one different and severall from another.

THOMAS MORLEY
(from *Plaine & Easie Introduction to Practical Musick*)

BACH BEFORE THE CONSISTORY COURT, ARNSTADT

Joh. S. Bach, Organist of the New Church, summoned respecting his prolonged absence and the discontinuance of the part-singing, 1706.

Actum, de Feb. 21. 1706.

Bach, Organist of the New Church, is required to state where he has been of late for so long a time and from whom he obtained leave of absence.

BACH. That he had been to Lubeck in order to learn perfectly certain things in connection with his art, and that he beforehand asked permission of the Superintendent.

THE SUPERINTENDENT. That Bach had requested this permission for four weeks only, but that he had been absent for fully four times that period.

BACH. Trusted that the organ would be played during the period by the substitute supplied by him in a manner such as would call for no complaint.

THE CONSISTORY. Charge Bach with having introduced astonishing variations into the Chorales, and mingling therein various strange sounds, by which the congregation was confounded. If henceforward he desires to introduce a foreign key, he shall adhere to it and not immediately stray beyond it, or, as he has been accustomed to do, indulge in eccentric harmonies. It is, moreover, contrary to order that hitherto he has held no rehearsals because he is not able to keep control of the scholars. Therefore he is to state whether he is willing to accompany the scholars both in part-singing and chorales, since it is not possible to employ another Capellmeister ; and if he is not willing to do so, let him state the fact freely and categorically, in order that someone who is willing to undertake this may be appointed to the position.

BACH. He was willing to accompany once more, if a proper Conductor of the choir be appointed.

IT IS RESOLVED that Bach explain his behaviour within eight days ; and that the scholar Rambach be summoned and be reprimanded for the disorders which have hitherto occurred between the scholars and the Organist in the New Church.

RAMBACH. The Organist, Bach, was in the habit of playing too long preludes, yet after this was pointed out to him by the Superintendent he immediately flew to the other extreme and now makes them too short.

331

THE CONSISTORY. Accuse him of having visited a wine-shop during the course of the sermon last Sunday.

RAMBACH. Was very sorry and would refrain from doing so again: their Reverences had dealt with him severely concerning it already. The Organist had no cause to complain of him in the matter of the conducting, for that was not undertaken by him, but by the young Schmidt.

THE CONSISTORY. His behaviour shall be very different in the future, and much better, otherwise the remuneration destined for him will not be paid. If he has any complaint against the Organist he must make it to the proper authority and not take the law into his own hands, but conduct himself satisfactorily in accordance with his promise. The servants of the Court are hereby ordered to instruct the Rector that Rambach is to be confined on four consecutive days for two hours each day.

(Quoted in SPITTA'S *Life of Bach*)

HANDEL

Man praises man. Desert in arts or arms
Wins public honor ; and ten thousand sit
Patiently present at a sacred song,
Commemoration-mad ; content to hear
(Oh wonderful effect of music's power !)
Messiah's eulogy for Handel's sake.
But less, methinks, than sacrilege might serve—
(For was it less, what heathen would have dar'd
To strip Jove's statue of his oaken wreath,
And hang it up in honor of a man ?)

332

Much less might serve, when all that we design
Is but to gratify an itching ear,
And give the day to a musician's praise.
Remember Handel? Who that was not born
Deaf as the dead to harmony, forgets,
Or can, the more than Homer of his age?
Yes—we remember him; and while we praise
A talent so divine, remember too
That His most holy book from whom it came
Was never meant, was never us'd before,
To buckram out the mem'ry of a man.

COWPER (from *The Task*)

George Frederick Handel was 73 years of age when he died. He was large in person, and his natural corpulency, which increased as he advanced in life, rendered his whole appearance of that bulky proportion as to give rise to Quin's inelegant, but forcible expression, that his hands were feet and his fingers toes. From a sedentary life he had contracted a stiffness in his joints which, in addition to his great weight and weakness of body, rendered his gait awkward : still his countenance was open, manly and animated, expressive of all that grandeur and benevolence which were the prominent features of his character. In temper he was irascible, impatient of contradiction, but not vindictive ; jealous of his musical pre-eminence, and tenacious in all points which regarded his professional honour.

He was averse to all restraint on his freedom. Being informed at the Spa that the King of Prussia was expected, and purposed to be witness of his musical powers, to the great disappointment of that monarch he quitted the place some days before his arrival.

W. COXE

(from Anecdotes of G-F Handel and Smith)

Opera in London, 1711

As I was walking in the streets about a fortnight ago, I saw an ordinary fellow carrying a cage full of little birds upon his shoulder; and, as I was wondering with myself what use he would put them to, he was met very luckily by an acquaintance, who had the same curiosity. Upon his asking what he had upon his shoulder, he told him that he had been buying sparrows for the opera. " Sparrows for the opera," says his friend, licking his lips; " what, are they to be roasted? "—" No, no," says the other, " they are to enter towards the end of the first act, and to fly about the stage." . . . At the same time I made this discovery, I found by the discourse of the actors, that there were great designs on foot for the improvement of the opera; that it had been proposed to break down a part of the wall, and to surprise the audience with a party of an hundred horse, and that there was actually a project of bringing the New-river into the house, to be employed in jetteaus and water-works. This project, as I have since heard, has been postponed till the summer season; when it is thought the coolness that proceeds from fountains and cascades will be more acceptable and refreshing to people of quality. In the mean time, to find out a more agreeable entertainment for the winter-season, the opera of *Rinaldo* is filled with thunder and lightning, illuminations and fire-works; which the audience may look upon without catching cold, and indeed without much danger of being burnt; for there are several engines filled with water, and ready to play at a minute's warning, in case any such accident should happen. . . .

It is no wonder that those scenes should be very surprising, which were contrived by two poets of different nations, and raised by two magicians of different sexes. Armida (as we are told in the argument) was an Amazonian enchantress, and poor Signior Cassani (as we learn from the persons represented) a Christian conjuror (*Mago Christiano*). I must confess I am very much puzzled to find how an Amazon should be versed in the black art, or how a good Christian, for such is the part of the magician, should deal with the devil.

To consider the poet after the conjurors, I shall give you a taste of the Italian from the first lines of his preface: " *Eccoti, benigno lettore, un parto di poche sere, che se ben nato di notte, non è però aborto di tenebre, ma si farà conoscere figlio d'Apollo con qualche raggio di Parnasso.*" " Behold, gentle reader, the birth of a few evenings, which, though it be the offspring of night, is not the abortive of darkness, but will make itself known to be the son of Apollo, with a certain ray of Parnassus." He afterwards proceeds to call Mynheer Handel the Orpheus of our age, and to acquaint us in the same sublimity of style, that he composed this opera in a fortnight. . . . Before I dismiss this paper, I must inform my reader, that I hear there is a treaty on foot between London and Wise (who will be appointed gardeners of the playhouse) to furnish the opera of *Rinaldo and Armida* with an orange-grove ; and that the next time it is acted, the singing-birds will be personated by tom-tits, the undertakers being resolved to spare neither pains nor money for the gratification of the audience.

ADDISON

(from *The Spectator*, 6th March, 1710/11)

ON THE FEUD OVER HANDEL AND BONONCINI

Strange ! all this difference should be
'Twixt Tweedle-DUM and Tweedle-DEE !

SWIFT

MUSICAL RULES

Poets seem to me rather like trumpeters with their mechanical tricks. If we composers were to stick as faithfully to our rules (which were very good at a time when no one knew any better), we should compose music as worthless as their libretti.

MOZART

There is no rule that may not be broken in the interests of a greater beauty.

BEETHOVEN

The oldest man was the youngest ; the last comer is the oldest. How is it, then, that we accept as laws the rules of past centuries ?

SCHUMANN

Music resembles poetry, in each
Are nameless graces which no methods teach,
And which a master-hand alone can reach.
If, where the rules not far enough extend
(Since rules were made but to promote their end),
Some lucky licence answer to the full
The intent proposed, that licence is a rule.
Thus Pegasus, a nearer way to take,
May boldly deviate from the common track;
From vulgar bounds with brave disorder part,
And snatch a grace beyond the reach of art,
Which, without passing through the judgment,
    gains
The heart, and all its end at once attains.

POPE

There is no rule which I have not considered that
I ought freely to sacrifice for the sake of effect.

GLUCK

Beethoven's piano-playing was not correct and his
manner of fingering was often faulty: he neglected
quality of tone. But who could think of the performer?
One was absorbed by his thoughts as expressed by his
hands, however those hands expressed them.

BARON DE TRÉMONT, 1809

Executants are merely the more or less intelligent instruments whose business it is to reveal the form and intimate meaning of the work. Their despotism is ended:

The master remains the master: it is for him to command.

Sound and sonority are second to the idea.

The idea is second to feeling and passion.

BERLIOZ

Music, today in the full power of her youth, is emancipated, free.—Many ancient rules are no longer current. They were made by inaccurate observers or by humdrum minds for other humdrum minds. New needs of the mind, the heart, and the sense of hearing impose new attempts and even, in certain cases, the infraction of ancient laws.—Various forms are too worn to be still admissible.—Besides, *everything is good* or *everything is bad* according to the use one makes of it and the reason for that use. . . . Sound and sonority are of less importance than idea. Idea is of less importance than sentiment and passion.

BERLIOZ (from A Travers Chants)

SOME VIEWS ON OPERA

I sought to reduce the music to its true function, that of aiding the poetry, in order to reinforce the expression of feeling and the interest of situation without interrupting the action and chilling it by superfluous ornament. I considered that the music ought to add to the poetry what vivacity of colouring and a happy concord of light and shade add, by animating the figures without altering their contours, to a correct and well-composed design.

GLUCK

The music must reign supreme : all else must be forgotten. In an opera it is absolutely necessary that poetry should be the obedient daughter of music.

MOZART (from The Letters)

In conjunction with drama, or merely with the chanted word, the music should always be in direct affinity with the feeling expressed by the word, with the character of the singer's rôle, often with the accent and vocal inflections which one feels would be most natural to the spoken language. . . .

Consequently it is mere madness to write for a *Kyrie eleison* (the humblest prayer of the Catholic Church) phrases which might be mistaken for a party of drunkards at an inn table.

BERLIOZ

A HAYDN WORSHIPPER

Whoever studies music, let his daily bread be Haydn. Beethoven indeed is admirable, he is incomparable, but he has not the same usefulness as Haydn : he is not a necessity.

Haydn composed no masterpieces; his masterpiece does not exist. True ! for he is masterpiece throughout.

Haydn the great musician, the first who created everything, discovered everything, taught everything to the rest ! Is it that I am old ? Anyhow, it is to Haydn that I always return with pleasure and calm, as to bread, the food of which one never tires.

INGRES

THE DEATH OF MOZART. 1791

When Mozart was taken ill, not knowing how serious the attack was, we made him a padded dressing-gown, so that when he got up he might be well protected from the cold. We constantly went to see him : he seemed to be very pleased with the dressing-gown. I went to town every day to see him, and while I was there one Saturday Mozart said to me : " Tell your mother, dear Sophie, that I am going on very well and that I shall be able to pay her a visit during the octave of her name-day, to bring her my congratulations." How delighted I was to take such good news to my mother, news which she could hardly have expected. I hurried home to reassure her, for he really seemed to me better and more cheerful.

The following day was a Sunday. I was still young and, I must confess, vain and fond of gay clothes ; but I never liked to go on foot, dressed in my best, from the suburbs to the town. To drive was expensive ; so I said to my mother: " Mozart was so well yesterday, my dear Mother, that I shall not go to see him today. Today, no doubt, he is even better, and one day more or less can not make much difference." " Make me a cup of coffee," said my mother, " and I will tell you what to do." . . . I went into the kitchen. The fire was out so I lit a candle and made it up again ; but Mozart was never out of my thoughts. The coffee was ready and the light still burning. I fixed my eyes steadily on the candle and thought : " I want to know how Mozart is." As I thought this and gazed at the candle, it suddenly went out as completely as if it had never been lit. Not a spark lingered on the thick wick, and I am quite sure that there was nowhere the smallest draught. I could not help shuddering and I ran to my mother and told her about it. She said : " Get dressed at once and go to town. Bring me back word immediately how he is : be sure not to stay long."

I hurried to town as quickly as I could. To my horror, my sister, almost in despair yet struggling to control herself, rushed to meet me. " Thank God you have come, Sophie," she said. " He was so ill during the night that I hardly expected him to live till the morning. Stay with me today, I beg you, for if he has another attack he will die tonight. Go to him and see how he is." I composed myself as well as I could and went to his bedside. As soon as he saw me he said : " O, my dear Sophie, it is good that you have come. You must stay tonight ; you must see me die." I tried to control my feelings and to distract his thoughts, but to all I said he only replied : " I have the taste of death on my tongue, I smell the grave ; and who will comfort my Constanze if you dont stay ? " " Yes, dear Mozart, but first I must return to my mother to tell her you want me to stay with you today, or she will think some misfortune has happened." " Yes, do. But come back soon."

I was terribly distressed. My poor sister followed me to

the door and begged me for God's sake to go to the priests of St Peter's and ask one of them to call as if by chance. I did so, but they hesitated for some time and I had the greatest difficulty in persuading one of these unchristian fathers to do as I asked. I then went as quickly as I could to my mother, who was anxiously expecting me. By this time it was quite dark. My poor mother was terribly shocked. I persuaded her to go for the night to the late Mr Hofer's eldest daughter and then ran back as quick as I could to my inconsolable sister.

I found Sussmayr sitting by Mozart's bed. The famous Requiem was lying on the counterpane and Mozart was explaining to Sussmayr how he wished him to complete it after his death. . . . Closset, the doctor, was sought in vain and was at last found at the theatre ; but he waited till the end of the play. When he came, he ordered cold compresses for Mozart's burning head and this gave him such a shock that he died without recovering consciousness.

The last movement of his lips was an attempt to tell where the kettledrums should be used in his Requiem. I think I still hear the sound.

SOPHIE WEBER, 1825

ROUSSEAU ON RAMEAU

The sky is represented by certain bluish rags hung on rods or ropes like a washing-line. . . . The chariots of gods and goddesses consist of a framework of four timbers suspended, like a swing, from a stout rope : between these timbers is a cross-plank upon which the deity sits, and in front hangs a piece of daubed canvas which serves as a cloud for this magnificent chariot. . . . The stage is furnished with small trap-doors which open, as occasion demands, portending the emergence of demons from the cellarage. When it becomes necessary for them to rise into the air, their place is taken by stuffed demons of brown canvas, or occasionally by real chimney-sweeps, who swing in mid-air, suspended by ropes, until they lose themselves majestically in the rags of heaven. . . . But what I cannot begin to convey to you is the appalling shrieks and long bellowings that ring through the theatre. . . . And the incredible thing is that these howls are almost the only thing that the spectators applaud. From their clapping one would guess that they were one and all deaf and (entranced to catch, here and there, a few piercing notes) were urging the singers to redouble their efforts. Personally I am persuaded that people applaud the shrieks of an opera-singer precisely as they applaud the feats of an acrobat at a fair. While these are in progress they suffer acutely, but they are so relieved to see them end without mishap that they are only too ready to signify their joy. . . . To these delightful sounds the orchestra supplies a fitting accompaniment. Imagine a ceaseless babel of instruments, totally without melody, and, for a bass, a long-drawn, perpetual purr, the most lugubrious, the most devastating thing I ever heard in my life. I could never endure it for half an hour without a violent head-ache. All this produces a kind of psalmody in which, for the most part, there is neither tune nor rhythm. But when there does happen to emerge some sign of a lively air, then there is a universal stampede. You hear the whole audience in movement, pursuing painfully and with much stamping a single member of the orchestra. Entranced at catching for a moment this cadence, of which they catch so little, they strain ears, voice, arms, feet, their whole bodies, in an attempt to run after the beat which is always on the point of escaping them.

ROUSSEAU (from La Nouvelle Héloïse)

BEETHOVEN CONDUCTS

2nd January, 1814

Beethoven mounted the conductor's desk. The orchestra, which was well aware of his infirmity, was filled with an anxiety which was only too soon justified, for no sooner had the music begun than its composer began to present a bewildering spectacle. At the *piano* passages he lowered himself to a kneeling posture, at the *forte* he sprang up, so that his figure shrank now to the size of a dwarf and vanished under the desk, now towered above it like a giant, his hands and arms gesticulating as if the music had instantly galvanized them into immeasurable energy. At first this did not upset the performance : the vanishing and reappearance of his body synchronized with the shrinking and swelling of the music. But suddenly the great man got ahead of his orchestra and vanished at the *fortes* and rose up at the *pianos*. Disaster was imminent. At the critical moment Capellmeister Umlauf took up the baton and it was somehow conveyed to the orchestra that thenceforward he would direct. For a long time Beethoven was unconscious of the change : when at last he discovered it, his lips curled to a smile which, of all smiles I have been fated to see, I can only describe as " heavenly."

FRANZ WILD (quoted in THAYER'S Beethoven)

BEETHOVEN'S EROICA SYMPHONY. FIRST PUBLIC PERFORMANCE

'I'll give another kreutzer if they'll stop the thing."
Voice from the Gallery (reported by CZERNY)

. . . .

Beethoven's particular friends maintain that this symphony is his masterpiece, that its style is the genuine style of great music, and that if it is not appreciated at present it is because the public is not sufficiently cultured to grasp its sublimities. After a few thousand years it will produce its proper effect. Another party asserts that the work has no artistic value and finds in it an unbridled straining after originality which fails everywhere to achieve beauty or true power and grandeur. By uncouth modulations and abrupt transitions, by combining the most incongruous elements, as for example when a pastoral in the broadest style is burst into by the basses, three horns, and so on, a certain unfortunate singularity can be produced without much difficulty ; but genius is revealed not in the exceptional and fantastic, but in the beautiful and sublime. Beethoven himself has proved this in his earlier works. The third party, which is a very small one, holds the mean between the other two. It allows that the symphony has many beauties, but agrees that the cohesion is often completely broken and that the immoderate length of this longest and perhaps most difficult of symphonies tires even the connoisseurs and is intolerable to the mere music-lover. It expresses the wish that H.v.B. would use his admittedly great powers in providing works like his Symphonies in C and D, his attractive Septet in E flat, the intellectual Quintet in D and other of his early work which has given him a permanent place among the greatest instrumental composers. But it fears that, if Beethoven continues to follow his present path, both he and his public will suffer for it. . . . The public and Herr van Beethoven, who conducted, were not very pleased with each other this evening. The audience found the symphony too heavy and too long and considered Beethoven ill-mannered because he did not bow to the applause given by a portion of the audience.

(from a Newspaper Report, quoted by THAYER)

THE RASOUMOWSKY QUARTETS, Op. 59

Perhaps no work of Beethoven's met with a more discouraging reception from musicians, than these now famous Quartets. One friendly contemporary voice alone is heard—that of the " Allg. Mus. Zeit." Czerny told Jahn, that " when Schuppanzigh first played the Rasoumowsky Quartet in F, they laughed and were convinced that Beethoven was playing a joke and that it was not the quartet which had been promised." And when Gyrowetz bought these Quartets he said : " Pity to waste the money ! " The Allegretto vivace of the first of these quartets was long a rock of offence. " When at the beginning of the year 1812," says Lenz, " the movement was to be played for the first time in the musical circle of Field Marshal Count Soltikoff in Moscow, Bernhard Romberg trampled under foot as a contemptible mystification the bass part which he was to play. The Quartet was laid aside. When, a few years later, it was played at the house of Privy Councillor Lwoff, father of the famous violinist, in St. Petersburg, the company broke out in laughter

when the bass played his solo on *one* note.—The Quartet
was again laid aside."

Thomas Appleby, father of Samuel Appleby, collector
of valuable papers referring to the violinist Bridgetower,
was a leader in the musical world of Manchester, England,
and principal director of concerts there. When these
quartets came out in London, Clementi sent a copy of
them to him. They were opened and thrown upon the
pianoforte. Next day Felix Radicati and his wife, Mme
Bertinotti, called and presented letters, they being upon
a concert tour. During the conversation the Italian went
to the pianoforte, took up the quartets and seeing what
they were, exclaimed (in substance) : " Have you got
these here ! Ha ! Beethoven, as the world says, and as I
believe, is music-mad ;—for these are not music. He sub-
mitted them to me in manuscript and, at his request, I
fingered them for him. I said to him, that he surely did
not consider these works to be music ?—to which he
replied, ' Oh, they are not for you, but for a later age ! ' "

THAYER

BEETHOVEN'S METHOD

I carry my ideas about me for a long time, often a very
long time, before I commit them to writing. My memory
is so good that I never forget a theme that has once come
to me, even if it is a matter of years. I alter much, reject,
try again until I am satisfied. Then, in my head, the thing
develops in all directions, and, since I know precisely
what I want, the original idea never eludes me. It rises
before me, grows, I hear it, see it in all its size and exten-
sion, standing before me like a cast, and it only remains for

347

me to write it down, which is soon done when I can find the time, for sometimes I take up other work, though I never confuse that with the other. You will ask where I find my ideas. I hardly know. They come uninvited, directly or indirectly. I can almost grasp them with my hands in the open air, in the woods, while walking, in the stillness of the night, early in the morning, called up by moods which the poet translates into words, I into musical tones. They ring and roar and swirl about me until I write them down in notes.

SCHLOESSER reporting BEETHOVEN
(quoted by THAYER)

BEETHOVEN IMPROVISES

Beethoven was present and was asked to play. As usual he took an unconscionable deal of persuading and finally allowed two ladies to haul him to the piano. With obvious irritation he snatched a second violin part of the Pleyel quartet from a music stand, flung it on to the piano, and fell to inprovising. Never had he improvised with more brilliance, originality and splendour. But throughout his improvisation there ran, in the middle voices, like a thread or *cantus firmus*, the notes, insignificant in themselves, which he had found on the casually opened page of the quartet, and on this he built up the most daring melodies and harmonies in a dazzling concerto style. Old Pleyel could only kiss his hands in astonishment. After these improvisations Beethoven invariably burst into loud and amused laughter.

CZERNY (quoted by THAYER)

CHOPIN PLAYS SOME ÉTUDES (Book 2, Op. 25)

Imagine that an Æolian harp possessed all the scales, and that an artist's hand struck these with all kinds of fantastic, elegant embellishments, always making audible a deep fundamental tone and a softly flowing upper voice, and you will have some idea of his playing. No wonder that, hearing them thus played by himself, we were instantly charmed by the pieces, and most of all with the first, in A flat major, which was rather a poem than a study. But don't imagine that he allowed us to hear every small note of it. It was, rather, an undulation of the A flat major chord, brought out more loudly here and there by the pedal; but, exquisitely entangled in the harmony, we followed a wonderful melody in the sustained tones, while, in the middle, a tenor voice broke clearly from the chords and joined the principal melody. And when the étude was ended we felt as if we had seen a lovely shape in a dream and, half awake, strove to seize it again. But such things cannot be described : still less can they be fitly praised. Then he played the second in the book, in F minor, one in which his individuality displays itself in a manner never to be forgotten. How charming, how dreamy it was ; soft as the song of a sleeping child. The one in F major followed ; fine again, but less novel in character ; and here he showed his admirable powers of bravura. But how can all this be expressed in words ? They are all models of bold, indwelling creative force, truly poetic creations, and, though not without minor blemishes in detail, powerful and arresting as a whole.

SCHUMANN
(from *Music and Musicians*)

His appearance was so harmonious that it seemed to call for no comment. His blue eyes were humorous rather than dreamy; his smile was sweet and subtle, never sour. The subtility and transparence of his colouring attracted the eye, his fair hair was silky, the curve of his nose was expressively accentuated, his limbs were frail, he was not tall. His gestures were graceful and many; the tone of his voice was somewhat muted, often suppressed almost to a whisper. He had so distinguished an air and his manners displayed such perfect breeding that instinctively one treated him as an aristocrat. His whole appearance in fact made one think of the convolvulus that swings its exquisitely coloured cups, of a texture so delicate that the least touch will tear them, on stalks of an incredible fineness.

In company he had the equability of those who are care-free because they are distracted by no ulterior object. He was habitually cheerful; his caustic mind rapidly extracted the ridiculous from points far beneath the surface on which it appears to the average intelligence. In mimicry he displayed a spirited drollery which seemed to be inexhaustible. He enjoyed making comic improvisations in which he reproduced the musical formulas and particular mannerisms of certain virtuosos, aping their gestures and movements, and the expression of their faces with a dexterity that provided in a flash a comment on their whole personalities. At such times his features became unrecognizable, so extraordinary were the changes he produced in them. But even while imitating the ugly and grotesque, he never lost his native grace; even grimaces never succeeded in making him ugly. His gaiety was

the more pointed that he kept it within its limits with
perfect good taste.

LISZT (from *Life of Chopin*)

SCHUBERT'S SYMPHONIES DISCOVERED

Doubtless many a young musician has wandered, like
me (1838), to the Währinger Cemetery after the first few
days of excitement in Vienna, to lay a gift of flowers on
those graves, even if it were only a wild rosebush such as
I found planted on the grave of Beethoven. Franz Schubert's resting-place was undecorated. One ardent desire
of my life was fulfilled, and I gazed long on those sacred
graves, almost envying the man buried between them, a
certain Earl O'Donnell if I am not mistaken. . . . It had
never been possible for me to meet either of these two
whom I most venerate of modern artists ; but after this
visit to their graves I stood by the side of a man who
loved one of them most dearly—his own brother. On the
way home, I remembered that Schubert's brother Ferdinand, to whom he had been much attached, was still
living. I sought him out. He bore, I found, a strong
resemblance to the bust that stands beside Schubert's
grave ; shorter than Franz, but strongly built, with a face
that expressed honesty as well as musical ability. He knew
me from that veneration for his brother which I have so
often publicly expressed. He showed me and spoke to me
of many things . . . and finally he allowed me to see those
treasures of Schubert's composition which he still possesses. The sight of this hoard of riches thrilled me profoundly. Where was I to begin, where leave off ? Among

other things he directed my attention to the scores of several symphonies, many of which, never yet heard, are laid on the shelf, prejudged as too heavy and turgid. One must understand Vienna, with its peculiar circumstances as regards concerts and the difficulties in the way of bringing together the necessary materials for great performances, before one can forgive the city where Schubert lived and laboured that only his songs, seldom or never his great instrumental works, are brought before the public. Who knows how long the Symphony in C major might not have lain buried in dust and darkness, had I not immediately arranged with Ferdinand Schubert to send it at once to the Director of the Gewandhaus concerts in Leipzig, whose fine discrimination detects even the most timid of budding genius and could therefore not fail to appreciate the dazzling splendours of a past master. My hopes were fulfilled. The symphony went to Leipzig, was heard, understood, heard again, and received with almost universal admiration. . . . It would be impossible to understand whence Schubert had acquired this sparkling, sportive mastery of the orchestra if we did not know that this symphony was preceded by six others, and that it was written in the years of his ripest power (on the score is the date " March, 1828 : " Schubert died in November). . . . Thus my visit to those honoured graves which reminded me of a relative of one of those great dead men, brought me a double reward.

SCHUMANN
(from *Music and Musicians*)

352

When I arrived, an actor in tights was seated before an object intended to represent an anvil; he wore a wig and a false beard; his white, well cared-for hands were not in the least those of the manual worker; his free and easy manner, prominent belly and the noticeable absence of muscle at once betrayed the actor. With an unbelievable hammer he was striking, as no one ever yet struck, a sword equally fantastic. One guessed that he was a dwarf because he walked with his legs bent at the knee. He uttered a long cry, holding his mouth strangely open. The orchestra also emitted curious sounds, beginnings that came to nothing. Then another actor came on with a horn slung over his shoulder, leading a man on all fours disguised as a bear. He loosed the bear at the dwarf who rushed away, forgetting this time to bend his legs. The actor with the human face represented the hero Siegfried. For some time he uttered cries and the dwarf replied in a similar fashion. A pilgrim came on: this was the god Wotan. Wigged like the other, he planted himself, with his lance, in an absurd attitude and proceeded to relate to Mime what Mime already knew, but what had to be somehow conveyed to the public. Then Siegfried seized the fragments which where supposed to represent the remains of the sword, forged them, and sang: " Heaho, heaho, hoho ! Hoho, hoho, hoho, hoho ! Hoheo, haho, haheo, hoho ! " and that was the end of the first act. It was all so false, so stupid, that I had difficulty in sitting it out. But my friends implored me to stay, assuring me that the second act would be better.

The scene is a forest. Wotan rouses the dragon. At first the dragon says : " I want to sleep." Then he emerges

from the cave. The dragon is represented by two men
covered with a green hide with scales attached. At one
end of the hide they switch the tail, at the other they open
a crocodile mouth from which comes fire. The dragon,
whose job it is to terrify—and doubtless, with children
of five, he would succeed—pronounces certain words in
a bass voice. It is so silly, so puerile, that one is amazed
to see various big-wigs in the audience; and yet thousands of so called intelligent folk watch, listen and go into
ecstasies. Here comes Siegfried with his horn. In a pause
that is considered very beautiful, he lies down. Sometimes he keeps quiet, sometimes he talks to himself. He
wants to imitate the song of the birds. He cuts a reed with
his sword and makes a flute of it. But he plays the flute
badly and falls to blowing the horn. This scene is un-
bearable. Not the least trace of music. It was exasperating
to see, all round me, three thousand people listening
obediently to this absurdity and admiring it because they
thought they ought to. With a courageous effort I managed to stay for the following scene, Siegfried's struggle
with the dragon,—roars, fire, brandishings of the sword;
—but after that I could bear it no longer and rushed from
the theatre with a feeling of disgust which I have not yet
been able to shake off.

TOLSTOI (from *What is Art?*)

ON A WAGNER CONCERT

I prefer late Wagner, as I prefer late Turner, to early
(which I suppose is all wrong in taste), the idiosyncrasies
of each master being more strongly shown in these strains.

When a man not contented with the grounds of his success goes on and on, and tries to achieve the impossible, then he gets profoundly interesting to me. Today it was early Wagner for the most part : fine music, but not so particularly his—no spectacle of the inside of a brain at work like the inside of a hive.

THOMAS HARDY
(from FLORENCE HARDY'S Life of Thomas Hardy)

WAGNER TO LISZT

London. May 16, 1855.

Cordial thanks, dearest Franz, for your kind note, which I had been expecting a long time. The hope which you open to me of seeing you in September is my only light in the night of this sad year. I live here like one of the lost souls in hell. I never thought that I could sink again so low. The misery I feel in having to live in these disgusting surroundings is beyond description, and I now realize that it was a sin, a crime, to accept this invitation to London, which in the luckiest case must have led me far away from my real path. I need not expatiate to you upon my actual situation. It is the consistent outgrowth of the greatest inconsistency I ever committed. I am compelled to conduct an English concert programme right down to the end : that says everything. I have got into the middle of a slough of conventionalities and customs, in which I stick up to the ears, without being able to lead into it the least drop of pure water for my recreation. " Sir, we are not accustomed to this,"—that is the eternal echo

I hear. Neither can the orchestra recompense me. It consists almost exclusively of Englishmen, that is, clever machines which cannot be got into the right swing ; handicraft and business kill everything. Then there is the public, which, I am assured, is very favourably inclined towards me, but can never be got out of itself, which accepts the most emotional and the most tedious things without ever showing that it has received a real impression. And, in addition to this, the ridiculous Mendelssohn worship !

And even if all this were better than it is, what business have I with such concerts ? I am not fit for them. It is quite a different thing if I conduct one of Beethoven's symphonies before a few friends, but to be a regular concert conductor, before whom they place the scores of concert pieces, etc., so that he may beat time to them—that, I feel, is the deepest disgrace. This thoroughly inappropriate character of my position led me to the resolution of sending in my resignation after the fourth concert. But of course I was talked out of it, and especially my regard for my wife, who would have heard of this sudden resignation and of all that would have been written about it with great grief, determined me to hold out till the last concert. The infernal torture this is to me I cannot express. All my pleasure in my work is disappearing more and more. I had made up my mind to finish the score of the *Valkyrie* during the four months here, but that is out of the question. I shall not even finish the second act, in so terribly dispiriting a manner does this false position act upon me. In July I wanted to begin *Young Siegfried* at Seelisberg, on the lake of Lucerne, but now I think of delaying that beginning till next spring. This dislike of work is the worst feature of all. I feel as if with it eternal night were closing around me, for what have I to do in this world if I cannot do my work?

Palazzo Giustiniani, Venice. September 27, 1858.

. . . You will be pleased to hear that Venice has not disappointed my expectations. The melancholy silence of the Grand Canal, on the banks of which I live in a stately palace with large rooms, is sympathetic to me. Amusement and an agreeable diversion of the mind are afforded by a daily walk in the square of St Mark, a trip in a gondola to the islands, walks there, etc. It will be the turn of the art treasures later on. The entirely new and interesting character of the surroundings is very pleasant to me. I am waiting for my grand piano, and hope to resume my work without interruption next month. My only thought is of completing *Tristan*, nothing else.

Venice. October 19, 1858.

I have at last got my Erard. It stands in the large echoing hall which serves me as a study. There *Tristan* is to be finished this winter. The first act, dearest friend, is quite complete ; ask Hartels to give you the proof-sheets of the full score, which is already engraved. In the completion of the second act, which I have only slightly sketched, I am continually interrupted by visits. I have just begun working at it again ; it will be very beautiful, and is to be finished and printed by the end of this year at the latest. By March the last act will follow, and if all goes well I shall witness the first performance about Easter.

Venice. January 2, 1859.

Believe me implicitly when I tell you that the only

357

reason for my continuing to live is the irresistible impulse of creating a number of works of art which have their vital force in me. I recognize beyond all doubt that this act of creating and completing alone satisfies me and fills me with a desire of life, which otherwise I should not understand. I can, on the other hand, do quite well without any chance of a performance. I see clearly that before the completion of *Tristan* my amnesty would absolutely place me in an awkward position ; no expectation, not even that of producing *Lohengrin*, could induce me to leave my present place of abode before I had finished my work. From this you may guess at other things. Any offer of a secured and comfortable existence would be of no value to me if it were coupled with the condition of my accepting the amnesty, and of doing certain services made possible thereby. I cannot and shall not accept an appointment or anything resembling it. What I demand, on the other hand, is the settlement upon me of an honourable and large pension, solely for the purpose of creating my works of art undisturbed and without regard for external success.

Lucerne. May 8, 1859.

It is very well to say : " Get *Tristan* ready, and then we shall see." But how if I did not get *Tristan* ready because I could not get it ready ? I feel as if I should break down pantingly in sight of the goal. Once at least every day I look at my book with a right good will, but my head is waste, my heart empty, and I stare at the mists and the rain-clouds, which, ever since I have been here, have debarred me even from the chance of shaking up my stagnant blood by pleasant excursions. People say : " Go to work, then all will be right." Very well in its way, but I, poor devil, lack routine, and if ideas do not come to me of themselves, I cannot make them. A pleasant state of things this ! and what is worse, there is no chance of helping myself in any other way. All is shut and locked against me. Work alone is to help me, but who is to help me to the possibility of work ? I have evidently too little of what you have too much . . . The last act of this child of sorrow is now on the verge of the " to be or not to be ; " a slight pressure of some spring of the vulgar fate, at whose mercy I am, might kill this child at the very moment of its birth. Everything with me depends now on the turning of a hand ; there may be a way and there may be a complete stoppage, for I, my Franz, am in a bad way.

I have heard nothing for a long time of any of my friends : they probably think I am very happy in my dear Switzerland, in this splendid solitude, in the joy of composing, forgetful of all the world. I am not angry with them because they make themselves such illusions. If they only knew that I had to threaten violence in order to get out of you the *Dante* symphony dedicated to me, they might draw further conclusions from this fact. What do you say to that ? I have, after all, arrived at *Dante*, of which I did not wish to speak to-day, because I love it too much to involve it in my present mood. Let me tell you, however, that we had better keep the dedication, written in my copy, to ourselves. I at least shall not mention it to a soul. Your words have positively made me blush, you may believe me. I cannot tell you too often how miserably weak I feel as a musician. I know, in the depth of my heart, that I am an absolute blunderer. You ought to watch me when I am at it ; now thinking " it must do after all," then going to the piano to puzzle out some wretched rubbish, and giving it up again in a state of idiocy. O how I feel then ! how thoroughly persuaded of my musical wretchedness ! And then you come, whose pores are running over as with streams, fountains, cataracts, and say such words as those which you have said to me. I find it difficult to think that this is not the purest irony, and I must recall your friendship in order to believe that you have not been cutting a joke at my expense after all. This is a peculiar story, dearest friend : believe me, I am not up to much.

. . . .

TELEGRAM

Weimar, August 9. *To Richard Wagner, Hotel Schweizerhof, Lucerne.*

On the completion of *Tristan* the most cordial congratulations of your invariably faithful Franciscus.

(from *Wagner and Liszt Correspondence—*
Trans. HUEFFER)

§ VI ARCHITECTURE

A DREAM PALACE

But as I sleep, me mette I was
Within a temple y-mad of glas ;
In whiche ther were mo images
Of gold, stondinge in sondry stages,
And mo riche tabernacles,
And with perree[1] mo pinacles,
And mo curious portreytures,
And queynte maner of figures
Of olde werke, then I saw ever.
For certeynly, I niste never
Wher that I was, but wel wiste I,
Hit was of Venus redely,
The temple ; for, in portreyture,
I saw anoon-right hir figure
Naked fletinge in a see.

. . . .

Al was of stone of beryle,
Bothe castel and the tour,
And eek the halle, and every bour,
Withouten peces or joininges.
But many subtil compassinges,
Babewinnes[2] and pinacles,
Imageries and tabernacles,
I saw ; and ful eek of windowes,
As flakes falle in grete snowes.
And eek in ech of the pinacles
Weren sondry habitacles,
In whiche stoden, al withoute—
Ful the castel, al aboute—
Of alle maner of minstrales,

[1] precious stones.   [2] baboons, grotesques.

363

And gestiours, that tellen tales
Bothe of weping and of game,
Of al that longeth unto Fame.

. . . .

I gan forth romen til I fond
The castel-yate on my right hond,
Which that so wel corven was
That never swich another nas ;
And yit hit was by aventure
Y-wrought, as often as by cure.
Hit nedeth noght yow for to tellen,
To make yow to longe dwellen,
Of this yates florisshinges,
Ne of compasses, ne of kervinges,
Ne how they hatte in masoneries,
As, corbets fulle of imageries.
But, lord ! so fair hit was to shewe,
For hit was al with gold behewe.

CHAUCER (from *The Hous of Fame*)

SOLOMON'S TEMPLE

The house which King Solomon built for the Lord, the
length thereof was threescore cubits and the breadth
thereof twenty, and the height thereof thirty cubits. And
the porch before the holy place, twenty cubits was the
length thereof, according to the breadth of the house ; and
ten cubits was the breadth thereof before the house. And
for the house he made windows of fixed lattice-work. And
against the wall of the house he built stories round about,
against the walls of the house that was about both the

holy place and the Holy of Holies. And he made side-chambers round about. The nethermost story was five cubits broad, and the middle was six cubits broad, and the third was seven cubits broad ; for on the outside he made rebatements in the wall of the house, round about, that the beams should not have hold in the walls of the house.

And the house, when it was in building, was built of stone made ready at the quarry ; and there was neither hammer nor axe nor any tool of iron heard in the house, while it was in building. The door for the lowest side-chambers was in the right side of the house, and they went up by winding stairs into the middle chambers, and out of the middle into the third. So he built the house and finished it ; and he covered the house with beams and planks of cedar. And he built the stories against all the house, each five cubits high ; and they rested on the house with timber of cedar. . . .

So Solomon built the house and finished it. And he built the walls of the house within with boards of cedar. From the floor of the house unto the beams of the cieling he covered them on the inside with wood. And he covered the floor of the house with boards of cypress. And he built twenty cubits on the hinder part of the house with boards of cedar from the floor unto the beams : he even built them for it within, for the most holy place, even for the Holy of Holies. And the house, that is, the holy place before the Holy of Holies, was forty cubits long. And there was cedar on the house within, carved with gourds and open flowers. All was cedar : there was no stone seen.

And he prepared a Holy of Holies in the midst of the house within, to set there the ark of the covenant of the Lord. And within the Holy of Holies was a space of twenty cubits in length, and twenty cubits in breadth, and twenty cubits in the height thereof. And he overlaid it with pure gold and he covered the altar with cedar. So Solomon overlaid the house within with pure gold, and he drew chains of gold across before the Holy of Holies, and he overlaid it with gold. And the whole house he overlaid with gold until the house was finished. Also the whole altar that belonged to the Holy of Holies he overlaid with gold.

And in the Holy of Holies he made two cherubs of olive-wood, each ten cubits high. And five cubits was the one wing of the cherub, and five cubits the other wing of the cherub : from the uttermost part of the one wing unto the uttermost part of the other were ten cubits. Both the cherubs were of equal measure and one form. And he set the cherubs within the inner house ; and the wings of the cherubs were stretched forth, so that the wing of the one touched the one wall and the wing of the other cherub touched the other wall, and their wings touched one another in the midst of the house.

And he overlaid the cherubs with gold, and he carved all the walls of the house round about with carved figures of cherubs and palm-trees and open flowers, within and without. And the floor of the house he overlaid with gold, within and without. And for the entering of the Holy of Holies he made doors of olive-wood. The lintel and door-posts were a fifth part of the wall. So he made two doors of olive-wood, and he carved upon them carvings of cherubs and palm-trees and open flowers, and overlaid them with gold ; and he spread the gold upon the cherubs and upon the palm-trees.

So also made he for the entering of the holy place doors of olive-wood out of a fourth part of the wall, and two doors of cypress-wood. The two leaves of the one door were folding and the two leaves of the other door were folding. And he carved thereon cherubs and palm-trees and open flowers, and he overlaid them with gold fitted upon the graven work. And he built the inner court with three rows of hewn stone and a row of cedar beams.

In the fourth year was the foundation of the house of the Lord laid, and in the month Ziv. And in the eleventh year, in the month Bul, which is the eight month, was the house finished throughout all the parts thereof, and according to the fashion of it. So was he seven years in building it.

THE BIBLE (I *Kings* vi)

EGYPT

And where within the surface of the river
   The shadows of the massy temples lie,
And never are erased—but tremble ever
   Like things which every cloud can doom to die,
Through lotus-paven canals, and wheresoever
   The works of man pierced that serenest sky
With tombs, and towers, and fanes, 'twas her
   delight
To wander in the shadow of the night.

SHELLEY (from *The Witch of Atlas*)

GREECE

. . . The windless and crystalline pool,
Where ever lies, on unerasing waves,

The image of a temple, built above,
Distinct with column, arch, and architrave,
And palm-like capital, and overwrought,
And populous with most living imagery,
Praxitelean shapes, whose marbles smiles
Fill the hushed air with everlasting love.

SHELLEY (from *Prometheus Unbound*)

ATHENS

The nodding promontories and blue isles,
And cloud-like mountains, and dividuous waves
Of Greece, basked glorious in the open smiles
Of favouring Heaven : from their enchanted caves
Prophetic echoes flung dim melody.
  On the unapprehensive wild
    The vine, the corn, the olive mild,
Grew savage yet, to human use unreconciled ;
And, like unfolded flowers beneath the sea,
Like the man's thought dark in the infant's brain,
Like aught that is which wraps what is to be,
Art's deathless dreams lay veiled by many a vein
Of Parian stone ; and, yet a speechless child,
Verse murmured, and Philosophy did strain
Her lidless eyes for thee ; when o'er the Aegean main

Athens arose : a city such as vision
Builds from the purple crags and silver towers
Of battlemented cloud, as in derision
Of kingliest masonry : the ocean-floors
Pave it ; the evening sky pavilions it ;

Its portals are inhabited
By thunder-zonèd winds, each head
Within its cloudy wings with sun-fire garlanded,—
A divine work ! Athens, diviner yet,
Gleamed with its crest of columns, on the will
Of man, as on a mount of diamond, set ;
For thou[1] wert, and thine all-creative skill
Peopled, with forms that mock the eternal dead
In marble immortality, that hill
Which was thine earliest throne and latest oracle.

Within the surface of Time's fleeting river
Its wrinkled image lies, as then it lay
Immovably unquiet, and for ever
It trembles, but it cannot pass away.

SHELLEY (from *Ode to Liberty*)

THE RUINES OF ROME

Great Babylon her haughtie walls will praise,
And sharped steeples high shot up in ayre ;
Greece will the olde Ephesian buildings blaze,
And Nylus nurslings their Pyramides faire ;
The same yet vaunting Greece will tell the storie
Of Joves great Image in Olympus placed ;
Mausolus worke will be the Carians glorie ;
And Crete will boast the Labyrinth, now raced :
The antique Rhodian will likewise set forth
The great Colosse, erect to Memorie ;
And what els in the world is of like worth,

[1] i.e. Liberty.

Some greater learned wit will magnifie :
But I will sing above all moniments
Seven Romane Hils, the worlds Seven Wonder-
    ments.

Thou stranger, which for Rome in Rome here seekest,
And nought of Rome in Rome perceiv'st at all,
These same olde walls, old arches, which thou seest,
Olde Palaces, is that which Rome men call.
Beholde what wreake, what ruine, and what wast,
And how that she, which with her mightie powr
Tam'd all the world, has tam'd herselfe at last ;
The pray of time, which all things doth devowre !
Rome now of Rome is th' onely funerall,
And onely Rome of Rome hath victorie ;
Ne nought save Tyber hastning to his fall
Remaines of all. O worlds inconstancie !
    That which is firme doth flit and fall away,
    And that is flitting doth abide and stay.

Ye sacred ruines, and ye tragick sights,
Which onely doo the name of Rome retaine,
Olde moniments, which of so famous sprights
The honour yet in ashes doo maintaine ;
Triumphant Arcks, spyres, neighbours to the skie,
That you to see doth th'heaven it selfe appall ;
Alas ! by little ye to nothing flie,
The peoples fable, and the spoyle of all :
And though your frames do for a time make warre
Gainst time, yet time in time shall ruinate
Your workes and names, and your last reliques marre.
My sad desires, rest therefore moderate ;
    For if that time make ende of things so sure,
    It als will ende the pain which I endure.

Thou that at Rome astonisht does behold
The antique pride which menaced the skie,
These haughtie heapes, these palaces of olde,
These wals, these arcks, these baths, these temples
    hie ;
Judge, by these ample ruines vew, the rest
The which injurious time hath quite outworne,
Since of all workmen helde in reckning best ;
Yet these olde fragments are for paternes borne :
Then also marke how Rome, from day to day,
Repayring her decayed fashion,
Renewes herselfe with buildings rich and gay ;
That one would judge, that the Romaine Dæmon
  Doth yet himselfe with fatall hand enforce,
  Againe on foote to reare her pouldred corse.

All that which Aegypte whilome did devise,
All that which Greece their temples to embrave
After th' Ionicke, Atticke, Doricke guise ;
Or Corinth skil'd in curious workes to grave ;
All that Lysippus practike arte could forme,
Apelles wit, or Phidias his skill,
Was wont this auncient Citie to adorne,
And the heaven it selfe with her wide wonders fill.
All that which Athens ever brought forth wise ;
All that which Afrike ever brought forth strange ;
All that which Asie ever had of prise,
Was here to see. O mervelous great change !
  Rome, living, was the worlds sole ornament,
  And, dead, is now the worlds sole moniment.

SPENSER (from The Ruines of Rome)

THE BUILDING OF SAINT SOPHIA

The principal church, which was dedicated by the founder of Constantinople to Saint Sophia, or the eternal wisdom, had been twice destroyed by fire; after the exile of John Chrysostom, and during the *Nika* of the blue and green factions. No sooner did the tumult subside, than the Christian populace deplored their sacrilegious rashness; but they might have rejoiced in the calamity, had they foreseen the glory of the new temple, which at the end of forty days was strenuously undertaken by the piety of Justinian. The ruins were cleared away, a more spacious plan was described. . . . Athemius formed the design, and his genius directed the hands of ten thousand workmen, whose payment in pieces of fine silver was never delayed beyond the evening. The emperor himself, clad in a linen tunic, surveyed each day their rapid progress, and encouraged their diligence by his familiarity, his zeal, and his rewards. The new cathedral of St. Sophia was consecrated by the patriarch, five years, eleven months, and ten days from the first foundation; and in the midst of the solemn festival, Justinian exclaimed with devout vanity, " Glory be to God, who hath thought me worthy to accomplish so great a work; I have vanquished thee, O Solomon ! " But the pride of the Roman Solomon, before twenty years had elapsed, was humbled by an earthquake, which overthrew the eastern part of the dome. Its splendour was again restored by the perseverance of the same prince; and in the thirty-sixth year of his reign, Justinian celebrated the second dedication of a temple, which remains, after twelve centuries, a stately monument of his fame. . . . The eye of the spectator is disappointed by an irregular prospect of half-domes and

372

shelving roofs : the western front, the principal approach, is destitute of simplicity and magnificence : and the scale of dimensions has been much surpassed by several of the Latin cathedrals. But the architect who first erected an *aerial* cupola is entitled to the praise of bold design and skilful execution. The dome of St. Sophia, illuminated by four-and-twenty windows, is formed with so small a curve, that the depth is equal only to one-sixth of its diameter ; the measure of that diameter is one hundred and fifteen feet, and the lofty centre, where a crescent has supplanted the cross, rises to the perpendicular height of one hundred and eighty feet above the pavement. The circle which encompasses the dome lightly reposes on four strong arches, and their weight is firmly supported by four massy piles, whose strength is assisted on the northern and southern sides by four columns of Egyptian granite. A Greek cross, inscribed in a quadrangle, represents the form of the edifice. . . . The memory of past calamities inspired Justinian with a wise resolution, that no wood, except for the doors, should be admitted into the new edifice ; and the choice of the materials was applied to the strength, the lightness, or the splendour of the respective parts. The solid piles which sustained the cupola were composed of huge blocks of freestone, hewn into squares and triangles, fortified by circles of iron, and firmly cemented by the infusion of lead and quicklime ; but the weight of the cupola was diminished by the levity of its substance, which consists either of pumice-stone that floats in the water, or of bricks from the isle of Rhodes, five times less ponderous than the ordinary sort. The whole frame of the edifice was constructed of brick ; but those base materials were concealed by a crust of marble ; and the inside of St. Sophia, the cupola, the two larger, and the six smaller, semi-domes, the walls, the hundred columns, and the pavement, delight even the eyes of barbarians, with a rich and variegated picture. A poet, who beheld the primitive lustre of St. Sophia, enumerates the colours, the shades, and the spots of ten or twelve marbles, jaspers, and porphyries, which nature had profusely diversified, and which were blended and contrasted as it were by a skilful painter. The triumph of Christ was adorned with the last spoils of Paganism, but the greater part of these costly stones was extracted from the quarries of Asia Minor, the isles and continent of Greece, Egypt, Africa, and Gaul. Eight columns of porphyry, which Aurelian had placed in the temple of the sun, were offered by the piety of a Roman matron ; eight others of green marble were presented by the ambitious zeal of the magistrates of Ephesus : both are admirable by their size and beauty, but every order of architecture disclaims their fantastic capitals. A variety of ornaments and figures was curiously expressed in mosaic ; and the images of Christ, of the Virgin, of saints, and of angels, which have been defaced by Turkish fanaticism, were dangerously exposed to the superstition of the Greeks. According to the sanctity of each object, the precious metals were distributed in thin leaves or in solid masses. The balustrade of the choir, the capitals of the pillars, the ornaments of the doors and galleries, were of gilt bronze ; the spectator was dazzled by the glittering aspect of the cupola ; the sanctuary contained forty thousand pound weight of silver ; and the holy vases and vestments of the altar were of the purest gold, enriched with inestimable gems.

GIBBON

(from *The Decline and Fall of the Roman Empire*)

I stood in Venice, on the Bridge of Sighs ;
A Palace and a prison on each hand :
I saw from out the wave her structures rise
As from the stroke of the Enchanter's wand :
A thousand Years their cloudy wings expand
Around me, and a dying Glory smiles
O'er the far times, when many a subject land
Looked to the wingèd Lion's marble piles,
Where Venice sate in state, throned on her hundred
    isles !

She looks a sea Cybele, fresh from Ocean,
Rising with her tiara of proud towers
At airy distance, with majestic motion,
A Ruler of the waters and their powers :
And such she was ;—her daughters had their dowers
From spoils of nations, and the exhaustless East
Poured in her lap all gems in sparkling showers :
In purple was she robed, and of her feast
Monarchs partook, and deemed their dignity
    increased.

In Venice Tasso's echoes are no more,
And silent rows the songless Gondolier ;
Her palaces are crumbling to the shore,
And Music meets not always now the ear :
Those days are gone—but Beauty still is here
States fall—Arts fade—but Nature doth not die,
Nor yet forgets how Venice once was dear,
The pleasant place of all festivity,
The Revel of the earth—the Masque of Italy !

        BYRON (from *Childe Harold's Pilgrimage*)

THE INTERIOR OF ST. MARK'S, VENICE

There opens before us a vast cave, hewn out into the form of a Cross, and divided into shadowy aisles by many pillars. Round the domes of its roof the light enters only through narrow apertures like large stars ; and here and there a ray or two from some far-away casement wanders into the darkness, and casts a narrow phosphoric stream upon the waves of marble that heave and fall in a thousand colours along the floor. What else there is of light is from torches, or silver lamps, burning ceaselessly in the recesses of the chapels ; the roof sheeted with gold, and the polished walls covered with alabaster, give back at every curve and angle some feeble gleaming to the flames ; and the glories round the heads of the sculptured saints flash out upon us as we pass them, and sink again into the gloom. Under foot and over head, a continual succession of crowded imagery, one picture passing into another, as in a dream ; forms beautiful and terrible mixed together ; dragons and serpents, and ravening beasts of prey, and graceful birds that in the midst of them drink from running fountains and feed from vases of crystal ; the passions and pleasures of human life symbolized together, and the mystery of its redemption ; for the mazes of interwoven lines and changeful pictures lead always at last to the Cross, lifted and carved in every place and upon every stone ; sometimes with the serpent of eternity wrapt round it, sometimes with doves beneath its arms, and sweet herbage growing forth from its feet, but conspicuous most of all on the great rood that crosses the church before the altar, raised in bright blazonry against the shadow of the apse.

RUSKIN (from *Stones of Venice*)

SANTA MARIA DELLA SALUTE, VENICE

A searchlight was playing on the basin of St. Mark's and on the mouth of the Canal. Suddenly it caught the Church of the Salute ; and the whole vast building, from the Queen of Heaven on its topmost dome, down to the water's brim, the figures of Saints and Prophets and Apostles which crowd its steps and ledges, the white whorls, like huge sea-shells, that make its buttresses, the curves and volutes of its cornices and doorways, rushed upon the eye in a white and blinding splendour, making the very darkness out of which the vision sprang alive and rich. Not a Christian church, surely, but a palace of Poseidon ! The bewildered gazer saw naiads and bearded sea-gods in place of angels and saints, and must needs imagine the champing of Poseidon's horses at the marble steps, straining towards the sea.

MRS. HUMPHRY WARD
(from *The Marriage of William Ashe*)

THE BUILDING OF DURHAM

They fasted and prayed three dayes with greate reverence and devotion, desiringe to know by revelation what they should doe with the holie bodye of Saint Cuthbert ; which thinge was granted unto them, and therein they were directed to carrye him to Dunholme. . . . And theruppon with great joy and gladnesse brought his body to Dunholme, Anno Domini 999, which was inculta tellus a barbarous and rude place replenished with nothinge but thornes and thick woods save only in the midst where the Church now standeth which was plaine and commodious for such a purpose, where they first builded a little Church of wands and branches wherein they did lay his body . . . till they did build a more sumptuous church, wherein they might enshrine him, which they assayed to doe with all theire power, Uthred Earle of northumberland aidinge them . . . which gave great encouragement to Alwinus the Bishop to hasten the finishinge of his church, which accordingly he did, and then did translate St. Cuthberts body from the wanded church to the white Chapell (for so it was called) which hee had newly built, which was a part of the great church, which was not yett finished, where it lay 4 yeares, but after the great church was finished and consecrated uppon the 20th of september hee translated his bodye out of the white Chapell into the great Church which hee made a Cathedrall erectinge his Bishops sea at Duresme (where it still remaineth) about 377 yeares after it was first founded in the holy Iland by St Aidaine and St Oswald. . . . Which said Aldwinus Bishop died 23 yeares after he had founded his Bishops sea in Duresme, and finished his Cathedrall church in the yeare 1020. . . . But William Carlipho beinge not well content with the smalnesse and homelinesse of that buildinge did pull it all downe 76 yeares after Aldwinus had finished it : and in stead thereof did erect the magnificent and famous buildinge which is now to bee seene, Malcolme kinge of Scotts, Turgott then prior of the church, and himselfe lyinge the first 3 stones in the new foundation uppon the 30 day of July (as some say) or uppon the 11 of August (as others affirme) Anno Domi : 1093 ; and caused the monkes to labour in that holy worke all the daye longe excepting onely meale times and times of prayer.

Rites of Durham

CANTERBURY

In the year of grace one thousand one hundred and seventy four, by the just but occult judgment of God, the church of Christ at Canterbury was consumed by fire, in the forty-fourth year from its dedication, that glorious choir, to wit, which had been so magnificently completed by the care and industry of Prior Conrad.

Now the manner of the burning and repair was as follows. In the aforesaid year, on the nones of September, at about the ninth hour, and during an extraordinary violent south wind, a fire broke out before the gate of the church, and outside the walls of the monastery, by which three cottages were half destroyed. From thence, while the citizens were assembling and subduing the fire, cinders and sparks carried aloft by the high wind, were deposited upon the church, and being driven by the fury of the wind between the joints of the lead, remained there amongst the half rotten planks, and shortly glowing with increasing heat, set fire to the rotten rafters ; from these the fire was communicated to the larger beams and their braces, no one yet perceiving or helping. For the well-painted ceiling below, and the sheet-lead covering above, concealed between them the fire that had arisen within.

Meanwhile the three cottages, whence the mischief had arisen, being destroyed, and the popular excitement having subsided, everybody went home again, while the neglected church was consuming with internal fire unknown to all. But beams and braces burning, the flames rose to the slopes of the roof ; and the sheets of lead yielded to the increasing heat and began to melt. Thus the raging wind, finding a freer entrance, increased the fury of the fire ; and the flames beginning to show themselves, a cry arose in the church-yard : " See ! see ! the church is on fire."

Then the people and the monks assemble in haste, they draw water, they brandish their hatchets, they run up the stairs, full of eagerness to save the church, already, alas ! beyond their help. But when they reach the roof and perceive the black smoke and scorching flames that pervade it throughout, they abandon the attempt in despair, and thinking only of their own safety, make all haste to descend.

And now that the fire had loosened the beams from the pegs that bound them together, the half-burnt timbers fell into the choir below upon the seats of the monks ; the seats, consisting of a great mass of woodwork, caught fire, and thus the mischief grew worse and worse. And it was marvellous, though sad, to behold how that glorious choir itself fed and assisted the fire that was destroying it. For the flames multiplied by this mass of timber, and extending upwards full fifteen cubits, scorched and burnt the walls, and more especially injured the columns of the church. . . .

In this manner the house of God, hitherto delightful as a paradise of pleasures, was now made a despicable heap of ashes, reduced to a dreary wilderness, and laid open to all the injuries of the weather. And many, both of the laity and monks, would rather have laid down their lives than that the church should have so miserably perished.

Bethink thee now what mighty grief oppressed the hearts of the sons of the Church under this great tribulation ; I verily believe that the afflictions of Canterbury were no less than those of Jerusalem of old ; neither can mind conceive, or words express, or writing teach, their grief and anguish. Truly that they might alleviate their miseries with a little consolation, they put together as well as they could, an altar and station in the nave of the church, where they might wail and howl, rather than sing, the diurnal and nocturnal services. So the brethren remained in grief and sorrow for five years in the nave of the church, separated from the people only by a low wall.

Meanwhile the brotherhood sought counsel as to how and in what manner the burnt church might be repaired, but without success; for the columns of the church were exceedingly weakened by the heat of the fire, and were scaling in pieces and hardly able to stand.

French and English artificers were therefore summoned, but even these differed in opinion. On the one hand, some undertook to repair the aforesaid columns without mischief to the walls above. On the other hand, there were some who asserted that the whole church must be pulled down if the monks wished to exist in safety. This opinion, true as it was, excruciated the monks with grief, and no wonder, for how could they hope that so great a work should be completed in their days by any human ingenuity.

However, amongst other workmen there had come a certain William of Sens, a man active and ready, and as a workman most skilful both in wood and stone. Him, therefore, they retained and to him and to the providence of God was the execution of the work committed.

And he, residing many days with the monks and carefully surveying the burnt walls in their upper and lower parts, within and without, did yet for some time conceal

381

what he found necessary to be done, lest the truth should kill them in their present state of pusillanimity.

But he went on preparing all things that were needful for the work, either of himself or by the agency of others. And when he found that the monks began to be somewhat comforted, he ventured to confess that the pillars rent with the fire and all that they supported must be destroyed if the monks wished to have a safe and excellent building. At length they agreed, and consented patiently, if not willingly, to the destruction of the choir.

And now he addressed himself to procuring stone from beyond sea. He constructed ingenious machines for loading and unloading ships, and for drawing cement and stones. He delivered molds for shaping the stones to the sculptors who were assembled, and diligently prepared other things of the same kind. The choir thus condemned to destruction was pulled down and nothing else was done in this year.

In the following year, before the winter, he erected four pillars, that is, two on each side, and after the winter two more were placed, so that on each side were three in order, upon which and upon the exterior wall of the aisles he framed seemly arches and a vault, that is, three *claves* on each side. I put *clavis* for the whole *ciborium* because the *clavis* placed in the middle locks up and binds together the parts which converge to it from every side.

In the third year he placed two pillars on each side, the two extreme ones of which he decorated with marble columns placed around them, and because at that place the choir and crosses were to meet, he constituted these principal pillars. To which, having added the keystones and vault, he intermingled the lower triforium from the great tower to the aforesaid pillars, that is, as far as the cross, with many marble columns. Over which he adjusted another triforium of other materials, and also the upper windows. And in the next place, three *claves* of the great vault, from the tower, namely, as far as the crosses. All which things appeared to us and to all who saw them, incomparable and most worthy of praise. And at so glorious a beginning we rejoiced and conceived good hopes of the end, and provided for the acceleration of the work with diligence and spirit. Thus was the third year occupied and the beginning of the fourth.

In the summer of which, commencing from the cross, he erected ten pillars, that is, on each side five. Of which the two first were ornamented with marble columns to correspond with the other two principal ones. Upon these ten he placed the arches and vaults. And having, in the next place, completed on both sides the triforia and upper windows, he was, at the beginning of the fifth year, in the act of preparing with machines for the turning of the great vault, when suddenly the beams broke under his feet, and he fell to the ground, stones and timbers accompanying his fall, from the height of the capitals of the upper vault, that is to say, of fifty feet. Thus sorely bruised by the blows from the beams and stones, he was rendered helpless alike to himself and for the work.

The master, thus hurt, remained in bed for some time under medical care in expectation of recovering, but was deceived in this hope, for his health amended not. Nevertheless, as the winter approached, and it was necessary to finish the upper vault, he gave charge of the work to a certain ingenious and industrious monk, who was the overseer of the masons. But the master reclining in bed commanded all things that should be done in order.

And thus was completed the ciborium between the four principal pillars. In the key-stone of this ciborium the choir and crosses seem as it were to meet. Two ciboria on each side were formed before the winter, when heavy rains beginning stopped the work.

And the master, perceiving that he derived no benefit from the physicians, gave up the work, and crossing the sea, returned to his home in France. And another succeeded him in charge of the works; William by name, English by nation, small in body, but in workmanship of many kinds acute and honest.

(from GERVASE—Trans. R. WILLIS: abbreviated)

SAINT HUGH AT LINCOLN. *c*. A.D. 1190

With wondrous art he built the fabric of the Cathedral; whereunto he supplied not only his own wealth, and the labours of his servants, but even the sweat of his own brow; for he oftentimes bore the hod-load of hewn stone or of building lime. In this structure, the art equals the precious materials; for the vault may be compared to a bird stretching out her broad wings to fly; planted on its firm columns, it soars to the clouds. On the other hand, the work is supported by precious columns of swarthy stone, not confined to one sole colour, nor loose of pore, but flecked with glittering stars and close-set in all its grain. This stone disdains to be tamed with steel until it have first been subdued by art; for its surface must be softened by long grinding with sand, and its hardness is relaxed with strong vinegar. Moreover, it may suspend the mind in doubt whether it be jasper or

marble ; it is dull indeed for jasper, yet, for marble, of a
most noble nature. Of this are formed those slender
columns which stand round the great piers, even as a
bevy of maidens stand marshalled for a dance.

(from *Metrical Life of St. Hugh*—Ed. DIMOCK)

THE CATHEDRAL, ANTWERP

The body of the church,—the interior and graceful
perspectives of which were not liable to the reproach
brought against many Netherland churches, of assimi-
lating themselves already to the municipal palaces which
they were to suggest—was completed in the fourteenth
century. The beautiful façade, with its tower, was not
completed till the year 1518. The exquisite and daring
spire, the gigantic stem upon which the consummate
flower of this architectural creation was to be at last
unfolded, was a plant of a whole century's growth. Rising
to a height of nearly five hundred feet, over a church of
as many feet in length, it worthily represented the upward
tendency of Gothic architecture. Externally and internally
the cathedral was a true expression of the Christian
principle of devotion. Amid its vast accumulation of
imagery, its endless ornaments, its multiplicity of episodes,
its infinite variety of details, the central, maternal principle was ever visible. Everything pointed upwards, from
the spire in the clouds to the arch which enshrined the
smallest sculptured saint in the chapels below. It was a
sanctuary, not like pagan temples, to enclose a visible
deity, but an edifice where mortals might worship an
unseen Being in the realms above.

The church, with the noisy streets of the metropolis eddying round its walls, was a sacred island in the tumultuous main. Through the perpetual twilight, tall columnar trunks in thick profusion grew from a floor chequered with lights and shadows. Each shaft of the forest rose to a preternatural height, the many branches intermingling in the space above, to form a stately canopy. Foliage, flowers, and fruit of colossal luxuriance, strange birds, beasts, griffins, and chimeras in endless multitudes, the rank vegetation and fantastic zoology of a fabulous world, seemed to decorate and to animate the serried trunks and pendant branches, while the shattering symphonies or dying murmurs of the organ suggested the rushing of the wind through the forest,—now the full diapason of the storm, and now the gentle cadence of the evening breeze.

Internally, the church was rich beyond expression. All that opulent devotion could devise, in wood, bronze, marble, silver, gold, precious jewelry, or sacramental furniture, had been profusely lavished. The penitential tears of centuries had encrusted the whole interior with their glittering stalactites. Divided into five naves, with external rows of chapels, but separated by no screens or partitions, the great temple forming an imposing whole, the effect was the more impressive, the vistas almost infinite in appearance. The wealthy citizens, the twenty-seven guilds, the six military associations, the rhythmical colleges, besides many other secular or religious sodalities, had their own chapels and altars. Tombs adorned with the effigies of mailed crusaders and pious dames covered the floor, tattered banners hung in the air, the escutcheons of the Golden Fleece, an order typical of Flemish industry, but of which Emperors and Kings were proud to be the chevaliers, decorated the columns. The vast and beautifully-painted windows glowed with scriptural scenes, antique portraits, homely allegories, painted in those brilliant and forgotten colours which Art has not ceased to deplore. The daylight melting into gloom or coloured with fantastic brilliancy, priests in effulgent robes chanting in unknown language, the sublime breathing of choral music, the suffocating odours of myrrh and spikenard, suggestive of the oriental scenery and imagery of Holy Writ, all combined to bewilder and exalt the senses. The highest and humblest seemed to find themselves upon the same level within those sacred precincts, where even the blood-stained criminal was secure, and the arm of secular justice was paralyzed.

MOTLEY (from *The Dutch Republic*)

THE OCTAGON OF ELY CATHEDRAL

When the brethren had made their procession to the shrines in honour of St Ermengilda, and were returning to the dormitory, scarce had one or two lain down upon their beds when, behold ! the central tower fell suddenly and overwhelmed the choir, with such a crash and din that men might have thought it an earthquake ; yet no man was hurt or crushed by its fall. Alan, our Sacrist, was sore grieved and afflicted at this most baleful and lamentable chance, not knowing whither to turn, or what possible means could be found of repairing so vast a ruin. But, plucking up courage, and putting all his trust in the help of God and His most gracious Mother, and in the merits of the holy virgin Etheldreda, put out his hand to

387

strong things. First, he spent great labour and much
money in removing from the cathedral the fallen stones
and beams; then he purged the holy building with all
possible haste from the masses of dust which lay there.
Finally he measured out in eight divisions, with the art
of an architect, the place where he thought to build the
new tower; and he set the workmen to dig and search
for the foundations of the eight stone columns whereupon
the whole building should be supported, and beneath
which the choir with its stalls might afterwards be built;
until at last he found solid and secure ground for all this
under-structure. Then, when these eight places had been
carefully dug out and firmly founded with stones and sand,
at last he began those eight columns, with the stonework
which they supported. This he completed in six years,
bringing it up to the upper string-course in the year of
our Lord 1328. Then, without delay, that cunningly-
wrought timber structure of the new tower was begun;
a structure designed with the utmost and most marvellous
subtlety of human thought, to be set upon the aforesaid
stonework. This in its turn was completed, with vast and
burdensome expense, especially in seeking far and wide
for the great beams which were needed to support this
building, which were found at last with the utmost difficulty and at great cost, and which were brought by land
or sea to Ely. These beams were carved and shaped by
skilful workmen and bound together into the fabric with
marvellous art; thus at length, with God's help, the tower
was brought to that honourable consummation which had
long been desired. The whole cost of this new tower,
during the twenty years of Alan de Walsingham's time,
was £2400 6s. 11d., whereof £206 1s. came from gifts.

(from *Historia Eliensis* in WHARTON'S *Anglia Sacra*)

Also all new fraternities or guilds made of men seem openly to run in this course. For they conspire many false errors against the common fraternity of Christ that all Christian men took in their christening, and against common charity and common profit of Christian men. And thereto they conspire to bear up each other, yea, in wrong, and oppress other men in the right by their wit and power And all the goodness that is in these guilds each man ought for to do by common fraternity of Christendom, by God's commandment. . . Also men of subtle craft, as freemasons and other, seem openly cursed by this sentence. For they conspire together that no man of their craft shall take less on a day than they have settled, though he should by good conscience take much less, and that none of them shall make serious true work that might hinder the earnings of other men of the craft, and that none of them shall do ought but only hew stone, though he might profit his master twenty pound by one day's work by laying a course on a wall without harm or paining himself. See how this wicked people conspireth against truth and charity and common profit of the land, and punisheth them that help freely their neighbours.

WYCLIF

(from *The Grete Sentens of Curs* : modernized)

Then thought I to ask the first of these four orders,
And posted to the Preachers to prove their will.
I hied to their house to hearken of more ;
And when I came to the court I gaped about,
Such a bold building built upon earth's height
Saw I not, for certain, since a long time.
I gazed upon the house and eagerly thereon looked
How the pillars were painted and polished full clean
And quaintly carven with curious knots ;
With windows well wrought wide up aloft ;
And then I entered in and even went forward ;
And all wall was that dwelling, wide though it were,
With private posterns to pass when they list,
Orchards and arbours well and fairly eaved
And a curious cross craftily graven,
Fitted with tabernacles to look all about.
The price of a ploughland of pennies so round
To provide that pillar were very little.
Then I mounted me forward the minster to know
And espied a dwelling wondrously well built,
With arches on every side and beautifully carven
With crockets on the corners, with knots of gold,
Wide windows wrought, painted full thickly,
Shine with shields shapen to show round about,
With the marks of merchants mingled between,
More than twenty and two twice numbered.
There is no herald that hath half such a roll,
Right as a register hath reckoned them new.
Tombs upon tabernacles tiled above,
Housed in corners set hard about,
Clad for the nonce in armed alabaster,

Made of marble in many manners,
Knights in their cognisance clad for the nonce ;
It seemed all saints sacred upon earth,
And lovely ladies wrought lay by their sides
In many gay ornaments that were beaten gold.
Though the tax of ten year were truly gathered,
It would not make half that house, as I trow.
Then came I to the cloister and gaped about,
How it was pillared and painted and fairly pictured,
And all covered with lead low to the stones,
And paved with square tiles, each after other ;
With conduits of pure tin closed all about,
With lavers of latten lovelily made ready.
I trow the gain from the ground in a great shire
Would not fit forth that place one point towards the
    other end.
Then was the Chapter House wrought as a great
    church,
Carven and covered and quaintly engraved
With seemly ceiling set aloft,
As a parliament house painted about.
Then fared I into the frator and found there another
A hall fit for a high king to have as his household,
With broad boards fairly benched about,
With windows of glass wrought as a church.
Then walked I farther and went all about
And saw halls full high and houses full noble,
Chambers with chimneys and chapels gay,
And kitchens for a high king to have in his castles ;
And its dormitory dight with doors full strong,
Infirmary and frater, with many more houses
And all strong stone wall, stern upon heath,

With gay garrets and great, and each hole glazed,
And other houses enough to harbour the queen.

LANGLAND
(from *The Crede of Piers Plowman* : modernized)

RULES FOR THE MASONS AT YORK MINSTER. 1370

It is ordained by the Chapter of the kirk of Saint Peter
of York that all the masons that shall work at the works
of the same kirk of Saint Peter, shall from Michaelmas
Day until the first Sunday of Lent, be every day at morn
at their work in the lodge that is ordained to the masons
at work within the close beside the foresaid kirk, as early
as they may see skilfully by daylight for to work ; and
they shall stand there truly working at their work all day
thereafter, as long as they may see skilfully for to work, if
it be all workday : or else till be it high noon smitten by
the clock, when holyday falls at noon. . . . And in time of
meat, at noon, they shall, no time of the year, stay away
from the lodges, nor from their work aforesaid, over the
space of time of an hour : and after noon they may drink
in the lodge : and for their drinking-time betwixt Michaelmas and Lent they shall not cease nor leave their work
passing the time of a mileway. And from the first Sunday of Lent until Michaelmas they shall be in the aforesaid lodge at their work at the sun rising, and stand there
truly and busily working upon the aforesaid work of the
kirk all the day, until it be no more space than time of
a mileway before sun set . . . and they shall not cease nor
leave their work in sleeping time, passing the time of a

mileway, nor in drinking-time after noon, passing the
time of a mileway. And they shall not sleep after noon no
time but between Saint Elenmas and Lammas; and if any
man stay away from the lodge and from the work aforesaid or make default any time of the year against this
aforesaid ordinance, he shall be chastised with abating of
his payment, at the looking and device of the master
mason; and all their times and hours shall be revealed
by a bell ordained therefor. And also it is ordained that
no mason shall be received at work, to the work of the
aforesaid kirk, but he be first proved a week or more upon
his well working; and, after that he is found sufficient
of his work, be received of the common assent of the
master and the keepers of the work, and of the master
mason, and swear upon the book that he shall truly . . .
hold and keep holy all the points of this aforesaid ordinance, . . . and whosoever come against this ordinance and
breaks it against the will of the aforesaid Chapter, have
he God's malison and Saint Peter's.

(from *Fabric Rolls of York Minster* : modernized)

KING'S COLLEGE CHAPEL

Tax not the royal Saint with vain expense,
With ill-matched aims the Architect who planned,
Albeit labouring for a scanty band
Of white-robed Scholars only, this immense
And glorious work of fine intelligence.
Give all thou canst; high Heaven rejects the lore
Of nicely-calculated less or more;
So deemed the man who fashioned for the sense
These lofty pillars, spread that branching roof

Self-poised, and scooped into ten thousand cells,
Where light and shade repose, where music dwells
Lingering, and wandering on as loth to die ;
Like thoughts whose very sweetness yieldeth proof
That they were born for immortality.

What awful perspective ! while from our sight
With gradual stealth the lateral windows hide
Their portraitures, their stone-work glimmers, dyed
In the soft chequerings of a sleepy light.
Martyr, or King, or sainted Eremite,
Whoe'er ye be, that thus, yourselves unseen,
Imbue your prison-bars with solemn sheen,
Shine on, until ye fade with coming Night !
But, from the arms of silence, list ! O list !
The music bursteth into second life ;
The notes luxuriate, every stone is kissed
By sound, or ghost of sound, in mazy strife ;
Heart-thrilling strains, that cast, before the eye
Of the devout, a veil of ecstasy.

WORDSWORTH

BRUNELLESCHI BUILDS THE CUPOLA
(*Florence*, 1420–1436)

The chain-work was now completed around all the
eight sides, and the builders, animated by success, worked
vigorously ; but being pressed more than usual by
Filippo, and having received certain reprimands concerning the masonry and in relation to other matters of
daily occurrence, they became discontented. Moved by
this circumstance and by their envy, the chiefs among

them drew together and got up a faction, declaring that the work was a laborious and perilous undertaking, and that they would not proceed with the vaulting of the Cupola, but on condition of receiving large payments, although their wages had already been increased and were much higher than was usual. By these means they hoped to injure Filippo and increase their own gains. This circumstance displeased the wardens greatly, as it did Filippo also; but the latter, having reflected on the matter, took his resolution, and one Saturday evening he dismissed them all. The men seeing themselves thus sent about their business and not knowing how the affair would turn, were very sullen; but on the following Monday Filippo set ten Lombards to work at the building, and by remaining constantly with them, and saying " do this here " and " do that there," he taught them so much in one day that they were able to continue the works during many weeks. The masons seeing themselves thus disgraced as well as deprived of their employment, and knowing that they would find no work equally profitable, sent messengers to Filippo saying that they would willingly return, and recommending themselves to his consideration. Filippo kept them for several days in suspense, and seemed not inclined to admit them again. They were eventually reinstated, but with lower wages than they had received at first: thus where they had thought to make gain they suffered loss, and by seeking to revenge themselves on Filippo, they brought injury and shame on their own heads.

The tongues of the envious were now silenced, and when the building was seen to proceed so happily, the genius of Filippo received its due consideration; and, by all who judged dispassionately, he was already held to have shown a boldness which has perhaps never before been displayed by any architect ancient or modern. This opinion was confirmed by the fact that Filippo now brought out his model, in which all might see the extraordinary amount of thought bestowed on every detail of the building. The varied invention displayed in the staircases, in the provision of lights, both within and without so that none might strike or injure himself in the darkness, were all made manifest, with the careful consideration evinced by the different supports of iron which were placed to assist the footsteps wherever the ascent was steep. In addition to this, Filippo had even thought of the irons for fixing scaffolds within the cupola, if ever they should be required for the execution of mosaics or paintings. He had selected the least dangerous positions for the places of the conduits, to be afterwards constructed for carrying off the rain-water ; had shown where these were to be covered and where uncovered ; and had moreover contrived various outlets and apertures, whereby the force of the winds should be diminished, to the end that neither vapours nor the vibrations of the earth should have power to do injury to the building : all which proved the extent to which he had profited by his studies during the many years of his residence in Rome. When in addition to these things, the superintendents considered how much he had accomplished in the shaping, fixing, uniting, and securing the stones of this immense pile, they were awe-struck at what the mind of one man had been capable of performing. His powers and facilities continually increased, and that to such an extent that there was no operation, however difficult and complex, that he did not render easy and simple. Of this he gave proof, in one instance among others, by the employment of wheels and counterpoises to raise heavy weights, so that one ox could draw more than six pairs could have moved by the ordinary methods.

The building had now reached such a height, that when a man had once arrived at the summit it was a very great labour to descend to the ground, and the workmen lost much time in going to their meals and to drink. They also suffered great inconvenience in the heat of the day from the same cause. Arrangements were therefore made by Filippo for opening wine-shops and eating-houses in the cupola, where the required food being sold, no one was compelled to leave his labour until the evening, which was a relief and convenience to the men as well as a very important advantage to the work.

Perceiving the building to proceed rapidly, and finding all his undertakings happily successful, Filippo increased in zeal and confidence, and he laboured unceasingly. He himself went to the ovens where the bricks were made, examined the clay, proved the quality of the working, and when they were baked he would select and set them apart with his own hands. In a like manner, while the stones were under the hands of the stone-cutters, he would look narrowly to see that they were hard and free from flaws. He supplied the stone-cutters with models in wood or wax, or hastily cut models on the spot from turnips, to direct them in the shaping and junction of the different masses. He did the same for the men who prepared the ironwork. He likewise invented hooked hinges, with the mode of fixing them to the doorposts, and greatly facilitated the practice of architecture, which was certainly brought by his labours to a perfection that it would else perhaps never have attained among the Tuscans.

VASARI (from *Lives of the Painters*)

FILIPPO STROZZI LAYS THE FOUNDATION-STONE OF THE STROZZI PALACE IN FLORENCE, AUGUST THE 16th, 1489

At the moment when the sun rose over the mountains I laid the first stone of the foundations in the name of God, as a good beginning for myself, my successors, and all who may have a share in the building. I caused a Mass of the Holy Ghost to be sung at the same hour by the brothers of San Marco, another by the nuns of Murate, a third in my own church Santa Maria di Lecceto, and a fourth by the monks there, who are under some obligation to me, together with a prayer for a blessing on the beginning of the work. The hour for the laying of the foundation-stone was determined by horoscope by Messer Benedetto Biliotti, Maestro Niccolò, and Messer Antonio Benevieni, doctors ; also Bishop Pagagnotti and Messer Marsilio Ficino, all of whom confirmed it as propitious. I sent twenty lire to the brothers of San Marco, to be doled out in alms as they thought good, and an equal sum to Murate. In lesser alms I disbursed ten lire. To Benedetto Biliotti I gave four ells of black damask which cost me twenty lire, and I invited to breakfast Maestro Jacopo the master-mason, Maestro Andrea the founder, Filippo Buondelmonte, Marcuccio Strozzi, Pietro Parenti, Simone Rudolfi, Donato Bonsi, Ser Agnolo, Lorenzo Fiorini, and other of my friends.

FILIPPO STROZZI
(quoted in REUMONT'S *Lorenzo de Medici*)

THE ABBEY MASON

The new-vamped Abbey shaped apace
In the fourteenth century of grace ;

Panel and circumscribing wall
Of latest feature, trim and tall,

Rose roundabout the Norman core
In prouder pose than heretofore,

Encasing magically the old
With parpend ashlars manifold.

The trowels rang out, and tracery
Appeared where blanks had used to be.

Men toiled for pleasure more than pay,
And all went smoothly day by day,

Till, in due course, the transept part
Engrossed the master-mason's art. . . .

Men now discerned as days revolved
The ogive riddle had been solved ;

Templates were cut, fresh lines were chalked
Where lines had been defaced and balked,

And the work swelled and mounted higher,
Achievement distancing desire ;

Here jambs with transoms fixed between,
Where never the like before had been—

There little mullions thinly sawn
Where meeting circles once were drawn.

Time passed, and like a living thing
The pile went on embodying,

And workmen died, and young ones grew,
And the old mason sank from view

And Abbots Wygmore and Staunton went
And Horton sped the embellishment. . . .

When longer yet dark death had wormed
The brain wherein the style had germed

From Gloucester church it flew afar—
The style called Perpendicular.—

To Winton and to Westminster
It ranged, and grew still beautifuller:

From Solway Firth to Dover Strand
Its fascinations starred the land,

Not only on cathedral walls
But upon courts and castle halls,

Till every edifice in the isle
Was patterned to no other style,

And till, long having played its part,
The curtain fell on Gothic art.

—Well: when in Wessex on your rounds,
Take a brief step beyond its bounds,

And enter Gloucester: seek the quoin
Where choir and transept interjoin,

And, gazing at the forms there flung
Against the sky by one unsung—

The ogee arches transom-topped,
The tracery-stalks by spandrils stopped,

Petrified lacework—lightly lined
On ancient massiveness behind—

Muse that some minds so modest be
As to renounce fame's fairest fee,

(Like him who crystallized on this spot
His visionings, but lies forgot,

And many a mediaeval one
Whose symmetries salute the sun)

While others boom a baseless claim
And upon nothing rear a name.

THOMAS HARDY

THE ABBEY OF THELEME

The architecture was in a figure *hexagonal*, and in such
a fashion that in every one of the six corners there was
built a great tower of threescore feet in diameter ; and
were all of a like form and bigness. Upon the north side
ran along the river of Loire, and on the bank thereof was
situated the tower called Arctic. Going towards the east,
there was another, called Calaer ; the next following
Anatole ; the next Mesembrine ; the next Hesperia, and
the last Criere. Every tower was distant from the other the

space of three hundred and twelve paces. The whole edifice was everywhere six stories high, reckoning the cellars underground for one. The second was arched after the fashion of a basket-handle. The rest were cieled with pure wainscoat, flourished with Flanders fret-work, in the form of the foot of a lamp ; and covered above with fine slates, with an indorsement of lead, carrying the antique figures of little puppets, and animals of all sorts, notably well suited to one another, and gilt, together with the gutters, which jetting without the walls, from betwixt the cross bars in a diagonal figure, painted with gold and azure, reached to the very ground, where they ended in great conduit pipes, which carried all away unto the river from under the house.

This same building was a hundred times more sumptuous and magnificent than ever was Bonnivet, Chambourg, or Chantilly. For there were in it nine thousand, three hundred, and two and thirty chambers ; every one whereof had a withdrawing room, a handsome closet, a wardrobe, an oratory, and neat passage, leading into a great and spacious hall. Between every tower, in the midst of the said body of building, there was a pair of winding stairs, whereof the steps were part of porphyry, part of *Numidian* stone, and part of *serpentine* marble ; each of those steps being two and twenty feet in length, and three fingers thick, and the just number of twelve betwixt every rest or landing-place. In every resting-place were two fair antique arches, where the light came in ; and by those they went into a cabinet (closet), made even with, and of the breadth of the said winding, a re-ascending above the roofs of the house ending *conically* in a pavillion. By that *vize*, or winding, they entered on every side into a great hall, and from the halls into the chambers. From the

Arctic tower unto the Criere, were the fair great libraries in Greek, Latin, Hebrew, French, Italian, and Spanish, respectively distributed in their respective cantons, according to the diversity of these languages. In the midst there was a wonderful winding stair, the entry whereof was without the house, in a vault or arch, six fathoms broad. It was made in such symmetry and largeness that six men-at-arms, with their lances in their rests, might together in a breast ride all up to the very top of all the palace. From the tower Anatole to the Mesembrine were spacious galleries, all coloured over and painted with the ancient prowesses, histories, and descriptions of the world. In the midst thereof there was likewise such another ascent and gate, as we said there was on the river side.

RABELAIS (Trans. URQUHART)

TUDOR HOUSES

The greatest part of our building in the cities and good towns of England consisteth only of timber; for as yet few of the houses of the commonalty (except here and there in the West country towns) are made of stone, although they may (in my opinion) in divers other places be builded so good cheap of the one as of the other. . . . Our houses are commonly strong and well timbered (so that in many places there are not above four, six, or nine inches between stud and stud), so, in the open and champaign countries they are forced, for want of stuff, to use no studs at all, but only frankposts, raisins, beans, prickposts, groundsels, summers (or domants), transoms, and such principals, with here and there a girding, where-unto they fasten their splints, or raddles, and then cast it all over with thick clay to keep out the wind, which other-wise would annoy them. . . .

As every countrey house is thus apparelled on the out-side, so it is inwardly divided into sundry rooms above and beneath ; and where plenty of wood is, they cover them with tiles, otherwise with straw, sedge or reed, except some quarry of slate be near hand, from whence they have for their money so much as may suffice them. The clay wherewith our houses are impannelled is either white, red or blue. . . .

Within their doors also, such as are of ability do oft make their floors and parget of fine abalaster burned, which they call plaster of Paris. . . . In plastering . . . we used to lay first a line or two of white mortar, tempered with hair upon laths, which are nailed one by another . . . and finally cover all with the aforesaid plaster. . . . The walls of our houses on the inner sides in like sort be either hanged with tapestry, arras work, or painted cloths, wherein either divers histories, or herbs, beasts, knots and such like are stained, or else they are ceiled with oak of our own, or wainscot brought hither out of the East countries.

. . . As for stoves, we have not hitherto used them greatly, yet do they now begin to be made in divers houses of the gentry and wealthy citizens, who build them not to work and feed in, as in Germany and else-where, but now and then to sweat in, as occasion and need shall require it. . . .

Horn in windows is now quite laid down in every place, so our lattices are also grown into less use, because glass is come to be so plentiful, and within a very little so good cheap, if not better than the other. . . . Heretofore also the houses of our princes and noblemen were often glazed with beryl . . . and in divers other places with fine crystal. . . . But now these are not in use, so that only the clearest glass is most esteemed. . . .

Moreover, the mansion houses of our country towns and villages . . . are builded in such sort generally as that they have neither dairy, stable, nor brewhouse annexed unto them under the same roof (as in many places beyond the sea and some of the north parts of our country), but all separate from the first and one of them from another. And yet, for all this, they are not so far distant in sunder but that the goodman lying in his bed may lightly hear what is done in each of them with ease, and call quickly unto his many, if any danger should attack him.

The ancient manors and houses of our gentlemen are yet and for the most part of strong timber, in framing whereof our carpenters have been and are worthily preferred before those of like science among all other nations. Howbeit such as be lately builded are commonly either of brick or hard stone, or both, their rooms large and comely, and houses of office further distant from their lodgings. . . .

The furniture of our houses also exceedeth, and is grown in manner even to passing delicacy : and herein I do not speak of the nobility and gentry only, but likewise of the lowest sort in most places of our south country that have anything at all to take to. Certes in noblemen's houses it is not rare to see abundance of arras, rich hangings of tapestry, silver vessel, and so much other plate as may furnish sundry cupboards to the sum oftentimes of a thousand or two thousand pounds at the least, whereby the value of this and the rest of their stuff doth grow to be almost inestimable. Likewise in the houses of knights, gentlemen, merchantmen, and some other wealthy citizens, it is not geson to behold generally their great provision of tapestry, Turkey work, pewter, brass, fine linen, and thereto costly cupboards of plate, worth five or six hundred or a thousand pounds to be deemed by estimation. . . .

There are old men yet dwelling in the village where I remain which have noted . . . things to be marvellously altered in England within their sound remembrance. . . . One is the multitude of chimneys lately erected, whereas in their young days there were not above two or three, if so many, in most uplandish towns of the realm (the religious houses and manor places of their lords always excepted, and peradventure some great personages), but each one made his fire against a reredos in the hall, where he dined and dressed his meat.

HARRISON (in HOLINSHED'S *Chronicles*)

PRAISE OF GOTHIC

The principle of the Gothic architecture is infinity made imaginable. It is, no doubt, a sublimer effort of genius than the Greek style ; but then it depends much more on execution for its effect.

COLERIDGE (from *Table Talk*)

The ancient Greek & Roman Architecture answer all the Perfections required in a faultless and accomplished Building ; such as for so many Ages were so renowned and reputed by the universal Suffrages of the civilised World, and would doubtless have still subsisted, & made good their Claim, and what is recorded of them ; had not the Goths, Vandals, and other barbarous Nations, subverted and demolished them, together with that glorious Empire, where those stately and pompous Monuments stood ; introducing in their stead, a certain fantastical and licentious Manner of Building, which we have since called Modern or Gothick. Congestions of heavy, dark, melancholy, and monkish Piles, without any just Proportion, Use or Beauty, compared with the truly ancient ; so as when we meet with the greatest Industry, and expensive Carving, full of Fret and lamentable Imagery ; sparing neither of Pains not Cost ; a judicious Spectator is rather distracted or quite confounded, than touched with that Admiration, which results from the true and just Symmetry, regular Proportion, Union, and Disposition ; and from the great and noble Manner in which the august and glorious Fabricks of the Ancients are executed.

It was after the Irruption & Swarms of those truculent People from the North ; the Moors and Arabs from the South and East, over-running the civilised World ; that where-ever they fixed themselves, they soon began to debauch this noble and useful Art ; when instead of those beautiful Orders, so majestical & proper for their Stations, becoming Variety, and other ornamental Accessories ; they set up those slender and misshapen Pillars, or rather Bundles of Staves and other incongruous Props, to support incumbent Weights, & ponderous arched Roofs, without Entablature; and though not without great Industry (as M. D'Aviler well observed) nor altogether naked of gaudy Sculpture, trite & busy Carvings; 'tis such as gluts the Eye, rather than gratifies and pleases it with any reasonable Satisfaction: For Proof of this (without travelling far abroad) I dare report myself to any Man of Judgment, and that has the least Taste of Order and Magnificence; if after he has looked a while upon King Henry the VIIth's Chapel at Westminster, gazed on its sharp Angles, Jetties, narrow Lights, lame Statues, Lace, and other Cut-work, and Crincle-crancle; and shall then turn his Eyes on the Banquetting-hall built at Whitehall by Inigo Jones, after the ancient Manner; or on what his Majesty's Surveyor, Sir Christopher Wren, has advanced at St Paul's, and consider what a glorious Object the Cupola, Porticoes, Colonades, and other Parts present to the Beholder, or compare the Schools and Library at Oxford with the Theatre there; or what he has built at Trinity-college, in Cambridge, & since all these, at Greenwich and other Places; by which Time our Home-traveller will begin to have a just Idea of the ancient and modern Architecture: I say, let him well consider, and compare them judicially, without Partiality and Prejudice; and then pronounce which of the two Manners strikes the Understanding as well as the Eye, with the more Majesty and solemn Greatness; tho' in so much a plainer and simple Dress, conform to the respective Orders and Entablature; and accordingly determine to whom the Preference is due: Not as we said, that there is not something of solid, and odly artificial too, after a Sort: but then the universal and unreasonable Thickness of the Walls, clumsy Buttresses, Towers, sharp-pointed Arches,

Doors, & other Apertures, without Proportion : non-sensical Insertions of various Marbles impertinently placed ; Turrets and Pinnacles thick set with Monkies and Chimeras, and Abundance of busy Work & other Incongruities dissipate and break the Angles of the Sight, and so confound it, that one cannot consider it with any Steadiness, where to begin or end ; taking off from that noble Air and Grandeur, bold and graceful Manner, which the Ancients had so well, and judiciously estab-lished : but, in this Sort have they and their Followers ever since filled not Europe alone, but Asia and Africa besides, with Mountains of Stone, vast and gigantick Buildings indeed, but not worthy the Name of Architec-ture.

EVELYN (from WREN'S *Parentalia*)

AFTER THE GREAT FIRE

I went this morning on foot from Whitehall as far as London Bridge, through the late Fleet Street, Ludgate Hill, by St. Paul's, Cheapside, Exchange, Bishopsgate, Aldersgate, and out to Moorfields, thence through Corn-hill, etc., with extraordinary difficulty, clambering over heaps of yet smoking rubbish, and frequently mistaking where I was. The ground under my feet so hot it even burnt the soles of my shoes. . . . At return I was infinitely concerned to find that goodly Church St. Paul's now a sad ruin, and that beautiful portico (for structure compar-able to any in Europe, as not long before repaired by the late king), now rent in pieces, flakes of vast stone split asunder, and nothing remaining entire but the inscrip-tion in the architrave. . . . It was astonishing to see what immense stones the heat had in a manner calcined, so that all the ornaments, columns, friezes, capitals, and projectures of massy Portland stone flew off, even to the very roof, where a sheet of lead covering a great space (no less than six acres by measure) was totally melted ; the ruins of the vaulted roof falling broke into St. Faith's. . . . Thus lay in ashes that most venerable Church, one of the most ancient pieces of early piety in the Christian world, besides near a hundred more. The lead, iron work, bells, plate, etc., melted, the exquisitely wrought Mercer's Chapel, the sumptuous Exchange, the august fabric of Christ Church, all the rest of the Companies' Halls, splendid buildings, arches, entries, all in dust.

EVELYN (from *The Diary*)

TO MY WORTHY FRIEND DR CHRISTOPHER WREN, PROFESSOR OF ASTRONOMY IN OXFORD. APRIL 25, 1668

SIR, As he said of old, *Prudentia est quædam divinatio,* so Science (at the Height you are Master of it) is prophetic too. What you whisper'd in my Ear at your last coming hither, is now come to pass. Our Work at the West-end of St. Paul's is fallen about our ears. Your quick Eye discern'd the Walls and Pillars gone off from their Perpendiculars, and I believe other Defects too, which are now expos'd to every common Observer.

About a Week since, we being at Work about the third Pillar from the West-end on the South-side, which we had new cased with Stone, where it was most defective, almost up to the Chapitre, a great Weight falling from the high Wall, so disabled the Vaulting of the Side-aile by it, that it threaten'd a sudden Ruin, so visibly, that the Workmen presently remov'd ; and the next Night the whole Pillar fell, & carry'd Scaffolds and all to the very Ground.

The second Pillar (which you know is bigger than the rest) stands now alone, with an enormous Weight on the Top of it ; which we cannot hope should stand long, and yet we dare not venture to take it down. . . .

Your very affectionate Friend, and Servant,

W. SANDCROFT
(Dean of St. Paul's)
(from WREN'S *Parentalia*)

THE KING'S COMMISSION

Whereas—Since the issuing out of our Commission (viz, Anno 1663, 15 Car. II) the late dreadful Fire in London hath destroyed & consumed the cathedral Church of St. Paul to such a Degree, that no Part of the ancient Walls or Structures can with any Safety be relied upon, or left standing ; insomuch, that it is now become absolutely necessary totally to demolish and raze to the Ground all the Relicks of the former Building, and in the same Place, but upon new Foundations, to erect a new Church ; (which that it may be done to the Glory of God, & for the promoting of his divine Worship and Service therein to the celebrated ; and to the End the same may equal, if not exceed the Splendor and Magnificence of the former cathedral Church, when it was in its best Estate, and so become much more than formerly, the principle Ornament of our royal City, to the Honour of our Government, and of this our Realm, we have caused several Designs to that Purpose to be prepared by Dr. Christopher Wren, Surveyor General of all our Works and Buildings, which we have seen, and one of which we do more especially approve, & have commanded a Model thereof to be made after so large & exact a Manner, that it may remain as a perpetual unchangeable Rule and Direction for the Conduct of the Whole Work) And whereas our former Commission, in which the upholding and repairing the ancient cathedral Church, is only designed and mentioned, doth not sufficiently authorize & impower our said Commissioners therein named, to begin and compleat a new Fabrick upon new Foundations. Know ye, &c.

(Preamble to King's Commission, Nov. 12th, 1673)

THE ROYAL WARRANT UNDER THE SIGN-MANUAL AND PRIVY-SEAL FOR BEGINNING THE WORKS OF THE NEW CATHEDRAL OF SAINT PAUL

CHARLES R.

Whereas We have been informed that a Portion of the Imposition laid on Coals, which by Act of Parliament is appointed and set apart for the rebuilding of the cathedral Church of St Paul, in our capital City of London, doth at present amount to a considerable Sum, which, tho' not proportionable to the greatness of the Work, is notwithstanding sufficient to begin the same ; & with all the

Materials, and other Assistances, which may probably be expected, will put a new Quire in great Forwardness; and whereas among divers Designs which have been presented to Us, We have particularly pitched upon one, as well because We found it very artificial, proper, and useful; as because it was so ordered that it might be built and finish'd by Parts: We do therefore by these Presents signify Our Royal Approbation of the said Design, hereunto annexed; and do will and require you forthwith to proceed according to the said Design, beginning with the East-end or Quire, and accomplishing the same with the present Stock of Money, & such Supplies as may probably accrue, according to the Tenor of the Commission to you directed; and for so doing this shall be your Warrant. Given at our Court at Whitehall, the 14th Day of May, 1675, in the 27th Year of our Reign.

By His Majesty's Command,

HENRY COVENTRY

To Our Commissioners for rebuilding
the Cathedral of St Paul, London.

THE DEMOLITION OF OLD SAINT PAUL'S

The pulling down of the Walls, being about 80 Feet high, and 5 Feet thick, was a great and troublesome Work; the Men stood above, and work'd them down with Pickaxes, whilst Labourers below moved away the Materials that fell, and dispersed them into Heaps: the want of Room made this Way slow, and dangerous, and some Men lost their Lives; the Heaps grew steep and large;

and yet this was to be done before the Masons could begin to lay the Foundations.

The City having Streets to pave anew, bought, from the Rubbish, most of the Stone, call'd Kentish-rag, which gave some Room to dig, and to lay Foundations; which yet was not easy to perform with any Exactness, but by this Method.

The Surveyor placed Scaffolds high enough to extend his Lines over the Heaps that lay in the Way; and then by Perpendiculars set out the Places below, from the Lines drawn with Care upon the level Plan of the Scaffold.

Thus he proceeded, gaining every Day more Room, till he came to the middle Tower that bore the Steeple: the Remains of the Tower being nearly 200 Feet high, the Labourers were afraid to work above, thereupon he concluded to facilitate the Work by the Use of Gunpowder.

He dug a Hole of about 4 Feet wide, down by the Side of the North-west Pillar of the Tower, the 4 Pillars of which were each about 14 feet diameter; when he had dug to the Foundation, he then, with Crows and Tools made on purpose, wrought a Hole 2 Feet square, level into the Center of the Pillar; there he placed a little Deal-box, containing eighteen Pounds of Powder, & no more: a Cane was fix'd to the Box with a Quick-match, (as Gunners call it) within the Cane, which reach'd from the Box to the Ground above, and along the Ground was laid a Train of Powder, with a Match: after the Mine was carefully clos'd up again with Stone and Mortar to the Top of the Ground, he then observ'd the Effect of the Blow.

This little Quantity of Powder not only lifted up the whole Angle of the Tower, with two great Arches which rested upon it, but also two adjoining Arches of the Ailes, and all above them ; and this it seem'd to do somewhat leisurely, cracking the Walls to the Top, lifting visibly the whole Weight about nine Inches, which suddenly jumping down, made a great Heap of Ruin in the Place without scattering, it was half a Minute before the Heap already fallen open'd in two or three Places, and emitted some Smoke. By this Description may be observ'd the incredible Force of Powder: 18 Pounds of which lifted up above 3000 Tun, & saved the Work of 1000 Labourers.

The Fall of so great a Weight from an Height of 200 Feet, gave a Concussion to the Ground, that the Inhabitants round about took for an Earthquake.

Encourag'd by this Success, he thought to proceed this Way, but being oblig'd to go out of Town in the King's Service, he left the Management of another Mine begun, to the Care of his next Officer, who too wise in his own Conceit, put in a greater Quantity of Powder, and neither went low enough, nor sufficiently fortified the Mouth of the Mine ; and tho' it had the Effect, yet one Stone was shot out to the opposite Side of the Church-yard, through an open Window, into a Room of a private House, where some Women were sitting at Work, without any Harm done ; this Accident frighted the Neighbours to that Degree, that he was importun'd to use no more Powder, and was so directed also by his Superiors ; tho' with due Caution it might have been executed without Hazard, and sav'd much Time and Money.

(from *Parentalia*)

It was necessary to give a greater Height than the Cupola would gracefully allow within, tho' it is considerably above the Roof of the Church; yet the old Church having had before a very lofty Spire of Timber and Lead, the world expected, that the new Work should not in this Respect fall short of the old (tho' that was but a Spit, and this is a Mountain). He was therefore obliged to comply with the Humour of the Age, (tho' not with ancient Example, as neither did Bramante) and to raise another structure over the first Cupola; & this was a Cone of Brick, so built as to support a Stone Lantern of an elegant Figure, and ending in Ornaments of Copper gilt.

As the whole Church above the Vaults is covered with a substantial oaken Roof, and Lead, (for no other Covering is so durable in our Climate) so he covered and hid out of Sight the Brick Cone with another Cupola of Timber and Lead; and between this and the Cone are easy Stairs that ascend to the Lantern. . . .

Altho' the Dome wants no Butment, yet, for greater Caution, it is hooped with Iron in this Manner; a Cbanel is cut in the Bandage of Portland-stone, in which is laid a double Chain of Iron strongly linked together at every ten Feet, and the whole chanel filled up with Lead.

Among all the Composures of the Ancients, we find no Cupolas raised above the necessary Loading of the Hemisphere, as is seen particularly in the Pantheon. In after Ages the Dome of Florence, and of the great Church of Venice, was raised higher. The Saracens mightily affected it, in Imitation of the first most eminent Pattern, given by Justinian, in his Temple of Sancta Sophia, at Constantinople. Bramante would not fall short of those

Examples; nor could the Surveyor do otherwise than gratify the general Taste of the Age, which had been so used to Steeples, that these round Designs were hardly digested, unless raised to a remarkable Height.

Thus St Paul's is lofty enough to be discerned at Sea Eastward, and at Windsor Westward; but our Air being frequently hazy, prevents those distant Views, except when the Sun shines out, after a Shower of Rain has washed down the Clouds of Sea-coal Smoke that hang over the City from so many Fires kindled every Morning, besides Glass-houses, Brew-houses, & Founderies, every one of which emits a blacker Smoke than twenty Houses.

In the beginning of the new Works of St Paul's, an Incident was taken notice of by some People as a memorable Omen, when the Surveyor in Person had set out upon the Place, the Dimensions of the great Dome, and fixed upon the Centre; a common Labourer was ordered to bring a flat Stone from the Heaps of Rubbish (such as should first come to Hand) to be laid for a Mark and Directions to the Masons; the Stone which was immediately brought & laid down for that Purpose, happened to be a piece of a Grave-stone, with nothing remaining of the Inscription but this single Word in large Capitals, RESURGAM.

(from *Parentalia*)

THE GOTHIC REVIVAL

We ought to have our Abbey back, you see.
It's different, preaching in basilicas,
And doing duty in some masterpiece
Like this of brother Pugin's, bless his heart!

I doubt if they're half baked, those chalk rosettes,
Ciphers and stucco-twiddlings everywhere ;
It's just like breathing in a lime-kiln : eh ?

BROWNING
(from *Bishop Blougram's Apology*)

A new Gothic building, or a new missal, is in reality
little less absurd than a *new ruin*. The Gothic architecture,
sculpture, and painting, belong to peculiar ages. The
feelings that guided their inventors are unknown to us.

CONSTABLE (from LESLIE'S *Life*)

THE TWENTIETH CENTURY

The most fundamental change in our technique is the
replacement of natural materials by *scientific* ones, and
more particularly the development of steel, steel-concrete
and steel-glass construction. The invention of steel and
the elaboration of systems of construction based on its
properties and those of its satellite materials, has in itself
been responsible for the most spectacular changes in our
social life, creating new *social*, as well as new *technical*,
design-situations.

Before our age, the technical problems of architecture
were concerned chiefly with the piling up of weights.
Great buildings were literally " stately piles " raised up
and supported by heavy masonry walls. But now the wall,
no longer an essential element of structure, becomes (truly
considered) an expression of its thermal and other insulat-
ing functions—to include or exclude the light, the view,

the weather, or the public—whose separate and relative values are to be determined by the requirements of the design-situation. Apertures are not so much cut out of the walls as left out of them. Without steel, none of the machines, engines, and processes incorporated into the modern building, such as heating, lighting, ventilating, refrigerating, and sanitary services, and the machines for vertical circulation, would be possible.

The work of integrating, unifying and synthesising a multitude of these new material details, processes and conditions, and of giving to the whole design a formal aspect of order and significance, calls for the utmost precision, vigilance, sincerity and clarity of vision on the part of the architect, who is, it must be remembered, not only the composer, but also the *conductor* of the many executants of his works. Again, the vital necessity for an *architectural* solution of the present social and economical problems calls for co-operation and mutual support amongst all architects of the same persuasion.

WELLS COATES (from *Unit One*)

All that has been achieved in the creation of new architectural form since the great autonomous efflorescence of mediaeval architecture and even during the most fruitful period of the baroque, down to the days of our own artistic exhaustion, is based in principle on the inherited forms and traditions of antique building art.

Precisely as there is no longer any connection between the principle of the antique world with its simple load and support, and the Gothic principle with column and vault,—both in the matter of construction and of ornamental architectonic expression,—so must we clearly recognize the fact that the first iron girder inspired an exalted feeling of liberation akin to that which the mediaeval masters felt when they had conquered the antique principle of construction by means of the vault. It is only from this point of departure that one is able to realize that the decisive features of the new constructive principle must be discovered again and again.

The regulation of our static sensation in accordance with the tensile power of reinforced concrete instead of, as hitherto, with the principle of direct load and support, necessitates a long and gradual approach and evolution. It is therefore particularly urgent to discover and emphasize this antithesis in order to be able to visualize the breadth and extent of this great change.

> Out of the columns and marble beams of the Greek
>   temple,
> Out of the pillars and stone vaults of the Gothic
>   cathedral,
> Evolves the girder rhythm of iron halls.

The balancing of the load practised by the ancients, the elevation of the load practised by the mediaevals, are succeeded by the dynamic tension of construction in steel and concrete.

ERICH MENDELSOHN
(Trans. H. G. SHEFFAUER)

RUINS

There was not, at that time, much to be seen in the Isle of Thanet besides the beauty of the country, and the fine prospects of the sea, which are nowhere surpassed except in the Isle of Wight, or upon some parts of the coast of Hampshire. One sight, however, I remember, engaged my curiosity, and I went to see it—a fine piece of ruins, built by the late Lord Holland at a great expense, which, the day after I saw it, tumbled down for nothing. Perhaps, therefore, it is still a ruin ; and if it is, I would advise you by all means to visit it, as it must have been much improved by this fortunate incident. It is hardly possible to put stones together with that air of wild and magnificent disorder which they are sure to acquire by falling of their own accord.

COWPER (*Letters*)

If thou would'st view fair Melrose aright,
Go visit it by the pale moonlight ;
For the gay beams of the lightsome day
Gild, but to flout, the ruins grey.
When the broken arches are black in night,
And each shafted oriel glimmers white ;
When the cold light's uncertain shower
Streams on the ruin'd central tower ;
When buttress and buttress, alternately,
Seem framed of ebon and ivory ;
When silver edges the imagery
And the scrolls that teach thee to live and die ;
When distant Tweed is heard to rave,

And the owlet to hoot o'er the dead man's grave,
Then go—but go alone the while—
Then view St. David's ruin'd pile ;
And, home returning, soothly swear,
Was never scene so sad and fair !

SCOTT

(from *The Lay of the Last Minstrel*)

Oh, Rome ! my Country ! City of the Soul !
The orphans of the heart must turn to thee,
Lone Mother of dead Empires ! and control
In their shut breasts their petty misery.
What are our woes and sufferance ? Come and see
The cypress, hear the owl, and plod your way
O'er steps of broken thrones and temples—Ye !
Whose agonies are evils of a day—
A world is at our feet as fragile as our clay.

The Niobe of nations ! there she stands,
Childless and crownless, in her voiceless woe ;
An empty urn within her withered hands,
Whose holy dust was scattered long ago ;
The Scipios' tomb contains no ashes now ;
The very sepulchres lie tenantless
Of their heroic dwellers : dost thou flow,
Old Tiber, through a marble wilderness ?
Rise, with thy yellow waves, and mantle her distress.

The Goth, the Christian, Time, War, Flood, and Fire,

Have dealt upon the seven-hilled City's pride ;
She saw her glories star by star expire,
And up the steep barbarian monarchs ride,
Where the car climbed the Capitol ; far and wide
Temple and tower went down, nor left a site :
Chaos of ruins ! who shall trace the void,
O'er the dim fragments cast a lunar light,
And say, " here was, or is," where all is doubly
    night ? . . .

But here, where Murder breathed her bloody
    steam ;
And here, where buzzing nations choked the ways,
And roared or murmured like a mountain stream
Dashing or winding as its torrent strays ;
Here, where the Roman million's blame or praise
Was Death or Life, the playthings of a crowd,
My voice sounds much, and fall the stars' faint
    rays
On the arena void, seats crushed, walls bowed,
And galleries where my steps seem echoes strangely
    loud.

A Ruin, yet what a Ruin ! from its mass
Walls, palaces, half-cities have been reared ;
Yet oft the enormous skeleton ye pass,
And marvel where the spoil could have appeared.
Hath it indeed been plundered, or but cleared ?
Alas ! developed, opens the decay,
When the colossal's fabric's form is neared :
It will not bear the brightness of the day,
Which streams too much on all years, man, have
    reft away.

But when the rising moon begins to climb
Its topmost arch and gently pauses there,
When the stars twinkle through the loops of Time,
And the low night-breeze waves along the air
The garland-forest which the gray walls wear,
Like laurels on the bald first Caesar's head,
When the light shines serene but does not glare,
Then in this magic circle raise the dead ;
Heroes have trod this spot, 'tis on their dust ye
    tread.

" While stands the Coliseum, Rome shall stand :
" When falls the Coliseum, Rome shall fall ;
" And when Rome falls, the World." From our
    own land
Thus spake the pilgrims o'er this mighty wall
In Saxon times, which we are wont to call
Ancient ; and these three mortal things are still
On their foundations, and unaltered all,—
Rome and her Ruin past Redemption's skill,
The World—the same wide den of thieves, or
    what ye will.

BYRON (from *Childe Harold's Pilgrimage*)

The weeds that feed on the marsh air have twisted
themselves into its crannies ; the polished fragments of
serpentine are split and rent out of their cells, and lie in
green ruins along its ledges ; the salt winds have eaten
away the fair shafting of its star window into a skeleton
of crumbling rays. It cannot stand much longer ; may
Heaven only in its benignity, preserve it from restoration,
and the sands of the Serchio give it honourable grave.

RUSKIN (from *The Stones of Venice*)

The cloud-capp'd towers, the gorgeous palaces,
The solemn temples, the great globe itself,
Yea, all which it inherit, shall dissolve
And, like this insubstantial pageant faded,
Leave not a rack behind.

SHAKESPEARE (from *The Tempest*)

§VII CONTEMPLATION

When Contemplation, like the night-calm felt
Through earth and sky, spreads widely, and sends
    deep
Into the soul its tranquillising power . . .

WORDSWORTH

But when the soul attends through her proper faculty,
she is instantly carried away into the other world of
purity, eternity, immortality and of unchanging things;
and there finding her own element she merges herself
in it (that is, so long as she is true to herself and keeps
herself whole); and she strays no longer, but thus always
in regard to it she remains steadfast, for that also in
which she has merged herself is steadfast. And the name
of this condition of the Soul is Understanding.

PLATO (from Phaedo)

Unthinking Heads, who have not learn'd to be alone,
are in a Prison to themselves, if they be not also with
others : Whereas on the contrary, they whose thoughts
are in a fair, and hurry within, are sometimes fain to
retire into Company, to be out of the crowd of themselves.
He who must needs have company, must needs have
sometimes bad Company. Be able to be alone. Loose not
the advantage of Solitude and the Society of thy self, nor
be only content, but delight to be alone and single with
Omnipresency. He who is thus prepared, the Day is not
uneasy nor the Night black unto him. Darkness may
bound his Eyes, not his Imagination. In his Bed he may

ly, like *Pompey* and his Sons, in all quarters of the Earth, may speculate the Universe and enjoy the whole World in the Hermitage of himself. Thus the old *Ascetick* Christians found a Paradise in a Desert, and with little converse on Earth held a conversation in Heaven ; thus they Astronomiz'd in Caves, and, though they beheld not the Stars, had the Glory of Heaven before them.

SIR THOMAS BROWNE
(from *Christian Morals*)

I am sure there is a common spirit that plays within us, yet makes no part of us ; and that is, the Spirit of God, the fire and scintillation of that noble and mighty Essence, which is the life and radical heat of Spirits, and those essences that know not the vertue of the Sun ; a fire quite contrary to the fire of Hell. This is that gentle heat that brooded on the waters, and in six days hatched the World ; this is that irradiation that dispels the mists of Hell, the clouds of horrour, fear, sorrow, despair, and preserves the region of the mind in serenity. Whosoever feels not the warm gale and gentle ventilation of this Spirit, though I feel his pulse, I dare not say he lives : for truely, without this, there is no heat under the Tropick ; nor any light, though I dwelt in the body of the Sun.

SIR THOMAS BROWNE
(from *Religio Medici*)

Think of things long past, and long to come : Acquaint thyself with the *choragium* of the Stars, and consider the vast expansion beyond them. Let Intellectual Tubes give thee a glance of things, which visive Organs reach not. Have a glimpse of incomprehensibles, and Thoughts of things, which Thoughts but tenderly touch. Lodge immaterials in thy Head : ascend unto invisibles : fill thy Spirit with Spirituals, with the mysteries of Faith, the magnalities of Religion, and thy Life with the Honour of God.

SIR THOMAS BROWNE
(from *Christian Morals*)

Dive deep into thy bosom ; learn the depth, extent, bias, and full fort of thy mind ; contract full intimacy with the stranger within thee ; excite and cherish every spark of intellectual light and heat, however smothered under former negligence, or scattered through the dull, dark mass of common thoughts ; and, collecting them into a body, let thy genius rise (if genius thou hast) as the sun from chaos ; and if I should then say, like an Indian, " Worship it," (though too bold,) yet should I say little more than my second rule enjoins ; namely, " Reverence thyself."

EDWARD YOUNG
(from *Conjectures on Original Composition*)

I shut myself in with my soul,
And the shapes come eddying forth.

ROSSETTI (a fragment)

If we examine our thoughts, we shall find them to be all set on the past and the future. Of the present we think hardly at all, and if we do, it is only that we may draw from it a light wherewith to control the future. The present is never our end ; past and present are our means ; the future alone is our end. Thus we never live, but we hope to live ; and it is inevitable that, ever preparing to be happy, we never are so.

.   .   .   .

When I set myself sometimes to consider the divers agitations of men, and the troubles and dangers to which they expose themselves, . . . I see that all their misfortunes come from one thing only, that they know not how to dwell in peace, in a room.

PASCAL (from *Les Pensées*)

An old man said : " The man who hath learned by experience the sweetness of the quietness which is in his cell, doth not flee from meeting his neighbour because he is as one who despiseth him, but because of the fruits which he plucketh from silence."

.   .   .   .

Abba Moses used to say : " The man who fleeth from the world is like unto ripe grapes, but he who dwelleth among the attractions of the children of men is like unto sour grapes."

.   .   .   .

An old man said : " Human care and worry and anxiety about the things of the body destroy the faculties of knowledge and expression in a man, and leave him like unto a piece of dry wood."

PALLADIUS
(from *The Paradise of the Fathers*—
Trans. E. A. WALLIS BUDGE)

Men seek retirement in lonely places and country houses, and you too have longed for these. But surely it is a mere whim, for it is in your power, whenever you desire it, to retire into yourself. The most serene and unperturbed place in the world is a man's own breast, for if he have a mind well stored he can gaze inwards and find himself at ease. Therefore make frequent use of this retirement for the refreshment of your virtue ; and to this end be always provided with brief and uncontentious thoughts, to keep your understanding true and make easy the duties that await you. What is it that troubles you ? The wickedness of the world ? Then apply your antidote and consider that mankind were made for mutual assistance, that forbearance is a part of justice, and that men do wrong against their will. Consider how men have embroiled themselves and spent their days in anger and disputes, and so gained more trouble and, maybe, less of life thereby. Be quiet, then. Or is it that your appointed lot does not please you ? Then consider this alternative : either Providence or Chaos sits at the helm. If the first, the administration cannot be questioned : if the latter, there's no mending it. Or you may reflect that the world is, as it were, one great city. Or does bodily affliction torment you ? Reflect that your mind does not lie in your lungs, nor your reason in your breath, so that if you be asthmatic or out of health, it is no great matter, if only you will let your mind retire and consider her own privilege and power and take rest in her adopted philosophy of pain and pleasure. Or is it that the concern of fame sits hard upon you ? If you are pinched there, consider how quickly all things vanish and are forgotten, what deserts of infinity lie on either side. Consider the emptiness of applause, the precarious tenure, the little judgment of those that give it, the narrow compass in which you are confined. For the whole globe is but a point, and how little of this is inhabited ; and of its inhabitants, how many, do you think, will admire you and what will be their quality ? Do not forget, then, to retire into the little enclosure of your self ; and above all, let there be no striving and struggling, but move freely and gracefully, and manage matters like a man of sense and spirit, a citizen of the world, and a creature that must shortly die. And, among the rest of your stock, let these two maxims be always ready. First, that it is not *things*, but *thoughts* which give disturbance ; for things keep their distance and are motionless. The second is to consider that all visible things are shifting and sliding off into nothing, and that even you yourself have seen great alterations. In a word, the world is all shifts and changes and life no more than a phantom.

Consider, for 'tis high time, that you have something more divine in you than the mechanism of passion, than the wires and tackling of a poppet. What then is my soul made of ? Is it fear, or jealousy, or lust ? Or anything of this coarse nature ? Certainly no.

Thoughts are, in a great measure, masters of things, and, which is more, it is in your own power to think as you please ; therefore do not suffer opinion to cheat you any longer. Disengage from the tyranny of fancy, and then, as if you had doubled some dangerous cape, you will have nothing but a steady course, a smooth sea, and a land-locked bay before you.

MARCUS AURELIUS
(Trans. JEREMY COLLIER: modified)

The Beings of the Mind are not of clay :
Essentially immortal, they create
And multiply in us a brighter ray
And more beloved existence : that which Fate
Prohibits to dull life, in this our state
Of mortal bondage, by these Spirits supplied,
First exiles, then replaces what we hate ;
Watering the heart whose early flowers have died,
And with a fresher growth replenishing the void.

Such is the refuge of our youth and age,
The first from Hope, the last from Vacancy ;
And this wan feeling peoples many a page
And, may be, that which grows beneath mine eye :
Yet there are things whose strong reality
Outshines our fairy-land ; in shape and hues
More beautiful than our fantastic sky,
And the strange constellations which the Muse
O'er her wild universe is skilful to diffuse :

I saw or dreamed of such, but let them go,
They came like Truth and disappeared like dreams ;
And whatsoe'er they were, are now but so :
I could replace them if I would ; still teems
My mind with many a form which aptly seems
Such as I sought for, and at moments found ;
Let these too go, for waking Reason deems
Such over-weening phantasies unsound,
And other voices speak, and other sights surround.

BYRON (from *Childe Harold's Pilgrimage*)

I imagine that whenever a man's personal habit is healthful and temperate, and when, before taking himself to rest, he has stimulated the rational part of him and feasted it on beautiful discussions and high enquiries by means of close and inward reflection ; while, on the other hand, he has neither stinted nor gorged his appetites, so that they are lulled to sleep instead of troubling with their joys and griefs that highest part, which may thus be permitted to pursue its studies in purity and independence and to strain forward until it perceives something till then unknown, either past, present, or future ; and when, in like manner, he has calmed the passionate element by avoiding every burst of anger which would send him to sleep with his spirit stirred,—when, I say, he proceeds to rest with two elements out of the three quieted, and the third, wherein wisdom resides, aroused, you are aware that at such moments he is best able to apprehend truth and that the visions which present themselves in his dreams are then anything but unlawful.

PLATO (from *The Republic*)

Silence is the element in which great things fashion themselves together ; that at length they may emerge, full-formed and majestic, into the daylight of Life, which they are henceforth to rule. Not William the Silent only, but all considerable men I have known, and the most undiplomatic and unstrategic of these, forbore to babble of what they were creating and projecting. Nay, in thy own mean perplexities, do thou thyself but *hold thy tongue for one day* : on the morrow, how much clearer are thy purposes, and duties ; what wreck and rubbish have those mute workmen within thee swept away, when intrusive noises were shut out! Speech is too often not, as the Frenchman defined it, the art of concealing Thought; but of quite stifling and suspending Thought, so that there is none to conceal. Speech too is great, but not the greatest. As the Swiss inscription says: *Sprechen ist silbern, Schweigen ist golden* (Speech is silvern, Silence is golden); or as I might rather express it: Speech is of Time, Silence is of Eternity.

CARLYLE (from Sartor Resartus)

Elected Silence, sing to me
And beat upon my whorlèd ear,
Pipe me to pastures still and be
The music that I care to hear.

Shape nothing, lips; be lovely dumb:
It is the shut, the curfew sent
From there where all surrenders come
Which only makes you eloquent.

Be shellèd, eyes, with double dark
And find the uncreated light:
This ruck and reel which you remark
Coils, keeps, and teases simple sight.

Palate, the hutch of tasty lust,
Desire not to be rinsed with wine:
The can must be so sweet, the crust
So fresh that come in fasts divine!

GERARD MANLEY HOPKINS

It came to pass (Thyself, as I believe, by Thy secret ways so ordering it), that she and I stood alone, leaning in a certain window, which looked into the garden of the house where we now lay, at Ostia; where removed from the din of men, we were recruiting from the fatigues of a long journey, for the voyage. We were discoursing then together, alone, very sweetly; and forgetting those things which are behind, and reaching forth unto those things which are before, we were enquiring between ourselves in the presence of the Truth, which Thou art, of what sort the eternal life of the saints was to be, which eye hath not seen, nor ear heard, nor hath it entered into the heart of man. But yet we gasped with the mouth of our heart, after those heavenly streams of Thy fountain, the fountain of life, which is with Thee; that being bedewed thence according to our capacity, we might in some sort meditate upon so high a mystery.

And when our discourse was brought to that point, that the very highest delight of the earthly senses, in the very purest material light, was, in respect of the sweetness of that life, not only not worthy of comparison, but not even of mention; we raising up ourselves with a more glowing affection towards the *Self Same*, did by degrees pass through all things bodily, even the very heaven, whence sun and moon, and stars shine upon the earth; yea, we were soaring higher yet, by inward musing, and discourse, and admiring of Thy works; and we came to our own minds, and went beyond them, that we might arrive at that region of never-failing plenty, where Thou feedest Israel for ever with the food of truth, and where life is the Wisdom by whom all things are made, and what have been, and what shall be, and she is not made, but is, as she hath been, and so shall she be ever; yea rather to *have been*, and *hereafter to be*, are not in her, but only *to be*, seeing she is eternal. For to *have been*, and to *be hereafter*, are not eternal. And while we were discoursing and panting after her, we slightly touched on her with the whole effort of our heart ; and we sighed, and there we leave bound the first-fruits of the Spirit ; and returned to vocal expressions of our mouth, where the word spoken has beginning and end. And what is like unto Thy Word, our Lord, who endureth in Himself without becoming old, and maketh all things new.

We were saying then : If to any the tumult of the flesh were hushed, hushed the images of earth, and waters, and air, hushed also the poles of heaven, yea the very soul be hushed to herself, and by not thinking on self surmount self, hushed all dreams and imaginary revelations, every tongue and every sign, and whatsoever exists only in transition, since if any could hear, all these say, We made not ourselves, but He made us that abideth for ever—If then having uttered this, they too should be hushed, having roused only our ears to Him who made them, and He alone speak, not by them, but by Himself, that we may hear His Word, not through any tongue of flesh, nor Angel's voice, nor sound of thunder, nor in the dark riddle of a similitude, but might hear Whom in these things we love, might hear His Very Self without these, (as we two now strained ourselves, and in swift thought touched on that Eternal Wisdom, which abideth over all ;)—could this be continued on, and other visions of kind far unlike be withdrawn, and this one ravish, and absorb, and wrap up its beholder amid these inward joys, so that life might be for ever like one moment of understanding which now we sighed after ; were not this, Enter into thy Master's joy ?

SAINT AUGUSTINE
(from *The Confessions*—Trans. PUSEY)

Wisdom and Spirit of the universe !
Thou Soul that art the eternity of thought
That givest to forms and images a breath
And everlasting motion, not in vain
By day or star-light thus from my first dawn
Of childhood didst thou intertwine for me
The passions that build up our human soul ;
Not with the mean and vulgar works of man,
But with high objects, with enduring things—
With life and nature—purifying thus
The elements of feeling and of thought,
And sanctifying, by such discipline,
Both pain and fear, until we recognise
A grandeur in the beatings of the heart.
. . . .

Imagination—here the Power so called
Through sad incompetence of human speech,
That awful Power rose from the mind's abyss
Like an unfathered vapour that enwraps,
At once, some lonely traveller. I was lost ;
Halted without an effort to break through ;
But to my conscious soul I now can say—
" I recognise thy glory : " in such strength
Of usurpation, when the light of sense
Goes out, but with a flash that has revealed
The invisible world, doth greatness make abode,
There harbours ; whether we be young or old,
Our destiny, our being's heart and home,
Is with infinitude, and only there ;
With hope it is, hope that can never die,
Effort, and expectation, and desire,
And something evermore about to be.
Under such banners militant, the soul

Seeks for no trophies, struggles for no spoils
That may attest her prowess, blest in thoughts
That are their own perfection and reward,
Strong in herself and in beatitude
That hides her, like the mighty flood of Nile
Poured from his fount of Abyssinian clouds
To fertilise the whole Egyptian plain.

. . . .

The moon hung naked in the firmament
Of azure without cloud, and at my feet
Rested a silent sea of hoary mist.
A hundred hills their dusky backs upheaved
All over this still ocean ; and beyond,
Far, far beyond, the solid vapours stretched,
In headlands, tongues, and promontory shapes,
Into the main Atlantic, that appeared
To dwindle, and give up his majesty,
Usurped upon far as the sight could reach.
Not so the ethereal vault ; encroachment none
Was there, nor loss ; only the inferior stars
Had disappeared, or shed a fainter light
In the clear presence of the full-orbed Moon,
Who, from her sovereign elevation, gazed
Upon the billowy ocean, as it lay
All meek and silent, save that through a rift—
Not distant from the shore whereon we stood,
A fixed, abysmal, gloomy breathing-place—
Mounted the roar of waters, torrents, streams
Innumerable, roaring with one voice !
Heard over earth and sea, and in that hour,
For so it seemed, felt by the starry heavens. . . .
There I beheld the emblem of a mind
That feeds upon infinity, that broods

441

Over the dark abyss, intent to hear
Its voices issuing forth to silent light
In one continuous stream ; a mind sustained
By recognitions of transcendent power,
In sense conducting to ideal form,
In soul of more than mortal privilege.
One function, above all, of such a mind
Had Nature shadowed there, by putting forth,
'Mid circumstances awful and sublime,
That mutual domination which she loves
To exert upon the face of outward things,
So moulded, joined, abstracted, so endowed
With interchangeable supremacy,
That men, least sensitive, see, hear, perceive,
And cannot choose but feel. The power, which all
Acknowledge thus when moved, which Nature thus
To bodily sense exhibits, is the express
Resemblance of that glorious faculty
That higher minds bear with them as their own.
This is the very spirit in which they deal
With the whole compass of the universe :
They from their native selves can sent abroad
Kindred mutations ; for themselves create
A like existence ; and, whene'er it dawns
Created for them, catch it, or are caught
By its inevitable mastery,
Like angels stopped upon the wing by sound
Of harmony from Heaven's remotest spheres.
Them the enduring and the transient both
Serve to exalt ; they build up greatest things
From least suggestions ; ever on the watch,
Willing to work and to be wrought upon,
They need not extraordinary calls

To rouse them ; in a world of life they live,
By sensible impressions not enthralled,
But by their quickening impulse made more
    prompt
To hold fit converse with the spiritual world,
And with the generations of mankind
Spread over time, past, present, and to come,
Age after age, till Time shall be no more.

WORDSWORTH (from *The Prelude*)

Hai Ebn Yokhdan began, therefore, to strip himself of all bodily properties, which he had made some progress in before, during the time of the former exercise, when he was employed in the imitation of the heavenly bodies ; but there still remained a great many relicks, as his circular motion (motion being one of the most proper attributes of the body), and his care of animals and plants, compassion upon them, and industry in removing whatever inconvenienced them. Now all these things belong to corporeal attributes, for he could not see these things at first, but by corporeal faculties ; and he was obliged to make use of the same faculties in preserving them. Therefore he began to reject and remove all those things from himself, as being in nowise consistent with that state which he was now in search of. So he continued, after confining himself to rest in the bottom of his cave, with his head bowed down and his eyes shut, and turning himself altogether from all sensible things and corporeal faculties, and bending all his thoughts and meditations upon the necessarily self-existent Being, without

443

admitting anything else besides him ; and if any other object presented itself to his imagination, he rejected it with his utmost force ; and exercised himself in this, and persisted in it to that degree, that sometimes he did neither eat nor stir for a great many days together. And whilst he was thus earnestly taken up in contemplation, sometimes all manner of beings whatsoever would be quite out of his mind and thoughts, except his own being only.

But he found that his own being was not excluded from his thoughts ; no, not at such times when he was most deeply immersed in the contemplation of the first, true, necessarily self-existent Being ; which concerned him very much. For he knew that even this was a mixture in his simple vision, and the admission of an extraneous object in that contemplation. Upon which he endeavoured to disappear from himself, and be wholly taken up in the vision of that true Being ; till at last he attained it ; and then both the heavens and the earth, and whatsoever is between them, and all spiritual forms, and corporeal faculties, and all those powers which are separate from matter, and all those beings which know the necessarily self-existent Being, all disappeared and vanished, and were as if they had never been ; and amongst these his own being disappeared too, and there remained nothing but this one, true, necessarily self-existent Being, who spoke thus in that saying of his (which is not a notion super-added to his essence) :—" To whom now belongs the kingdom ? To this one, Almighty God." Which words of his Hai Ebn Yokhdan understood and heard his voice ; nor was his being unacquainted with words, and not being able to speak, any hindrance at all to understanding him. Wherefore he deeply immersed himself into this state, and witnessed that which neither eye hath seen nor ear heard, nor hath it ever entered into the heart of man to conceive.

ABU JAAFER EBN TOPHAIL
(from *The Improvement of Human Reason*—
Trans. SIMON OCKLEY, 1708)

Thou hast another eye, an eye within, far more piercing than the other thou speakest of,—one that beholds at once the past, the present, and the future ; which diffuses through all things the keen brightness of its vision ; which penetrates what is hidden, investigates what is impalpable ; which needs no foreign light wherewith to see, but gazes by a light of its own, proper unto itself.

HUGO OF ST. VICTOR
(from *De Vanitate Mundi*—Trans. R. A. VAUGHAN)

Look ! are not the fields covered with a delightful verdure ? Is there not something in the woods and groves, in the rivers and clear springs, that soothes, that softens, that transports the soul ? At the prospect of the wide and deep ocean, or some huge mountain whose top is lost in the sky, or of an old gloomy forest, are not our minds filled with a pleasing horror ? Even in rocks and desarts, is there not an agreable wildness ? How sincere a pleasure is it to behold the natural beauties of the earth ! To preserve and renew our relish for them, is not the veil of night alternately drawn over her face, and does she not

445

change her dress with the seasons? How aptly are the elements disposed! What variety and use in stones and minerals! What delicacy, what beauty, what contrivance, in animal and vegetable bodies! How exquisitely are all things suited, as well to their particular ends as to constitute apposite parts of the whole! And while they mutually aid and support, do they not also set off and illustrate each other? Raise now your thoughts from this ball of earth to all those glorious luminaries that adorn the high arch of heaven. The motion and situation of the planets, are they not admirable for use and order? Were those (miscalled *erratique*) globes once known to stray, in their repeated journies through the pathless void? Do they not measure areas round the sun, ever proportioned to the times? So fixed, so immutable are the laws by which the unseen Author of Nature actuates the universe. How vivid and radiant is the lustre of the fixed stars! How magnificent and rich that negligent profusion with which they appear to be scattered through the whole azure vault! Yet, if you take the telescope, it brings into your view a new host of stars that escape the naked eye. Here they seem contiguous and minute, but, to a nearer view, immense orbs of light at various distances far sunk in the abyss of space. Now you must call imagination to your aid: The feeble, narrow sense cannot descry innumerable worlds revolving round the central fires, and, in those worlds, the energy of an all-perfect mind displayed in endless forms. But neither sense nor imagination are big enough to comprehend the boundless extent, with all its dazzling furniture. Though the labouring mind exert and strain each power to its utmost reach, there still stands out ungrasped a surplusage immeasurable. Yet all the vast bodies that compose this mighty frame, how distant and remote soever, are, by some secret mechanism, some divine art and force, linked in a mutual dependence and intercourse with each other, even with this earth, which almost slipt from my thoughts, and was lost in the crowd of worlds. Is not the whole system immense, beautiful, glorious beyond expression and beyond thought ? What treatment then do those Philosophers deserve, who would deprive these noble and delightful scenes of all reality ? How should those principles be entertained, that lead us to think all the visible beauty of the creation a false imaginary glare ?

BERKELEY (from *Dialogues*)

The everlasting universe of things
Flows through the mind, and rolls its rapid waves,
Now dark, now glittering, now reflecting gloom,
Now lending splendour, where from secret springs
The source of human thought its tribute brings
Of waters, with a sound but half its own. . . .

Thou art the path of that unresting sound,
Dizzy Ravine ! and when I gaze on thee
I seem as in a trance sublime and strange
To muse on my own separate fantasy,
My own, my human mind, which passively
Now renders and receives fast influencings,
Holding an unremitting interchange
With the clear universe of things around ;
One legion of wild thoughts, whose wandering
    wings

447

Now float above thy darkness, and now rest
Where that or thou art no forbidden guest,
In the still cave of the witch Poesy,
Seeking among the shadows that pass by
Ghosts of all things that are, some shade of thee,
Some phantom, some faint image ; till the breast
From which they fled recalls them, thou art there !

Some say that gleams of a remoter world
Visit the soul in sleep,—that death is slumber,
And that its shapes the busy thoughts outnumber
Of those who wake and live.—I look on high ;
Has some unknown omnipotence unfurled
The veil of life and death ? or do I lie
In dream, and does the mightier world of sleep
Spread far around and inaccessibly
Its circles ? For the very spirit fails,
Driven like a homeless cloud from steep to steep
That vanishes among the viewless gales !
Far, far above, piercing the infinite sky,
Mont Blanc appears, still, snowy, and serene :
Its subject mountains their unearthly forms
Pile around it, ice and rock ; broad vales between
Of frozen floods, unfathomable deeps,
Blue as the overhanging heaven, that spread
And wind among the accumulated steeps . . .

The fields, the lakes, the forests, and the streams,
Ocean, and all the living things that dwell
Within the daedal earth ; lightning, and rain,
Earthquake, and fiery flood, and hurricane,
The torpor of the year when feeble dreams
Visit the hidden buds, or dreamless sleep

Holds every future leaf and flower ; the bound
With which from that detested trance they leap ;
The works and ways of man, their death and birth,
And all of him and all that his may be ;
All things that move and breathe with toil and
    sound
Are born and die ; revolve, subside, and swell.
Power dwells apart in its tranquillity,
Remote, serene, and inaccessible :
And this, the naked countenance of earth,
On which I gaze, even these primaeval mountains
Teach the adverting mind.

SHELLEY (from *Mont Blanc*)

When the act of reflection takes place in the mind, when
we look at ourselves in the light of thought, we discover
that our life is embosomed in beauty. Behind us, as far
as we go, all things assume pleasing forms, as clouds do
far off. Not only things familiar and stale, but even the
tragic and terrible, are comely, as they take their place in
the pictures of memory. The river-bank, the weed at the
water-side, the old house, the foolish person,—however
neglected in the passing,—have a grace in the past. Even
the corpse that has lain in the chambers has added a
solemn ornament to the house. The soul will not know
either deformity or pain. If, in the hours of clear reason,
we should speak the severest truth, we should say, that
we had never made a sacrifice. In these hours the mind
seems so great, that nothing can be taken from us that
seems much. All loss, all pain, is particular ; the universe

Pl   449

remains to the heart unhurt. Neither vexations nor calamities abate our trust. No man ever stated his griefs as lightly as he might. Allow for exaggeration in the most patient and sorely ridden hack that was ever driven. For it is only the finite that has wrought and suffered ; the infinite lies stretched in smiling repose. . . .

Not in nature but in man is all the beauty and worth he sees. The world is very empty, and is indebted to this gilding, exalting soul for all its pride. " Earth fills her lips with splendours " *not her own.* The vale of Tempe, Tivoli, and Rome are earth and water, rocks and sky. There are as good earth and water in a thousand places, yet how unaffecting !

EMERSON (from *The Essays*)

Within a cavern of man's trackless spirit
    Is throned an Image, so intensely fair
That the adventurous thoughts that wander near it
    Worship, and as they kneel, tremble and wear
The splendour of its presence, and the light
    Penetrates their dreamlike frame
Till they become charged with the strength of
    flame.

SHELLEY (fragment)

When contemplation raises itself from nature to soul, and from this to intellect, the contemplations always becoming more close and familiar, and united with the contemplating individuals, they become surely in intellect one through essence, because in intellect essence is

450

the same with intellection. For there it cannot be any longer said that *this* is one thing and *that* another ; for if this was admitted, there must be some other nature in which essence and intellection are one. It is requisite therefore that in intellect both should be truly one ; and this is no other than a vital contemplation.

But since it is *through* and *with* intellect that intelligent natures derive their knowledge of other things, by what collected intuition can we perceive a nature exalted above intellect itself ? We answer, that this can be accomplished only by something resident in our souls as like as possible to the first ; for we possess in our inmost recesses something of this exalted nature ; or rather, there is not any thing endued with a power of partaking of this first divinity in which he does not abide. Indeed wherever any thing subsists capable of receiving this divine principle, it partakes of something from thence : just as if a voice should occupy a solitary place and, together with this solitude, a number of men ; for then in whatever part the hearing is placed the whole voice is received, and yet again not the whole. What is it then which, by the use of our intellect, we receive ?

Now it is necessary that intellect should depend on another nature, which is no longer conversant with a discursive energy, but is the principle of transition, the source of life, and the origin of intellect and of all things.

What then shall we say it is ? The power of all things, without whose subsistence the universality of things would never have had being ; nor would intellect have been, which is the first and universal life ; for that which subsists above life is the cause of life ; since the energy of life, which is all things, is not the first, but emanates from this principle as its ineffable fountain. Conceive then

451

a fountain possessing no other principle, but imparting itself to all rivers, without being exhausted by any one of them, and abiding quietly in itself; but the streams which emanate from this fountain, before they flow in different directions, as yet abiding together and, as it were, already knowing what rivulets will proceed from their defluxions. Or conceive the life of a mighty tree, propagating itself through the whole tree, the principle at the same time remaining without being divided through the whole, but, as it were, established in the root: this then will afford an universal and abundant life to the tree, but will abide itself, without multiplication, and subsisting as the principle of multitude.

Intellect indeed is beautiful, and the most beautiful of all things, being situated in a pure light and a pure splendour, and comprehending in itself the nature of beings, of which indeed this our beautiful material world is but the shadow and image; but intellect, that true intelligible world, is situated in universal splendour, living in itself a blessed life, and containing nothing unintelligible, nothing dark, nothing without measure; which divine world whoever perceives will immediately be astonished, if, as is requisite, he profoundly and intimately merges himself into its inmost recesses, and becomes one with its all-beauteous nature. And as he who diligently surveys the heavens and contemplates the splendour of the stars, should immediately think upon and search after their artificer, so it is requisite that he who beholds and admires the intelligible world should diligently enquire after its author, investigating who he is, where he resides, and how he produced such an offspring as intellect, a son beautiful and pure and full of his ineffable fire. But his father is neither intellect nor himself a son, but superior to both; for intellect has an ulterior subsistence and is of itself lacking in nourishment and intelligence, being placed the next in order to that nature which is above every kind of want. Intellect, however, enjoys true plenitude and intelligence, because it possesses the first of all things; but that which is prior to intellect neither lacks nor possesses, for if this were the case it would not be the Good itself.

PLOTINUS
(Trans. TAYLOR: modified and abridged)

Like as a falcon or an eagle tiring after wide circuits in the windy spaces of heaven foldeth his wings and droppeth to quiet cover, so urgeth the spirit towards that state whose repose no desire troubleth nor delusion entereth. That is its true being, from yearnings, from evil, and from fear delivered. Like unto a man in the embrace of a beloved wife, unaware of things without or things within, is the spirit that is embraced by the all-discerning self.

(from *The Upanishads*)

Com pensive Nun, devout and pure,
Sober, stedfast, and demure,
All in a robe of darkest grain,
Flowing with majestick train,
And sable stole of Cipres Lawn,
Over thy decent shoulders drawn.
Com, but keep thy wonted state,
With even step and musing gate,

453

And looks commercing with the skies,
Thy rapt soul sitting in thine eyes :
There held in holy passion still,
Forget thy self to Marble, till
With a sad leaden downward cast,
Thou fix them on the earth as fast.
And joyn with thee calm Peace, and Quiet,
Spare Fast, that oft with gods doth diet,
And hears the Muses in a ring,
Ay round about Joves Altar sing.
And adde to these retired Leasure,
That in trim Gardens takes his pleasure ;
But first, and chiefest, with thee bring,
Him that yon soars on golden wing,
Guiding the fiery-wheeled throne,
The Cherub Contemplation,
And the mute Silence hist along,
'Less Philomel will daign a Song,
In her sweetest, saddest plight,
Smoothing the rugged brow of night,
While Cynthia checks her Dragon yoke,
Gently o're th'accustom'd Oke ;
Sweet Bird that shunn'st the noise of folly,
Most musicall, most melancholy !
Thee Chauntress oft the Woods among,
I woo to hear thy eeven-song ;
And missing thee, I walk unseen
On the dry smooth-shaven Green,
To behold the wandring Moon,
Riding neer her highest noon,
Like one that hath bin led astray
Through the Heav'ns wide pathles way ;
And oft, as if her head she bow'd,

Stooping through the fleecy cloud.
Oft on a Plat of rising ground,
I hear the far-off Curfeu sound,
Over som side-water'd shoar,
Swinging slow with sullen roar ;
Or if the Ayr will not permit,
Som still removed place will fit,
Where glowing Embers through the room
Teach light to counterfeit a gloom,
Far from all resort of mirth,
Save the Cricket on the hearth,
Or the Belmans drousie charm,
To bless the dores from nightly harm :
Or let my Lamp at midnight hour
Be seen in som high lonely Towr,
Where I may oft out-watch the Bear,
With thrice great Hermes, or unsphear
The spirit of Plato to unfold
What worlds, or what vast Regions hold
The immortal mind that hath forsook
Her mansion in this fleshly nook.

MILTON (from *Il Penseroso*)

What is more easy and sweet than meditation ? Yet
in this hath God commended his Love, that by meditation
it is enjoyed. As nothing is more easy than to think, so
nothing is more difficult than to think well. The easiness
of thinking we received from God, the difficulty of thinking well proceeded from ourselves. Yet in truth, it is far
more easy to think well than ill, because good thoughts

be sweet and delightful : Evil thoughts are full of discontent and trouble. So that an evil habit and custom have made it difficult to think well, not Nature. For by nature nothing is so difficult as to think amiss.

.   .   .   .   .   .

Is it not easy to conceive the World in your Mind ? To think the Heavens fair ? The Sun Glorious ? The Earth fruitful ? The Air Pleasant ? The Sea Profitable ? And the Giver bountiful ? Yet these are the things which it is difficult to retain. For could we always be sensible of their use and value, we should be always delighted with their wealth and glory.

TRAHERNE (from *Centuries of Meditations*)

How vainly men themselves amaze
To win the Palm, the Oke, the Bayes ;
And their uncessant Labours see
Crown'd from some single Herb or Tree,
Whose short and narrow verged Shade
Does prudently their Toyles upbraid ;
While all Flow'rs and all Trees do close
To weave the Garlands of repose.

Fair quiet, have I found thee here,
And Innocence thy Sister dear !
Mistaken long, I sought you then
In busie Companies of Men.
Your sacred Plants, if here below,
Only among the Plants will grow.
Society is all but rude,
To this delicious Solitude.

456

No white nor red was ever seen
So am'rous as this lovely green.
Fond Lovers, cruel as their Flame,
Cut in these Trees their Mistress name.
Little, Alas, they know, or heed,
How far these Beauties Hers exceed !
Fair Trees ! where s'eer your barkes I wound,
No Name shall but your own be found.

When we have run our Passions heat,
Love hither makes his best retreat.
The *Gods*, that mortal Beauty chase,
Still in a Tree did end their race.
Apollo hunted *Daphne* so,
Only that She might Laurel grow.
And *Pan* did after *Syrinx* speed,
Not as a Nymph, but for a Reed.

What wond'rous Life is this I lead !
Ripe Apples drop about my head ;
The Luscious Clusters of the Vine
Upon my Mouth do crush their Wine ;
The Nectaren, and curious Peach,
Into my hands themselves do reach
Stumbling on Melons, as I pass,
Insnar'd with Flow'rs, I fall on Grass.

Mean while the Mind, from pleasure less,
Withdraws into its happiness :
The Mind, that Ocean where each kind
Does streight its own resemblance find ;
Yet it creates, transcending these,
Far other Worlds, and other Seas ;

Annihilating all that's made
To a green Thought in a green Shade.

Here at the Fountains sliding foot,
Or at some Fruit-trees mossy root,
Casting the Bodies Vest aside,
My Soul into the boughs does glide :
There like a Bird it sits, and sings,
Then whets, and combs its silver Wings ;
And, till prepar'd for longer flight,
Waves in its Plumes the various Light.

Such was that happy Garden-state,
While Man there walk'd without a Mate :
After a Place so pure, and sweet,
What other Help could yet be meet !
But 'twas beyond a Mortal's share
To wander solitary there :
Two Paradises 'twere in one
To live in Paradise alone.

How well the skilful Gardner drew
Of flow'rs and herbes this Dial new ;
Where from above the milder Sun
Does through a fragrant Zodiack run ;
And, as it works, th' industrious Bee
Computes its time as well as we.
How could such sweet and wholsome Hours
Be reckon'd but with herbs and flow'rs !

MARVELL

At the time . . . when I am tired with amusement and company, and have indulged a reverie in my chamber, or a solitary walk by a river side, I feel my mind all collected within itself, and am naturally inclined to carry my view into all those subjects about which I have met with so many disputes in the course of my reading and conversation. I cannot forbear having a curiosity to be acquainted with the principles of moral good and evil, the nature and foundation of government, and the cause of those several passions and inclinations, which actuate and govern me. I am uneasy to think I approve of one object, and disapprove of another; call one thing beautiful, and another deformed; decide concerning truth and falsehood, reason and folly, without knowing upon what principles I proceed. I am concerned for the condition of the learned world, which lies under such a deplorable ignorance in all these particulars. I feel an ambition to arise in me of contributing to the instruction of mankind, and of acquiring a name by my inventions and discoveries. These sentiments spring up naturally in my present disposition; and should I endeavour to banish them, by attaching myself to any other business or diversion, I feel I should be a loser in point of pleasure; and this is the origin of my philosophy.

HUME (from *A Treatise of Human Nature*)

I am certain of nothing but of the holiness of the heart's affections, and the truth of Imagination. What the Imagination seizes as Beauty must be Truth, whether it existed before or not—for I have the same idea of all our

459

passions as of Love : they are all, in their sublime, creative of essential Beauty. In a word, you may know my favourite speculation by my first book, and the little song I sent in my last, which is a representation from the fancy of the probable mode of operating in these matters. The Imagination may be compared to Adam's dream : he woke and found it truth. I am more zealous in this affair, because I have never yet been able to perceive how anything can be known for truth by consecutive reasoning— and yet so it must be. Can it be that even the greatest philosopher ever arrived at his goal without putting aside numerous objections ? However it may be, O for a life of sensations rather than of thoughts ! It is " a Vision in the form of Youth," a shadow of reality to come—and this consideration has further convinced me—for it has come as auxiliary to another favourite speculation of mine— that we shall enjoy ourselves hereafter by having what we called happiness on earth repeated in a finer tone. And yet such a fate can only befall those who delight in Sensation, rather than hunger, as you do, after Truth. Adam's dream will do here, and seems to be a conviction that Imagination and its empyreal reflection is the same as human life and its spiritual repetition. But, as I was saying, the simple imaginative mind may have its rewards in the repetition of its own silent working coming continually on the spirit with a fine suddenness. To compare great things with small, have you never, by being surprised with an old melody, in a delicious place, by a delicious voice, *felt* over again your very speculations and surmises at the time it first operated on your soul ? Do you not remember forming to yourself the singer's face—more beautiful than it was possible, and yet, with the elevation of the moment, you did not think so ? Even then you were mounted on the wings of Imagination, so high that the prototype must be hereafter—that delicious face you will see. Sure this cannot be exactly the case with a complex mind—one that is imaginative, and at the same time careful of its fruits—who would exist partly on sensation, partly on thought—to whom it is necessary that " years should bring the philosophic mind " ? Such a one I consider yours, and therefore it is necessary to your eternal happiness that you not only drink this old wine of Heaven, which I shall call the redigestion of our most ethereal musings upon earth, but also increase in knowledge, and know all things.

KEATS (from *The Letters*)

Hampstead. 19 February, 1818.

MY DEAR REYNOLDS,

I had an idea that a man might pass a very pleasant life in this manner—let him on a certain day read a certain page of full poesy or distilled prose, and let him wander with it, and muse upon it, and reflect from it, and bring home to it, and prophesy upon it, and dream upon it, until it becomes stale. But will it do so ? Never. When man has arrived at a certain ripeness of intellect, any one grand and spiritual passage serves him as a starting-post towards all " the two-and-thirty palaces." How happy is such a voyage of conception, what delicious diligent indolence ! A doze upon a sofa does not hinder it, and a nap upon clover engenders ethereal finger-pointings ; the prattle of a child gives it wings, and the converse of middle-age the strength to beat them ; a strain of music conducts to " an odd angle of the Isle," and when the leaves whisper, it puts a girdle round the earth. Nor will this sparing touch of noble books be any irreverence to their writers ; for perhaps the honours paid by man to man are trifles in comparison to the benefit done by great works to the " spirit and pulse of good " by their mere passive existence. Memory should not be called knowledge. Many have original minds who do not think it : they are led away by custom. Now it appears to me that almost any man may, like the spider, spin from his own inwards, his own airy citadel. The points of leaves and twigs on which the spider begins her work are few, and she fills the air with a beautiful circuiting. Man should be content with as few points to tip with the fine web of his soul, and weave a tapestry empyrean—full of symbols for his spiritual eye, of softness for his spiritual touch, of space for his wanderings, of distinctness for his luxury. But the minds of mortals are so different, and bent on such diverse journeys, that it may at first appear impossible for any common taste and fellowship to exist between two or three under these suppositions. It is however quite the contrary. Minds would leave each other in contrary directions, traverse each other in numberless points, and at last greet each other at the journey's end.

KEATS (from *The Letters*)

It is not a Man's cloistering himself up in his Study, nor his continual Poring upon Books, that makes him a Wise Man : No ; this property is to be acquired only by Meditation and Converse. For Reading may very properly be compared to Eating, and Meditating to Digesting ; as therefore to one hour Eating, we allow many hours for

Digesting; so to one hours Reading we should assign a sufficient time for Meditating, and Digesting what we have read. Or else, as the one by breeding ill humours and obstructing the passages, impairs the Health of the Body; so will the other be of no less prejudice to the understanding, by occasioning Diseases to the mind. Thus do many Men, through not observing this Rule, instead of improving, really impair themselves by their Studies. For by over-much Reading they clog and oppress their Minds, and so digest nothing. They stuff themselves so full of other Mens Notions, that there is no room for their Faculties to display themselves. Whereas the Man of Thought and Meditation moves in a larger Sphere; he does not thus pinion his Fancy, but puts it upon the Wing, which seldom returns home without some noble Quarry. And did Men but know how much the pleasure of Thinking transcends all other pleasures, they would certainly put greater value upon it. For nothing is comparable to the pleasure of an active and a prevailing Thought: a Thought prevailing over the difficulty and obscurity of the Object, and refreshing the Soul with new Discoveries and Images of things, and thereby extending the bounds of Apprehension, and (as it were) enlarging the Territories of Reason. But the Learned Man that daily plods on in his Reading, and that never makes use of this thinking Faculty, by reflecting upon what he hath read, quite loseth the *Intellectual Enjoyments*; nor is he sensible of that *Suavissima Vita*, as the Poet calls it, of *Descending into himself, and being daily sensible of his own improvement*: but like the Carriers Horse, he still keeps the old Track; and his Learning (to continue the Simile) like the Pack is but a Burthen to the Beast that carries it. But now, after all that hath been said against Learning, thus much I must own and acknowledge, That Learning when it meets with an ingenuous temper, and is joyn'd to a pregnancy of mind, is then of excellent use and Advantage : For there is no Man but will speak the better, where he knows what others have said upon the same subject. But on the other hand, if Learning happens to be in the possession of a Fool, 'tis then but a Bawble, and, like Dr *Donne's Sun-Dial in the Grave*, a trifle, and of no use.

SIR THOMAS BLOUNT (from *Essays*, 1692)

Who then, that has a mind well strung and tun'd
To contemplation, and within his reach
A scene so friendly to his fav'rite task,
Would waste attention at the chequer'd board,
His host of wooden warriors to and fro
Marching and counter-marching, with an eye
As fixt as marble, with a forehead ridg'd
And furrow'd into storms, and with a hand
Trembling, as if eternity were hung
In balance of his conduct of a pin ?
Nor envies he aught more their idle sport,
Who pant with application misapplied
To trivial toys, and, pushing iv'ry balls
Across the velvet level, feel a joy
Akin to rapture, when the bawble finds
Its destin'd goal, of difficult access.
Nor deems he wiser him, who gives his noon
To Miss, the Mercer's plague, from shop to shop
Wandr'ing, and litt'ring with unfolded silks
The polish'd counter, and approving none,
Or promising with smiles to call again.

COWPER (from *The Task*)

Mrs Millamant : My dear liberty, shall I leave thee? my
faithful solitude, my darling contemplation, must I bid
you then adieu? Ay-h adieu! my morning thoughts,
agreeable wakings, indolent slumbers, all ye *douceurs*, ye
sommeils du matin, adieu?—I can't do it, 'tis more than
impossible—positively, Mirabell, I'll lie abed in a morning as long as I please.

CONGREVE (from *The Way of the World*)

I remember that Sam Cox, the counsel, walking by the
seaside as if in deep contemplation, was questioned about
what he was musing on. He replied " I was wondering
that such an almost infinite and unwieldy element should
produce a *sprat*."

COWPER (from *The Letters*)

I was yesterday about sunset walking in the open fields,
till the night insensibly fell upon me. I at first amused
myself with all the richness and variety of colours, which
appeared in the western parts of heaven : in proportion
as they faded away and went out, several stars and planets
appeared one after another, till the whole firmament was
in a glow. The blueness of the ether was exceedingly
heightened and enlivened by the season of the year, and
by the rays of all those luminaries that passed through it.
The galaxy appeared in its most beautiful white. To complete the scene, the full moon rose at length in that clouded
majesty which Milton takes notice of, and opened to the
eye a new picture of nature, which was more finely shaded,

and disposed among softer lights, than that which the sun had before discovered to us.

As I was surveying the moon walking in her brightness, and taking her progress among the constellations, a thought rose in me which I believe very often perplexes and disturbs men of serious and contemplative natures. David himself fell into it in that reflection, " When I consider the heavens, the works of thy fingers, the moon and the stars which thou hast ordained ; what is man that thou art mindful of him, and the son of man that thou regardest him ? " In the same manner, when I had considered that infinite host of stars, or, to speak more philosophically, of suns, which were then shining upon me, with those innumerable sets of planets or worlds, which were moving round their respective suns ; when I still enlarged the idea, and supposed another heaven of suns and worlds rising still above this which we discovered, and these still enlightened by a superior firmament of luminaries, which are planted at so great a distance that they may appear to the inhabitants of the former as the stars do to us ;—in short, whilst I pursued this thought, I could not but reflect on that little insignificant figure which I myself bore amidst the immensity of God's works.

Were the sun, which enlightens this part of the creation, with all the host of planetary worlds that move about him, utterly extinguished and annihilated, they would not be missed more than a grain of sand upon the seashore. The space they possess is so exceedingly little in comparison of the whole, that it would scarce make a blank in the creation. The chasm would be imperceptible to an eye, that could take in the whole compass of nature, and pass from one end of the creation to the other, as it is possible there may be such a sense in ourselves hereafter, or in creatures which are at present more exalted than ourselves. We see many stars by the help of glasses, which we do not discover with our naked eyes ; and the finer our telescopes are, the more still are our discoveries. Huygenius carries this thought so far, that he does not think it impossible there may be stars whose light is not yet travelled down to us, since their first creation. There is no question but the universe has certain bounds set to it ; but when we consider that it is the work of infinite power, prompted by infinite goodness, with an infinite space to exert itself in, how can our imagination set any bounds to it ?

To return therefore to my first thought, I could not but look upon myself with secret horror, as a being that was not worth the smallest regard of one who had so great a work under his care and superintendency. I was afraid of being overlooked amidst the immensity of nature, and lost among that infinite variety of creatures, which in all probability swarm through all these immeasurable regions of matter.

In order to recover myself from this mortifying thought, I considered that it took its rise from those narrow conceptions, which we are apt to entertain of the divine nature. We ourselves cannot attend to many different objects at the same time. If we are careful to inspect some things, we must of course neglect others. This imperfection which we observe in ourselves, is an imperfection that cleaves in some degree to creatures of the highest capacities, as they are creatures, that is, beings of finite and limited natures. The presence of every created being is confined to a certain measure of space, and consequently his observation is stinted to a certain number of objects. The sphere in which we move and act and understand,

467

is of a wider circumference to one creature than another,
according as we rise one above another in the scale of
existence. But the widest of these our spheres has its
circumference. When therefore we reflect on the divine
nature, we are so used and accustomed to this imperfection in ourselves, that we cannot forbear in some measure
ascribing it to him in whom there is no shadow of imperfection. Our reason indeed assures us that his attributes
are infinite, but the poorness of our conceptions is such,
that it cannot forbear setting bounds to everything it contemplates, till our reason comes again to our succour, and
throws down all those little prejudices which rise in us
unawares, and are natural to the kind of man.

ADDISON (*Essays*)

What links are ours with orbs that are
    So resolutely far :
The solitary asks, and they
Give radiance as from a shield :
    Still at the death of day,
    The seen, the unrevealed.
    Implacable they shine
To us who would of Life obtain
An answer for the life we strain
    To nourish with one sign.
Nor can imagination throw
The penetrative shaft : we pass
The breath of thought, who would divine
    If haply they may grow
As Earth ; have our desire to know ;

468

If life comes there to grain from grass,
And flowers like ours of toil and pain ;
  Has passion to beat bar,
  Win space from cleaving brain ;
  The mystic link attain,
  Whereby star holds on star.

Those visible immortals beam
  Allurement to the dream :
Ireful at human hungers brook
  No question in the look.
For ever virgin to our sense,
Remote they wane to gaze intense :
Prolong it, and in ruthlessness they smite
The beating heart behind the ball of sight
  Till we conceive their heavens hoar,
  Those lights they raise but sparkles frore,
And Earth, our blood-warm Earth, a shuddering
      prey
To that frigidity of brainless ray.

Yet space is given for breath of thought
Beyond our bounds when musing : more
When to that musing love is brought,
And love is asked of love's wherefore.
'Tis Earth's, her gift ; else have we nought :
Her gift, her secret, here our tie.
And not with her and yonder sky ?
Bethink you : were it Earth alone
Breeds love, would not her region be
  The sole delight and throne
  Of generous Deity ?

To deeper than this ball of sight
Appeal the lustrous people of the night.
Fronting yon shoreless, sown with fiery sails,
    It is our ravenous that quails,
Flesh by its craven thirsts and fears distraught.
    The spirit leaps alight,
    Doubts not in them is he,
The binder of his sheaves, the sane, the right :
Of magnitude to magnitude is wrought,
To feel it large of the great life they hold :
In them to come, or vaster intervolved,
The issues known in us, our unsolved solved :
That there with toil Life climbs the self-same
    Tree,
Whose roots enrichment have from ripeness
    dropped.
So may we read and little find them cold :
Let it but be the lord of Mind to guide
Our eyes ; no branch of Reason's growing
    lopped ;
Nor dreaming on a dream ; but fortified
By day to penetrate black midnight ; see,
Hear, feel, outside the senses ; even that we,
The specks of dust upon a mound of mould,
We who reflect those rays, though low our place,
    To them are lastingly allied.

So may we read, and little find them cold :
Not frosty lamps illumining dead space,
Not distant aliens, not senseless Powers.
The fire is in them whereof we are born ;
The music of their motion may be ours.

Spirit shall deem them beckoning Earth and
    voiced
Sisterly to her, in her beams rejoiced.
Of love, the grand impulsion, we behold
    The love that lends her grace
    Among the starry fold.
Then at new flood of customary morn,
    Look at her through her showers,
    Her mists, her streaming gold,
A wonder edges the familiar face :
She wears no more the robe of printed hours ;
Half strange seems Earth, and sweeter than her
    flowers.

GEORGE MEREDITH

Then the Lord answered Job out of the whirlwind,
    and said,
Who is this that darkeneth counsel
By words without knowledge ?
Gird up now thy loins like a man ;
For I will demand of thee, and declare thou unto me.
Where wast thou when I laid the foundations of the
    earth ?
Declare, if thou hast understanding ?
Who determined the measures thereof, if thou
    knowest ?
Or who stretched the line upon it ?
Whereupon were the foundations thereof fastened ?
Or who laid the corner stone thereof ;
When the morning stars sang together,

471

And all the sons of God shouted for joy ?
Or who shut up the sea with doors,
When it brake forth, as if it had issued out of the
      womb ;
When I made the cloud the garment thereof,
And thick darkness a swaddlingband for it,
And prescribed it for my boundary,
And set bars and doors,
And said, Hitherto shalt thou come, but no further ;
And here shall thy proud waves be stayed ?
Hast thou commanded the morning since thy days
      began,
And caused the dayspring to know its place ;
That it might take hold of the ends of the earth,
And the wicked be shaken out of it ?
It is changed as clay under the seal ;
And all things stand forth as a garment :
And from the wicked their light is witholden,
And the high arm is broken.
Hast thou entered into the springs of the sea ?
Or hast thou walked in the recesses of the deep ?
Have the gates of death been revealed unto thee ?
Or hast thou seen the gates of the shadow of death ?
Hast thou comprehended the breadth of the earth ?
Declare if thou knowest it all.
Where is the way to the dwelling of light,
And as for darkness, where is the place thereof ;
That thou shouldest take it to the bound thereof,
And that thou shouldest discern the paths to the
      house thereof ?
Doubtless, thou knowest, for thou wast then born,
And the number of thy days is great !
Hast thou entered the treasuries of the snow,

Or hast thou seen the treasuries of the hail,
Which I have reserved against the time of trouble,
Against the day of battle and war ?
By what way is the light parted,
Or the east wind scattered upon the earth ?
Who hath cleft a channel for the waterflood,
Or a way for the lightning of the thunder ;
To cause it to rain on a land where no man is ;
On the wilderness, wherein there is no man ;
To satisfy the waste and desolate ground ;
And to cause the tender grass to spring forth ?
Hath the rain a father ?
Or who hath begotten the drops of dew ?
Out of whose womb came the ice ?
And the hoary frost of heaven, who hath gendered it ?
The waters are congealed like stone,
And the face of the deep cohereth.
Canst thou bind the cluster of the Pleiades,
Or loose the bands of Orion ?
Canst thou lead forth the Signs of the Zodiac in
    their season ?
Or canst thou guide the Bear with her train ?
Knowest thou the ordinances of the heavens ?
Canst thou establish the dominion thereof in the
    earth ?
Canst thou lift up thy voice to the clouds,
That abundance of waters may cover thee ?
Canst thou send forth lightnings, that they may go,
And say unto thee, Here we are ?
Who hath put wisdom in the inward parts
Or who hath given understanding to the mind ?
Who can number the clouds by wisdom ?
Or who can pour out the bottles of heaven,

When the dust runneth into a mass,
And the clods cleave fast together ? . . .
Moreover the Lord answered Job, and said,
Shall he that cavilleth contend with the Almighty ?
He that argueth with God, let him answer it.

Then Job answered the Lord, and said,
Behold, I am of small account ; what shall I answer
thee ?
I lay my hand upon my mouth.

THE BIBLE (from *Job*)

O how contemptible a thing is man except he raise
himselfe above humane things ! As long as we struggle
with affections, what doe we that deserveth praise ?
Although we get the upper hand, yet overcome we but
monsters. What cause have we to boast of our selves
because we are unlike the worst men of the world ? I see
not why hee should take pleasure in himselfe that is
stronger than a sicke man. There is great difference betwixt strength and good health. Thou hast escaped from
the vices of the minde ; thou art no hypocrite, nor
flatterer, nor double, nor soyled with avarice, which
denieth her selfe that, which she hath taken from all men,
nor grounded in dissolution, which spendeth his goods
and mony basely, and getteth them likewise most villein-
ously ; neyther travailed with ambition, which will not
leade thee to dignity but by indignities. Thou hast as yet
gotten nothing, thou hast escaped many mens hands, but
not thine owne. For that vertue which we affect is magnificent, not because it is a blessed thing of it selfe to have

wanted evill, but because it freeth the minde, and pre-
pareth it to the knowledge of heavenly things, and
maketh it worthy to come and accompanie God. Then
enjoyeth the minde the consummate and complete good
of humane condition, whenas (treading all evil under-foot)
he flieth to heaven and nestleth in the secret bosome of
nature. Then taketh he delight in wandering amidst the
starres, to laugh at the pavements of the rich, and to
deride the earth with all her golde, not onely that I meane
which she hath delivered out and given to make money of,
but that also which she keepeth close hidden, to content
the avarice of prosperitie. He cannot contemne the
porches, nor the house beams that are burnished with
Ivory, nor the groves planted upon the tops of houses,
nor the rivers drawne and convayed thorow chambers,
before he hath circled the whole world, and beholding
the globe thereof from above, small and for the most part
covered with the Sea, and in that place where it dis-
covereth it selfe, hugely desart, and eyther burnt or frozen,
without saying to himselfe : Is this the point that is divided
amongst so many Nations by fire and sword ? O how
ridiculous are the bounds of mortall men ? Let not the
Dane passe by the river of Ister, let Strimo include the
Thracians, let Euphrates bound the Parthians, Danubia
separate the Samaritans and the Romanes, let Rhene
border Germany, the Pyrinean mountaines raise their
heads betwist France and Spaine ; let the desolate vast-
nesse of sands divide Egypt from the Ethiopians. If we
should give humane understanding unto Ants, would they
not likewise divide a little Mole-hill of earth into Provinces ? Whenas thou hast raised thy selfe to those things
that are truly great, as often as thou shalt see whole armies
marching with displayed engines, and as if there were som

great matter in hand, the horse-men now scowting and discovering before, now flancking the battell, thou mayest freely say, *The blacker Squadron trotteth through the Plaines*. All this is but a businesse of Ants that labour in a Mole-hill.

SENECA
(from *Of National Questions*—Trans. THOMAS LODGE)

This morning saw I, fled the shower,
The earth reclining in a lull of power :
The heavens, pursuing not their path,
Lay stretched out naked after bath,
Or so it seemed ; field, water, tree, were still,
Nor was there any purpose on the calm-browed
    hill.

The hill, which sometimes visibly is
Wrought with unresting energies,
Looked idly ; from the musing wood,
And every rock, a life renewed
Exhaled like an unconscious thought
When poets, dreaming unperplexed,
Dream that they dream of nought.
Nature one hour appears a thing unsexed,
Or to such serene balance brought
That her twin natures cease their sweet alarms,
And sleep in one another's arms.
The sun with resting pulses seems to brood,
And slacken its command upon my unurged
    blood.

The river has not any care
Its passionless water to the sea to bear ;

476

The leaves have brown content ;
The wall to me has freshness like a scent,
And takes half animate the air,
Making one life with its green moss and stain ;
And life with all things seems too perfect blent
For anything of life to be aware.
The very shades on hill, and tree, and plain,
Where they have fallen doze, and where they
    doze remain.

No hill can idler be than I ;
No stone its inter-particled vibration
Investeth with a stiller lie ;
No heaven with a more urgent rest betrays
The eyes that on it gaze.
We are too near akin that thou shouldst cheat
Me, Nature, with thy fair deceit.
In poets floating like a water-flower
Upon the bosom of the glassy hour,
In skies that no man sees to move,
Lurk untumultuous vortices of power,
For joy too native, and for agitation
Too instant, too entire for sense thereof,
Motion like gnats when autumn suns are low,
Perpetual as the prisoned feet of love
On the heart's floors with painèd pace that go.
From stones and poets you may know,
Nothing so active is, as that which least seems
    so.

For he, that conduit running wine of song,
Then to himself does most belong
When he his mortal house unbars

To the importunate and thronging feet
That round our corporal walls unheeded beat;
Till, all containing, he exalt
His stature to the stars, or stars
Narrow their heaven to his fleshly vault:
When, like a city under ocean,
To human things he grows a desolation,
And is made a habitation
For the fluctuous universe
To lave with unimpeded motion.
He scarcely frets the atmosphere
With breathing, and his body shares
The immobility of rocks;
His heart's a drop-well of tranquillity;
His mind more still is than the limbs of fear,
And yet its unperturbed velocity
The spirit of the simoon mocks.
He round the solemn centre of his soul
Wheels like a dervish, while his being is
Streamed with the set of the world's harmonies,
In the long draft of whatsoever sphere
He lists the sweet and clear
Clangour of his high orbit on to roll,
So gracious is his heavenly grace;
And the bold stars does hear,
Every one in his airy soar,
For evermore
Shout to each other from the peaks of space,
As 'thwart ravines of azure shouts the
        mountaineer.

FRANCIS THOMPSON

They whose bodies only are creative, betake themselves to women and beget children—this is the character of their love ; their offspring, as they hope, will preserve their memory and give them the blessedness and immortality which they desire in the future. But creative souls—for there certainly are men who are more creative in their souls than in their bodies—conceive that which is proper for the soul to conceive or retain. And what are these conceptions ?—wisdom and virtue in general. And such creators are poets and all artists who are deserving of the name inventor. But the greatest and fairest sort of wisdom by far is that which is concerned with the ordering of states and families, and which is called temperance and justice. And he who in youth has the seed of these implanted in him and is himself inspired, when he comes to maturity desires to beget and generate. He wanders about seeking beauty that he may beget offspring—for in deformity he will beget nothing—and naturally embraces the beautiful rather than the deformed body ; above all when he finds a fair and noble and well-nurtured soul, he embraces the two in one person, and to such an one he is full of speech about virtue and the nature and pursuits of a good man ; and he tries to educate him ; and at the touch of the beautiful which is ever present to his memory, even when absent, he brings forth that which he had conceived long before, and in company with him tends that which he brings forth ; and they are married by a far nearer tie and have a closer friendship than those who beget mortal children, for the children which are their offspring are fairer and more immortal. Who, when he thinks of Homer and Hesiod and other great poets, would not rather have their children than ordinary human ones ? Who would not emulate them in the creation of children such as theirs, which have preserved their memory and given them everlasting glory? Or who would not have such children as Lycurgus left behind him to be the saviours, not only of Lacedaemon, but of Hellas, as one may say? There is Solon, too, who is the revered father of Athenian laws; and many others there are in many other places, both among Hellenes and barbarians. All of them have given to the world many noble works, and have been the parents of virtue of every kind, and many temples have been raised in their honour for the sake of their children; which were never raised in honour of any one, for the sake of his mortal children.

These are the lesser mysteries of love, into which even you, Socrates, may enter; to the greater and more hidden ones which are the crown of these, and to which, if you pursue them in a right spirit, they will lead, I know not whether you will be able to attain. But I will do my utmost to inform you, and do you follow if you can. For he who would proceed aright in this matter should begin in youth to visit beautiful forms; and first, if he be guided by his instructor aright, to love one such form only—out of that he should create fair thoughts; and soon he will of himself perceive that the beauty of one form is akin to the beauty of another; and then if beauty of form in general is his pursuit, how foolish would he be not to recognize that the beauty in every form is one and the same! And when he perceives this he will abate his violent love of the one, which he will despise and deem a small thing, and will become a lover of all beautiful forms; in the next stage he will consider that the beauty of the mind is more honourable than the beauty of the outward form. So that if a virtuous soul have but a little comeliness, he will be content to love and tend him, and will search out and bring to the birth thoughts which may improve the young, until he is compelled to contemplate and see the beauty of institutions and laws, and to understand that the beauty of them all is of one family, and that personal beauty is a trifle ; and after laws and institutions he will go on to the sciences, that he may see their beauty, being not like a servant in love with the beauty of one youth or man or institution, himself a slave mean and narrow-minded, but drawing towards and contemplating the vast sea of beauty, he will create many fair and noble thoughts and notions in boundless love of wisdom ; until on that shore he grows and waxes strong, and at last the vision is revealed to him of a single science, which is the science of beauty everywhere. To this I will proceed ; please to give me your very best attention.

He who has been instructed thus far in the things of love, and who has learned to see the beautiful in due order and succession, when he comes toward the end will suddenly perceive a nature of wondrous beauty (and this, Socrates, is the final cause of all our former toils)—a nature which in the first place is everlasting, not growing and decaying, or waxing and waning ; in the next place not fair in one point of view and foul in another, or at one time or in one relation or at one place fair, at another time or in another relation or at another place foul, as if fair to some and foul to others, or in the likeness of a face or hands or any other part of the bodily frame, or in any form of speech or knowledge, or existing in any other being ; as for example, in an animal, or in heaven, or in earth, or in any other place, but beauty only, absolute, separate, simple, and everlasting, which without diminution and without increase, or any change, is imparted to the ever-growing and perishing beauties of all

other things. He who under the influence of true love
rising upward from these begins to see that beauty, is not
far from the end. And the true order of going or being
led by another to the things of love, is to use the beauties
of earth as steps along which he mounts upwards for the
sake of that other beauty, going from one to two, and from
two to all fair forms, and from fair forms to fair practices,
and from fair practices to fair notions, until from fair
notions he arrives at the notion of absolute beauty, and at
last knows what the essence of beauty is. This, my dear
Socrates . . ., is that life above all others which man
should live, in the contemplation of beauty absolute ; a
beauty which if you once beheld, you would see not to be
after the measure of gold, and garments, and fair boys and
youths, whose presence now entrances you ; and you and
many a one would be content to live seeing only and
conversing with them without meat or drink, if that were
possible—you only want to be with them and to look at
them. But what if man had eyes to see the true beauty—
the divine beauty, I mean, pure and clear and unalloyed,
not clogged with the pollutions of mortality, and all the
colours and vanities of human life—thither looking, and
holding converse with the true beauty divine and simple ?
Do you not see that in that communion only, beholding
beauty with the eye of the mind, he will be enabled to
bring forth, not images of beauty, but realities (for he has
hold not of an image but of a reality), and bringing forth
and nourishing true virtue to become the friend of God
and be immortal, if mortal man may ?

PLATO
(from *Symposium*—Trans. JOWETT)

482

Too late loved I Thee, O Thou Beauty of ancient days, yet ever new! too late I loved Thee! And behold, Thou wert within, and I abroad, and there I searched for Thee, deformed I, plunging amid those fair forms, which Thou hadst made. Thou wert with me, but I was not with Thee. Things held me far from Thee, which, unless they were in Thee, were not at all. Thou calledst, and shoutedst, and burstedst my deafness. Thou flashedst, shonest, and scatteredst my blindness. Thou breathedst odours, and I drew in breath and pant for Thee. I tasted, and hunger and thirst. Thou touchedst me, and I burned for Thy peace. When I shall with my whole self cleave to Thee, I shall no where have sorrow, or labour; and my life shall wholly live, as wholly full of Thee.

SAINT AUGUSTINE (Trans. PUSEY)

§VIII FOOD

'Tis not the food, but the content
That makes the Tables merriment.
Where Trouble serves the board, we eate
The Platters there, as soone as meat.
A little Pipkin with a bit
Of Mutton, or of Veale in it,
Set on my Table, (Trouble-free)
More than a Feast contenteth me.

HERRICK

Eaten I have ; and though I had good cheere,
I did not sup, because no friends were there.
Where Mirth and friends are absent when we Dine
Or Sup, there wants the Incense and the Wine.

HERRICK

The world and all that has ever been in it will one day
be as much forgotten as what we ate for dinner forty years
ago. Very likely, but the fact that we shall not remember
much about a dinner forty years hence does not make it
less agreeable now, and after all it is only the accumulation
of these forgotten dinners that makes the dinner of forty
years hence possible.

SAMUEL BUTLER (from *The Notebooks*)

In banquets remember that you entertain two guests,
body and soul ; and whatever you shall have given to the
body you will soon eject, but what you shall have given
to the soul you will keep for ever.

EPICTETUS

Let not him that eateth despise him that eateth not ;
and let not him which eateth not judge him that eateth ;
for God hath received him.

SAINT PAUL

In Gluttony there must be Eating, in Drunkenness
there must be Drinking : 'tis not the eating, nor 'tis not
the drinking that is to be blamed, but the Excess.

SELDEN (from *Table Talk*)

This Thou hast taught me, that I should set myself to
take food as physic. But while I am passing from the discomfort of emptiness to the content of replenishing, in
the very passage the snare of concupiscence besets me.
For that passing, is pleasure, nor is there any other way
to pass thither, whither we needs must pass. And health
being the cause of eating and drinking, there joineth itself
as an attendant a dangerous pleasure, which mostly
endeavours to go before it, so that I may for her sake do
what I say I do, or wish to do, for health's sake. Nor have
each the same measure ; for what is enough for health,
is too little for pleasure. And often it is uncertain, whether
it is the necessary care of the body which is yet asking
for sustenance, or whether a voluptuous deceivableness
of greediness is proffering its services.

SAINT AUGUSTINE
(from the *Confessions*—Trans. PUSEY)

THE FIRST COOK

If, according to Petavius and Le Clerc, the world was created in autumn, when fruits of the earth were both plentiful and in the highest perfection, the first man had little occasion for much culinary knowledge ; roasting or boiling the cruder productions, with modes of preserving those which were better ripened, seem to be all that was necessary for him in the way of *Cury*. And even after he was displaced from Paradise, I conceive, as many others do, he was not permitted the use of animal food (Gen. i. 29) ; but that this was indulged to us, by an enlargement of our charter, after the Flood (Gen. ix. 3).

SAMUEL PEGGE (1780)

PILGRIMS' FARE

A Cook they hadde with hem for the nones,
To boille the chiknes with the marybones,
And poudre-marchant tart, and galingale.
Wel coude he knowe a draughte of London ale.
He coude roste, and sethe, and broille, and frye,
Maken mortreux, and wel bake a pye. . .
    For blankmanger, that made he with the beste.

CHAUCER
(from Prologue : *The Canterbury Tales*)

DINNER IN PARADISE

So saying, with dispatchful looks in haste
She turns, on hospitable thoughts intent
What choice to chuse for delicacie best,

What order, so contriv'd as not to mix
Tastes, not well joynd, inelegant, but bring
Taste after taste upheld with kindliest change,
Bestirs her then, and from each tender stalk
Whatever Earth all-bearing Mother yeilds
In *India* East or West, or middle shoare
In *Pontus* or the *Punic* Coast, or where
Alcinous reign'd, fruit of all kindes, in coate,
Rough, or smooth rin'd, or bearded husk, or shell
She gathers, Tribute large, and on the board
Heaps with unsparing hand ; for drink the Grape
She crushes, inoffensive moust, and meathes
From many a berrie, and from sweet kernels prest
She tempers dulcet creams, nor these to hold
Wants her fit vessels pure, then strews the ground
With Rose and Odours from the shrub unfum'd.
. . . Rais'd of grassie terf
Thir Table was, and mossie seats had round,
And on her ample Square from side to side
All *Autumn* pil'd, though *Spring* and *Autumn* here
Danc'd hand in hand. A while discourse they hold ;
No fear lest Dinner coole ; when thus began
Our Authour. Heav'nly stranger, please to taste
These bounties which our Nourisher, from whom
All perfet good unmeasur'd out, descends,
To us for food and for delight hath caus'd
The Earth to yeild ; unsavourie food perhaps
To spiritual Natures ; only this I know,
That one Celestial Father gives to all.

To whom the Angel. Therefore what he gives
(Whose praise be ever sung) to man in part
Spiritual, may of purest Spirits be found
No ingrateful food : and food alike those pure

Intelligential substances require
As doth your Rational ; and both contain
Within them every lower facultie
Of sense, whereby they hear, see, smell, touch, taste
Tasting concoct, digest, assimilate,
And corporeal to incorporeal turn.
For know, whatever was created, needs
To be sustaind and fed ; of Elements
The grosser feeds the purer, earth and sea,
Earth and the Sea feed Air, the Air those Fires
Ethereal, and as lowest first the Moon ;
Whence in her visage round those spots, unpurg'd
Vapours not yet into her substance turn'd.
Nor doth the Moon no nourishment exhale
From her moist Continent to higher Orbes.
The Sun that light imparts to all, receives
From all his alimental recompence
In humid exhalations, and at Even
Sups with the Ocean : though in Heav'n the Trees
Of life ambrosial frutage bear, and vines
Yeild Nectar, though from off the boughs each Morn
We brush mellifluous Dewes, and find the ground
Cover'd with pearly grain : yet God hath here
Varied his bounty so with new delights,
As may compare with Heaven ; and to taste
Think not I shall be nice. So down they sat,
And to their viands fell, nor seemingly
The Angel, nor in mist, the common gloss
Of Theologians, but with keen dispatch
Of real hunger, and concoctive heate
To transubstantiate ; what redounds, transpires
Through Spirits with ease ; nor wonder ; if by fire
Of sooty coal the Empiric Alchimist

Can turn, or holds it possible to turn
Metals of drossiest Ore to perfect Gold
As from the Mine. Mean while at Table *Eve*
Ministerd naked, and thir flowing cups
With pleasant liquors crown'd : O innocence
Deserving Paradise ! if ever, then,
Then had the Sons of God excuse to have bin
Enamour'd at that sight ; but in those hearts
Love unlibidinous reign'd, nor jealousie
Was understood, the injur'd Lovers Hell.

MILTON (from *Paradise Lost*)

AN ITALIAN ON ENGLISH FARE

They take pleasure in having a quantity of excellent
victuals, and also in remaining a long time at table, being
very sparing of wine when they drink it at their own
expense. And this, it is said, they do in order to induce
their other English guests to drink wine in moderation
also ; not considering it any inconvenience for three or
four persons to drink out of the same cup. Few people
keep wine in their own houses, but buy it for the most
part at a tavern ; and when they mean to drink a great
deal, they go to the tavern, and this is done not only by
the men, but by ladies of distinction. The deficiency of
wine, however, is amply supplied by the abundance of
ale and beer, to the use of which these people are become
so habituated, that, at an entertainment where there is
plenty of wine, they will drink them in preference to it,
and in great quantities.

(Italian Relation of England under Henry VII.
About A.D. 1500)

FOOD AND DRINK UNDER THE TUDORS

In number of dishes and change of meat the nobility of England (whose cooks are for the most part musical-headed Frenchmen and strangers) do most exceed, sith there is no day in manner that passeth over their heads wherein they have not only beef, mutton, veal, lamb, kid, pork, cony, capon, pig, or so many of these as the season yieldeth, but also some portion of the red or fallow deer, besides great variety of fish and wild fowl, and thereto sundry other delicates wherein the sweet hand of the sea-faring Portugal is not wanting. . . .

The chief part likewise of their daily provision is brought in before them (commonly in silver vessels, if they be of the degree of barons, bishops and upwards) and placed on their tables, whereof when they have taken what it pleaseth them, the rest is reserved, and afterward sent down to their serving men and waiters, who feed thereon in like sort with convenient moderation, their reversion also being bestowed upon the poor which lie ready at their gates in great number to receive the same. . . .

As for drink, it is usually filled in pots, goblets, jugs, bowls of silver in noblemen's houses, also in fine Venice glasses of all forms ; and for want of these elsewhere, in pots of earth of sundry colours and moulds, whereof many are garnished with silver, or at the leastwise in pewter. . . .

The gentlemen and merchants keep much about the same rate, and each of them contenteth himself with four, five, or six dishes, when they have but small resort, or peraventure with one, or two, or three the most, when they have no strangers to accompany them at their tables. . . .

At such times as the merchants do make their ordinary or voluntary feasts, it is a world to see what great provision is made of all manner of delicate meats, from every quarter of the country. . . . In such cases also jellies of all colours, mixed with a variety in the representation of sundry flowers, herbs, trees, forms of beasts, fish, fowls, and fruits, and thereunto marchpane wrought with no small curiosity, tarts of divers hues and sundry denomination, conserves of old fruits, foreign and home-bred, suckets . . . gingerbread, florentines, wild fowl, venison of all sorts, and sundry outlandish confections, altogether seasoned with sugar . . . do generally bear the sway. . . . And as all estates do exceed herein, I mean for strangeness and number of costly dishes, so these forget not to use the like excess in wine. . . . Neither do I mean this of small wines only, as Claret, White, Red, French, etc., which amount to about fifty-six sorts . . . but also of the thirty kinds of Italian, Grecian, Spanish, Canari, etc., whereof Vervage, Cate pument, Raspis, Muscadell, Romnie, Bastard, Tire, Oseie, Caprike, Clareie, and Malmeseie are not least of all accompted of, because of their strength and flavour.

HARRISON (in HOLINSHED'S *Chronicles*)

THE FOOD OF FANTASY

My meat shall all come in, in Indian shells,
    Dishes of agat set in gold, and studded
With emeralds, sapphires, hyacinths, and rubies.
The tongues of carps, dormice, and camels'
    heels,

Boiled in the spirit of sol, and dissolved pearl,
Apicius' diet, 'gainst the epilepsy:
And I will eat these broths with spoons of amber,
Headed with diamond and carbuncle.
My foot-boy shall eat pheasants, calvered
    salmons,
Knots, godwits, lampreys: I myself will have
The beards of barbel served, instead of salads;
Oiled mushrooms; and the swelling unctuous
    paps
Of a fat pregnant sow, newly cut off,
Drest with an exquisite and poignant sauce;
For which, I'll say unto my cook, *There's gold,
Go forth, and be a knight.*

BEN JONSON (from *The Alchemist*)

.   .   .   .

Then will we triumph, banquet, and carouse;
Cooks shall have pensions to provide us cates,
And glut us with the dainties of the world;
Lachryma Christi and Calabrian wines
Shall common soldiers drink in quaffing bowls,
Ay, liquide gold (when we have conquered him)
Mingled with coral and with orient pearl.
Come, let us banquet and carouse the whiles.

MARLOWE
(from *Tamburlaine the Great : Part II*)

I usher
Such unexpected dainty bit for breakfast
As never yet I cooked ; 'tis not Botargo,
Fried frogs, potatoes marrow'd, cavear,
Carps' tongues, the pith of an English chine of
    beef,
Nor our Italian delicate, oil'd mushrooms,
And yet a drawer-on too ; and if you show not
An appetite, and a strong one, I'll not say
To eat it, but devour it, without grace too,
(For it will not stay a preface) I am shamed,
And all my past provocatives will be jeer'd at.

          MASSINGER (from *The Guardian*)

On some, a priest succinct in amice white
Attends ; all flesh is nothing in his sight !
Beeves, at his touch, at once to jelly turn,
And the huge boar is shrunk into an urn ;
The board with spacious miracles he loads,
Turns hares to larks, and pigeons into toads.
Another (for in all what one can shine ?)
Explains the *sève* and *verdeur* of the wine,
What cannot copious sacrifice atone ?
Thy truffles, Perigord ! thy hams, Bayonne !
With French libation, and Italian strain,
Wash Bladen white and expiate Hays's stain.
Knight lifts the head, for what are crowds undone,
To three essential partridges in one ?
Gone every blush, and silent all reproach,
Contending princes mount them in their coach.

          POPE (from *The Dunciad*)

Breads we have of several grains, roots, and kernels ; yea and some of flesh and fish dried ; with divers kinds of leavenings and seasonings : so that some do extremely move appetites ; some do nourish so as divers do live of them without any other meat, who live very long. So for meats, we have some of them so beaten and made tender and mortified, yet without all corrupting, as a weak heat of the stomach will turn them into good chylus, as well as a strong heat would meat otherwise prepared. We have some meats also, and breads and drinks, which, taken by men, enable them to fast long after ; and some other that used make the very flesh of men's bodies sensibly more hard and tough, and their strength far greater than otherwise it would be.

BACON (from *The New Atlantis*)

GLUTTONY

And in that day did the Lord, the Lord of hosts, call to weeping and to mourning, and to baldness, and to girding with sackcloth : and, behold, joy and gladness, slaying oxen and killing sheep, eating flesh and drinking wine : let us eat and drink, for tomorrow we shall die.

(from *Isaiah*)

But they thought there was no life after this, or if there were, it was without pleasure, and every soul thrust into a hole, and a dorter of a spans length allowed for his rest and for his walk ; and in the shades below no numbring of healths by the numerical letters of *Philenium's* name, no fat Mullets, no Oysters of *Lucrinus*, no *Lesbian* or *Chian* Wines. Τοῦτο σαφῶς ἄνθρωπε μαθὼν εὔφραινε

497

σεαυτὸν. Therefore now enjoy the delicacies of Nature, and feel the descending wines distilled through the limbeck of thy tongue & *larynx*, and suck the delicious juice of fishes, the Marrow of the laborious Oxe, and the tender lard of *Apulian* Swine, and the condited bellies of the *Scarus* ; but lose no time ; for the Sunne drives hard, and the shadow is long, and *the dayes of mourning are at hand*, but the number of the dayes of darknesse and the grave cannot be told.

JEREMY TAYLOR (from *Sermons*)

. . . .

Strange therefore is it that for the stomach which is scarce a span long there should be provided so many furnaces and ovens, huge fires and an army of cooks, cellars swimming with wine & granaries sweating with corn ; that into one belly should enter the vintage of many Nations, the spoils of distant Provinces, and the shell-fishes of severall seas. When the Heathens feasted their Gods, they gave nothing but a fat oxe, a ram, or a kid ; they poured a little wine upon the Altar & burned a handfull of gum ; but when they feasted themselves, they had many vessels fill'd with Campanian wine, turtles of *Liguria*, *Sicilian beeves*, and *wheat* from *Egypt*, wilde boars from *Illyrium*, and *Grecian* sheep, variety, and load, and cost, and curiosity : and so do we. It is so little we spend in Religion, and so very much upon ourselves : so little to the poor, and so without measure to make our selves sick, that we seem to be in love with our own mischief, & so passionate for necessity and want that we strive all the ways we can to make our selves need more than Nature intended.

JEREMY TAYLOR (from *Sermons*)

ADAPTATION

i. The Man to the Food

I am of a constitution so general, that it consorts and sympathiseth with all things. I have no antipathy, or rather Idiosyncrasie, in dyet, humour, air, any thing. I wonder not at the French for their dishes of Frogs, Snails, and Toadstools, nor at the Jews for Locusts and Grasshoppers ; but being amongst them, make them my common Viands, and I find they agree with my Stomach as well as theirs. I could digest a Salad in a Church-yard as well as in a Garden.

SIR THOMAS BROWNE (from *Religio Medici*)

ii. The Food to the Man

Though Reason be so strictly to be preserved at our tables as well as at our prayers, and we can never have leave to do any violence to it ; yet the measures of Nature may be enlarged beyond the bounds of prime and common necessity. For besides hunger and thirst, there are some labours of the body and others of the mind, and there are sorrows and loads upon the spirit by its communications with the indispositions of the body. And as the labouring man may be supplied with bigger quantities, so the *student* and *contemplative* man with more delicious and spritefull nutriment : for as the tender and more delicate easily-digested meats will not help to carry burthens upon the neck and hold the plough in society and yokes of the laborious oxen, so neither will the pulse and leeks, *Lavinian* sausages, and the *Cisalpine* suckets or gobbets of condited buls flesh minister such delicate spirits to the

499

thinking man ; but his notion will be flat as the noise of the *Arcadian* porter and thick as the first juice of his countrey lard, unlesse he makes his body a fit servant to the soul, & both fitted for the imployment.

JEREMY TAYLOR (from Sermons)

TRANSCENDENTAL GASTRONOMY

Step up, my gluttonous friends ; a universal sage is about to instruct you in the art of living. . . . Come and listen to the Professor of Transcendental Gastronomy and learn to dine well. To dine is everything : the rest is but a long—too long an interval between a play that is always too short. To dine is the end of all human action. . . .

But before offering yourself for initiation into the mysteries of the maw, consider well your powers and natural dispositions ; examine without presumption *quid valeat stomachus, quid ferre recuset*. Has Nature given you that sure and exquisite sense of taste which can distinguish the finest shades among sapid molecules and nutritive substances ? And what of the nervous ganglia, papillae, and suckers which are the furniture of your degustatory apparatus ? Are they endowed with that selective wisdom which induces a delicious orgasm at the lightest contact with a classic condiment ? When you bite into a beccafico, cooked to a turn, do you feel your mouth deluged with a torrent of bliss unknown to the vulgar ? . . . If you can answer these questions in the affirmative you are worthy of the Professor and you may dine with him. But if unkindly Nature has given you a papier mâché stomach, if your appetite is no more than a feeble fancy in perpetual danger of extinction, then out you go ; haunt the provinces which are still back in the Middle Ages of gastronomy, and gorge yourselves on potatoes, Sauerkraut, porridge, peas-pudding, or polenta.

HOFFMAN on BRILLAT-SAVARIN

(*Journal des Débats*, 1825)

THE PROFESSOR APHORIZES

The destiny of nations depends upon the manner in which they eat.

Tell me what you eat and I will tell you what you are.

The discovery of a new dish does more for the happiness of the human race than the discovery of a new star.

They that bring upon themselves indigestion or drunkenness know neither how to eat nor how to drink.

A dessert lacking cheese is a pretty face that lacks an eye.

The Creator, while compelling Man to eat to live, invites him to it by Appetite and rewards him with Pleasure.

Animals feed ; Man eats ; but the Man of Taste knows how to eat.

BRILLAT-SAVARIN (from *Physiologie du Goût*)

A GLASSE FOR GLUTTONS

Where we are to eat to live, these only live to eat.

THOMAS FULLER (from *Sermons*)

THE EPICURE'S MEASURES

Let Pleasure be the lesse principall and used as a servant. It may be modest and prudent to strew the dish with Sugar or to dip thy bread in vinegar, but to make thy meal of sauces, and to make the accessory become the principall, and pleasure to rule the table and all the regions of thy soul, is to make a man lesse and lower than an Oglio, of a cheaper value than a Turbat, a servant and a worshipper of *sauces*, and *cooks*, and *pleasures*, and *folly*.

JEREMY TAYLOR (from *Sermons*)

. . . .

The constant aim of the wise man, in keeping the harmony of the body in tune, is to preserve the symphony which resides in the soul.

PLATO

. . . .

The art of pleasant meals or the art of good living is not the art of self-indulgence. On the contrary, it is the art of moderation in the enjoyment of all that is best in the world. Excess and ignorance, the lack of control and the lack of knowledge have been the cause of the misuse, abuse or distruction of the good things of the earth. Sad in the extreme is the thought of all the internal disorders —dispepsia and divorces—which could so easily have been avoided had the food been better cooked or the drink been less watery.

ANDRÉ SIMON (from *Tables of Content*)

NICETIES OF TASTE

We have been brought up to cherish the belief that of all the creatures that walk, swim, crawl, or fly, Man is the one with the most perfect sense of taste. . . .

In short, what is there left to desire in a faculty capable of such perfection that the epicures of Rome could distinguish by its taste the fish caught between the bridges from that caught lower down ? And have not our own days seen the discovery of that special flavour of the leg on which the partridge roosts ? And have we not around us epicures who can indicate the latitude under which a wine has matured as surely as a pupil of Biot or Arago can predict an eclipse ?

.　　.　　.　　.　　.　　.　　.

Game, too, owes a great part of its value to the nature of its native soil. The taste of a Perigord partridge is not the same as that of a partridge from Sologne ; and while a hare killed on the plains about Paris is a merely insignificant dish, a leveret born on the sun-scorched hills of Valromey or High Dauphiné is perhaps the most deliciously perfumed of all quadrupeds.

BRILLAT-SAVARIN (from *Physiologie du Goût*)

HOW TO EAT SMALL BIRDS

Few people know how to eat small birds. Here is the method as it was imparted to me in confidence by Canon Charcot, epicure by profession and, thirty years before the name became known, the perfect gastronome.

Take a properly plump little bird by the beak, sprinkle it with a little salt, remove the gizzard, thrust it neatly into the mouth, bite it off quite close to the fingers, and masticate vigorously. There will result a juice sufficiently abundant to envelop the whole organ of taste, and you will experience a pleasure unknown to the vulgar :

Odi profanum vulgus et arceo. HORACE.

The quail is, among game properly so called, the sweetest thing in the world. A plump quail pleases equally by its taste, its form, and its colour. It is an act of gross ignorance to serve it otherwise than roast, or cooked in paper, because its aroma is very fugitive and will dissolve, evaporate, and be lost if ever the creature is in contact with a liquid.

BRILLAT-SAVARIN (from *Physiologie du Goût*)

THE REVEREND DOCTOR FOLLIOTT AT BREAKFAST

" God bless my soul, sir ! " exclaimed the Reverend Doctor Folliott, bursting, one fine May morning, into the breakfast-room at Crotchet Castle, " I am out of all patience with this march of mind. Here has my house been nearly burned down, by my cook taking it into her head to study hydrostatics, in a sixpenny tract, published by the Steam Intellect Society, and written by a learned friend who is for doing all the world's business as well as his own, and is equally well qualified to handle every branch of human knowledge. I have a great abomination of this learned friend ; as author, lawyer, and politician, he is *triformis*, like Hecate : and in every one of his three forms he is *bifrons*, like Janus ; the true Mr. Facing-both-ways of Vanity Fair. My cook must read his rubbish in bed; and as might naturally be expected, she dropped suddenly fast asleep, overturned the candle, and set the curtains in a blaze. Luckily, the footman went into the room at the moment, in time to tear down the curtains and throw them into the chimney, and a pitcher of water on her nightcap extinguished her wick: she is a greasy subject, and would have burned like a short mould."

The reverend gentleman exhaled his grievance without looking to the right or to the left; at length, turning on his pivot, he perceived that the room was full of company, consisting of young Crotchet and some visitors whom he had brought from London. The Reverend Doctor Folliott was introduced to Mr. Mac Quedy, the economist: Mr. Skionar, the transcendental poet: Mr. Firedamp, the meteorologist; and Lord Bossnowl, son of the Earl of Foolincourt, the member for the borough of Rogueingrain.

The divine took his seat at the breakfast-table, and began to compose his spirits by the gentle sedative of a large cup of tea, the demulcent of a well-buttered muffin, and the tonic of a small lobster.

THE REV. DR. FOLLIOTT. You are a man of taste, Mr. Crotchet. A man of taste is seen at once in the array of his breakfast-table. It is the foot of Hercules, the far-shining face of the great work, according to Pindar's doctrine: ἀρχομένου ἔργου, πρόσωπον χρὴ θέμεν τηλαυγές. The breakfast is the πρόσωπον of the great work of the day. Chocolate, coffee, tea, cream, eggs, ham, tongue, cold fowl,—all these are good, and bespeak good knowledge in him who sets them forth: but the touchstone is fish: anchovy is the first step, prawns and shrimps the second; and I laud him who reaches even to these: potted char and lampreys are the third, and a fine stretch of progression; but lobster is, indeed, matter for a May morning, and demands a rare combination of knowledge and virtue in him who sets it forth.

MR. MAC QUEDY. Well, sir, and what say you to a fine fresh trout, hot and dry, in a napkin? or a herring out of the water into the frying pan, on the shore of Loch Fyne?

THE REV. DR. FOLLIOTT. Sir, I say every nation has some eximious virtue; and your country is pre-eminent in the glory of fish for breakfast. We have much to learn from you in that line at any rate.

MR. MAC QUEDY. And in many others, sir, I believe. Morals and metaphysics, politics and political economy, the way to make the most of all the modifications of smoke; steam, gas, and paper currency; you have all these to learn from us; in short, all the arts and sciences. We are the modern Athenians.

THE REV. DR. FOLLIOTT. I, for one, sir, am content to learn nothing from you but the art and science of fish for breakfast. Be content, sir, to rival the Boeotians, whose redeeming virtue was in fish, touching which point you may consult Aristophanes and his scholiast, in the passage of Lysistrata, ἀλλ' ἄφελε τὰς ἐγχέλεις, and leave the name of Athenians to those who have a sense of the beautiful, and a perception of metrical quantity.

MR. MAC QUEDY. Then, sir, I presume you set no value on the right principles of rent, profit, wages, and currency?

THE REV. DR. FOLLIOTT. My principles, sir, in these things are, to take as much as I can get, and to pay no more than I can help. These are every man's principles, whether they be the right principles or no. There, sir, is political economy in a nutshell.

MR. MAC QUEDY. The principles, sir, which regulate production and consumption, are independent of the will of any individual as to giving and taking, and do not lie in a nutshell by any means.

THE REV. DR. FOLLIOTT. Sir, I will thank you for a leg of that capon.

LORD BOSSNOWL. But, sir, by the bye, how came your footman to be going into your cook's room? It was very providential to be sure, but——

THE REV. DR. FOLLIOTT. Sir, as good came of it, I shut my eyes, and asked no questions. I suppose he was going to study hydrostatics, and he found himself under the necessity of practising hydraulics.

MR. FIREDAMP. Sir, you seem to make very light of science.

THE REV. DR. FOLLIOTT. Yes, sir, such science as the learned friend deals in : every thing for every body, science for all, and sense for none. I say, sir, law for lawyers, and cookery for cooks : and I wish the learned friend, for all his life, a cook that will pass her time in studying his works ; then every dinner he sits down to at home, he will sit on the stool of repentance.

LORD BOSSNOWL. Now really that would be too severe : my cook should read nothing but Ude.

THE REV. DR. FOLLIOTT. No, sir ! let Ude and the learned friend singe fowls together ; let both avaunt from my kitchen. Θύρας δ'ἐπίθεσθε βεβήλοις. Ude says an elegant supper may be given with sandwiches. *Horresco referens.* An elegant supper ! *Di meliora piis.* No Ude for me. Conviviality went out with punch and suppers. I cherish their memory. I sup when I can, but not upon sandwiches. To offer me a sandwich, when I am looking for a supper, is to add insult to injury. Let the learned friend, and the modern Athenians, sup upon sandwiches.

MR. MAC QUEDY. Nay, sir; the modern Athenians know better than that. A literary supper in sweet Edinbroo' would cure you of the prejudice you seem to cherish against us.

THE REV. DR. FOLLIOTT. Well, sir, well; there is cogency in a good supper; a good supper, in these degenerate days, bespeaks a good man; but much more is wanted to make up an Athenian. Athenians, indeed! Where is your theatre? Who among you has written a comedy? where is your attic salt? which of you can tell me who was Jupiter's great grandfather? or what metres will successively remain, if you take off the three first syllables, one by one, from the pure antispastic acatalectic tetrameter? Now, sir, there are three questions for you; theatrical, mythological, and metrical; to every one of which an Athenian would give me an answer that would lay me prostrate in my own nothingness.

PEACOCK (from *Crotchet Castle*)

THE CURÉ'S OMELETTE

Everyone knows that for the last twenty years Madame R . . . has occupied, by common consent, the throne of beauty in Paris. It is also known that she is extremely charitable and that at a certain period she took an interest in almost all the enterprises which had for their end the relief of poverty, often more severe in the capital than anywhere else.

Having to confer on this subject with the Curé of . . . , she called at his house at about five o'clock in the afternoon and was much surprised to find him already at table. The dear lady, who lived in the Rue du Mont-Blanc, believed that everyone in Paris dined at six : she was unaware that ecclesiastics in general begin early, because many of them make a light meal in the evening.

Madame R. . . desired to withdraw, but the Curé pressed her to stay, either because the matter they had to discuss was not of a kind to interrupt dinner or because at such a time a pretty woman is anything but an interruption . . . The table was laid with remarkable taste ; an old wine sparkled in a crystal decanter ; the white porcelain was of the first quality, the dishes kept hot by boiling water, and a serving-woman, at once canonical and neatly turned out, was on duty. The repast was nicely balanced between the frugal and the exquisite. A shrimp soup had just been removed, and the lady observed on the table a salmon trout, an omelette, and a salad. . . .

Execution had begun with the trout, of which the fore-part was under discussion ; the sauce betrayed a skilled hand, and an internal satisfaction began to appear on the pastor's brow. After this first dish he attacked the omelette, which was round, full-bellied, and cooked to perfection. At the first stroke of the spoon the pouch gave forth a thick juice which flattered at once the eye and the nose ; the dish seemed to be full of it and our dear Juliette confessed that her mouth watered.

This movement of sympathy did not escape the Curé, accustomed as he was to keep guard over the passions of mankind, and with the air of answering a question which

Madame R. . . had been careful not to ask, he remarked :
" It is a tunny omelette : my cook understands these
things to perfection, and few of my friends have tasted
it without congratulating me."

" I'm not surprised," exclaimed the fair inhabitant of
the Chaussée-d'Antin ; " no such appetising omelette has
ever appeared on the tables of our people of fashion."

The salad followed. (I recommend the salad to all those
who have given me their confidence ; the salad refreshes
without impairing the appetite, comforts without irrita-
ting ; I am in the habit of asserting that it rejuvenates.)

Dinner did not interrupt conversation. They talked of
the business which had occasioned the visit, of the war
which was at the time all the rage, of topical matters, of
the hopes of the Church, and other table talk such as
beguiles a bad dinner and embellishes a good one. Dessert
came in its turn. It consisted of a Septmoncel cheese,
three Calville apples and a pot of preserves.

At last the servant brought a small round table on which
she set a cup of moka, very clear, very hot, whose aroma
filled the room. After sipping it, the Curé said his grace,
and added as he rose from his chair : " I never take
liqueurs ; they are a superfluity which I always offer to
my guests but never myself partake of. Thus I reserve
some assistance for my old age, if God in His goodness
allows me to survive."

While all this was occurring, time had flown, six oclock
had come : Madame R. . . hastened to her carriage, for
on that evening she had various friends coming to dinner,
including myself. *According to her custom*, she got home
late, but home she got at last, still thrilled and excited by
what she had seen and inhaled.

BRILLAT-SAVARIN (from *Physiologie du Goût*)

510

GAME

August 22, 1800.

DEAR MANNING,

You needed not imagine any apology necessary. Your fine hare and fine birds (which are just now dangling by our kitchen blaze) discourse most eloquent music in your justification. You just nicked my palate. For with all due decorum and leave may it be spoken, my worship hath taken physic to-day, and being low and puling, requireth to be pampered. Foh! how beautiful and strong those buttered onions come to my nose! For you know we extract a divine spirit of gravy from those materials, which, duly compounded with a consistence of bread and cream (y'clept bread-sauce), each to each giving double grace, do mutually illustrate and set off (as skilful gold foils to rare jewels) your partridge, pheasant, woodcock, snipe, teal, widgeon, and the other lesser daughters of the ark. My friendship, struggling with my carnal and fleshly prudence (which suggests that a bird a man is the proper allotment in such cases), yearneth sometimes to have thee here to pick a wing or so. I question if your Norfolk sauces match our London culinaric. . . .

God bless me, here are the birds, smoking hot! All that is gross and unspiritual in me rises at the sight!

Avaunt friendship, and all memory of absent friends!

C. LAMB

BRAWN

DEAR MANNING,

I have been very unwell since I saw you ; a sad depression of spirits, a most unaccountable nervousness ; from which I have been partially relieved by an odd accident. You knew Dick Hopkins, the swearing scullion of Caius ? This fellow, by industry and agility, has thrust himself into the important situations (no sinecures, believe me) of cook to Trinity Hall and Caius College : and the generous creature has contrived, with the greatest delicacy imaginable, to send me a present of Cambridge brawn. What makes it the more extraordinary is, that the man never saw me in his life that I know of. I suppose he has *heard* of me. I did not immediately recognise the donor ; but one of Richard's cards, which had accidentally fallen into the straw, detected him in a moment. Dick, you know, was always remarkable for flourishing. His card imports, that " orders (to wit, for brawn) from any part of England, Scotland, or Ireland, will be duly executed," etc. At first, I thought of declining the present ; but Richard knew my blind side when he pitched upon brawn. 'Tis of all my bobbies the supreme in the eating way. He might have sent sops from the pan, skimmings, crumpets, chips, hog's lard, the tender brown judiciously scalped from a fillet of veal (dexterously replaced by a salamander), the tops of asparagus, fugitive livers, runaway gizzards of fowls, the eyes of martyred pigs, tender effusions of laxative woodcocks, the red spawn of lobsters, leverets' ears, and such pretty filchings common to cooks ; but these had been ordinary presents, the everyday courtesies of dish-washers to their sweethearts. Brawn was a noble thought. It is not every common gullet-fancier that can properly esteem it. It is like a picture of one of the choice old Italian masters. Its gusto is of that hidden sort. As Wordsworth sings of a modest poet,—" you must love him, ere to you he will seem worthy of your love ; " so brawn, you must taste it ere to you it will seem to have any taste at all. But 'tis nuts to the adept : those that will send out their tongue and feelers to find it out. It will be wooed, and not unsought be won. Now, ham-essence, lobsters, turtle, such popular minions, absolutely *court you*, lay themselves to strike you at first smack, like one of David's pictures (they call him *Darveed*) compared with the plain russet-coated wealth of a Titian or a Correggio, as I illustrated above. Such are the obvious glaring heathen virtues of a corporation dinner, compared with the reserved collegiate worth of brawn. Do me the favour to leave off the business which you may be at present upon, and go immediately to the kitchens of Trinity and Caius, and make my most respectful compliments to Mr. Richard Hopkins, and assure him that his brawn is most excellent ; and that I am moreover obliged to him for his innuendo about salt water and bran, which I shall not fail to improve. I leave it to you whether you shall choose to pay him the civility of asking him to dinner while you stay in Cambridge, or in whatever other way you may best like to show your gratitude to *my friend*. Richard Hopkins, considered in many points of view, is a very extraordinary character. Adieu. I hope to see you to supper in London soon, where we will taste Richard's brawn, and drink his health in a cheerful but moderate cup. We have not many such men in any rank of life as Mr. R. Hopkins. Crisp, the barber, of St. Mary's, was just such another. I wonder *he* never sent me any little token, some chestnuts, or a puff, or two pound of hair : just to remember him by. Gifts are like nails. *Praesens ut absens ;* that is, your *present* makes amends for your absence.

Yours,

C. LAMB

SALMO SALAR

THE REV. DR. FOLLIOTT. Here is a very fine salmon before me : and May is the very *point nommé* to have salmon in perfection. There is a fine turbot close by, and there is much to be said in his behalf ; but salmon in May is the king of fish.

MR. CROTCHET. That salmon before you, doctor, was caught in the Thames this morning.

THE REV. DR. FOLLIOTT. Παπαπαι̃ ! Rarity of rarities ! A Thames salmon caught this morning. Now, Mr. Mac Quedy, even in fish your Modern Athens must yield, *Cedite Graii*.

MR. MAC QUEDY. Eh ! sir, on its own ground, your Thames salmon has two virtues over all others : first, that it is fresh ; and, second, that it is rare ; for I understand you do not take half a dozen in a year.

THE REV. DR. FOLLIOTT. In some years, sir, not one. Mud, filth, gas dregs, lock-weirs, and the march of mind, developed in the form of poaching, have ruined the fishery. But when we do catch a salmon, happy the man to whom he falls.

MR. MAC QUEDY. I confess, sir, this is excellent ; but I

cannot see why it should be better than a Tweed salmon at Kelso.

THE REV. DR. FOLLIOTT. Sir, I will take a glass of Hock with you.

MR. MAC QUEDY. With all my heart, sir. There are several varieties of the salmon genus : but the common salmon, the *salmo salar*, is only one species, one and the same everywhere, just like the human mind. Locality and education make all the difference.

THE. REV. DR. FOLLIOTT. Education ! Well, sir, I have no doubt schools for all are just as fit for the species *salmo salar* as for the genus *homo*. But you must allow that the specimen before us has finished his education in a manner that does honour to his college. However, I doubt that the *salmo salar* is only one species, that is to say, precisely alike in all localities. I hold that every river has its own breed, with essential differences ; in flavour especially.

PEACOCK (from *Crotchet Castle*)

ROAST PIG

Spokes, when he sees a rosted Pig, he swears
Nothing he loves on't but the chaps and ears :
And carve to him the fat flanks, and he shall
Rid these, and those, and part by part eat all.

HERRICK

515

DEAR COLERIDGE,

It gives me great satisfaction to hear that the pig turned out so well; they are interesting creatures at a certain age. What a pity such buds should blow out into the maturity of rank bacon ! You had all some of the crackling and brain sauce. Did you remember to rub it with butter, and gently dredge it a little, just before the crisis ? Did the eyes come away kindly with no Œdipean avulsion ? Was the crackling the colour of the ripe pomegranate ? Had you no complement of boiled neck of mutton before it, to blunt the edge of delicate desire ? Did you flesh maiden teeth in it ? Not that I sent the pig, or can form the remotest guess what part Owen could play in the business. I never knew him give any thing away in my life. He would not begin with strangers. I suspect the pig, after all, was meant for me ; but at the unlucky juncture of time being absent, the present somehow went round to Highgate. To confess an honest truth, a pig is one of those things which I could never think of sending away. Teal, widgeon, snipes, barndoor fowls, ducks, geese— your tame villactic things—Welsh mutton, collars of brawn, sturgeon, fresh or pickled, your potted char, Swiss cheeses, French pies, early grapes, muscadines, I impart as freely unto my friends as to myself. They are but self-extended : but pardon me if I stop somewhere. Where the fine feeling of benevolence giveth a higher smack than the sensual rarity, there my friends (or any good man) may command me ; but pigs are pigs, and I myself therein am nearest to myself. Nay, I should think it an affront, an undervaluing done to Nature who bestowed such a boon upon me, if in a churlish mood I parted with the precious gift. One of the bitterest pangs of remorse I ever felt was when a child—when my kind old aunt had strained her pocket strings to bestow a six-penny whole plum cake upon me. In my way home through the Borough I met a venerable old man, not a mendicant, but thereabouts ; a look-beggar, not a verbal petitionist ; and in the coxcombry of taught charity I gave away the cake to him. I walked on a little in all the pride of an Evangelical peacock, when of a sudden my old aunt's kindness crossed me ; the sum it was to her ; the pleasure she had a right to expect that I—not the old imposter—should take in eating her cake ; the ingratitude by which, under the colour of a Christian virtue, I had frustrated her cherished purpose. I sobbed, wept, and took it to heart so grievously, that I think I never suffered the like ; and I was right. It was a piece of unfeeling hypocrisy, and it proved a lesson to me ever after. The cake has long been masticated, consigned to the dunghill with the ashes of that unseasonable pauper.

But when Providence, who is better to us all than our aunts, gives me a pig, remembering my temptation and my fall, I shall endeavour to act towards it more in the spirit of the donor's purpose.

Yours (short of pig) to command in everything,

C. LAMB

POET INVITES POET

I entreat you, Alfred Tennyson,
Come and share my haunch of venison.
I have too a bin of claret,
Good, but better when you share it.
Tho' 'tis only a small bin,

There's a stock of it within.
And as sure as I'm a rhymer,
Half a butt of Rudesheimer.
Come ; among the sons of men is one
Welcomer than Alfred Tennyson ?

LANDOR

A LETTER OF THANKS

We have received beef, tongues, and tea,
And certainly from none but thee ;
Therefore with all our power of songs,
Thanks for the beef, and tea, and tongues.

COWPER

ANABOLISM

MAMMON. I love to see you eat, to see you drink.
The foolish flesh, the herbs and grains and fruit
You take into your body, I love them too,
For they are you. In gardens, orchards, fields,
Vineyards and seas and rivers you grow all day ;
All night your roots drain treasure from the earth ;
And herds and shoals and harvests change in you
To beauty, passion and the world's desire.

GUENDOLEN. And these, the herds, the harvests, and the
    shoals
That turn to love and manhood in my lord,
Are of the very substance of the stars.

MAMMON. The stars are we ; we live upon the stars ;
We eat, and drink, and are the Universe.

JOHN DAVIDSON (from *Mammon and his Message*)

LUNCHEON AT OXBRIDGE

It is part of the novelist's convention not to mention soup and salmon and ducklings, as if soup and salmon and ducklings were of no importance whatsoever, as if nobody ever smoked a cigar or drank a glass of wine. Here, however, I shall take the liberty to defy that convention and to tell you that the lunch on this occasion began with soles, sunk in a deep dish, over which the college cook had spread a counterpane of the whitest cream, save that it was branded here and there with brown spots like the spots on the flanks of a doe. After that came the partridges, but if this suggests a couple of bald, brown birds on a plate you are mistaken. The partridges, many and various, came with all their retinue of sauces and salads, the sharp and the sweet, each in its order ; their potatoes, thin as coins but not so hard ; their sprouts, foliated as rosebuds but more succulent. And no sooner had the roast and its retinue been done with than the silent serving-man, the Beadle himself perhaps in a milder manifestation, set before us, wreathed in napkins, a confection which rose all sugar from the waves. To call it pudding and so relate it to rice and tapioca would be an insult. Meanwhile the wineglasses had flushed yellow and flushed crimson ; had been emptied ; had been filled. And thus by degrees was lit, halfway down the spine, which is the seat of the soul, not that hard little electric light which we call brilliance, as it pops in and out upon our lips, but the more profound, subtle and subterranean glow which is the rich yellow flame of rational intercourse. No need to hurry. No need to sparkle. No need to be anybody but oneself. We are all going to heaven and Vandyck is of the company—in other words, how good life seemed, how sweet its rewards, how trivial this grudge or that grievance, how admirable friendship and the society of one's kind, as, lighting a good cigarette, one sunk among the cushions in the window-seat.

VIRGINIA WOOLF

(from *A Room of One's Own*)

DINNER AT FERNHAM

Everybody was assembled in the big dining-room. Dinner was ready. Here was the soup. It was a plain gravy soup. There was nothing to stir the fancy in that. One could have seen through the transparent liquid any pattern that there might have been on the plate itself. But there was no pattern. The plate was plain. Next came beef with its attendant greens and potatoes—a homely trinity, suggesting the rumps of cattle in a muddy market, and sprouts curled and yellowed at the edge, and bargaining and cheapening, and women with string bags on Monday morning. There was no reason to complain of human nature's daily food, seeing that the supply was sufficient and coal-miners doubtless were sitting down to less. Prunes and custard followed. And if anyone complains that prunes, even when mitigated by custard, are an uncharitable vegetable (fruit they are not), stringy as a miser's heart and exuding a fluid such as might run in misers' veins who have denied themselves wine and warmth for eighty years and yet not given to the poor, he should reflect that there are people whose charity embraces even the prune. Biscuits and cheese came next, and here the water-jug was liberally passed round, for it is in the nature of biscuits to be dry, and these were biscuits to the core. That was all. The meal was over. Everybody scraped their chairs back; the swing-doors swung violently to and fro; soon the hall was emptied of every sign of food and made ready no doubt for breakfast next morning.

VIRGINIA WOOLF

(from *A Room of One's Own*)

A VEGETARIAN PICNIC

Dispatch, and to the myrtle grove convey
Whatever with the natural palate suits
The dairy's store, with salads, roots, and fruits ;
I mean to play the epicure to-day.
Let nought be wanting to complete
     Our bloodless treat :
But bloodless let it be, for I've decreed
The grape alone for this repast shall bleed.
Sit, worthy friends. But e'er we feed,
Let Love b'expelled the company :
Let no man's mirth here interrupted be
With thought of any scornful little She !
Fall to, my friends ! Trust me, the cheer is good !
Ah ! (if our bliss we understood)
How should we bless th'indulgent Fates,
Indulgent Fates that with content have stored
     Our rural board,
A rarity never found among the cates
Of most voluptuous potentates.

NAHUM TATE

521

We had long promised the old schools a dinner, as a bribe for good behaviour during our absence, and the prospect of the feast, as they called it, was a charm so captivating, that it procured many a task to be learned with pleasure, for the sake of obtaining one good dinner. On the 4th of August, on Callow Hill, a high part of Mendip, all our children were assembled (except the new schools—without them we had five hundred and seventeen). We left Cowslip Green in the morning, with some friends, mounted in a waggon, dressed out with greens, flowers, etc. Another followed with the servants, thirteen large pieces of beef, forty-five great plum-puddings, six hundred cakes, several loaves, and a great cask of cider. The children by order were concealed in a valley, whilst all the preparations were making, such as railing in a large piece of ground, and placing the dinner upon the grass to the best advantage. In the meantime we were arranging the children below. At the sound of the horn, the procession began. A boy of the best character carried a little flag ; we walked next, then Ma'am Baber, followed by the Cheddar children, and so on according to seniority ; all the schools, one after another, singing psalms. Upwards of four thousand people were assembled to see this interesting sight. After marching round our little railing, all were seated in pairs as they walked. The dinner was then carved, and each child had laid at his feet a large slice of beef, another of plum-pudding, and a cake. The instant they were served, all arose, and six clergymen, who were present, said grace. All were again seated, and were permitted to eat as much as their stomachs would hold and talk as fast as their tongues would go. When the children were properly feasted, and the company had regaled themselves with their leavings, grace was said again, when some little examination into their acquirements took place. One girl could repeat twenty-four chapters, another fifteen ; and many questions put to them, which were answered to the satisfaction of the company, and to the credit of the children. As the design of the day was to prove to them the possibility of being *merry and wise*, we all joined in singing " God save the King," and amusing them by a little mirthful chat. At four oclock all the pleasure was over, and the children marched out of the circle in the order they entered, each school headed by their master and mistress, singing psalms and halle-lujahs, till they were lost in the valley. Thus were five hundred and seventeen children, and three hundred others, made happy, and really feasted for the sum of £15.

MARTHA MORE (from *Mendip Annals*)

BAUCIS AND PHILEMON ENTERTAIN THE GODS

The good old housewife, tucking up her gown,
The table sets ; the invited gods lie down.
The trivet-table of a foot was lame,
A blot which prudent Baucis overcame,
Who thrust beneath the limping leg a sherd,
So was the mended board exactly rear'd :
Then rubb'd it o'er with newly gather'd mint ;
A wholesome herb, that breathed a grateful scent.
Pallas began the feast, where first was seen
The party-colour'd olive, black and green :
Autumnal cornels next in order served,

In lees of wine well pickled and preserved :
A garden salad was the third supply,
Of endive, radishes, and succory :
Then curds and cream, the flower of country fare,
And new-laid eggs, which Baucis' busy care
Turn'd by a gentle fire, and roasted rare.
All these in earthenware were served to board ;
And, next in place, an earthen pitcher, stored
With liquor of the best the cottage could afford.
This was the table's ornament and pride,
With figures wrought : like pages at his side
Stood beechen bowls ; and these were shining clean,
Varnish'd with wax without, and lined within.
By this the boiling kettle had prepared,
And to the table sent the smoking lard ;
On which with eager appetite they dine,
A savoury bit, which served to relish wine :
The wine itself was suiting to the rest,
Still working in the must, and lately press'd.
The second course succeeds like that before ;
Plums, apples, nuts, and, of their wintry store,
Dry figs and grapes, and wrinkled dates were set
In canisters, to enlarge the little treat :
All these a milk-white honeycomb surround,
Which in the midst the country banquet crown'd.
But the kind hosts their entertainment grace
With hearty welcome, and an open face ;
In all they did, you might discern with ease
A willing mind, and a desire to please.

DRYDEN
(from *Philemon and Baucis* : after OVID)

524

A BAD SUPPER

To sup with thee thou didst me home invite ;
And mad'st a promise that mine appetite
Sho'd meet and tire on such lautitious meat,
The like not Heliogabalus did eat :
And richer Wine wo'dst give to me (thy guest)
Than Roman Sylla powr'd out at his feast.
I came ; (tis true) and lookt for Fowle of price,
The bastard Phenix ; bird of Paradice ;
And for no less than Aromatick Wine
Of Maydens-blush, commixt with Jessimine.
Cleane was the herth, the mantle larded jet,
Which wanting Lar and smoke, hung weeping wet ;
At last, i' th' noone of winter, did appeare
A ragd-soust-neats-foot with sick vineger ;
And in a burnisht Flagonet stood by
Beere small as Comfort, dead as Charity.
At which amaz'd and pondring on the food,
How cold it was, and how it chil'd my blood,
I curst the master and I damn'd the souce,
And swore I'de got the ague of the house.
Well, when to eat thou dost me next desire,
Ile bring a Fever, since thou keep'st no fire.

HERRICK

A BAD LUNCHEON

Something I wrote lately has brought me a letter from
a witty and ill-used reader, not known to me personally,
drawing my attention to the fact that I have ignored, in

my consideration of English meals, the meals served on railway dining-cars. My kind and amusing correspondent travels, it would seem, weekly to —— and is condemned to consume on his way a meal that would appear to be more suited to the Channel passage than to land travel— " Have you lunched ? " asked the English steward of the Channel-crossing Frenchman, to receive the pithy answer, " *Au contraire !* " ... The menu included " some sloshy fish with a stickfast sauce " (" ' Turbot, sir,' said the waiter, placing before me two fishbones, two eyeballs, and a bit of black mackintosh ") ; some overdone beef, underdone potatoes, and clammy greens ; and a sweet which my correspondent describes as being either " a dollop of trifle or a trifle of dollop."

T. EARLE WELBY (from *The Dinner Knell*)

NAVAL RATIONS IN THE XVIIIth CENTURY

Seamen in the King's ships have made buttons for their Jackets and Trowses with the Cheese they were served with, having preferred it, by reason of its tough and durable quality, to buttons made of common metal ; and Carpenters in the Navy-Service have made Trucks to their Ships' flagstaffs with whole Cheeses, which have stood the weather equally with any timber.

The flour in the King's ships has been devoured by weevils, and become so intolerably musty, and cemented into such hard rocks, that the men have been obliged to use instruments, with all their feeble power, to break and pulverise it, as though, in a comparative degree, they had been stubbing to pieces the ruins of an old fortification.

Their bread has been so full of large black-headed maggots and they have so nauseated the thoughts of it, as to be obliged to shut their eyes to confine that sense from being offended before they could bring their minds into a resolution of consuming it.

WILLIAM THOMPSON
(from *An Appeal to the Public . . . to prevent the Navy of England being supplied with pernicious Provisions . . .* 1761)

SAUCES

Homer has not, if I rightly remember, ever said a word about sauces.

PLATO

.   .   .   .

The English have a hundred religions, but only one sauce.

VOLTAIRE

.   .   .   .

Whereas on the Continent sauce usually means something newly made with particular regard to the needs of the dish in question, in England it is a liquid out of a bottle to be spattered indiscriminately into soup, on to fish and butcher's meat and poultr , and even in some wicked households in and on a salad.

To be sure, at least two of the English bottled sauces, each aristocratic in origin, are among the more considerable achievements of our race. In the latter part of the eighteenth century, Captain Charles Combers, a follower of the Quorn Hunt, had the habit of staying at the George

Inn, Bedford, always accompanied by a bottle of his special sauce. On an occasion, he left the precious bottle there against his imminent return ; the host, Peter Harvey, brother of the eventually not less celebrated Elizabeth Lazenby, rashly served some of it to a company of strangers, who insisted on finishing the lot. On Captain Comber's return, there followed apologies, and the Captain's good-natured offer to give the landlord the recipe, and eventually a sale by Harvey of the recipe for an annuity of £400. Many years later, round about 1830, " a Nobleman of the County " accidentally left his recipe for Worcester sauce on the counter of a chemist with a mere and vile medical prescription.

T. EARLE WELBY (from *The Dinner Knell*)

THE REV. DR. FOLLIOTT. By the bye, Captain, you remember a passage in Athenæus, where he cites Menander on the subject of fish-sauce : ὀψάριον ἐπὶ ἰχθύος. The science of fish-sauce, Mr. Mac Quedy, is by no means brought to perfection ; a fine field of discovery still lies open in that line.

MR. MAC QUEDY. Nay, sir, beyond lobster sauce, I take it, ye cannot go.

THE REV. DR. FOLLIOTT. In their line, I grant you, oyster and lobster sauce are the pillars of Hercules. But I speak of the cruet sauces, where the quintessence of the sapid is condensed in a phial. I can taste in my mind's palate a combination, which, if I could give it reality, I would christen with the name of my college, and hand it down to posterity as a seat of learning indeed.

PEACOCK (from *Crotchet Castle*)

This feast is named the Carnaval, which being
Interpreted, implies " farewell to flesh " :
So called, because the name and thing agreeing,
Through Lent they live on fish both salt and fresh.
But why they usher Lent with so much glee in,
Is more than I can tell, although I guess
'Tis as we take a glass with friends at parting,
In the stage-Coach or Packet, just at starting.

And thus they bid farewell to carnal dishes,
And solid meats, and highly spiced ragouts,
To live for forty days on ill-dressed fishes,
Because they have no sauces to their stews ;
A thing which causes many " poohs " and " pishes "
And several oaths (which would not suit the Muse),
From travellers accustomed from a boy
To eat their salmon, at the least, with soy ;

And therefore humbly I would recommend
" The curious in fish-sauce," before they cross
The sea, to bid their cook, or wife, or friend,
Walk or ride to the Strand, and buy in gross
(Or if set out beforehand, these may send
By any means least liable to loss),
Ketchup, Soy, Chili-vinegar, and Harvey,
Or, by the Lord, a Lent will wellnigh starve ye.

BYRON (from Beppo)

SIX DRINK

WINE AND THE GRAPE

Mihi est propositum in taberna mori ;
Vinum sit appositum morientis ori,
Ut dicant, cum venerint Angleorum chori,
" Deus sit propitius huic potatori."

WALTER MAPES

Born I was to be old,
    And for to die here ;
After that, in the mould
    Long for to lye here.
But before that day comes,
    Still I be Bousing ;
For I know, in the Tombs
    There's no Carousing.

HERRICK

Wine by its moisture quencheth my thirst, whether I
consider it or no : but to see it flowing from His love who
gave it unto man, quencheth the thirst even of the Holy
Angels. To consider it, is to drink it spiritually. To rejoice
in its diffusion is to be of a public mind. And to take
pleasure in all the benefits it doth to all is Heavenly, for
so they do in Heaven.

TRAHERNE (from Centuries of Meditations)

Solon, having been asked by Periander over their cups,
since he did not speak, whether he was silent for want of
words or because he was a fool, replied : A fool is never
silent over his cups.

EPICTETUS

Drink no longer water, but use a little wine for thy stomach's sake and thine often infirmities.

ST. PAUL to TIMOTHY

Come, come ; good wine is a good familiar creature, if it be well used.

SHAKESPEARE (from *Othello*)

He causeth the grass to grow for the cattle, and herb for the service of man, that he may bring forth food out of the earth, and wine that maketh glad the heart of man, and oil to make his face to shine, and bread which strengtheneth man's heart.

THE BIBLE (from *The Psalms*)

And in this mountain shall the Lord of Hosts make unto all people a feast of fat things, a feast of wines on the lees, of fat things full of marrow, of wines on the lees well refined.

THE BIBLE (from *Isaiah*)

And they went out into the fields, and gathered their vineyards, and trode the grapes, and made merry.

THE BIBLE (from *Judges*)

Let your drink so serve your meat, as your meat doth your health ; that it be apt to convey and digest it, and refresh the spirits ; but let it never go beyond such a refreshment as may a little lighten the present load of a sad or troubled spirit.

JEREMY TAYLOR

. . . That salutary, though dangerous, liquor.

GIBBON

O thou invisible spirit of wine ! if thou hast no name to be known by, let us call thee devil.

. . . .

O God ! that men should put an enemy in their mouths to steal away their brains ; that we should, with joy, pleasance, revel, and applause, transform ourselves into beasts.

SHAKESPEARE (from *Othello*)

Wine is a mocker, strong drink is raging, and whosoever is deceived thereby is not wise.

. . . .

Who hath woe ? who hath sorrow ? who hath contentions ? who hath babbling ? who hath wounds without cause ? who hath redness of eyes ? They that tarry long at the wine ; they that go to seek mixed wine. Look not upon the wine when it is red, when it giveth his colour in the cup, when it moveth itself aright. At the last it biteth like a serpent and stingeth like an adder.

THE BIBLE (from *Proverbs*)

Were the Pleasure of Drinking accompanied, the very moment a Man takes off his Glass, with that sick Stomach and aking Head which in some Men are sure to follow not many hours after, I think no body, whatever Pleasure he had in his Cups, would, on these Conditions, ever let Wine touch his Lips ; which yet he gaily swallows and the evil side comes to be chosen only by the fallacy of a little difference of time.

LOCKE

(from Essay on the Human Understanding)

A DIALOGUE BETWEEN JUNO AND JUPITER

JUNO. I should blush, Jupiter, to have such a Sonne, so effeminate and lost in wine : who weares a Miter, lies with mad women, more womanish than they ; dances after Timbrels, Pipes, and Cimbales ; and resembles every body more than you his Father.

JUPITER. This Miter-wearer, and wencher, Juno, not only subdued Lydia, and the Inhabitants of Tmolus ; also the Thracians ; but went against the Indians, with his female Army, took their Elephants, possest their Countrey, and brought away their King, who made resistance, captive. All this he did revelling, and dancing, and carrying roddes twined with Ivye, and drunk, as you say, and beside himselfe. But those who reviled him, or blasphemed his rites, either he punish't with shackles of Vines, or caused to be dismembred, by their mothers, like Fawnes. Are not those valiant Acts, and worthy of me his Father ? Nor let it be any disparagement that he mingled Maskes, and Revellings with his Conquests; but rather consider what he would do sober, who can do thus drunk.

JUNO. Methinks, Husband, you should have made a panegyrick of his invention of Grapes, and wine. Though you see how men reele when they are drunk and incline to quarrels, and forget themselves in their drink; and how that Icarius, to whom he first taught the use of the Vines, was kill'd by his Companions, and slain with pitch-forkes.

JUPITER. This is nothing to the purpose: For 'tis not Wine, or Bacchus which do this, but excesse of wine, and drink taken beyond fit measure. But whosoever drinkes moderately is cheered, and made the merrier. And as for Icarius it wrought no so upon any of his Company. But you show your jealousie, Juno, and spleen to Semele, when you accuse Bacchus of those things which are most commendable.

LUCIAN (Trans. JASPER MAYNE)

WINE FOR MELANCHOLY

I say with him in A. Gellius, " let's maintain the vigour of our souls with a moderate cup of wine, *Natis in usum lætitiæ scyphis*, and drink to refresh our mind; if there be any cold sorrow in it, or torpid bashfulness, let's wash it all away."—*Nunc vino pellite curas;* so saith Horace, so saith Anacreon,

> Μεθύοντα γαρ με κεῖσθαι
> Πολὺ κρεισσον ἢ θανόντα.

537

Let's drive down care with a cup of wine ; and so say I too (though *I drink none* myself), for all this may be done, so that it be modestly, soberly, opportunely used : so that " they be not drunk with wine, wherein is excess," which our Apostle forewarns ; for as Chrysostom well comments on that place, *ad lætitiam datum est vinum, non ad ebrietatem*, 'tis for mirth wine, but not for madness : and will you know where, when, and how that is to be understood ? *Vis dicere ubi bonum sit vinum ? Audi quid dicat Scriptura*, hear the Scriptures, " Give wine to them that are in sorrow," or as Paul bid Timothy drink wine for his stomach's sake, for concoction, health, or some such honest occasion. Otherwise, as Pliny tells us ; if singular moderation be not had, " nothing so pernicious, 'tis mere vinegar, *blandus dæmon*, poison itself." But hear a more fearful doom, Habac. ii. 15 & 16. " Woe be to him that makes his neighbour drunk, shameful spewing shall be upon his glory." Let not good fellows triumph therefore (saith Matthiolus), that I have so much commended wine ; if it be immoderately taken, " instead of making glad, it confounds both body and soul, it makes a giddy head, a sorrowful heart." And 'twas well said of the poet of old, " Wine causeth mirth and grief," nothing so good for some, so bad for others, especially as one observes, *qui a causa calida male habent*, that are hot or inflamed.

ROBERT BURTON
(from *The Anatomy of Melancholy*)

THE RUINED VINEYARD

My wellbeloved hath a vineyard in a very fruitful hill.
And he fenced it and gathered out the stones thereof, and
planted it with the choicest vine, and built a tower in the
midst of it, and also made a winepress therein. And he
looked that it should bring forth grapes, and it brought
forth wild grapes.

And now, O inhabitants of Jerusalem and men of Judah,
judge, I pray you betwixt me and my vineyard. What
could have been done more to my vineyard, that I have
not done in it? wherefore, when I looked that it should
bring forth grapes, brought it forth wild grapes?

And now go to; I will tell you what I will do to my
vineyard. I will take away the hedge thereof, and it shall
be eaten up; and break down the wall thereof, and it
shall be trodden down. And I will lay it waste; and it
shall not be pruned, nor digged; but there shall come up
briars and thorns. I will also command the clouds that
they rain no rain upon it.

THE BIBLE (from *Isaiah*)

HOW THEY CHIRPED OVER THEIR CUPS

Then did they fall upon the chat of the afternoon's
collation; and forthwith began flagons to go, gammons to
trot, goblets to fly, great bowls to ting, glasses to ring,
draw, reach, fill, mix, give it me without water, so, my
friend, so, whip me off this glass neatly, bring me hither
some claret, a full weeping glass till it run over, a cessation and truce with thirst. Ha! thou false fever, wilt thou

not be gone ? By my figgins, godmother, I cannot as yet enter in the humour of being merry, nor drink so currently as I would ; you have catched a cold, Gammer ; yea forsooth, sir ; by the belly of Sanct Buff let us talk of our drink, I never drink but at my hours, like the pope's mule ; and I never drink but in my breviary, like good father Gardian. Which was first, thirst or drinking ? Thirst, for who in the time of innocence would have drunk without being athirst ? nay, sir, it was drinking ; for *privatio praeponit habitum.* I am learned you see. *Faecundi calices quem non fecere disertum ?* We poor innocents drink but too much without thirst. Not I truly, who am a sinner, for I never drink without thirst, either present or future, to prevent it (as you know) I drink for the thirst to come ; I drink eternally, this is to me an eternity of drinking, and drinking of an eternity. Let us sing, let us drink, now for a catch, dust it away, where is my nogging ? what, it seems I do not drink but by proxy. Do you wet yourselves to dry, or do you dry to wet you ? Pish, I understand not the rhetoric (theoric I should say), but I help myself somewhat by the practice. Enough ; I sup, I wet, I humect, I moisten my gullet, I drink, and all for fear of dying ; drink always and you shall never die. If I drink not, I am aground, and lost. I am stark dead without drink, and my soul ready to fly into some marsh among frogs ; the soul never dwells in a dry place.

O, you butlers, creators of new forms, make me of no drinker a drinker ; a perennity and everlastingness of sprinkling and bedewing me through these my parched and sinewy bowels. He drinks in vain that feels not the pleasure of it.

RABELAIS (Trans. URQUHART)

540

FALSTAFF ON SHERRIS-SACK

Good faith, this same young sober-blooded boy doth not love me ; nor a man cannot make him laugh ; but that's no marvel, he drinks no wine. There's never none of these demure boys come to any proof ; for thin drink doth so over-cool their blood, and making many fish-meals, that they fall into a kind of male green-sickness ; and then, when they marry, they get wenches : they are generally fools and cowards ; which some of us should be too, but for inflammation. A good sherris-sack hath a two-fold operation in it. It ascends me into the brain ; dries me there all the foolish and dull and crudy vapours which environ it ; makes it apprehensive, quick, forgetive, full of nimble, fiery and delectable shapes ; which, de-livered o'er to the voice, the tongue, which is the birth, becomes excellent wit. The second property of your excel-lent sherris is, the warming of the blood ; which, before cold and settled, left the liver white and pale, which is the badge of pusillanimity and cowardice ; but the sherris warms it and makes it course from the inwards to the parts extreme : it illumineth the face, which as a beacon gives warning to all the rest of this little kingdom, man, to arm ; and then the vital commoners and inland petty spirits muster me all to their captain, the heart, who, great and puffed up with this retinue, doth any deed of cour-age ; and this valour comes of sherris. So that skill in the weapon is nothing without sack, for that sets it a-work ; and learning a mere hoard of gold kept by a devil, till sack commences it and sets it in act and use. Hereof comes it that Prince Harry is valiant ; for the cold blood he did naturally inherit of his father, he hath, like a lean sterile and bare land, manured, husbanded and tilled with excellent endeavour of drinking good and good store of fertile sherris, that he is become very hot and valiant. If I had a thousand sons, the first humane principle I would teach them should be, to forswear thin potations, and to addict themselves to sack.

SHAKESPEARE (from *King Henry IV, Part II*)

THE WELCOME TO SACK

So soft streams meet, so springs with gladder smiles
Meet after long divorcement by the Iles :
When Love (the child of likenesse) urgeth on
Their Christal natures to an union.
So meet stolne kisses, when the Moonie nights
Call forth fierce Lovers to their wisht Delights :
So Kings & Queens meet, when Desire convinces
All thoughts, but such as aime at getting Princes,
As I meet thee. Soule of my life, and fame !
Eternall Lamp of Love ! whose radiant flame
Out-glares the Heav'ns Osiris ; and thy gleams
Out-shine the splendour of his mid-day beams.
Welcome, O welcome my illustrious Spouse ;
Welcome as are the ends unto my Vowes :
I ! far more welcome than the happy soile,
The Sea-scourg'd Merchant, after all his toile,
Salutes with tears of joy ; when fires betray
The smoakie chimneys of his Ithaca.
Where hast thou been so long from my embraces,
Poore pittyed Exile ? Tell me, did thy Graces
Flie discontented hence, and for a time
Did rather choose to blesse another clime ?

542

Or went'st thou to this end, the more to move me,
By thy short absence, to desire and love thee?
Why frowns my Sweet? Why won't my Saint confer
Favours on me, her fierce Idolater?
Why are Those Looks, Those Looks the which have
been
Time-past so fragrant, sickly now drawn in
Like a dull Twi-light? Tell me; and the fault
Ile expiate with Sulphur, Haire, and Salt:
And with the Christal humour of the spring,
Purge hence the guilt, and kill this quarrelling.
Wo't thou not smile, or tell me what's amisse?
Have I been cold to hug thee, too remisse,
Too temp'rate in embracing? Tell me, has desire
To thee-ward dy'd i'th'embers, and no fire
Left in this rak't-up Ash-heap, as a mark
To testifie the glowing of a spark?
Have I divorc't thee onely to combine
In hot Adult'ry with another Wine?
True, I confesse I left thee, and appeale
'Twas done by me, more to confirme my zeale,
And double my affection on thee; as doe those,
Whose love growes more inflam'd, by being Foes.
But to forsake thee ever, co'd there be
A thought of such like possibilitie?
When thou thy selfe dar'st say, thy Iles shall lack
Grapes, before Herrick leaves Canarie Sack.
Thou mak'st me ayrie, active to be born,
Like Iphyclus upon the tops of Corn.
Thou mak'st me nimble, as the wingèd howers,
To dance and caper on the heads of flowers,
And ride the Sun-beams. Can there be a thing
Under the heavenly Isis, that can bring

More love unto my life, or can present
My Genius with a fuller blandishment ?
Illustrious Idoll ! co'd th' Ægyptians seek
Help from the Garlick, Onyon, and the Leek,
And pay no vowes to thee ? who wast their best
God, and far more transcendent than the rest ?
Had Cassius, that weak Water-drinker, known
Thee in thy Vine, or had but tasted one
Small Chalice of thy frantick liquor ; He
As the wise Cato had approv'd of thee.
Had not Joves son, the brave Tyrinthian Swain,
(Invited to the Thespian banquet) ta'ne
Full goblets of thy gen'rous blood ; his spright
Ne'r had kept heat for fifty Maids that night.
Come, come and kisse me ; Love and lust commends
Thee, and thy beauties ; kisse, we will be friends
Too strong for Fate to break us ; Look upon
Me, with that full pride of complexion,
As Queenes meet Queenes ; or come thou unto me,
As Cleopatra came to Anthonie ;
When her high carriage did at once present
To the Triumvir, Love and wonderment.
Swell up my nerves with spirit ; let my blood
Run through my veines, like to a hasty flood.
Fill each part full of fire, active to doe
What thy commanding soule shall put it to.
And till I turne Apostate to thy love,
Which here I vow to serve, doe not remove
Thy Fiers from me ; but Apollo's curse
Blast these-like actions, or a thing that's worse ;
When these Circumstants shall but live to see
The time that I prevaricate from thee.
Call me the sonne of Beere, and then confine

544

Me to the Tap, the Tost, the Turfe ; Let Wine
Ne'r shine upon me ; May my Numbers all
Run to a sudden Death, and Funerall.
And last, when thee (deare Spouse) I disavow,
Ne'r may Prophetique Daphne crown my Brow.

HERRICK

A SPECIFIC AGAINST WATER

MR. FIREDAMP. There is another great question, greater
than all these, seeing that it is necessary to be alive in
order to settle any question ; and this is the question
of water against human woe. Wherever there is water,
there is *malaria*, and wherever there is *malaria*, there
are the elements of death. The great object of a wise
man should be to live on a gravelly hill, without so
much as a duck-pond within ten miles of him, eschewing cisterns and water-butts, and taking care that there
be no gravel-pits for lodging the rain. The sun sucks
up infection from water, wherever it exists on the face
of the earth.

THE REV. DR. FOLLIOTT. Well, sir, you have for you the
authority of the ancient mystagogue, who said : Ἔστιν
ὕδωρ ψυχῇ θάνατος. For my part I care not a rush (or
any other aquatic and inesculent vegetable) who or what
sucks up either the water or the infection. I think the
proximity of wine a matter of much more importance
than the longinquity of water. You are here within a
mile of the Thames ; but in the cellar of my friend,

Mr. Crotchet, there is the talismanic antidote of a thousand dozen of old wine; a beautiful spectacle, I assure you, and a model of arrangement.

MR. FIREDAMP. Sir, I feel the malignant influence of the river in every part of my system. Nothing but my great friendship for Mr. Crotchet would have brought me so nearly within the jaws of the lion.

THE REV. DR. FOLLIOTT. After dinner, sir, after dinner, I will meet you on this question. I shall then be armed for the strife. You may fight like Hercules against Achelous, but I shall flourish the Bacchic thyrsus, which changed rivers into wine: as Nonnus sweetly sings, Οἴνῳ κυματόεντι μέλας κελάρυζεν Ὑδάσπης.

PEACOCK (from *Crotchet Castle*)

WHITE WINE

Appetite comes with eating, says Angeston; but the thirst goes away with drinking. I have a remedy against thirst quite contrary against that which is against the biting of a mad dog: keep running after a dog and he will never bite you; drink always before the thirst and it will never come upon you. There I catch you, I awake you. Argus had a hundred eyes for his sight; a butler should have (like Briarius) a hundred hands wherewith to fill us wine indefatigably. Ha, now lads, let us wet; it will be time to dry hereafter. White wine, here, wine boys, pour out all, *per le diable*, fill, I say, fill and fill till it be full. My tongue peels. *Lans, tringue*: to thee, countryman, I drink to thee, good fellow. Comrade, to thee, lusty, lively, ha, la, la, that was drunk to some purpose, and bravely gulped over. *O lachryma Christi*, it is of the best grape ; i' faith, pure Greek, Greek. O the fine white wine ! Upon my conscience it is a kind of taffetas wine, him, him, it is of one ear, well wrought and of good wool. Courage, comrade ; up thy heart, Billy ; we will not be beasted at this bout, for I have got one trick. *Ex hoc in hoc.* There is no enchantment nor charm there ; everyone of you hath seen it ; my prenticeship is out ; I am a free man at this trade. I am an abbot. (Pshaw, I should say.) O, the drinkers, those that are dry ; O, poor thirsty souls ! Good page, my friend, fill me here some, and crown the cup, I prithee, *à la cardinale ; natura abhorret vacuum.* Would you say that a fly could drink in this ? *A la mode de Bretagne.*—Clear off neat, *supernaculum*, swill it over heartily, no deceit in a brimmer ; nectar and ambrosia.

RABELAIS (Trans. URQUHART)

DR. JOHNSON DISCUSSES WINE

Desirous of calling Johnson forth to talk, and exercise his wit, though I should myself be the object of it, I resolutely ventured to undertake the defence of convivial indulgence in wine, though he was not tonight in the most genial humour. After urging the common plausible topicks, I at last had recourse to the maxim, *in vino veritas*, a man who is well warmed with wine will speak truth. JOHNSON. " Why, Sir, that may be an argument for drinking, if you suppose men in general to be liars. But, Sir, I would not keep company with a fellow, who lyes as long as he is sober, and whom you must make drunk before you can get a word of truth out of him."

. . . .

A gentleman having to some of the usual arguments for drinking added this : " You know, Sir, drinking drives away care, and makes us forget whatever is disagreeable. Would you not allow a man to drink for that reason ? " JOHNSON. " Yes, Sir, if he sat next *you*."

. . . .

Johnson and I supped this evening at the Crown and Anchor tavern, in company with Sir Joshua Reynolds, Mr. Langton, Mr. Nairne, now one of the Scotch Judges with the title of Lord Dunsinan, and my very worthy friend, Sir William Forbes of Pitsligo.

We discussed the question, whether drinking improved conversation and benevolence. Sir Joshua maintained it did. JOHNSON. " No, Sir : before dinner men meet with great inequality of understanding ; and those who are conscious of their inferiority, have the modesty not to talk. When they have drunk wine, every man feels himself happy, and loses that modesty, and grows impudent and vociferous : but he is not improved : he is only not sensible of his defects." Sir Joshua said the Doctor was talking of the effects of excess in wine ; but that a moderate glass enlivened the mind, by giving a proper circulation to the blood. " I am, (said he,) in very good spirits when I get up in the morning. By dinner-time I am exhausted ; wine puts me in the same state as when I got up : and I am sure that moderate drinking makes people talk better." JOHNSON. " No, Sir ; wine gives not light, gay, ideal hilarity ; but tumultuous, noisy, clamorous merriment. I have heard none of those drunken,—nay, drunken is a

coarse word,—none of those *vinous* flights." SIR JOSHUA.
"Because you have sat by, quite sober, and felt an envy
of the happiness of those who were drinking." JOHNSON.
"Perhaps, contempt.—And, Sir, it is not necessary to be
drunk one's self, to relish the wit of drunkenness. Do we
not judge of the drunken wit of the dialogue between Iago
and Cassio, the most excellent of its kind, when we are
quite sober ? Wit is wit, by whatever means it is produced ; and, if good, will appear so at all times."

On Wednesday, April 7, I dined with him at Sir Joshua
Reynolds's. I have not marked what company was there.
Johnson harangued upon the qualities of different liquors ;
and spoke with great contempt of claret, as so weak that
" a man would be drowned by it before it made him
drunk." He was persuaded to drink one glass of it, that
he might judge, not from recollection which might be
dim, but from immediate sensation. He shook his head
and said, " Poor stuff ! No, Sir, claret is the liquor for
boys ; port for men ; but he who aspires to be a hero
(smiling) must drink brandy. In the first place, the flavour
of brandy is most grateful to the palate ; and then brandy
will do soonest for a man what drinking *can* do for him.
There are, indeed, few who are able to drink brandy. That
is a power rather to be wished for than attained. And yet
(proceeded he), as in all pleasure hope is a considerable
part, I know not but fruition comes too quick by brandy.
Florence wine I think the worst ; it is wine only to the
eye ; it is wine neither while you are drinking it, nor after
you have drunk it ; it neither pleases the taste nor exhil-
arates the spirits." I reminded him how heartily he and
I used to drink wine together, when we were first

acquainted; and how I used to have a head-ache after sitting up with him. He did not like to have this recalled, or, perhaps, thinking that I boasted improperly, resolved to have a witty stroke at me : " Nay, Sir, it was not the *wine* that made your head ache, but the *sense* that I put into it." BOSWELL. " What, Sir ! will sense make the head ache ? " JOHNSON. " Yes, Sir, (with a smile) when it is not used to it."

.   .   .   .

Talking of drinking wine, he said, " I did not leave off wine because I could not bear it ; I have drunk three bottles of port without being the worse for it. University College has witnessed this." BOSWELL. " Why then, Sir, did you leave it off ? " JOHNSON. " Why, Sir, because it is so much better for a man to be sure that he is never to be intoxicated, never to lose the power over himself. I shall not begin to drink wine again till I grow old, and want it."

.   .   .   .

We talked of drinking wine. JOHNSON. " I require wine only when I am alone. I have then often wished for it, and often taken it." SPOTTISWOODE. " What, by way of companion, Sir ? " JOHNSON. " To get rid of myself, to send myself away. Wine gives great pleasure ; and every pleasure is of itself a good. It is a good, unless counterbalanced by evil. A man may have a strong reason not to drink wine ; and that may be greater than the pleasure. Wine makes a man better pleased with himself. I do not say that it makes him more pleasing to others. Wine gives a man nothing. It neither gives him knowledge nor wit ; it only animates a man, and enables him to bring out what a dread of the company has repressed. It only puts in motion what has been locked up in frost. But this may be good, or it may be bad."

I mentioned a nobleman who I believed was really uneasy if his company would not drink hard. JOHNSON. " This is from having had people about him whom he has been accustomed to command." BOSWELL. " Supposing I should be tête-à-tête with him at table." JOHNSON. " Sir, there is no more reason for your drinking with *him*, than his being sober with *you*." BOSWELL. " Why, that is true ; for it would do him less hurt to be sober, than it would do me to get drunk." JOHNSON. " Yes, Sir ; and from what I have heard of him, one would not wish to sacrifice himself to such a man. If he must always have somebody to drink with him, he should buy a slave, and then he would be sure to have it. They who submit to drink as another pleases, make themselves 'his slaves." BOSWELL. " But, Sir, you will surely make allowance for the duty of hospitality. A gentleman who loves drinking comes to visit me." JOHNSON. " Sir, a man knows whom he visits ; he comes to the table of a sober man." BOSWELL. " But, Sir, you and I should not have been so well received in the Highlands and Hebrides if I had not drunk with our worthy friends. Had I drunk water only as you did, they would not have been so cordial." JOHNSON. " Sir William Temple mentions that in his travels through the Netherlands he had two or three gentlemen with him ; and when a bumper was necessary, he put it on *them*. Were I to travel again through the islands, I would have Sir Joshua with me to take the bumpers." BOSWELL. " But, Sir, let me put a case. Suppose Sir Joshua should take a jaunt into Scotland ; he does me the honour to pay me a visit at my house in the country ; I am overjoyed at seeing him ; we are quite by ourselves ; shall I unsociably and churlishly let him sit drinking by himself ? No, no, my dear Sir Joshua, you shall not be treated so, I *will* take a bottle with you."

BOSWELL (from The Life of Samuel Johnson)

IN VINO VERITAS

I promised, if you'd watch a dinner out,
We'd see truth dawn together—truth that peeps
Over the glass's edge when dinner's done,
And body gets its sop and holds its noise
And leaves soul free a little.

BROWNING (from Bishop Blougram's Apology)

KEATS ON CLARET

I never drink above three glasses of wine, and never any spirits and water ; though, by the bye, the other day Woodhouse took me to his coffee-house, and ordered a bottle of claret. How I like claret ! When I can get claret, I must drink it. 'Tis the only palate affair that I am at all sensual in. Would it not be a good spec. to send you some vine-roots ? Could it be done ? I'll enquire. If you could make some wine like claret, to drink on summer evenings in an arbour ! It fills one's mouth with a gushing freshness, then goes down cool and feverless : then, you do not feel it quarrelling with one's liver. No ; 'tis rather a peace-maker, and lies as quiet as it did in the grape.

552

Then it is as fragrant as the Queen Bee, and the more ethereal part mounts into the brain, not assaulting the cerebral appartments, like a bully looking for his trull, and hurrying from door to door, bouncing against the wainscot, but rather walks like Aladdin about his enchanted palace, so gently that you do not feel his step. Other wines of a heavy and spirituous nature transform a man into a Silenus, this makes him a Hermes, and gives a woman the soul and immortality of an Ariadne, for whom Bacchus always kept a good cellar of claret, and even of that he never could persuade her to take above two cups. I said this same claret is the only palate-passion I have ; I forgot game ; I must plead guilty to the breast of a partridge, the back of a hare, the back-bone of a grouse, the wing and side of a pheasant, and a wood-cock *passim*.

KEATS (from *The Letters*)

THE CRYSTAL CUP

Fill me my Wine in Christall ; thus, and thus
I see't in's *puris naturalibus* :
Unmixt. I love to have it smirke and shine,
'Tis sin I know, 'tis sin to throtle Wine.
What Mad-man's he, that when it sparkles so,
Will coole his flames, or quench his fires with
   snow !

HERRICK

553

SEX AND TEMPERAMENT OF WINES

If Claret is the queen of natural wines, Burgundy is the king : their places being taken in the other realm of the artificial by Madeira and Port.

. . . . . .

Port—*red* Port, as one of its earliest celebrants after the Methuen treaty no less justly than emphatically calls it, White Port being a mere albino—is incomparable when good. It is not a wine-of-all-work like Sherry— Mr. Pendennis was right when he declined to drink it *with* his dinner. It has not the almost feminine grace and charm of Claret ; the transcendental qualities of Burgundy and Madeira ; the immediate inspiration of Champagne ; the rather unequal and sometimes palling attractions of Sauterne and Moselle and Hock. But it strengthens while it gladdens as no other wine can do ; and there is something about it which must have been created in pre-established harmony with the best English character.

. . . . . .

I think Madeira and Burgundy carry combined intensity and complexity of vinous delights further than any other wines.

SAINTSBURY (from *Notes on a Cellar Book*)

A QUESTION OF PRECEDENCE

THE REV. DR. FOLLIOTT. A glass of wine after soup is, as the French say, the *verre de santé*. The current opinion sets in favour of Hock ; but I am for Madeira ; I do not fancy Hock till I have laid a substratum of Madeira.

PEACOCK (from *Crotchet Castle*)

CHARACTER IN WINES

The *Margaux* 1900 was simply beautiful : sweet and gentle, well balanced and complete . . . The *Haut Brion* 1899 was bigger than the 1900, and it had an even finer bouquet. It promised to be the better of the two, but it did not stay the course. It is a remarkable wine. It comes in with a most stately bow—quite the Grand Seigneur— but departs on tip-toe like a page-boy. It has lost some of its fruit and does not finish sweetly.

The '20 *Margaux* was light and pleasing, but not great : very little bouquet and none of that quiet but firm assurance that a well-bred wine should possess.

The 1900 *Lafite* was ever so much finer. It was not Château bottled, but it had been very well bottled ; its bouquet had great distinction ; its body was full and firm ; it still had plenty of sugar and was probably at the top of its form. A really interesting and enjoyable wine. Yet how quickly the '78 put it in the shade was astounding !

The '78, in spite of its slightly drier finish, was much finer ; it belonged to another class even more than to another age. It reminded me of the late Lord Curzon being announced immediately after the late Lord Lever-hulme.

ANDRÉ SIMON (from *Tables of Content*)

INCOMPATIBILITIES

A glass of very much iced sweet Champagne is not a fit and proper companion for a very hot and properly *assaisonnée* clear soup. A small glass of Madeira—not too small a glass—would have met the case ever so much better.

With the lobster, the *Moet & Chandon* 1906 would have been much more enjoyable than the *Quart de Chaume*. It was a delightful wine and served exactly at the right temperature : full, rich, lively, luscious, a truly splendid specimen of Anjou at its best, but decidedly a dessert wine *en pleine beauté*. . . .

The capons were White Sussex . . . and were gorgeous : so tender and tasty ! Of course they were also distinctly on the rich side, and a little too much so for the *Quart de Chaume*, which stood by during the whole of this course. I couldn't help closing my eyes for a second or two and thinking how delicious a glass of *Margaux* 1900 would have tasted at this stage.

. . . .

The 1893 (*Marcobrunner feinste Beeren Auslese*) still had a fascinating bouquet, with just a touch of cedar-wood in it, but it was a little worn, and I also was beginning to feel a little tired of so much cold white wine on this December night. The partridge which come with the '93 was as tender as tender could be, and I couldn't help thinking that it would have called, had it dare raise its voice, for a drop of Burgundy or Claret to be quite happy. But it never said a word and we had one more white wine.

ANDRÉ SIMON (from *Tables of Content*)

THE WINE WORKS

The Wine is murmuring in the gloom,
Because he feels that Spring is come
To gladden everything outside . . .

To wing the dove to meet his bride
And not disdainfully to pass
Even the snail along the grass ;
Because he feels that on the slope
Of his own hill the vine-flowers ope ;
Because he feels that never more
Will earth or heaven *his* past restore.
He beats against the ribs of iron
Which him and all his strength environ ;
He murmurs, swells, and beats again,
But murmurs, swells, and beats in vain . . .

LANDOR

THE WINE-BREWERS

—Scelus est jugulare Falernum,
Et dare Campano toxica sæva mero.

(*Martial*)

There is in this city a certain fraternity of chymical
operators, who work under ground in holes, caverns,
and dark retirements, to conceal their mysteries from
the eyes and observation of mankind. These subter-
raneous philosophers are daily employed in the trans-
mutation of liquors, and, by the power of magical drugs
and incantations, raising under the streets of London
the choicest products of the hills and valleys of France.
They can squeeze Bordeaux out of the sloe, and draw
Champagne from an apple. Virgil, in that remarkable
prophecy,

557

Incultisque rubens pendebit sentibus uva,
The ripening grape shall hang on every thorn,

seems to have hinted at this art, which can turn a plantation of northern hedges into a vineyard. These adepts are known among one another by the name of wine-brewers, and, I am afraid, do great injury, not only to her Majesty's customs, but to the bodies of many of her good subjects.

Having received sundry complaints against these invisible workmen, I ordered the proper officer of my court to ferret them out of their respective caves, and bring them before me, which was yesterday executed accordingly.

The person who appeared against them was a merchant, who had by him a great magazine of wines that he had laid in before the war : but these gentlemen (as he said) had so vitiated the nation's palate, that no man could believe his to be French, because it did not taste like what they sold for such. And as a man never pleads better than where his own personal interest is concerned, he exhibited to the court, with great eloquence, that this new corporation of druggists had inflamed the bills of mortality, and puzzled the college of physicians with diseases, for which they neither knew a name or cure. He accused some of giving all their customers cholics and megrims ; and mentioned one who had boasted, he had a tun of claret by him, that in a fortnight's time should give the gout to a dozen of the healthfullest men in the city, provided that their constitutions were prepared for it by wealth and idleness. He then enlarged, with a great show of reason, upon the prejudice which these mixtures and compositions had done to the brains of the English nation ; as is too visible, said he, from many late pamphlets, speeches, and sermons, as well as from the ordinary conversations of the youth of this age. He then quoted an ingenious person, who would undertake to know by a man's writings, the wine he most delighted in ; and on that occasion named a great satirist, whom he had discovered to be the author of a lampoon, by the manifest taste of the sloe, which showed itself in it by much roughness and little spirit.

In the last place, he ascribed to the unnatural tumults and fermentations which these mixtures raise in our blood, the divisions, heats, and animosities that reign among us ; and, in particular, asserted most of the modern enthusiasms and agitations to be nothing else but the effects of adulterated port.

The counsel for the brewers had a face so extremely inflamed and illuminated with carbuncles, that I did not wonder to see him an advocate for these sophistications. His rhetoric was likewise such as I should have expected from the common draught, which I found he often drank to great excess. Indeed, I was so surprised at his figure and parts, that I ordered him to give me a taste of his usual liquor ; which I had no sooner drank, than I found a pimple rising in my forehead ; and felt such a sensible decay in my understanding, that I would not proceed in the trial till the fume of it was entirely dissipated. . . .

When I had sent out my summons to these people, I gave at the same time orders to each of them to bring the several ingredients he made use of in distinct phials, which they had done accordingly, and ranged them into two rows on each side of the court. The workmen were drawn up in ranks behind them. The merchant informed me, that in one row of phials were the several colours they dealt with, and in the other the tastes. He then showed me, on the right hand, one who went by the name of Tom Tintoret, who (as he told me) was the greatest master in his colouring of any vintner in London. To give me a proof of his art, he took a glass of fair water, and by the infusion of three drops out of one of his phials, converted it into a most beautiful pale Burgundy. Two more of the same kind heightened it into a perfect Languedoc : from thence it passed into a florid Hermitage ; and after having gone through two or three other changes, by the addition of a single drop, ended in a very deep Pontac. This ingenious virtuoso, seeing me very much surprised at his art, told me, that he had not an opportunity of showing it in perfection, having only made use of water for the groundwork of his colouring ; but that if I were to see an operation upon liquors of stronger bodies, the art would appear to a much greater advantage. . . .

The artists on my other hand were ordered, in the second place, to make some experiments of their skill before me : upon which the famous Harry Sippet stepped out, and asked me, what I would be pleased to drink ? At the same time he filled out three or four white liquors in a glass, and told me, that it should be what I pleased to call for ; adding very learnedly, that the liquor before him was as the naked substance or first matter of his compound, to which he and his friend, who stood over against him, could give what accidents or form they pleased. Finding him so great a philosopher, I desired that he would convey into it the qualities and essence of right Bordeaux. " Coming, coming, sir," said he, with the air of a drawer ; and after having cast his eye on the several tastes and flavours that stood before him, he took up a little cruet that was filled with a kind of inky juice, and pouring some of it out into the glass of white wine, presented it to me, and told me, this was the wine over which most of the business of the last term had been dispatched. I must confess, I looked upon that sooty drug, which he held up in his cruet, as the quintessence of English Bordeaux, and therefore desired him to give me a glass of it by itself, which he did with great unwillingness. My cat at that time sat by me upon the elbow of my chair ; and as I did not care for making the experiment upon myself, I reached it to her to sip of it, which had like to have cost her her life ; for notwithstanding it flung her at first into freakish tricks, quite contrary to her usual gravity, in less than a quarter of an hour she fell into convulsions ; and, had it not been a creature more tenacious of life than any other, would certainly have died under the operation . . .

For my own part, I have resolved hereafter to be very careful in my liquors ; and have agreed with a friend of mine in the army, upon their next march, to secure me two hogsheads of the best stomach-wine in the cellars of Versailles, for the good of my lucubrations, and the comfort of my old age.

The Tatler.   *Thursday, February 9, 1709.*

ADDISON

DRINKS IN THE NEW ATLANTIS

I will not hold you long with recounting of our brewhouses, bakehouses, and kitchens, where are made divers drinks, breads, and meats, rare, and of special effects.

Wines we have of grapes ; and drinks of other juice, of fruits, of grains, and of roots ; and mixtures with honey, sugar, manna, and fruits dried, and decocted : also of the tears or woundings of trees ; and of the pulp of canes. And these drinks are of several ages ; some to the age or last of forty years. We have drinks also brewed with several herbs, and roots, and spices ; yea, with several fleshes and white meats ; whereof some of the drinks are such as they are in effect meat and drink both : so that divers, especially in age, do desire to live with them, with little or no meat, or bread. And above all we strive to have drinks of extreme thin parts, to insinuate into the body, and yet without all biting, sharpness, or fretting ; in so much as some of them, put upon the back of your hand, will, with a little stay, pass through to the palm, and yet taste mild to the mouth. We have also waters which we ripen in that fashion, as they become nourishing ; so that they are indeed excellent drink ; and many will use no other.

BACON

HOT DRINKS

Towards the middle of the sixteenth century, the Spaniards imported chocolate from Mexico. Rather more than half a century later, tea was introduced from China and Japan. It had been noticed by Marco Polo as early as the thirteenth century, but it was probably first brought to Europe by the Jesuit missionaries in the first years of the seventeenth century, and it was soon after largely imported by the Dutch. In 1636 we find it in usage in France, and enthusiastically patronised by the Chancellor

Séguier. The earliest notice of it in England is in an Act of Parliament of 1660. The discovery of the circulation of blood, which produced an exaggerated estimate of the medical value of bleeding and of hot drinks, and the writings of two physicians named Tulpius and Bontekoe, gave a great impulse to its popularity. In a letter written in 1680, Madame de Sévigné observes that the Marchioness de la Sablière had just introduced the custom of drinking it with milk. About the middle of the same century, coffee began to pour in from Turkey. The properties of this berry had been noticed in 1591 by the Venetian physician Alpinus, and soon afterwards by Bacon in his "Natural History," and the drink was introduced into England in 1652 by an English Turkey merchant named Edwards. In France the first coffee-house was established at Marseilles in 1664. A few years later, Soliman Aga, the ambassador of Mahomet IV., made the new beverage very fashionable in Paris; and in 1672 an Armenian named Pascal established a coffee-house in that city. He had soon countless imitators; and it was observed that this new taste gave a serious and almost instantaneous check to drunkenness, which had been very prevalent in France. Coffee-houses were the true precursors of the clubs of the eighteenth century. They became the most important centres of society, and they gave a new tone to the national manners. In England, though they were once even more popular than in France, and though they were indissolubly associated with one of the most brilliant periods of literary history, they have not taken root; but the effect of hot drinks upon domestic life has probably been even greater than on the Continent. Checking the boisterous revels that had once been universal, and raising woman to a new position in the domestic circle, they have

contributed very largely to refine manners, to introduce a
new order of tastes, and to soften and improve the
character of men.

LECKY (from *History of Rationalism*)

MR. AND MRS. PEPYS TAKE TEA

1660, Sept. 25th.—I did send for a cup of tee (a China
drink), of which I never had drunk before. . . .

1667, June 28th.—Home, and there find my wife making of tea ; a drink which Mr. Pelling, the Potticary, tells
her is good for her cold.

PEPYS (from *The Diary*)

COFFEE-HOUSES VINDICATED

Though the happy Arabia, nature's spicery, prodigally
furnishes the voluptuous world with all kinds of aromatics
and divers other rareties ; yet I scare know whether mankind be not still as much obliged to it for the excellent
fruit of the humble coffee-shrub, as for any other of its
more specious productions : for since there is nothing we
here enjoy, next to life, valuable beyond health, certainly
those things that contribute to preserve us in good plight
and eucracy, and fortify our weak bodies against the continual assaults and batteries of diseases, deserve our
regards much more than those which only gratify a
liquorish palate, or otherwise prove subservient to our
delights.

As for this salutiferous berry, of so general a use through

all the regions of the East, it is sufficiently known, when prepared, to be moderately hot, and of a very drying, attenuating, and cleansing quality ; whence reason infers, that its decoction must contain many good physical properties, and cannot but be an incomparable remedy to dissolve crudities, comfort the brain, and dry up all humours in the stomach.

(from a Pamphlet, 1675)

BELINDA TAKES COFFEE

For lo ! the board with cups and spoons is crowned,
The berries crackle, and the mill turns round ;
On shining altars of Japan they raise
The silver lamp ; the fiery spirits blaze ;
From silver spouts the grateful liquors glide,
While China's earth receives the smoking tide :
At once they gratify their scent and taste,
And frequent cups prolong the rich repast.
Straight hover round the fair her airy band ;
Some, as she sipped, the fuming liquor fanned,
Some o'er her lap their careful plumes displayed,
Trembling, and conscious of the rich brocade.
Coffee (which makes the politician wise,
And see through all things with his half-shut eyes)
Sent up in vapours to the baron's brain
New stratagems, the radiant lock to gain.
Ah cease, rash youth ! desist ere 'tis too late,
Fear the just Gods, and think of Scylla's fate !
Changed to a bird, and sent to flit the air,
She dearly pays for Nisus' injured hair !

POPE (from *The Rape of the Lock*)

THE SCIENCE OF COFFEE

An ancient tradition has it that coffee was discovered by a goatherd who observed his flock to be in a particular agitation and hilarity every time it had browsed on the berries of the coffee-shrub.

Whatever be the truth of this old story, not more than a half of the honour of discovery belongs to the observant goatherd : the balance is incontestably due to him who first had the idea of torrefying this bean.

In effect, the decoction of raw coffee is an insignificant drink ; but carbonization develops an aroma and forms an oil which are the characteristics of coffee as we take it and which would remain eternally unknown without the intervention of heat.

The Turk, who is our master in this department, never employs a mill for the trituration of coffee. He brays it in mortars with wooden pestles, and when these instruments have been long employed to this end they become precious and fetch high prices.

It belonged to me, in more capacities than one, to discover whether, in the result, there was any difference in these two methods and which was preferable. Consequently I carefully torrefied a pound of good moka. This I separated into two equal portions, one of which was milled, the other brayed after the manner of the Turk. With both the powders I made coffee, taking an equal weight of each, pouring upon each equal weight of boiling water, acting in all respects with a perfect equality. This coffee I tasted myself and had tasted by the greatest connoisseurs. The unanimous opinion was that the coffee resulting from the brayed powder was evidently superior to that from the milled. . . .

Some years since, all thoughts were fixed simultaneously upon the best way of making coffee,—the result, though few suspected it, of the fact that the head of the government was a great coffee-drinker. It was proposed to make it without burning, without grinding, by infusing it cold, by boiling three quarters of an hour, by submitting it to the autoclave, etc. I have in course of time tried all these methods and all those proposed up to the present day, and I have fixed, for excellent reasons, on that known as the Dubelloy method, which consists in pouring boiling water on coffee placed in a porcelain or silver receptacle pierced with very small holes. Take this first decoction, heat it to boiling-point, pass it through again, and you will have a coffee as clear and good as is possible. . . . It is past doubt that coffee produces a great excitation of the cerebral powers : moreover, everyone who drinks it for the first time is certain to be robbed of a portion of his night's sleep. . . .

Voltaire and Buffon took a great deal of coffee. Perhaps the first owed to this habit the admirable clarity observable in his works, and the second, the ecstatic harmony found in his style. It is evident that many pages of the treatises on Man, the Dog, the Tiger, the Lion, and the Horse were written in a state of extraordinary cerebral exaltation. . . .

The bootmaker, author of the tragedy La Reine de Palmyre, whom a few years ago all Paris heard read, took a great deal of coffee. Accordingly he rose higher than the Miller of Nevers who was merely a drunkard. . . .

Coffee is a very much more energetic liquor than is commonly believed. A man of good constitution who drinks two bottles of wine a day can live to a good old age. The same man would not so long resist an equal quantity of coffee : either he would become imbecile or die of consumption.

In London, on Leicester Square, I saw a man whom an immoderate indulgence in coffee had reduced to a cripple : he no longer suffered, had grown accustomed to his state, and had reduced himself to five or six cups a day.

Papas and Mammas are under an obligation to forbid coffee to their children, unless they wish to be the parents of little desiccated machines, old and stunted by the time they are twenty.

BRILLAT-SAVARIN (from *Physiologie du Goût*)

THE CUP THAT DOES NOT CHEER

It may seem odd that I have said nothing, in the chapter on Champagne, as to Saumur, Vouvray, and the Swiss imitations. These last I have never drunk. As to the first, I should feel inclined to borrow the saying of the innocent accomplice to whom a villain had imparted a share of stolen Champagne. Interrogated as to the various liquors which had been given to him, he said that there was one which was " like ginger-beer, but not so nice." If he had said this of Saumur I should not have found much fault with him. Vouvray has not the same coarseness, but seems to me feeble.

. . . .

As to Italian, I suppose it does not travel well, though Chianti, like Carlowitz, can be drunk. I remember some very " wersh " sparkling Asti ; but I think I preferred it to some sparkling Lacrima Cristi, which suggested ginger-beer alternately stirred up with a stick of chocolate and a large sulphur match.

. . . .

I believe that elder wine can be made less deleterious by putting an equal quantity of brandy in it. But why not drink the brandy by itself?

SAINTSBURY (from *Notes on a Cellar Book*)

THE SODA FOUNTAIN

As far as my observation goes the national drink of England is now either something sold from the urban soda-fountain or something by the wayside where a hideous white and blue enamelled sign announces " Minerals."

Why the soda-fountain was ever introduced into England and how mere aerated waters came to be called minerals are questions wholly beyond me. Let it suffice that these extraordinary beverages have always been regarded by the wise as very dangerous. Did not George Meredith, long ago, by word of mouth, give us the cautionary tale of the man who exclusively drank gasified waters, and died suddenly; whereupon his friends, instead of accepting the obvious explanation, insisted upon an autopsy, which had to be conducted by a physician wearing blue glasses to shield his eyes from the glare of the stalactites in the poor wretch's interior? With these deplorable drinks must be lumped those half-hearted frauds, cider which is not cider, beer which is not beer, things condemned even in the country of Prohibition, as by the negro waiter who said of some such fluid: " It looks like beer, it smells like beer, but when it gets into you it has no authority."

T. EARLE WELBY (from *The Dinner Knell*)

BRYNG US IN GOOD ALE

Bryng us in good ale, and bryng us in good ale ;
For our blyssyd Lady sak, bryng us in good ale.

> Bryng us in no browne bred, for that is made of
> brane,
> Nor bryng us in no whyt bred, for therein is no
> game.
But bryng us in good ale, bryng us in good ale ;
For our blyssyd Lady sak, bryng us in good ale.

> Bryng us in no befe, for there is many bonys,
> But bryng us in good ale, for that goth down at
> onys ;
And bryng us in good ale, etc.

> Bryng us in no bacon, for that is passing fat,
> But bryng us in good ale, and gife us i-nough of
> that ;
And bryng us in good ale, etc.

> Bryng us in no mutton, for that is often lene,
> Nor bryng us in no trypes, for thei be syldom
> clene ;
But bryng us in good ale, etc.

> Bryng us in no eggys, for there are many schelles,
> But bryng us in good ale, and give us nothyng ellys ;
And bryng us in good ale, etc.

> Bryng us in no butter, for therein are many herys ;
> Nor bryng us in no pygges flesch, for that will
> make us borys[1] ;
But bryng us in good ale, etc.

[1] boars.

Bryng us in no podynges, for therein is al Godes
    good ;
Nor bryng us in no venesen, for that is not for our
    blod ;
But bryng us in good ale, etc.

Bryng us in no capon's flesch, for that is often der ;
Nor bryng us in no dokes flesch, for thei slober in
    the mer ;
But bryng us in good ale, etc.

(XVth Century Song)

THE NEW IS BETTER

Beer abides, and the best of it is now as good as English
beer ever was. This is not a fashionable thing to say. For
years the air has been full of the moanings of those who
imagine a golden age for beer, and suppose it to have been
destroyed by the wickedness of the great breweries.
The truth of the matter is that, until the nineteenth
century was pretty well advanced, most small brewers
and vendors, secure in local monopoly, adopted the most
vicious methods with beer.

As late as 1824, the author of *The Private Brewery*
wrote : " It has seldom been my fortune in a great number
of years to taste unadulterated purchased ale, whether
brewed in the metropolis or in the brewing districts of
the country." For years before that date and for some
years later an extremely harmful and highly intoxicat-
ing drug, the Indian berry (coccollus Indicus) was freely
used in beer ; and willow bark, walnut leaf, quassia,
gentian, aloes, entered into the production of what was

sold in hundreds of establishments and more particularly in the abominable beer-houses produced by the Duke of Wellington's Act. However the limited number of favourably placed individuals may have fared, the nation as a whole never had pure beer, wholesome and maintained to the standard of the particular brewery, until such great concerns as Barclay, Allsop, Bass, rose into command of the market. But that the evil continued longer than is commonly supposed is made manifest in a piece of evidence which will probably be unfamiliar to most people in this country. I call as witness Baudelaire, who, writing to Alfred de Vigny, I think somewhere about the year 1860, most earnestly warned him against drinking any English beer available in Paris except that emanating from Messieurs Allsop, or Messieurs Bass, a touching proof of one great poet's solicitude for the health of another, but more pertinently for us a reminder that the evil continued into a time within the memory of still-living veterans.

T. EARLE WELBY (from The Dinner Knell)

BAD BEER

The brewers have gotten the art to sophisticate beer with broom instead of hops, and ashes instead of malt, and (to make it look the more lively) to pickle it with salt water, so that whilst it is new, it shall seemingly be worthy of praise, but in one month wax worse than stinking water.

NATHANIEL KNOTT
(from An Advice of a Seaman, 1634)

WORSE BEER

Their beer has stunk as abominably as the foul stagnant water which is pumped out of many cellars in London
at midnight hour ; and they were under a necessity of
shutting their eyes, and stopping their breath by holding
of their noses before they could conquer their aversion,
so as to prevail upon themselves in their extreme necessities to drink it.

WILLIAM THOMPSON
(from *An Appeal to the Public . . . to prevent the
Navy of England being supplied with pernicious
Provisions . . .* 1761)

THE DOMESTICITY OF BEER

There is no beverage I have liked " to live with " more
than Beer ; but I have never had a cellar large enough to
accommodate much of it, or an establishment numerous
enough to justify the accommodation. In the good old
days when servants expected beer, but did not expect
to be treated otherwise than as servants, a cask or two
was necessary ; and the persons who were " quite "
generally took care that the small beer they drank should
be the same as that which they gave to their domestics,
though they might have other sorts as well. For these
better sorts at least the good old rule was, when you
began one cask always to have in another. Even Cobbett,
whose belief in beer was the noblest features in his character, allowed that it required *some* keeping.

SAINTSBURY (from *Notes on a Cellar Book*)

THE TOPERS

Come sit we by the fire side,
And roundly drinke we here ;
Till that we see our cheekes Ale-dy'd
And noses tann'd with Beere.

HERRICK

574

§X NATURE AND THE SIMPLE LIFE

See, the day begins to break,
And the light shoots like a streak
Of subtle fire ; the wind blows cold,
Whilst the morning doth unfold ;
Now the birds begin to rouse,
And the squirrel from the boughs
Leaps, to get him nuts and fruit :
The early lark, that erst was mute,
Carols to the rising day
Many a note and many a lay !

. . . .

        Here be woods as green
As any ; air likewise as fresh and sweet
As where smooth Zephyrus plays on the fleet
Face of the curled streams ; with flowers as many
As the young spring gives, and as choice as any ;
Here be all new delights, cool streams and wells,
Arbours o'ergrown with woodbines, caves, and dells.

. . . . . .

Through yon same bending plain,
That flings his arms down to the main,
And through these thick woods, have I run,
Whose bottom never kissed the sun
Since the lusty spring began.

FLETCHER (from *The Faithful Shepherdess*)

Rise up, my Love, my Fair One, and come away. For,
lo, the winter is past, the rain is over and gone ; the
flowers appear on the earth ; the time of the singing of
birds is come, and the voice of the turtle is heard in our

land. The fig tree putteth forth her green figs, and the vines with the tender grape give a good smell. Arise, my Love, my Fair One, and come away.

O my Dove, that art in the clefts of the rock, in the secret places of the stairs, let me see thy countenance, let me hear thy voice ; for sweet is thy voice and thy countenance is comely.

Take us the little foxes, the little foxes that spoil the vines, for our vines have tender grapes.

My Beloved is mine and I am his : he feedeth among the lilies. Until the day break and the shadows flee away, turn, my Beloved, and be thou like a roe or a young hart upon the mountains of Bether.

Come, my Beloved, let us go forth into the field, let us lodge in the villages. Let us get up early to the vineyards ; let us see if the vine flourish, whether the tender grape appear and the pomegranates bud forth. There will I give thee my loves. The mandrakes give a smell, and at our gates are all manner of pleasant fruits, new and old, which I have laid up for thee, O my Beloved.

(from *The Song of Solomon*)

Every little thing can blast an infant blossome ; and the breath of the South can shake the little rings of the Vine, when first they begin to curle like the locks of a new weaned boy ; but when by age and consolidation they stiffen into the hardnesse of a stem, and have by the warm embraces of the Sunne and the kisses of heaven brought forth their clusters, they can endure the storms of the

North, and the loud noises of a tempest, and yet never be broken.

So have I seen the Sunne kiss the frozen earth which was bound up with the images of death and the colder breath of the North; and then the waters break from their inclosures, and melt with joy, and runne in usefull channels; and the flies to rise againe from their little graves in walls and dance a while in the air, to tell that there is joy within and that the great mother of creatures will open the stock of her new refreshment, become usefull to mankinde, and sing praises to her Redeemer.

. . . .

God is glorified in the Sun and Moon, in the rare fabrick of the honeycombs, in the discipline of Bees, in the œconomy of Pismires, in the little houses of birds, in the curiosity of an eye, God being pleased to delight in those little images and reflexes of himself from those pretty mirrours, which like a crevice in a wall thorow a narrow perspective transmit the species of a vast excellency.

JEREMY TAYLOR (from *Sermons*)

I set out one morning before five o'clock, the moon shining through a dark and misty autumnal air, and got to the sea-coast time enough to be at the sun's levee. I saw the clouds and dark vapours open gradually to right and left, rolling over one another in great smoky wreaths, and the tide (as it flowed gently in upon the sands) first whitening, then slightly tinged with gold and blue; and all at once a little line of insufferable brightness that (before I can write these five words) was grown to half an orb, and now to a whole one, too glorious to be distinctly seen. It is very odd it makes no figure on paper ; yet I shall remember it as long as the sun, or at least as long as I endure. I wonder whether any body ever saw it before ? I hardly believe it.

THOMAS GRAY (from *The Letters*)

Sweet is the breath of morn, her rising sweet,
With charm of earliest Birds ; pleasant the Sun
When first on this delightful Land he spreads
His oriend Beams, on herb, tree, fruit, and flour,
Glistring with dew ; fragrant the fertil earth
After soft showers ; and sweet the coming on
Of grateful Evening milde, then silent Night
With this her solemn Bird and this fair Moon,
And these the Gemms of Heav'n, her starrie train :
But neither breath of Morn when she ascends
With charm of earliest Birds, nor rising Sun
On this delightful Land, nor herb, fruit, floure,
Glistring with dew, nor fragrance after showers,
Nor grateful Evening mild, nor silent Night
With this her solemn Bird, nor walk by Moon,
Or glittering Starr-light without thee is sweet.

. . . .

As one who long in populous City pent,
Where Houses thick and Sewers annoy the Aire,
Forth issuing on a Summers Morn to breathe
Among the pleasant Villages and Farmes

Adjoynd, from each thing met conceaves delight,
The smell of Grain, or tedded Grass, or Kine,
Or Dairie, each rural sight, each rural sound ;
If chance with Nymphlike step fair Virgin pass,
What pleasing seemd, for her now pleases more,
She most, and in her looks summs all Delight.

MILTON (from *Paradise Lost*)

Most high, omnipotent good Lord ;
   Thine are the praises, the glory and the honour and
      every blessing.
   To Thee alone, Most High, do they belong
   and no man is worthy to speak of Thee.

Praise be to Thee, my Lord, with all thy creatures, especi-
      ally Master Sun, my brother,
   who maketh day, and Thou givest light through him.
   And he is beautiful and radiant with great splendour ;
   Of Thee, Most High, he beareth the signification.

Praise be to thee, my Lord, for sister Moon and the Stars ;
   in the heaven hast Thou formed them, clear, precious
      and beautiful.

Praise be to Thee, my Lord, for brother Wind
   and for air and cloud and clear and every weather,
   through which Thou givest sustenance unto Thy
      creatures.

Praise be to Thee, my Lord, for sister Water,
   who is very useful, and humble, and precious, and
      chaste.

Praise be to Thee, my Lord, for brother Fire,
    by whom Thou dost illumine the night ;
    and he is beautiful and jocund, robust and strong.

Praise be to Thee, my Lord, for our sister Mother Earth,
    who sustaineth and governeth us
    and bringeth forth divers fruits, with coloured flowers
        and grass.

Praise be to Thee, my Lord, for them that pardon for
        love of Thee
    and bear infirmity and tribulation ;
    blessed are they that endure in peace,
    for by Thee, Most High, they shall be crowned.

Praise be to Thee, my Lord, for our sister bodily Death,
    from whom no man living may escape ;
    woe unto them that die in mortal sin,
    but blessed are they that shall find themselves in Thy
        most holy will,
    for unto them shall the second death do no evil.

Praise ye and bless my Lord, and give thanks and service
    unto Him with great humility.

SAINT FRANCIS OF ASSISI

I dreamed that, as I wandered by the way,
    Bare Winter suddenly was changed to Spring,
And gentle odours led my steps astray,
    Mixed with a sound of waters murmuring

Along a shelving bank of turf, which lay
   Under a copse, and hardly dared to fling
Its green arms round the bosom of the stream,
But kissed it and then fled, as thou mightest in a
    dream.

There grew pied wind-flowers and violets,
   Daisies, those pearled Arcturi of the earth,
The constellated flower that never sets ;
   Faint oxslips ; tender bluebells, at whose birth
The sod scarce heaved ; and that tall flower that
    wets—
   Like a child, half in tenderness and mirth—
Its mother's face with Heaven's collected tears,
When the low wind, its playmate's voice, it hears.

And in the warm hedge grew lush eglantine,
   Green cowbind and the moonlight-coloured may,
And cherry-blossoms, and white cups, whose wine
   Was the bright dew, yet drained not by the day ;
And wild roses, and ivy serpentine,
   With its dark buds and leaves, wandering astray ;
And flowers azure, black, and streaked with gold,
Fairer than any wakened eyes behold.

And nearer to the river's trembling edge
   There grew broad flag-flowers, purple pranked
    with white,
And starry river buds among the sedge,
   And floating water-lilies, broad and bright,
Which lit the oak that overhung the hedge
   With moonlight beams of their own watery light ;
And bulrushes, and reeds of such deep green
As soothed the dazzled eye with sober sheen.

Methought that of these visionary flowers
   I made a nosegay, bound in such a way
That the same hues, which in their natural bowers
   Were mingled or opposed, in like array
Kept these imprisoned children of the Hours
   Within my hand,—and then, elate and gay,
I hastened to the spot whence I had come,
That I might there present it !—Oh ! to whom ?

SHELLEY

Thursday. 15th April. 1802.—When we were in the
woods beyond Gowbarrow Park we saw a few daffodils
close to the water-side. We fancied that the lake had
floated the seeds ashore, and that the little colony had so
sprung up. But as we went along there were more and
yet more ; and at last, under the boughs of the trees, we
saw that there was a long belt of them along the shore,
about the breadth of a country turnpike road. I never
saw daffodils so beautiful. They grew among the mossy
stones about and above them ; some rested their heads
upon these stones, as on a pillow, for weariness ; and the
rest tossed and reeled and danced, and seemed as if they
verily laughed with the wind, that blew upon them over
the lake ; they looked so gay, ever glancing, ever changing.
This wind blew directly over the lake to them. There
was here and there a little knot, and a few stragglers higher
up ; but they were so few as not to disturb the simplicity,
unity, and life of that one busy highway.

DOROTHY WORDSWORTH (from *The Journals*)

I wandered lonely as a cloud
That floats on high o'er vales and hills,
When all at once I saw a crowd,
A host, of golden daffodils;
Beside the lake, beneath the trees,
Fluttering and dancing in the breeze.

Continuous as the stars that shine
And twinkle on the milky way,
They stretched in never-ending line
Along the margin of a bay:
Ten thousand saw I at a glance,
Tossing their heads in sprightly dance.

The waves beside them danced; but they
Out-did the sparkling waves in glee:
A poet could not but be gay,
In such a jocund company:
I gazed, and gazed, but little thought
What wealth the show to me had brought:

For oft, when on my couch I lie
In vacant or in pensive mood,
They flash upon that inward eye
Which is the bliss of solitude;
And then my heart with pleasure fills,
And dances with the daffodils.

WORDSWORTH (composed 1804)

Consider what we owe merely to the meadow grass, to the covering of the dark ground by that glorious enamel, by the companies of those soft, and countless, and peaceful spears. The fields ! Follow but forth for a little time the thoughts of all that we ought to recognize in those words. All spring and summer is in them,—the walks by silent, scented paths,—the rests in noonday heat,—the joy of herds and flocks,—the power of all shepherd life and meditation,—the life of sunlight upon the world, falling in emerald streaks, and falling in soft blue shadows, where else it would have struck upon the dark mould, or scorching dust,—pastures beside the pacing brooks,—soft emerald banks and knolls of lowly hills,—thymy slopes of down overlooked by the blue line of lifted sea,—crisp lawns all dim with early dew, or smooth in evening warmth of barred sunshine, dinted by happy feet, and softening in their fall the sound of loving voices ; all these are summed in those simple words ; and these are not all. We may not measure to the full the depth of this heavenly gift in our own land ; though still, as we think of it longer, the infinite of all that meadow sweetness, Shakespeare's peculiar joy, would open on us more and more, yet we have it but in part. Go out, in the spring-time, among the meadows that slope from the shores of the Swiss lakes to the roots of their lower mountains. There, mingled with the taller gentians and the white narcissus, the grass grows deep and free ; and as you follow the winding mountain paths, beneath arching boughs all veiled and dim with blossom,—paths that for ever droop and rise over the green banks and mounds sweeping down in scented undulation, steep to the blue water, studded here and there with new mown heaps filling all the air with fainter sweetness,—look up towards

the higher hills, where the waves of everlasting green roll
silently into their long inlets among the shadows of the
pines ; and we may, perhaps, at last know the meaning
of those quiet words of the 147th Psalm, " He maketh
grass to grow upon the mountains."

RUSKIN (from *Modern Painters*)

In somer when the shawes be sheyne,
 And the leves be large and long,
Hit is full mery in feyre foreste
 To here the foulys song.

To se the dere draw to the dale
 And leve the hilles hee,
And shadow him in the leves grene
 Under the grene-wode tree.

Hit befel on Witsontide.
 Early in a May mornyng,
The Sonne up faire can shyne,
 And the briddis mery can syng.

This is a mery mornyng," said Litulle Johne,
 " Be Hym that dyed on tre ;
A more mery man than I am one
 Lyves not in Christiante.

" Pluk up thi hert, my dere mayster,"
 Litulle John can say,
" And thynk hit is a fulle fayre tyme
 In a mornynge of May."

ANONYMOUS

587

But Master, first let me tell you, that that very hour when you were absent from me, I sate down under a Willow tree by the water side, and considered what you had told me of the owner of the pleasant Meadow in which you then left me, that he had a plentiful estate, and not a heart to think so ; that he had at this time many Law Suites depending, and that they both damp'd his mirth and took up so much of his time and thoughts, that he himselfe had not leisure to take the sweet content that I, who pretended no title, took in his fields ; for I could sit there quietly, and looking on the water, see Fishes leaping at Flies of several shapes and colours ; looking on the Hils, could behold them spotted with Woods and Groves ; looking down the Meadows, could see here a Boy gathering *Lillies* and *Lady-smocks*, and there a Girle cropping *Culverkeys* and *Cowslips*, all to make Garlands sutable to this pleasant Month of *May* ; these and many other Field-flowers so perfum'd the air, that I thought this Meadow like the field in *Sicily* (of which *Diodorus* speaks) where the perfumes arising from the place, makes all the dogs that hunt in it, to fall off, and lose their hottest sent.

IZAAK WALTON (from *The Compleat Angler*)

I love England—I like its living men—give me a long brown plain for my money, so that I may meet with some of Edmund Ironside's descendants ; give me a barren mould, so I may meet with some shadowing of Alfred in the shape of a gipsy, a huntsman, or a shepherd. Scenery is fine, but human nature is finer ; the sward is richer for the tread of a real nervous English foot ; the eagle's nest is finer, for the mountaineer having looked into it.

KEATS (from *The Letters*)

In the country it is as if every tree said to me " Holy ! Holy ! " Who can ever express the ecstasy of the woods ? If all else fails, there remains the country, even in winter.

BEETHOVEN

Did I see a man sitting in a chair, as long as he was quiet, I could not tell but his body was inanimate ; but if he stirred, if he moved his legs, or stretched forth his arms, if he breathed or twinkled with his eyes, I could easily tell he had a soul within him. Motion being a far greater evidence of life, than all lineaments whatsoever. Colours and features may be in a dead picture, but motion is always attended with life. What shall I think therefore when the winds blow, the seas roar, the waters flow, the vapours ascend, the clouds fly, the drops of rain fall, the stars march forth in armies, the sun runneth swiftly round about the world ? Can all these things move so without a life, or spring of motion ? But the wheels in watches move, and so doth the hand that pointeth out the figures : this being a motion of dead things. Therefore hath God created living ones : that by lively motions, and sensible desires, we might be sensible of a Deity. They breathe, they see, they feel, they grow, they flourish, they know, they love. O what a world of evidences ! We are lost in abysses, we now are absorpt in wonders, and swallowed up of demonstrations. Beasts, fowls, and fishes teaching and evidencing the glory of their creator. But these by an endless generation might succeed each other from everlasting. Let us therefore survey their order, and see by that whether we cannot discern their governor. The sun, and moon, and stars shine, and by shining minister influences to herbs and flowers. These grow and feed the cattle : the seas also and springs minister unto them, as they do unto fowls and fishes. All which are subservient unto man, a more noble creature endued with understanding to admire his Creator. Who being king and lord of this world, is able to prize all in a reflexive manner, and render praises for all with joy, living blessedly in the fruition of them. None can question the being of a Deity but one that is ignorant of man's excellencies, and the glory of his dominion over all the creatures.

TRAHERNE (from *Centuries of Meditations*)

It may indeed be phantasy when I
Essay to draw from all created things
Deep, heartfelt, inward joy that closely clings ;
And trace in leaves and flowers that round me
    lie
Lessons of love and earnest piety.
So let it be ; and if the wide world rings
In mock of this belief, it brings
Nor fear, nor grief, nor vain perplexity.
So will I build my altar in the fields,
And the blue sky my fretted dome shall be,
And the sweet fragrance that the wild flower
    yields

Shall be the incense I will yield to Thee,
Thee only God ! and thou shalt not despise
Even me, the priest of this poor sacrifice.

COLERIDGE

It seems as if the day was not wholly profane in which
we have given heed to some natural object. The fall of
snowflakes in a still air, preserving to each crystal its
perfect form ; the blowing of sleet over a wide sheet of
water, and over plains ; the waving ryefields ; the mimic
waving of acres of houstonia, whose innumerable florets
whiten and ripple before the eye ; the reflections of trees
and flowers in glassy lakes ; the musical steaming odorous
south wind, which converts all trees to wind-harps ; the
crackling and spurting of hemlock in the flames ; or of
pine-logs, which yield glory to the walls and faces in the
sitting-room,—these are the music and pictures of the
most ancient religion. My house stands in low land, with
limited outlook, and on the skirt of the village. But I go
with my friend to the shore of our little river, and with
one stroke of the paddle I leave the village politics and
personalities behind, and pass into a delicate realm of
sunset and moonlight, too bright almost for spotted man
to enter without noviciate and probation. We penetrate
bodily this incredible beauty : we dip our hands in this
painted element : our eyes are bathed in these lights and
forms. A holiday, a villeggiatura, a royal revel, the
proudest, most heart-rejoicing festival that valour and
beauty, power and taste, ever decked and enjoyed,
establishes itself on the instant. These sunset clouds,
these delicately emerging stars, with their private and

ineffable glances, signify and proffer it. I am taught the poorness of our invention, the ugliness of towns and palaces. Art and luxury have early learned that they must work as enhancement and sequel to this original beauty.

EMERSON (from *The Essays*)

Ye Presences of Nature in the sky
And on the earth ! Ye Visions of the hills !
And Souls of lonely places ! can I think
A vulgar hope was yours when ye employed
Such ministry, when ye, through many a year
Haunting me thus among my boyish sports,
On caves and trees, upon the woods and hills,
Impressed, upon all forms, the characters
Of danger or desire ; and thus did make
The surface of the universal earth,
With triumph and delight, with hope and fear,
Work like a sea ?

. . . . . .

I would walk alone,
Under the quiet stars, and at that time
Have felt whate'er there is of power in sound
To breathe an elevated mood, by form
Or image unprofaned ; and I would stand,
If the night blackened with a coming storm,
Beneath some rock, listening to notes that are
The ghostly language of the ancient earth,
Or make their dim abode in distant winds.
Thence did I drink the visionary power ;
And deem not profitless those fleeting moods

Of shadowy exultation : not for this,
That they are kindred to our purer mind
And intellectual life ; but that the soul,
Remembering how she felt, but what she felt
Remembering not, retains an obscure sense
Of possible sublimity, whereto
With growing faculties she doth aspire,
With faculties still growing, feeling still
That whatsoever point they gain, they yet
Have something to pursue.

     I, at this time,
Saw blessings spread around me like a sea.
Thus while the days flew by, and years passed on,
From Nature and her overflowing soul
I had received so much, that all my thoughts
Were steeped in feeling ; I was only then
Contented, when with bliss ineffable
I felt the sentiment of Being spread
O'er all that moves and all that seemeth still ;
O'er all that, lost beyond the reach of thought
And human knowledge, to the human eye
Invisible, yet liveth to the heart ;
O'er all that leaps and runs, and shouts and sings,
Or beats the gladsome air ; o'er all that glides
Beneath the wave, yea, in the wave itself,
And mighty depth of waters. Wonder not
If high the transport, great the joy I felt,
Communing in this sort through heaven and earth
With every form of creature, as it looked
Towards the Uncreated with a countenance
Of adoration, with an eye of love.
One song they sang, and it was audible,

Most audible, then, when the fleshly ear,
O'ercome by humblest prelude of that strain,
Forgot her functions, and slept undisturbed.

Ye motions of delight, that haunt the sides
Of the green hills ; ye breezes and soft airs,
Whose subtle intercourse with breathing flowers,
Feelingly watched, might teach Man's haughty race
How without injury to take, to give
Without offence ; ye who, as if to show
The wondrous influence of power gently used,
Bend the complying heads of lordly pines,
And, with a touch, shift the stupendous clouds
Through the whole compass of the sky ; ye brooks,
Muttering along the stones, a busy noise
By day, a quiet sound in silent night ;
Ye waves, that out of the great deep steal forth
In a calm hour to kiss the pebbly shore,
Not mute, and then retire, fearing no storm ;
And you, ye groves, whose ministry it is
To interpose the covert of your shades,
Even as a sleep, between the heart of man
And outward troubles, between man himself,
Not seldom, and his own uneasy heart :
Oh ! that I had a music and a voice
Harmonious as your own, that I might tell
What ye have done for me. The morning shines,
Nor heedeth Man's perverseness ; Spring returns,—
I saw the Spring return, and could rejoice,
In common with the children of her love,
Piping on boughs, or sporting on fresh fields,
Or boldly seeking pleasure nearer heaven
On wings that navigate cerulean skies.

594

So neither were complacency, nor peace,
Nor tender yearnings, wanting for my good
Through these distracted times ; in Nature still
Glorying, I found a counterpoise in her,
Which, when the spirit of evil reached its height,
Maintained for me a secret happiness.

.   .   .   .   .

O Soul of Nature ! excellent and fair !
That didst rejoice with me, with whom I, too,
Rejoiced through early youth, before the winds
And roaring waters, and the lights and shades
That marched and countermarched about the hills
In glorious apparition, Powers on whom
I daily waited, now all eye and now
All ear ; but never long without the heart
Employed, and man's unfolding intellect :
O Soul of Nature ! that, by laws divine
Sustained and governed, still dost overflow
With an impassioned life, what feeble ones
Walk on this earth ! how feeble have I been
When thou wert in thy strength !

               WORDSWORTH (from *The Prelude*)

Natura nihil agit frustra, is the only undisputed Axiome
in Philosophy. There are no Grotesques in Nature ; not
anything framed to fill up empty Cantons and unnecessary
spaces. In the most imperfect Creatures, and such as were
not preserved in the Ark, but, having their Seeds and
Principles in the womb of Nature, are everywhere, where
the power of the Sun is, in these is the Wisdom of His

hand discovered. Out of this rank Solomon chose the object of his admiration. Indeed, what Reason may not go to School to the wisdom of Bees, Ants, and Spiders ? what wise hand teacheth *them* to do what Reason cannot teach *us* ? Ruder heads stand amazed at those prodigious pieces of Nature, Whales, Elephants, Dromidaries, and Camels ; these, I confess, are the Colossus and majestick pieces of her hand : but in these narrow Engines there is more curious Mathematicks ; and the civility of these little Citizens more neatly sets forth the Wisdom of their Maker. . . I could never content my contemplation with those general pieces of wonder, the Flux and Reflux of the Sea, the increase of Nile, the conversion of the Needle to the North ; and have studied to match and parallel those in the more obvious and neglected pieces of Nature, which without further travel I can do in the Cosmography of myself. We carry with us the wonders we seek without us : there is all Africa and her prodigies in us ; we are that bold and adventurous piece of Nature which he that studies wisely learns in a compendium what others labour at in a divided piece and endless volume.

Thus there are two Books from whence I collect my Divinity ; besides that written one of God, another of His servant Nature, that universal and publick Manuscript, that lies expans'd unto the Eyes of all : those that never saw Him in the one have discover'd Him in the other. This was the Scripture and Theology of the Heathens : the natural motion of the Sun made *them* more admire Him than its supernatural station did the Children of Israel ; the ordinary effects of Nature wrought more admiration in *them* than in the other all his Miracles. Surely the Heathens knew better how to joyn and read these mystical Letters than we Christians, who cast a more

careless Eye on these common Hieroglyphicks and disdain
to suck Divinity from the flowers of Nature.

SIR THOMAS BROWNE (from *Religio Medici*)

London, September 24, 1802.

MY DEAR MANNING,

Since the date of my last letter I have been a traveller.
A strong desire seized me of visiting remote regions. My
first impulse was to go and see Paris. It was a trivial
objection to my aspiring mind, that I did not understand
a word of the language, since I certainly intend some
time in my life to see Paris, and equally certainly intend
never to learn the language ; therefore that could be no
objection. However, I am very glad I did not go, because
you had left Paris (I see) before I could have set out. I
believe, Stoddart promising to go with me another year
prevented that plan. My next scheme (for to my restless,
ambitious mind London was become a bed of thorns)
was to visit the far-famed peak in Derbyshire, where the
Devil sits, they say, without breeches. *This* my purer
mind rejected as indelicate. And my final resolve was, a
tour to the Lakes. I set out with Mary to Keswick, without giving Coleridge any notice, for my time, being
precious, did not admit of it. He received us with all the
hospitality in the world, and gave up his time to show
us all the wonders of the country. He dwells upon a small
hill by the side of Keswick, in a comfortable house, quite
enveloped on all sides by a net of mountains ; great
floundering bears and monsters they seemed, all couchant
and asleep. We got in in the evening, travelling in a post-
chaise from Penrith, in the midst of a gorgeous sunshine,

597

which transmuted all the mountains into colours, purple, etc., etc. We thought we had got into fairyland. But that went off (as it never came again; while we stayed we had no more fine sunsets), and we entered Coleridge's comfortable study just in the dusk, when the mountains were all dark with clouds upon their heads. Such an impression I never received from objects of sight before, nor do I suppose I ever can again. Glorious creatures, fine old fellows, Skiddaw, etc. I never shall forget ye, how ye lay about that night, like an intrenchment; gone to bed, as it seemed for the night, but promising that ye were to be seen in the morning. Coleridge had got a blazing fire in his study; which is a large antique, ill-shaped room, with an old-fashioned organ, never played upon, big enough for a church, shelves of scattered folios, an Æolian harp, and an old sofa, half bed, etc. And all looking out upon the last fading view of Skiddaw, and his broad-breasted brethren : what a night ! Here we stayed three full weeks, in which time I visited Wordsworth's cottage, where we stayed a day or two with the Clarksons (good people, and most hospitable, at whose house we tarried one day and night), and saw Lloyd. The Wordsworths were gone to Calais. They have since been in London, and past much time with us : he is now gone into Yorkshire to be married. So we have seen Keswick, Grasmere, Ambleside, Ulswater (where the Clarksons live), and a place at the other end of Ulswater ; I forget the name ; to which we travelled on a pretty sultry day, over the middle of Helvellyn. We have clambered up to the top of Skiddaw, and I have waded up the bed of Lodore. In fine, I have satisfied myself that there is such a thing as that which tourists call *romantic*, which I very much suspected before ; they make such a spluttering about it, and toss their splendid epithets around them, till they give as dim a light as at four o'clock next morning the lamps do after an illumination. Mary was excessively tired when she got about half-way up Skiddaw, but we came to a cold rill (than which nothing can be imagined more cold, running over cold stones), and with the reinforcement of a draught of cold water she surmounted it most manfully. Oh, its fine black head, and the bleak air atop of it, with a prospect of mountains all about and about, making you giddy ; and then Scotland afar off, and the border countries so famous in song and ballad ! It was a day that will stand out, like a mountain, I am sure, in my life. But I am returned (I have now been come home near three weeks ; I was a month out), and you cannot conceive the degradation I felt at first, from being accustomed to wander free as air among mountains, and bathe in rivers without being controlled by any one, to come home and *work*. I felt very *little*. I had been dreaming I was a very great man. But that is going off, and I find I shall conform in time to that state of life to which it has pleased God to call me. Besides, after all, Fleet Street and the Strand are better places to live in for good and all than amidst Skiddaw. Still, I turn back to those great places where I wandered about, participating in their greatness. After all, I could not *live* in Skiddaw. I could spend a year, two, three years among them, but I must have a prospect of seeing Fleet Street at the end of that time, or I should mope and pine away, I know. Still, Skiddaw is a fine creature.

LAMB (from *The Letters*)

                                   Now, my friends emerge
Beneath the wide wide Heaven—and view again
The many-steepled tract magnificent
Of hilly fields and meadows, and the sea,
With some fair bark, perhaps, whose sails light up
The slip of smooth clear blue betwixt two Isles
Of purple shadow ! Yes ! they wander on
In gladness all ; but thou, methinks, most glad,
My gentle-hearted Charles ! for thou hast pined
And hungered after Nature, many a year,
In the great City pent, winning thy way
With sad yet patient soul, through evil and pain
And strange calamity ! Ah ! slowly sink
Behind the western ridge, thou glorious Sun !
Shine in the slant beams of the sinking orb,
Ye purple heath-flowers ! richlier burn, ye clouds
Live in the yellow light, ye distant groves !
And kindle, thou blue Ocean ! So my Friend
Struck with deep joy may stand, as I have stood,
Silent with swimming sense ; yea, gazing round
On the wide landscape, gaze till all doth seem
Less gross than bodily ; and of such hues
As veil the Almighty Spirit, when yet he makes
Spirits perceive his presence.

                                   COLERIDGE
                    (from *This Lime-Tree Bower* . . .
                    addressed to CHARLES LAMB)

. . . Rarely are Mountains seen in such combined majesty and grace as here. The rocks are of that sort called Primitive by the mineralogists, which always arrange themselves in masses of a rugged, gigantic character ; which ruggedness, however, is here tempered by a singular airiness of form, and softness of environment : in a climate favourable to vegetation, the gray cliff, itself covered with lichens, shoots up through a garment of foliage or verdure ; and white, bright cottages, tree-shaded, cluster round the everlasting granite. In fine vicissitude, Beauty alternates with Grandeur : you ride through stony hollows, along strait passes, traversed by torrents, overhung by high walls of rock ; now winding amid broken shaggy chasms, and huge fragments ; now suddenly emerging into some emerald valley, where the streamlet collects itself into a Lake, and man has again found a fair dwelling, and it seems as if Peace had established herself in the bosom of Strength. . . .

Now the Valley closes in abruptly, intersected by a huge mountain mass, the stony waterworn ascent of which is not to be accomplished on horseback. Arrived aloft, he finds himself again lifted into the evening sunset light ; and cannot but pause, and gaze round him, some moments there. An upland irregular expanse of wold, where valleys in complex branchings are suddenly or slowly arranging their descent towards every quarter of the sky. The mountain-ranges are beneath your feet, and folded together : only the loftier summits look down here and there as on a second plain ; lakes also lie clear and earnest in their solitude. No trace of man now visible ; unless indeed it were he who fashioned that little visible link of Highway, here, as would seem, scaling the inaccessible, to unite Province with Province. But sunwards, to you ! how it towers sheer up, a world of Mountains, the diadem and centre of the mountain region ! A hundred and a hundred savage peaks, in the last light of Day ; all glowing, of gold and amethyst, like giant spirits of the wilderness ; there in their silence, in their solitude, even as on the night when Noah's Deluge first dried !

CARLYLE (from *Sartor Resartus*)

O God ! methinks it were a happy life
To be no better than a homely swain :
To sit upon a hill, as I do now,
To carve out dials quaintly point by point,
Thereby to see the minutes, how they run :
How many make the hour full complete,
How many hours bring about the day,
How many days will finish up the year,
How many years a mortal man may live.
When this is known, then to divide the times :
So many hours must I tend my flock ;
So many hours must I take my rest ;
So many hours must I contemplate ;
So many hours must I sport myself ;
So many days my ewes have been with young ;
So many weeks ere the poor fools will yean ;
So many years ere I shall shear the fleece ;
So minutes, hours, days, months and years,
Pass'd over to the end they were created,
Would bring white hairs unto a quiet grave.
Ah, what a life were this, how sweet, how lovely !

Gives not the hawthorn bush a sweeter shade
To shepherds, looking on their silly sheep,
Than doth a rich embroider'd canopy
To kings, that fear their subjects' treachery ?
O yes it doth ; a thousand-fold it doth.
And to conclude ; the shepherd's homely curds,
His cool thin drink out of his leather bottle,
His wonted sleep under a fresh tree's shade,
All which secure and sweetly he enjoys,
Is far beyond a prince's delicates,
His viands sparkling in a golden cup,
His body couchèd in a curious bed,
When care, mistrust, and treason wait on him.

SHAKESPEARE (from *Henry VI, Part III*)

Ah, yet, ere I descend to the grave
May I a small house and large garden have ;
And a few friends, and many books, both true,
Both wise, and both delightful too !
   And since love ne'er will from me flee,
A Mistress moderately fair,
And good as guardian angels are,
   Only beloved and loving me.

O fountains ! when in you shall I
Myself eased of unpeaceful thoughts espy ?
O fields ! O woods ! when, when shall I be made
The happy tenant of your shade ?
   Here's the spring-head of Pleasure's flood ;

Here's wealthy Nature's treasury,
Where all the riches lie that she
  Has coin'd and stamp'd for good.

Pride and ambition here
Only in far-fetch'd metaphors appear ;
Here nought but winds can hurtful murmurs
    scatter,
And nought but Echo flatter.
  The gods, when they descended, hither
From heaven did always choose their way :
And therefore we may boldly say
  That 'tis the way too thither.

How happy here should I
And one dear She live, and embracing die !
She who is all the world, and can exclude
In deserts solitude.
  I should have then this only fear :
Lest men, when they my pleasures see,
Should hither throng to live like me,
  And so make a city here.

COWLEY (from *The Wish*)

When I came into the country, and being seated among
silent trees, and meads and hills, had all my time in mine
own hands, I resolved to spend it all, whatever it cost
me, in the search of happiness, and to satiate that burning thirst which Nature had enkindled in me from my
youth. In which I was so resolute, that I chose rather to

live upon ten pounds a year, and to go in leather clothes, and feed upon bread and water, so that I might have all my time clearly to myself, than to keep many thousands per annum in an estate of life where my life would be devoured in care and labour. And God was so pleased to accept of that desire, that from that time to this, I have had all things plentifully provided for me, without any care at all, my very study of Felicity making me more to prosper, than all the care in the whole world. So that through His blessing I live a free and kingly life as if the world were turned again into Eden, or much more, as it is at this day.

TRAHERNE (from *Centuries of Meditations*)

Sweet Country life to such unknown,
Whose lives are others, not their own !
But serving Courts, and Cities, be
Less happy, less enjoying thee.
Thou never Plow'st the Oceans foame
To seek, and bring rough Pepper home :
Nor to the Eastern Ind dost rove
To bring from thence the scorchèd Clove.
Nor, with the losse of thy lov'd rest,
Bring'st home the Ingot from the West.
No, thy Ambition's Master-piece
Flies no thought higher than a fleece :
Or how to pay thy Hinds, and cleere
All scores ; and so to end the yeere :
But walk'st about thine own dear bounds,
Not envying others larger grounds :

For well thou know'st, *'tis not th'extent*
Of Land makes Life, but sweet content.
When now the Cock (the Plow-man's Horne)
Calls forth the lily-wristed Morne ;
Then to thy corn-fields thou dost goe,
Which though well soyl'd, yet thou dost know
That the best compost for the Lands
Is the wise Masters Feet, and Hands.
There at the Plough thou find'st thy Teame,
With a Hind whistling there to them :
And cheer'st them up, by singing how
The Kingdoms portion is the Plow.
This done, then to th'enameld Meads
Thou go'st, and as thy foot there treads,
Thou seest a present God-like Power
Imprinted in each Herbe and Flower ;
And smell'st the breath of great-ey'd Kine,
Sweet as the blossomes of the Vine.
Here thou behold'st thy large sleek Neat
Unto the Dew-laps up in meat :
And, as thou look'st, the wanton Steere,
The Heifer, Cow, and Oxe draw neere
To make a pleasing passtime there.
These seen, thou go'st to view thy flocks
Of sheep, (safe from the Wolfe and Fox)
And find'st their bellies there as full
Of short sweet grasse, as backs with wool.
And leav'st them (as they feed and fill)
A Shepherd piping on the hill.
For Sports, for Pagentrie, and Playes,
Thou hast thy Eves, and Holydayes :
On which the young men and maids meet,
To exercise their dancing feet :

Tripping the comely country Round,
With Daffodils and Daisies crown'd.
Thy Wakes, thy Quintels, here thou hast,
Thy May-poles too with Garlands grac't :
Thy Morris-dance ; thy Whitsun-ale ;
Thy Sheering-feast, which never faile.
Thy Harvest home ; thy Wassaile bowle,
That's tost up after Fox i' th' Hole.
Thy Mummeries ; thy Twelfe-tide Kings
And Queenes ; thy Christmas revellings :
Thy Nut-browne mirth ; thy Russet wit ;
And no man payes too deare for it.
To these, thou hast thy time to goe
And trace the Hare i' th'trecherous Snow :
Thy witty wiles to draw, and get
The Larke into the Trammell net :
Thou hast thy Cockrood, and thy Glade
To take the precious Phesant made :
Thy Lime-twigs, Snares, and Pit-falls then
To catch the pilfring Birds, not Men.
O happy life ! if that their good
The Husbandmen but understood !
Who all the day themselves doe please,
And Younglings, with such sports as these.
And, lying down, have nought t'affright
Sweet sleep, that makes more short the night.

HERRICK

607

Though Clock,
To tell how night drawes hence, I've none,
A Cock
I have, to sing how day drawes on.
I have
A maid (my Prew) by good luck sent,
To save
That little Fates me gave or lent.
A Hen
I keep, which creeking day by day,
Tells when
She goes her long white egg to lay.
A Goose
I have, which, with a jealous eare,
Lets loose
Her tongue, to tell what danger's neare.
A Lamb
I keep (tame) with my morsells fed,
Whose Dam
An Orphan left him (lately dead.)
A Cat
I keep, that playes about my House,
Grown fat
With eating many a miching Mouse.
To these
A Trasy[1] I do keep, whereby
I please
The more my rurall privacie :
Which are
But toyes, to give my heart some ease :
Where care
None is, slight things do lightly please.

HERRICK

[1] his dog.

It was, and still my care is,
To worship ye, the Lares,
With crowns of greenest Parsley,
And Garlick chives not scarcely :
For favours here to warme me,
And not by fire to harme me.
For gladding so my hearth here,
With inoffensive mirth here ;
That while the Wassaile Bowle here
With North-down Ale doth troule here,
No sillable doth fall here
To marre the mirth at all here.
For which, O Chimney-keepers !
(I dare not call ye Sweepers)
So long as I am able
To keep a countrey-table,
Great be my fare, or small cheere,
Ile eat and drink up all here.

HERRICK

How sweet is the Shepherd's sweet lot !
From the morn to the evening he strays ;
He shall follow his sheep all the day,
And his tongue shall be filled with praise.

For he hears the lamb's innocent call,
And he hears the ewe's tender reply ;
He is watchful while they are at peace,
For they know when their Shepherd is nigh.

BLAKE

On a certain day the blessed Francis was journeying to Siena, and he found near to the city a great flock of sheep. And he gave them salutation, as was his wont, and the sheep ceased their feeding and went after him and gazed into his face and made him such welcome that the shepherds wondered greatly.

And once when the blessed Francis was at Santa Maria di Porziuncola, there was given to him a ewe-lamb, which he received gladly because of her simplicity and innocence, and he recommended her to be intent in praising God and to be careful to give no offence to the brethren; and the ewe-lamb fully observed the command of the blessed Francis, as if she manifestly knew his piety. And when she heard the brethren chant in the choir, she ran thither straightway and, without receiving any instruction, she knelt before the altar of the Virgin Mary and bleated as though she had human sense, and at the elevation of the Body of Christ she knelt down like a human creature shaming the slothful by her readiness.

At a time when the Blessed Francis was at Rome, he tended a lamb there for a certain while, and when he departed he left it in charge of a lady, by name Madonna Iacopa di Sette Soli, and whenever she went to church the lamb went with her, as if it were an animal reasonable and instructed in the things of the Spirit; and if the lady did not rise betimes in the morning, it roused her with its horns and with its voice and so persuaded her to go to Church. And so this Lamb, disciple of the blessed Francis, became by these means a teacher of doctrine and godly devotion.

At another time, when the blessed Francis was at the place Greccio, there was presented to him alive a wild leveret; and he took it in his hands. Then he set it on the ground; but it fled into his bosom. And the blessed Francis let it go, recommending it not to suffer itself to be caught again. And many times he set it on the ground so that it should go, yet it returned into his bosom, and in the end it was taken to the forest and was let go. . . .

And once when the blessed Francis was going by the lake of Rieti to the hermitage of Greccio, a fisherman brought him a water-fowl, which he received gladly, and when he held it in his hands he opened them, to let it go, and the bird would not go; and the blessed Francis raised his eyes to God and remained thus a long time in prayer. And when he was come to himself he bade the bird to go and to praise God, and then the bird, when it had received his blessing, departed, showing great gladness with the movements of its body.

Likewise in that same lake was taken a fish and brought to the blessed Francis, which, when he had received, he set back in the water, and staying there it played with him for a good while and would not go before the blessed Francis had given it leave and his blessing.

On a day when the blessed Francis was going through the Venetian marshes, a great flock of birds was singing upon the bushes; and when the blessed Francis saw them he said to his companion: Hark how our brothers the birds are praising the Lord. Let us go into the midst of them and sing our canonical Hours. And the birds, when they had entered into their midst, did not move: and when he and his companion could not hear one another because of the noise of the birds' song, the blessed Francis said to them: Our brothers the birds, cease your singing, that we may say the Hours. And instantly the birds were silent until they had sung the office at great leisure, and, having received the blessing of the blessed Francis, the birds began to sing as before.

The blessed Francis being in his cell at Santa Maria di Porziuncola, there was a grasshopper making a great singing upon a fig-tree. And many times he said to her: Well done! Praise the Lord! And at last he called her; and instantly, as if bidden by God, she came upon his hand, and the blessed Francis said to her: Sing, my sister. And she sang. And then he said: Sing no more. And she went to a place near by, and for full eight days she stayed there singing, and the blessed Francis said: Let us now give our sister grasshopper leave to depart, for she has afforded us much refreshment. And instantly, receiving his permission, she departed and returned no more, as if she dared not to transgress his commandment.

SAINT BONAVENTURA
(from *The Life of St. Francis*)

Is that beast better that hath two or three Mountains to graze on, than a little Bee that feeds on Dew or Manna and lives upon what falls every morning from the Store-houses of Heaven, Clouds and Providence? Can a Man quench his thirst better out of a river than a full Urn, or drink better from the Fountain when it is finely paved with Marble, than when it swels over the green Turf?

JEREMY TAYLOR (from *Holy Living*)

My meat shall be what these wild woods afford,
Berries and chestnuts, plantains, on whose cheeks
The sun sits smiling, and the lofty fruit
Pulled from the fair head of the straight-grown pine;
On these I'll feed with free content, and rest,
When night shall blind the world.

FLETCHER
(from *The Faithful Shepherdess*)

The first age of man was much happy that was contented with such as the fields brought forth without
labour of man, and was not hurt with great excess of
meats and drinks; they were wont to satisfy their long
hunger with little acorns of the oak, they sought not for
dainty meats, nor knew how to mingle the wine with
honey. That is to say, they knew not pleasant drinks
nor how to dye the white fleeces of wool with the blood of
shell-fishes of Tyre, a country where there be many such
fishes, but were contented with such colours as the sheep
did bear. They could then be contented to take wholesome sleeps upon the grass and knew no beds of down,
and drink fair running water for lack of wine and ale,
also dwell under the shadow of the high pine tree for
lack of curious houses. Then had no stranger or merchant
sailed on the seas with ship, or seen strange coasts to
convey their merchandise to divers countries and places.
Then the cruel trumpets of war made no noise to call
men to battle, nor shedding of blood with mortal hate
had imbrued the fearful armour. What cruel enemy
would first move war before he saw cruel wounds, or
saw some profit by battle or war? I would our conditions

were turned again into those old manners. But the great greedy covetousness to catch and have riches burneth more fervently than the hill called Etna. Alas, who was he that first delved up the pieces of gold that lay hid in the earth and the precious stones that were contented to have lain hid and unknown?

BOETHIUS

(from *De Consolatione*—Trans. GEORGE COLVILLE, 1556: spelling modernized)

But art thou not too sensible, my lad,
Of those few losses thou hast lately had?
Thou art not yet in want, thou still dost eat
Bread of the finest flour of purest wheat;
Who better cider drinks, what Shepherd's board
Does finer curds, butter, or cheese afford?
Who wears a frock, to grace a Holy-day,
Spun of a finer wool, or finer grey?
Whose cabin is so neatly swept as thine,
With flowers and rushes kept so sweet and fine?
Whose name amongst our many Shepherds' swains
So great as thine is throughout all these plains?
Who has so many friends, so pretty loves?
Who by our bubbling fountains and green groves
Passes away the summer heats so well?
And who but thee in singing does excel?
So that the swains, when Clotten sings or plays,
Lay down their pipes, and listen to his lays?

COTTON (from *An Eclogue*)

We entered by the cow-house, the house-door being within, at right angles to the other door. The woman was distressed that she had a bad fire, but she heaped up some dry peats and heather, and, blowing it with her breath, in a short time raised a blaze that scorched us into comfortable feelings. A small part of the smoke found its way out of the hole of the chimney, the rest through the open window-panes, one of which was within the recess of the fireplace, and made a frame to the little picture of the restless lake and the opposite shore, seen when the outer door was open. The woman of the house was very kind : whenever we asked her for anything it seemed a fresh pleasure to her that she had it for us ; she always answered with a sort of softening down of the Scotch exclamation, " Hoot ! " " Ho ! yes, ye'll get that," and hied to her cupboard in the spence. . . . We got oatmeal, butter, bread and milk, made some porridge, and then departed. It was rainy and cold, with a strong wind. . . .

The evening began to darken, and it rained so heavily before we had gone two miles that we were completely wet. It was dark when we landed, and on entering the house I was sick with cold.

The good woman had provided, according to her promise, a better fire than we had found in the morning ; and indeed when I sate down in the chimney-corner of her smoky biggin' I thought I had never been more comfortable in my life. Coleridge had been there long enough to have a pan of coffee boiling for us, and having put our clothes in the way of drying, we all sate down, thankful for a shelter. We could not prevail on the man of the house to draw near the fire, though he was cold and wet, or to suffer his wife to get him dry clothes till she had served us, which she did, though most willingly, not very expeditiously. . . . He did not, however, refuse to let his wife bring out the whiskey-bottle at our request : " She keeps a dram," as the phrase is ; indeed, I believe there is scarcely a lonely house by the wayside in Scotland where travellers may not be accommodated with a dram. We asked for sugar, butter, barley-bread, and milk, and with a smile and a stare more of kindness than wonder, she replied, " Ye'll get that," bringing each article separately.

We caroused our cups of coffee, laughing like children at the strange atmosphere in which we were ; the smoke came in gusts, and spread along the walls and above our heads in the chimney, where the hens were roosting like light clouds in the sky. We laughed and laughed again, in spite of the smarting of our eyes, yet had a quieter pleasure in observing the beauty of the beams and rafters gleaming between the clouds of smoke. They had been crusted over and varnished by many winters, till, where the firelight fell upon them, they were as glossy as black rocks on a sunny day cased in ice. When we had eaten our supper we sate about half an hour, and I think I had never felt so deeply the blessing of a hospitable welcome and a warm fire. . . .

I went to bed some time before the family. The door was shut between us, and they had a bright fire, which I could not see ; but the light it sent up among the varnished rafters and beams, which crossed each other in almost as intricate and fantastic a manner as I have seen the under-boughs of a large beech-tree withered by the depth of the shade above, produced the most beautiful effect that can be conceived. It was like what I should suppose an underground cave or temple to be, with a dripping or moist roof, and the moonlight entering in upon it by some means or other, and yet the colours were more like melted gems. I lay looking up till the light of the fire faded away, and the man and his wife and child had crept into their bed at the other end of the room. I did not sleep much, but passed a comfortable night, for my bed, though hard, was warm and clean : the unusualness of my situation prevented me from sleeping. I could hear the waves beat against the shore of the lake ; a little " syke " close to the door made a much louder noise ; and when I sate up in my bed I could see the lake through an open window-place at the bed's head. Add to this, it rained all night. I was less occupied by remembrance of the Trossachs, beautiful as they were, than the vision of the Highland hut, which I could not get out of my head.

DOROTHY WORDSWORTH (from *The Journals*)

Farewell thou busy World, amd may
   We never meet again :
Here I can eat and sleep, and pray,
And do more good in one short day
Than he who his whole age out-wears
Upon thy most conspicuous theatres,
Where nought but vice and vanity do reign.

Good God ! how sweet are all things here !
How beautiful the fields appear !
How cleanly do we feed and lie !

Lord! what good hours do we keep!
   How quietly we sleep!
What peace! what unanimity!
How innocent from the lewd fashion,
Is all our bus'ness, all our conversation!

Oh how happy here's our leisure!
Oh how innocent our pleasure!
Oh ye valleys, oh ye mountains
Oh ye groves and crystal fountains,
   How I love at liberty
By turn to come and visit ye!

O solitude, the soul's best friend,
That man acquainted with himself dost make,
And all his maker's wonders to intend;
   With thee I here converse at will,
   And would be glad to do so still;
For it is thou alone that keep'st the soul awake.

How calm and quiet a delight
   It is alone
To read, and meditate, and write,
By none offended, nor offending none;
To walk, ride, sit, or sleep at one's own ease,
And pleasing a man's self, none other to displease!

Oh my beloved Nymph! fair Dove,
Princess of rivers, how I love
Upon thy flow'ry banks to lie,
   And view thy silver stream,
When gilded by a summer's beam
And in it all thy wanton fry
   Playing at liberty,

And with my angle upon them,
   The all of treachery
   I ever learn'd to practise and to try !

Oh my beloved rocks ! that rise
To awe the earth, and brave the skies,
From some aspiring mountain's crown
   How dearly do I love,
   Giddy with pleasure, to look down,
And from the vales to view the noble heights above!

Lord ! would men let me alone,
What an over-happy one
Should I think myself to be,
Might I in this desert place,
Which most men by their voice disgrace,
   Live but undisturbed and free !
   Here, in this despised recess,
   Would I maugre Winter's cold,
   And the summer's worst excess,
Try to live out to sixty full years old,
   And all the while
   Without an envious eye
   On any thriving under Fortune's smile,
   Contented live, and then contented die.

COTTON

With what deep murmurs through times silent stealth
Doth thy transparent, cool and watry wealth
            Here flowing fall,
            And chide, and call,

As if his liquid, loose Retinue staid
Lingring, and were of this steep place afraid,
>   The common pass
>   Where, clear as glass,
>   All must descend
>   Not to an end :
But quickened by this deep amd rocky grave
Rise to a longer course more bright and brave.

Dear stream ! dear bank, where often I
Have sate, and pleas'd my pensive eye,
Why, since each drop of thy quick store
Runs thither, whence it flowed before,
Should poor souls fear a shade or night,
Who came (sure) from a sea of light ?
Or since those drops are all sent back
So sure to thee, that none doth lack,
Why should frail flesh doubt any more
That what God takes, He'll not restore ?

O useful Element and clear !
My sacred wash and cleanser here,
My first consigner unto those
Fountains of life, where the Lamb goes !
What sublime truths, and wholesome themes,
Lodge in thy mystical, deep streams !
Such as dull man can never finde
Unless that Spirit lead his minde,
Which first upon thy face did move,
And hatch'd all with his quickning love.
As this loud brooks incessant fall
In streaming rings restagnates all,
Which reach by course the bank, and then

Are no more seen, just so pass men.
O my invisible estate,
My glorious liberty, still late !
Thou art the channel my soul seeks,
Not this with Cataracts and Creeks.

VAUGHAN

Jolif and gay, ful of gladnesse,
Toward a river I gan me dresse,
That I herde renne faste by :
For fairer playing non saugh I
Than playen me by that riveer,
For from an hille that stood ther neer
Cam doun the streem ful stif and bold.
Cleer was the water, and as cold
As any welle is, sooth to seyne ;
And somdel lasse it was than Seine,
But it was straighter wel away.
And never saugh I, er that day,
The water that so wel lyked me ;
And wonder glad was I to see
That lusty place, and that riveer ;
And with that water that ran so cleer
My face I wissh. Tho saugh I wel
The botme paved everydel
With gravel, ful of stones shene.
The medewe softe, swote, and grene,
Beet right on the water-syde.

CHAUCER
(from The Romaunt of the Rose)

August 11th.—Scheideck to Meiringen. It is impossible to imagine a more beautiful descent than was before us to the vale of Hasli. The roaring stream was our companion ; sometimes we looked down upon it from the edge of a lofty precipice ; sometimes descended towards it, and could trace its furious course for a considerable way. The torrent bounded over rocks, and still went foaming on, no pausing-places, no gentle windings, no pools under the innumerable smaller cataracts ; the substance and the grey hue still the same, whether the stream rushed in one impetuous current down a regularly rough part of its steep channel, or laboured among rocks in cloud-shaped heavings, or in boisterous fermentation... We saw the cataract through an open window. It is a tremendous one, but, wanting the accompaniments of overhanging trees, and all the minor graces which surround our waterfalls—overgrowings of lichen, moss, fern, and flowers—it gives little of what may be called pleasure. It was astonishment and awe—an overwhelming sense of the powers of nature for the destruction of all things, and of the helplessness of man—of the weakness of his will if prompted to make a momentary effort against such a force. What weight and speed of waters ! and what a tossing of grey mist ! Though at a considerable distance from the fall, when standing at the window, a shower of misty rain blew upon us. . . .

August 24th.—Airola. . . . Cascades of pure unsullied water tumble down the hills in every conceivable variety of form and motion—and never, I think, distant from each other a quarter of a mile in the whole of our course from Airola. Sometimes, those cascades are seen to fall in one snow-white line from the highest ridge of the steep ; or, sometimes, gleaming through the woods (no traceable bed above them) they seem to start out at once from beneath the trees, as from their source, leaping over the rocks. One full cataract rose up like a geyser of Iceland, a silvery pillar that glittered, as it seemed, among lightly tossing snow.

DOROTHY WORDSWORTH (from *The Journals*)

Waters above ! eternal springs !
The dew that silvers the Dove's wings !
O welcome, welcome to the sad !
Give dry dust drink ; drink that makes glad !
Many fair ev'nings, many flow'rs
Sweeten'd with rich and gentle showers
Have I enjoy'd, and down have run
Many a fine and shining sun ;
But never, till this happy hour,
Was blest with such an evening-shower !

VAUGHAN

I lay awake last night listening to the rain, with a sense of being drowned and rotted like a grain of wheat.

KEATS (from *The Letters*)

This Sycamore, oft musical with bees,—
Such tents the Patriarchs loved ! O long unharmed
May all its aged boughs o'er-canopy
The small round basin, which this jutting stone
Keeps pure from falling leaves. Long may the
    Spring,
Quietly as a sleeping infant's breath,
Send up cold waters to the traveller
With soft and even pulse, nor ever cease
Yon tiny cone of sand its soundless dance,
Which at the bottom, like a Fairy's Page,
As merry and no taller, dances still,
Nor wrinkles the smooth surface of the Fount.
Here twilight is and coolness : here is moss,
A soft seat, and a deep and ample shade.
Thou may'st toil far and find no second tree.
Drink, Pilgrim, here ! Here rest ! and if thy heart
Be innocent, here too shalt thou refresh
Thy spirit, listening to some gentle sound,
Or passing gale or hum of murmuring bees.

COLERIDGE

On September the 21st, 1741, being then on a visit,
and intent on field-diversions, I rose before daybreak :
when I came into the enclosures, I found the stubbles
and clover-grounds matted all over with a thick coat of
cobweb, in the meshes of which a copious and heavy dew
hung so plentifully that the whole face of the country
seemed, as it were, covered with two or three setting-
nets drawn one over another. When the dogs attempted

to hunt, their eyes were so blinded and hoodwinked that they could not proceed, but were obliged to lie down and scrape the incumbrances from their faces with their fore feet; so that, finding my sport interrupted, I returned home, musing in my mind on the oddness of the occurrence.

As the morning advanced, the sun became bright and warm, and the day turned out one of those most lovely ones which no season but the autumn produces; cloudless, calm, serene, and worthy of the south of France itself.

About nine, an appearance very unusual began to demand our attention—a shower of cobwebs falling from very elevated regions, and continuing, without any interruption, till the close of the day.

These webs were not single filmy threads, floating in the air in all directions, but perfect flakes or rags; some near an inch broad, and five or six long, which fell with a degree of velocity, that showed they were considerably heavier than the atmosphere.

On every side, as the observer turned his eyes, he might behold a continual succession of fresh flakes falling into his sight, and twinkling like stars, as they turned their sides towards the sun.

How far this wonderful shower extended, would be difficult to say; but we know that it reached Bradley, Selborne, and Alresford, three places which lie in a sort of triangle, the shortest of whose sides is about eight miles in extent.

At the second of those places there was a gentleman (for whose veracity and intelligent turn we have the greatest veneration) who observed it the moment he got abroad; but concluded that, as soon as he came upon the hill above his house where he took his morning rides, he should be higher than this meteor, which he imagined might have been blown, like thistle-down, from the common above : but, to his great astonishment, when he rode to the most elevated part of the down, 300 feet above his fields, he found the webs in appearance still as much above him as before ; still descending into sight in a constant succession, and twinkling in the sun, so as to draw the attention of the most incurious.

Neither before nor after was any such fall observed ; but on this day the flakes hung in the trees and hedges so thick, that a diligent person sent out might have gathered baskets full.

The remark that I shall make on these cobweb-like appearances, called gossamer, is, that strange and superstitious as the notions about them were formerly, nobody in these days doubts but that they are the real production of small spiders, which swarm in the fields in fine weather in autumn, and have a power of shooting out webs from their tails, so as to render themselves buoyant and lighter than air. But why these apterous insects should that day take such a wonderful aerial excursion, and why their webs should at once become so gross and material as to be considerably more weighty than air, and to descend with precipitation, is a matter beyond my skill. If I might be allowed to hazard a supposition, I should imagine that those filmy threads, when first shot, might be entangled in the rising dew, and so drawn up, spiders and all, by a brisk evaporation, into the regions where clouds are formed : and if the spiders have a power of coiling and thickening their webs in the air, as Dr. Lister says they have, (see his letters to Mr. Ray), then, when they were become heavier than air, they must fall.

Every day in fine weather, in autumn chiefly, do I see

those spiders shooting out their webs and mounting aloft ; they will go off from your finger if you will take them into your hand. Last summer one alighted on my book as I was reading in the parlour ; and, running to the top of the page, and shooting out a web, took its departure from thence. But what I most wondered at was, that it went off with considerable velocity in a place where no air was stirring ; and I am sure that I did not assist it with my breath. So that these little crawlers seem to have, while mounting, some locomotive power without the use of wings, and to move in the air faster than the air itself.

GILBERT WHITE (from *Natural History of Selborne*)

November 24th, 1822.

On we trotted up a pretty green lane ; and, indeed, we had been coming gently and generally up hill for a good while. The lane was between highish banks and pretty high stuff growing on the banks, so that we could see no distance from us, and could receive not the smallest hint of what was so near at hand. The lane had a little turn towards the end ; so that, out we came, all in a moment, at the very edge of the hanger ! And, never, in all my life, was I so surprised and so delighted ! I pulled up my horse, and sat and looked ; and it was like looking from the top of a castle down into the sea, except that the valley was land and not water. . . These hangers are woods on the sides of very steep hills. The trees and underwood *hang*, in some sort, to the ground, instead of *standing on* it. Hence these places are called *Hangers*. From the summit of that which I had now to descend, I looked down upon the villages of Hawkley, Greatham, Selborne and some others.

From the south-east, round, southward, to the north-west, the main valley has cross-valleys running out of it, the hills on the sides of which are very steep, and, in many parts, covered with wood. The hills that form these cross-valleys run out into the main valley, like piers into the sea. Two of these promontories, of great height, are on the west side of the main valley, and were the first objects that struck my sight when I came to the edge of the hanger, which was on the south. The ends of these promontories are nearly perpendicular, and their tops so high in the air, that you cannot look at the village below without something like a feeling of apprehension. The leaves are all off, the hop-poles are in stack, the fields have little verdure ; but, while the spot is beautiful beyond description even now, I must leave to imagination to suppose what it is, when the trees and hangers and hedges are in leaf, the corn waving, the meadows bright, and the hops upon the poles. . . .

I forgot to mention, that in going from Hawkley to Greatham, the man, who went to show me the way, told me at a certain fork, " that road goes to *Selborne*." This put me in mind of a book, which was once recommended to me, but which I never saw, entitled *The History and Antiquities of Selborne*, (or something of that sort) written, I think, by a parson of the name of *White*, brother of Mr. *White*, so long a Bookseller in Fleet-street. This parson had, I think, the living of the parish of Selborne. The book was mentioned to me as a work of great curiosity and interest.

. . . .

August 7th, 1823.

At Tisted I crossed the turnpike-road before mentioned, and entered a lane which, at the end of about four miles, brought me to this village of Selborne. . . . I was desirous of seeing this village, about which I have read in the book of Mr. White, and which a reader has been so good as to send me. From Tisted I came generally up hill till I got within half a mile of this village, when, all of a sudden, I came to the edge of a hill, looked down over all the larger vale of which the little vale of this village makes a part. Here Hindhead and Blackdown Hill came full in my view. . . . This hill, from which you descend down into Selborne, is very lofty ; but, indeed, we are here amongst some of the highest hills in the island, and amongst the sources of rivers. The hill over which I have come this morning sends the Itchen river forth from one side of it, and the river Wey, which rises near Alton, from the opposite side of it. Hindhead, which lies before me, sends . . . the Arun forth towards the south, and a stream forth towards the north, which meets the river Wey, somewhere above Godalming. I am told that the springs of these two streams rise in the Hill of Hindhead, or, rather, on one side of the hill, at not many yards from each other. The village of Selborne is precisely what it is described by Mr. White. A straggling irregular street, bearing all the marks of great antiquity, and showing, from its lanes and its vicarage generally, that it was once a very considerable place. I went to look at the spot where Mr. White supposes the convent formerly stood. It is very beautiful. Nothing can surpass in beauty these dells and hillocks and hangers, which last are so steep that it is impossible to ascend them except by means of a serpentine path. I found here deep hollow ways, with beds

629

and sides of solid white stone ; but not quite so white and
so solid, I think, as the stone which I found in the roads
at Hawkley. The churchyard of Selborne is most beautifully situated. The land is good, all about it. The trees are
luxuriant and prone to be lofty and large. I measured the
yew-tree in the churchyard, and found the trunk to be,
according to my measurement, twenty-three feet, eight
inches, in circumference.

COBBETT (from *Rural Rides*)

Between the upright shafts of those tall elms
We may discern the thresher at his task.
Thump after thump, resounds the constant flail,
That seems to swing uncertain, and yet falls
Full on the destin'd ear. Wide flies the chaff ;
The rustling straw sends up a frequent mist
Of atoms, sparkling in the noon-day beam.

COWPER (from *The Task*)

The day's grown old, the fainting sun
Has but a little way to run,
And yet his steeds, with all his skill,
Scarce lug the chariot down the hill.

With labour spent, and thirst opprest,
Whilst they strain hard to gain the West,
From fetlocks hot drops melted light,
Which turn to meteors in the night.

The shadows now so long do grow,
That brambles like tall cedars show,
Mole-hills seem mountains, and the ant
Appears a monstrous elephant.

A very, very little flock
Shades thrice the ground that it would stock;
Whilst the small stripling following them
Appears a mighty Polypheme.

These being brought into the fold,
And by the thrifty master told,
He thinks his wages are well paid,
Since none are either lost, or stray'd.

Now lowing herds are each-where heard,
Chains rattle in the villain's yard,
The cart's on tail set down to rest,
Bearing on high the Cuckold's crest.

The hedge is stripped, the clothes brought in,
Nought's left without should be within,
The bees are hiv'd, and hum their charm,
Whilst every house does seem a swarm.

The cock now to the roost is prest;
For he must call up all the rest;
The sow's fast pegg'd within the sty,
To still her squeaking progeny.

Each one has had his supping mess,
The cheese is put into the press,
The pans and bowls clean scalded all,
Rear'd up against the milk-house wall.

And now on benches all are sat
In the cool air to sit and chat,
Till Phoebus, dipping in the West,
Shall lead the world the way to rest.

COTTON

. . . Once, above Milan, over in the direction of Lake Maggiore, I saw a cloud shaped like a huge mountain made up of banks of fire, because the rays of the sun which was then setting red on the horizon had dyed it with their colour. This great cloud drew to itself all the little clouds which were round about it. And the great cloud remained stationary and retained the light of the sun on its apex for an hour and a half after sunset, so enormous was its size. And about two hours after night had fallen there arose a stupendous and phenomenal wind storm.

LEONARDO DA VINCI
(from *The Notebooks*—Trans. E. MCCURDY)

Upon the mountain's edge with light touch resting,
There a brief while the globe of splendour sits
And seems a creature of the earth, but soon,
More changeful than the Moon,
To wane fantastic his great orb submits,
Or cone or mow of fire : till sinking slowly
Even to a star at length he lessens wholly.

Abrupt, as Spirits vanish, he is sunk.
A soul-like breeze possesses all the wood.
    The boughs, the sprays have stood
As motionless as stands the ancient trunk.
But every leaf through all the forest flutters,
And deep the cavern of the mountain mutters.

COLERIDGE

I saw old Autumn in the misty morn
Stand shadowless like Silence, listening
To silence, for no lonely bird would sing
Into his hollow ear from woods forlorn,
Nor lowly hedge nor solitary thorn ;
Shaking his languid locks all dewy bright
With tangled gossamer that fell by night,
Pearling his coronet of golden corn.

Where are the songs of Summer ? With the sun,
Oping the dusky eyelids of the south,
Till shade and silence waken up as one,
And Morning sings with a warm odorous mouth.
Where are the merry birds ? Away, away,
On panting wings through the inclement skies,
   Lest owls should prey
   Undazzled at noon-day,
And tear with horny beak their lustrous eyes.

Where are the blooms of Summer ? In the west,
Blushing their last to the last sunny hours,
When the mild Eve by sudden Night is prest
Like tearful Proserpine, snatch'd from her
 flow'rs
   To a most gloomy breast.

Where is the pride of Summer, the green pine,
The many, many leaves all twinkling ? Three
On the moss'd elm ; three on the naked lime
Trembling, and one upon the old oak tree !
Where is the Dryads' immortality ?
Gone into mournful cypress and dark yew,
Or wearing the long gloomy Winter through
In the smooth holly's green eternity.

The squirrel gloats on his accomplish'd hoard,
The ants have brimm'd their garners with ripe
   grain,
              And honey bees have stor'd
The sweets of Summer in their luscious cells;
The swallows all have wing'd across the main;
But here the Autumn Melancholy dwells,
              And sighs her tearful spells
Amongst the sunless shadows of the plain.
              Alone, alone,
              Upon a mossy stone,
She sits and reckons up the dead and gone
With the last leaves of a love-rosary.
Whilst all the wither'd world looks drearily,
Like a dim picture of the drowned past
In the hush'd mind's mysterious far away,
Doubtful what ghostly thing will steal the last
Into that distance, grey upon the grey.

O go and sit with her, and be o'ershaded
Under the languid downfall of her hair:
She wears a coronal of flowers faded
Upon her forehead, and a face of care;
There is enough of wither'd every where
To make her bower, and enough of gloom;
There is enough of sadness to invite,
If only for the rose that died, whose doom
Is Beauty's, she that with the living bloom
Of conscious cheeks most beautifies the light;
There is enough of sorrowing, and quite
Enough of bitter fruits the earth doth bear,
Enough of chilly droppings for her bowl;

Enough of fear and shadowy despair,
To frame her cloudy prison for the soul.

HOOD

See, how the wind-enamoured aspen leaves
    Turn up their silver lining to the sun !
And hark ! the rustling noise, that oft deceives
    And makes the sheep-boy run :
The sound so mimics fast-approaching showers,
        He thinks the rain's begun,
        And hastes to sheltering bowers.

CLARE (from *Summer Images*)

If you are on the side from whence the wind is blowing,
you will see the trees look much lighter than you would
see them from the other sides, and this is due to the fact
the wind turns up the reverse side of the leaves, which is
in all cases much paler than their right side ; and especially
will they be very light if the wind blows from the quarter
where the sun happens to be, and if you have your back
turned to it.

LEONARDO DA VINCI
(from *The Notebooks*—Trans. E. MCCURDY)

I

O wild West Wind, thou breath of Autumn's being,
Thou from whose unseen presence the leaves dead
Are driven, like ghosts from an enchanting fleeing,

Yellow, and black, and pale, and hectic red,
Pestilence-stricken multitudes : O thou
Who chariotest to their dark wintry bed

The wingèd seeds, where they lie cold and low,
Each like a corpse within its grave, until
Thine azure sister of the Spring shall blow

Her clarion o'er the dreaming earth, and fill
(Driving sweet buds like flocks to feed in air)
With living hues and odours plain and hill :

Wild Spirit, which art moving everywhere ;
Destroyer and preserver, hear, oh, hear !

II

Thou on whose stream, mid the steep sky's commo-
    tion,
Loose clouds like earth's decaying leaves are shed,
Shook from the tangled boughs of Heaven and Ocean,

Angels of rain and lightning : there are spread
On the blue surface of thine aery surge,
Like the bright hair uplifted from the head

Of some fierce Maenad, even from the dim verge
Of the horizon to the zenith's height,
The locks of the approaching storm. Thou dirge

Of the dying year, to which this closing night
Will be the dome of a vast sepulchre,
Vaulted with all thy congregated might

Of vapours, from whose solid atmosphere
Black rain, and fire, and hail will burst : oh, hear

III

Thou who didst waken from his summer dreams
The blue Mediterranean, where he lay,
Lulled by the coil of his crystalline dreams,

Beside a pumice isle in Baiae's bay,
And saw in sleep old palaces and towers
Quivering within the wave's intenser day,

All overgrown with azure moss and flowers
So sweet, the sense faints picturing them. Thou
For whose path the Atlantic's level powers

Cleave themselves into chasms, while far below
The sea-blooms and the oozy woods which wear
The sapless foliage of the ocean, know

Thy voice, and suddenly grow grey with fear,
And tremble and despoil themselves : oh, hear !

IV

If I were a dead leaf thou mightest bear ;
If I were a swift cloud to fly with thee ;
A wave to pant beneath thy power, and share

The impulse of thy strength, only less free
Than thou, O uncontrollable ! If even
I were as in my boyhood, and could be

The comrade of thy wanderings over Heaven,
As then, when to outstrip thy skiey speed
Scarce seemed a vision ; I would ne'er have striven

As thus with thee in prayer in my sore need.
Oh, lift me as a wave, a leaf, a cloud !
I fall upon the thorns of life. I bleed.

A heavy weight of hours has chained and bowed
One too like thee : tameless, and swift, and proud.

V

Make me thy lyre, even as the forest is :
What if my leaves are falling like its own !
The tumult of thy mighty harmonies

Will take from both a deep, autumnal tone,
Sweet though in sadness. Be thou, Spirit fierce,
My spirit ! Be thou me, impetuous one !

Drive my dead thoughts over the universe
Like withered leaves to quicken a new birth !
And, by the incantation of this verse,

Scatter, as from an unextinguished hearth
Ashes and sparks, my words among mankind !
Be through my lips to unawakened earth

The trumpet of a prophecy ! O, Wind,
If Winter comes, can Spring be far behind ?

SHELLEY

638

On stern Blencartha's perilous height
   The winds are tyrannous and strong ;
And flashing forth unsteady light
From stern Blencartha's skiey height,
   As loud the torrents throng.
Beneath the moon, in gentle weather,
They bind the earth and sky together.
But oh ! the sky and all its forms, how quiet !
The things that seek the earth, how full of noise
   and riot !

COLERIDGE

Blow, blow, thou winter wind,
Thou art not so unkind
   As man's ingratitude ;
Thy tooth is not so keen
Because thou art not seen,
   Although thy breath be rude.
Heigh ho ! sing, heigh ho ! unto the green holly :
Most friendship is feigning, most loving mere
   folly :
   Then, heigh ho ! the holly !
   This life is most jolly.

Freeze, freeze, thou bitter sky,
Thou dost not bite so nigh
   As benefits forgot :
Though thou the waters warp,
Thy sting is not so sharp
   As friend remember'd not.
Heigh ho ! sing, heigh ho ! unto the green holly :

> Most friendship is feigning, most loving mere
> folly :
> Then, heigh ho ! the holly !
> This life is most jolly.

SHAKESPEARE

The wind, indeed, seemed made for the scene, as the scene seemed made for the hour. Part of its tone was quite special ; what was heard there could be heard nowhere else. Gusts in innumerable series followed each other from the north-west, and when each one of them raced past, the sound of its progress resolved into three. Treble, tenor, and bass notes were to be found therein. The general ricochet of the whole over pits and prominences had the gravest pitch of the chime. Next there could be heard the baritone buzz of a holly tree. Below these in force, above them in pitch, a dwindled voice strove hard at a husky tune, which was the peculiar local sound alluded to. Thinner and less immediately traceable than the other two, it was far more impressive than either. In it lay what may be called the linguistic peculiarity of the heath . . .

Throughout the blowing of these plaintive November winds that note bore a great resemblance to the ruins of human song which remain to the throat of fourscore and ten. It was a worn whisper, dry and papery, and it brushed so distinctly across the ear that, by the accustomed, the material minutiae in which it originated could be realized as by touch. It was the united products of infinitesimal vegetable causes, and these were neither stems, leaves, fruit, blades, prickles, lichen, nor moss.

They were the mummied heath-bells of the past summer, originally tender and purple, now washed colourless
by Michaelmas rains, and dried to dead skins by October
suns. So low was an individual sound from these that
a combination of hundreds only just emerged from silence,
and the myriads of the whole declivity reached the . . .
ear but as a shrivelled and intermittent recitative. Yet
scarcely a single accent amongst the many afloat to-night
could have such power to impress a listener with thoughts
of its origin. One inwardly saw the infinity of those combined multitudes ; and perceived that each of the tiny
trumpets was seized on, entered, scoured and emerged
from by the wind as thoroughly as if it were as vast as
a crater.

THOMAS HARDY (from *The Return of the Native*)

So now my yeare drawes to his latter terme,
My spring is spent, my sommer burnt up quite ;
My harveste hasts to stirre up Winter sterne,
And bids him clayme with rigorous rage hys right :
So nowe he stormes with many a sturdy stoure ;
So nowe his blustring blast eche coste dooth scoure.

The carefull cold hath nypt my rugged rynde,
And in my face deepe forrowes eld hath pight :
My head besprent with hoary frost I fynd,
And by myne eie the Crow his clawe dooth wright :
Delight is layd abedde ; and pleasure past ;
No sonne now shines ; clouds han all overcast.

Now leave, ye shepheards boyes, your merry glee ;
My Muse is hoarse and wearie of thys stounde ;
Here will I hang my pype upon this tree :
Was never pype of reede did better sounde.
Winter is come that blowes the bitter blaste,
And after Winter dreerie death does hast.

Gather together ye my little flocke,
My little flock, that was to me so liefe ;
Let me, ah ! lette me in your foldes ye lock,
Eere the breme Winter breede you greater griefe.
Winter is come, that blowes the balefull breath,
And after Winter commeth timely death.

SPENSER (from *The Shepheards Calender*)

When biting Boreas, fell and doure,
Sharp shivers thro' the leafless bow'r ;
When Phoebus gies a short-liv'd glow'r
    Far south the lift,
Dim dark'ning through the flaky show'r,
    Or whirling drift :

Ae night the storm the steeples rocked,
Poor labour sweet in sleep was locked,
While burns, wi' snawy wreaths up-choked,
    Wild-eddying swirl,
Or thro' the mining outlet bocked,
    Down headlong hurl.

List'ning, the doors and winnocks rattle,
I thought me on the ourie cattle,
Or silly sheep, who bide this brattle
    O' winter war,
And thro' the drift, deep-lairing sprattle,
    Beneath a scaur.

Ilk happing bird, wee, helpless thing!
That, in the merry months o' spring,
Delighted me to hear thee sing,
    What comes o' thee?
Whare wilt thou cow'r thy chittering wing,
    An' close thy e'e?

BURNS (from *A Winter Night*)

Poor naked wretches, wheresoe'er you are,
That bide the pelting of this pitiless storm,
How shall your houseless heads and unfed sides,
    Your loop'd and window'd raggedness, defend
      you
From seasons such as these? O! I have ta'en
To little care of this. Take physic, pomp;
Expose thyself to feel what wretches feel,
That thou mayst shake the superflux to them,
And show the heavens more just.

   .   .   .   .   .

Away! the foul fiend follows me! Through the sharp
hawthorn blow the winds. Hum! go to thy bed and warm
thee . . . Who gives anything to poor Tom? whom the
foul fiend hath led through fire and through flame,
through ford and whirlpool, o'er bog and quagmire;

that hath laid knives under his pillow, and halters in his
pew; set ratsbane by his porridge; made him proud of
heart, to ride on a bay trotting-horse over four-inched
bridges, to course his own shadow for a traitor. Bless thy
five wits! Tom's a-cold. O! do de, do de, do de. Bless
thee from whirlwinds, star-blasting, and taking! Do poor
Tom some charity, whom the foul fiend vexes.

SHAKESPEARE (from *King Lear*)

The keener tempests rise: and fuming dun
From all the livid east, or piercing north,
Thick clouds ascend; in whose capacious womb
A vapoury deluge lies, to snow congeal'd.
Heavy they roll their fleecy world along;
And the sky saddens with the gathered storm.
Thro' the hush'd air the whitening shower
    descends,
At first thin wavering, till at last the flakes
Fall broad, and wide, and fast, dimming the day,
With a continual flow. The cherish'd fields
Put on their winter-robe of purest white.
'Tis brightness all; save where the new snow melts
Along the mazy current. Low, the woods
Bow their hoar head; and, ere the languid sun
Faint from the west emits his evening ray,
Earth's universal face, deep hid, and chill,
Is one wild dazzling waste, that buries wide
The works of Man. Drooping, the labourer-ox
Stands cover'd o'er with snow, and then demands
The fruit of all his toil. The fowls of heaven,

Tam'd by the cruel season, crowd around
The winnowing store, and claim the little boon
Which Providence assigns them. One alone,
The red-breast, sacred to the household gods,
Wisely regardful of th' embroiling sky,
In joyless fields, and thorny thickets, leaves
His shivering mates, and pays to trusted Man
His annual visit.

THOMSON (from *The Seasons*)

Ill fares the traveller now, and he that stalks
In pond'rous boots beside his reeking team.
The wain goes heavily, impeded sore
By congregated loads adhering close
To the clogg'd wheels ; and in its sluggish pace,
Noiseless, appears a moving hill of snow.
The toiling steeds expand the nostril wide,
While ev'ry breath, by respiration strong
Forc'd downward, is consolidated soon
Upon their jutting chests. He, form'd to bear
The pelting brunt of the tempestuous night,
With half-shut eyes, and pucker'd cheeks, and
    teeth
Presented bare against the storm, plods on.
One hand secures his hat, save when with both
He brandishes his pliant length of whip,
Resounding oft, and never heard in vain.

.   .   .   .   .   .

The streams are lost amid the splendid blank,
O'erwhelming all distinction. On the flood,
Indurated and fixt, the snowy weight
Lies undissolv'd ; while silently beneath,
And unperceiv'd, the current steals away.
Not so, when scornful of a check it leaps
The mill-dam, dashes on the restless wheel,
And wantons in the pebbly gulph below :
No frost can bind it there ; its utmost force
Can but arrest the light and smokey mist
That in its fall the liquid sheet throws wide.
And see where it has hung th' embroider'd banks
With forms so various, that no pow'rs of art,
The pencil or the pen, may trace the scene !
Here glitt'ring turrets rise, upbearing high
(Fantastic misarrangement) on the roof
Large growth of what may seem the sparkling
    trees
And shrubs of fairy land. The crystal drops
That trickle down the branches, fast congeal'd,
Shoot into pillars of pellucid length,
And prop the pile they but adorn'd before.
Here grotto within grotto safe defies
The sun-beam : there imboss'd and fretted wild,
The growing wonder takes a thousand shapes
Capricious, in which fancy seeks in vain
The likeness of some object seen before.

COWPER (from *The Task*)

I had a dream, which was not all a dream.
The bright sun was extinguished, and the stars
Did wander darkling in eternal space,
Rayless, and pathless, and the icy Earth
Swung blind and blackening in the moonless air ;
Morn came and went—and came, and brought no
    day,
And men forgot their passions in the dread
Of this their desolation ; and all hearts
Were chilled into a selfish prayer for light :
And they did live by watchfires ; and the thrones,
The palaces of crownèd kings, the huts,
The habitations of all things which dwell,
Were burnt for beacons ; cities were consumed,
And men were gathered round their blazing homes
To look once more into each other's face ;
Happy were those who dwelt within the eye
Of the volcanoes, and their mountain torch :
A fearful hope was all the World contained ;
Forests were set on fire, but hour by hour
They fell and faded, and the crackling trunks
Extinguished with a crash, and all was black.
The brows of men by the despairing light
Wore an unearthly aspect, as by fits
The flashes fell upon them ; some lay down
And hid their eyes and wept ; and some did rest
Their chins upon their clenchèd hands, and smiled ;
And others hurried to and fro, and fed
Their funeral piles with fuel, and looked up
With mad disquietude on the dull sky,
The pall of a past World ; and then again
With curses cast them down upon the dust,

And gnashed their teeth and howled; the wild
    birds shrieked.
And, terrified, did flutter on the ground,
And flap their useless wings; the wildest brutes
Came tame and tremulous; and vipers crawled
And twined themselves among the multitude,
Hissing, but stingless—they were slain for food:
And War, which for a moment was no more,
Did glut himself again; a meal was bought
With blood, and each sate sullenly apart
Gorging himself in gloom; no Love was left;
All earth was but one thought, and that was Death,
Immediate and inglorious; and the pang
Of famine fed upon all entrails, men
Died, and their bones were tombless as their flesh;
The meagre by the meagre were devoured,
Even dogs assailed their masters, all save one,
And he was faithful to a corse, and kept
The birds and beasts and famished men at bay,
Till hunger clung them, or the dropping dead
Lured their lank jaws; himself sought out no food,
But with a piteous and perpetual moan,
And a quick desolate cry, licking the hand
Which answered not with a caress, he died.
The crowd was famished by degrees; but two
Of an enormous city did survive,
And they were enemies; they met beside
The dying embers of an altar-place
Where had been heaped a mass of holy things
For an unholy usage; they raked up,
And shivering scraped with their cold skeleton
    hands
The feeble ashes, and their feeble breath

Blew for a little life, and made a flame
Which was a mockery; then they lifted up
Their eyes, as it grew lighter, and beheld
Each other's aspects, saw, and shrieked, and
    died,
Even of their mutual hideousness they died,
Unknowing who he was upon whose brow
Famine had written Fiend. The World was void,
The populous and the powerful was a lump,
Seasonless, herbless, treeless, manless, lifeless,
A lump of death, a chaos of hard clay.
The rivers, lakes, and ocean all stood still,
And nothing stirred within their silent depths;
Ships sailorless lay rotting on the sea,
And their masts fell down piecemeal: as they
    dropped
They slept on the abyss without a surge—
The waves were dead; the tides were in their
    grave,
The Moon, their mistress, had expired before;
The winds were withered in the stagnant air,
And the clouds perished; Darkness had no need
Of aid from them, She was the Universe.

BYRON

Through that pure virgin-shrine,
That sacred veil drawn o'er thy glorious noon,
That men might look and live, as glow-worms shine
    And face the moon:
Wise Nicodemus saw such light
As made him know his God by night.

Most blest believer he !
Who in that land of darkness and blind eyes
Thy long-expected healing wings could see
    When thou didst rise,
    And, what can never more be done,
    Did at midnight speak with the Sun !

O who will tell me, where
He found thee at that dead and silent hour ?
What hallowed solitary ground did bear
    So rare a flower
    Within whose sacred leaves did lie
    The fullness of the Deity ?

No mercy-seat of gold,
No dead and dusty cherub, nor carved stone,
But his own living works did my Lord hold
    And lodge alone ;
    Where trees and herbs did watch and peep
    And wonder, while the Jews did sleep.

Dear Night ! this world's defeat ;
The stop to busy fools ; care's check and curb ;
The day of spirits ; my soul's calm retreat
    Which none disturb !
    Christ's progress, and his prayer-time ;
    The hours to which high heaven doth chime.

God's silent, searching flight :
When my Lord's head is fill'd with dew and all
His locks are wet with the clear drops of night ;
    His still, soft call ;
    His knocking-time ; the soul's dumb watch,
    When spirits their fair kindred catch.

Were all my loud, evil days
Calm and unhaunted as is thy dark tent,
Whose peace but by some angel's wing or voice
    Is seldom rent;
  Then I in heaven all the long year
  Would keep, and never wander here.

  But living where the sun
Doth all things wake, and where all mix and tire
Themselves and others, I consent and run
    To every mire;
  And by this world's ill-guiding light,
  Err more than I can do by night.

  There is in God (some say)
A deep, but dazzling darkness; as men here
Say it is late and dusky, because they
    See not all clear.
  O for that night! where I in him
  Might live invisible and dim.

                        VAUGHAN

THESEUS
  The iron tongue of midnight hath told twelve:
  Lovers, to bed; 'tis almost fairy time.
  I fear we shall outsleep the coming morn
  As much as we this night have overwatch'd.
  This palpable gross play hath well beguiled
  The heavy gait of night. Sweet friends, to bed.
  A fortnight hold we this solemnity,
  In nightly revels and new jollity.
                    [*Exeunt.*   *Enter* PUCK.

PUCK

Now the hungry lion roars,
 And the wolf behowls the moon ;
Whilst the heavy ploughman snores,
 All with weary task fordone.
Now the wasted brands do glow,
 Whilst the screech-owl, screeching loud,
Puts the wretch that lies in woe
 In remembrance of a shroud.
Now it is the time of night
 That the graves all gaping wide,
Every one lets forth his sprite,
 In the church-way paths to glide :
And we fairies, that do run
 By the triple Hecate's team,
From the presence of the sun,
 Following darkness like a dream,
Now are frolic : not a mouse
 Shall disturb this hallow'd house :
I am sent with broom before,
 To sweep the dust behind the door.

[*Enter* OBERON *and* TITANIA *with their train.*

OBERON

Through the house give glimmering light,
 By the dead and drowsy fire :
Every elf and fairy sprite
 Hop as light as bird from brier ;
And this ditty, after me,
 Sing, and dance it trippingly.

TITANIA

First, rehearse your song by rote,
 To each word a warbling note :

652

Hand in hand, with fairy grace,
   Will we sing, and bless this place.

OBERON
   Now, until the break of day,
     Through this house each fairy stray.
   To the best bride-bed will we,
     Which by us shall blessed be ;
   And the issue there create
     Ever shall be fortunate.
   So shall all the couples three
     Ever true in loving be ;
   And the blots of Nature's hand
     Shall not in their issue stand ;
   Never mole, hare lip, nor scar,
     Nor mark prodigious such as are
   Despised in nativity,
     Shall upon their children be.
   With this field-dew consecrate,
     Every fairy take his gait ;
   And each several chamber bless,
     Through this palace, with sweet peace ;
   And the owner of it blest
     Ever shall in safety rest.
   Trip away ; make no stay ;
     Meet me all by break of day.

SHAKESPEARE
(from *A Midsummer Night's Dream*)

Care-charming Sleep, thou easer of all woes,
Brother to Death, sweetly thyself dispose
On this afflicted prince ; fall like a cloud,
In gentle showers ; give nothing that is loud,
Or painful to his slumbers ; easy, light,
And as a purling stream, thou son of Night,
Pass by his troubled senses ; sing his pain,
Like hollow murmuring wind or silver rain ;
Into this prince gently, oh, gently slide,
And kiss him into slumbers like a bride.

FLETCHER (from *Valentinian*)

Sleep, Silence' child, sweet father of soft rest,
Prince, whose approach peace to all mortals brings,
Indifferent host to shepherds and to kings,
Sole comforter of minds with grief opprest ;
Lo, by thy charming rod all breathing things
Lie slumbering, with forgetfulness possest,
And yet o'er me to spread thy drowsy wings
Thou spares, alas ! who cannot be thy guest.
Since I am thine, O come, but with that face
To inward light which thou art wont to show,
With feigned solace ease a true-felt woe ;
Or if, deaf god, thou do deny that grace,
Come as thou wilt, and what thou wilt bequeath :
I long to kiss the image of my death.

DRUMMOND

Sweet are the thoughts that savour of content ;
　The quiet mind is richer than a crown ;
Sweet are the nights in careless slumber spent ;
　The poor estate scorns fortune's angry frown ;
Such sweet content, such minds, such sleep, such
　　　bliss,
Beggars enjoy, when princes oft do miss.

The homely house that harbours quiet rest,
　The cottage that affords no pride nor care,
The mean that 'grees with country music best,
　The sweet consort of mirth and music's fare,
Obscured life sets down a type of bliss ;
A mind content both crown and kingdom is.

GREENE

ACKNOWLEDGMENTS

I am grateful to the following writers, publishers, and others, for permission to use copyright material :

Mrs. Thomas Hardy, the author's executors, and Messrs. Macmillan & Co. Ltd. for extracts from *The Life of Thomas Hardy*, *The Collected Poems*, and *The Return of the Native* ; Messrs. Macmillan for extracts from Matthew Arnold's *Essays in Criticism* and Pater's *Renaissance* ; Mr. W. B. Yeats and Messrs. Macmillan for poems from *The Collected Poems of W. B. Yeats* ; Mr. Christopher Saintsbury and Messrs. Macmillan for extracts from George Saintsbury's *Notes on a Cellar Book* ; Messrs. Jonathan Cape Ltd. for extracts from *The Notebooks of Samuel Butler* ; the Trustees of the Meredith Estate and Messrs. Constable & Co. Ltd. for a poem from George Meredith's *Poetical Works* ; Mr. André Simon and Messrs. Constable for extracts from *Tables of Content* ; Messrs. Constable for extracts from *The Letters of Vincent van Gogh* ; Mr. Wilfred Meynell for two poems from *The Poems of Alice Meynell* and for two poems and a prose extract from *The Works of Francis Thompson* ; Mr. Edward McCurdy and Messrs. Duckworth & Co. Ltd. for extracts from *Leonardo da Vinci's Notebooks* ; Sir E. A. Wallis Budge for extracts from *The Paradise of the Fathers* ; Messrs. G. Bell & Sons Ltd. for two poems from *Coventry Patmore's Poems* ; Professor Herbert Read and Messrs. Faber & Faber Ltd. for extracts from *Art Now* ; Mr. Wells Coates and Messrs. Cassell & Co. Ltd. for an extract from *Unit One* ; The Hogarth Press for two extracts from Virginia Woolf's *A Room of One's Own* ; Mr. Roger Fry and Messrs. A. Zwemmer for an extract from *Henri-Matisse* ; Messrs. Field Roscoe & Co. for the extract from George Moore's *Impressions and Opinions* ; Messrs. William Heinemann Ltd. for two poems from *Swinburne's Poems* and extracts from *The Letters of Paul Gaugin* ; Messrs. P. J. and A. E. Dobell for extracts from Traherne's *Centuries of Meditations* ; Messrs. Ernest Benn Ltd. and Messrs. Ernst Wasmuth for an extract from *Erich Mendelsohn : Structures & Sketches* ; Messrs. John Murray for an extract from Mrs. Humphry Ward's *The Marriage of William Ashe* ; the Executors of T. Earle Welby and Messrs. Methuen & Co. Ltd. for extracts from *The Dinner Knell* ; the Family of Gerard Manley Hopkins and the Oxford University Press for two poems from *Poems of Gerard Manley Hopkins* ; the Jowett Trustees and The Clarendon Press for the passage from Jowett's translation of Plato's *Symposium*.

INDEX OF AUTHORS

660

KANT, 11
KEATS, 17, 74, 114, 116, 144, 173, 259, 260, 261, 459, 461, 552, 588, 623
KEMPIS, À, 282
KNOTT, NATHANIEL, 572

LA BRUYÈRE, 13, 238
LAMB, 30, 60, 75, 86, 104, 174, 511, 512, 516, 597
LANDOR, 104, 124, 125, 163, 250, 303, 517, 556
LANGLAND, 390
LAW, WILLIAM, 22
LECKY, 252, 562
LEONARDO DA VINCI, 11, 136, 169, 205, 245, 632, 635
LESLIE, 137, 178, 418
LISZT, 350, 360
LOCKE, 34, 536
LUCIAN, 536

MAPES, WALTER, 533
MARCUS AURELIUS, 433
MARLOWE, 495
MARVELL, 208, 456
MASSINGER, 496
MATISSE, 200
MENDELSOHN, ERICH, 419
MEREDITH, GEORGE, 468
MERYON, CHARLES, 107
MEYNELL, ALICE, 53, 327
MICHAEL ANGELO, 168
MILTON, 30, 45, 46, 70, 75, 301, 302, 309, 310, 453, 489, 580
MONTESQUIEU, 50
MOORE, GEORGE, 189

MORE, MARTHA, 522
MORLEY, THOMAS, 329
MOTLEY, 385
MOZART, 336, 339

OSBORNE, DOROTHY, 210

PACHECO, 167
PALLADIUS, 243, 289, 432
PASCAL, 124, 432
PATER, 142, 149, 170
PATMORE, 270, 276
PAUL, SAINT, 282, 488, 534
PEACHAM, 305
PEACOCK, 504, 514, 528, 545, 554
PEGGE, SAMUEL, 489
PEPYS, 296, 564
PLATO, 12, 24, 141, 245, 295, 429, 436, 479, 502, 527
PLOTINUS, 450
PLUTARCH, 296
POPE, 47, 49, 81, 295, 318, 337, 496, 565
PURCHAS, 100, 101, 102

QUARLES, 281

RABELAIS, 20, 401, 539, 546
READ, HERBERT, 143, 189, 201
REYNOLDS, SIR JOSHUA, 48, 141, 142, 161
RICHTER, J. P., 296
ROSSETTI, D. G., 152, 174, 180, 303, 431
ROUSSEAU, 342
RUSKIN, 134, 144, 184, 186, 376, 424, 586

661

INDEX OF FIRST LINES OF VERSE

667

668